PENGUIN BOOKS

THE BEST MINDS

Jonathan Rosen is the author of two novels, *Eve's Apple* and *Joy Comes in the Morning*, and two other works of nonfiction, *The Talmud and the Internet: A Journey Between Worlds* and *The Life of the Skies: Birding at the End of Nature*. His essays and articles have appeared in *The New York Times*, *The New Yorker*, *The Atlantic*, *The Wall Street Journal*, and numerous anthologies. He lives with his family in New York City.

❋

Praise for *The Best Minds*

"The absolute best book of 2023: a real genre-bender, complex and moving."
—Alexandra Jacobs, *The New York Times*

"Haunting . . . Rosen tells this story with such a keen mix of compassion and eloquence we can't help but hope there will be a twist that somehow saves everyone from the inevitably heartbreaking outcome. . . . Throughout the book—which is part memoir, part manifesto—Rosen asks uncomfortable but crucial questions, some of them unanswerable, all of them compelling, and the result is an incisive but intimate tour de force that's as much about Michael's story as it is about the stories we tell as a culture—what we value, what we see, and what we do our best not to see even when it's right in front of us. . . . Masterful."
—*The Washington Post*

"This engrossing memoir centers on the author's childhood friend Michael Laudor, who developed schizophrenia and, in his thirties, committed a horrific murder. . . . Rosen thoughtfully interweaves this story with an account of changing attitudes toward mental illness." —*The New Yorker*

"Jonathan Rosen's *The Best Minds: A Story of Friendship, Madness, and the Tragedy of Good Intentions* takes its title from Allen Ginsberg's *Howl* and could end up as just as enduring a work of American writing. Expect to see it on 'Best Of' lists and plan to make space for its nearly 600 pages on your shelf. A memoir, a love letter, and a biblical tragedy all at once, it avoids easy answers but clings to difficult questions. A tale told with humility, it charts the path to hell by noting every good intention along the way." —*The New York Sun*

"A shattering narrative." —Sue Halpern, *Yale Alumni Magazine*

"It's the darkest of literary triumphs, and the most gripping of unbearable reads." —Simon Ings, *The Telegraph* (five stars)

"Dazzling . . . both a breathtaking and tragic portrait of a man with vast potential and a reckoning on how schizophrenia is treated and understood. This is a tough one to forget." —*Publishers Weekly* (starred review)

"Rosen is a novelist, and his literary imagination shapes the book like a novel. . . . This artful, reflective, and even entertaining book—one of the best of this or any year—is his powerful effort to take responsibility for changing minds, to persuade us of the danger of allowing compassion to obscure truth. *The Best Minds* manages to honor both."
—Elaine Showalter, *The Times Literary Supplement*

"I think it's the best book about mental illness I've ever read."
—Freddie deBoer

"Intelligent, absorbing, and heartbreaking, an intensely personal story."
—Kevin Canfield, *CrimeReads*

"Rosen captures many worlds in this attentive, nuanced narrative, evoking boyhood discovery, the life of post-Shoah Jews in America, the rise of predatory capitalism, and the essential inability of one friend to comprehend fully the 'delicate brain' of the other. It's an undeniably tragic story, but Rosen also probes meaningfully into the nature of mental illness. Throughout, he is keenly sensitive, as when he writes of the perils of self-awareness, 'The flip side of the idea that writing heals you, perhaps, was the fear that failing to tell your story, and fulfill your dreams, cast you into outer darkness.' An affecting, thoughtfully written portrait of a friendship broken by mental illness and its terrible sequelae." —*Kirkus Reviews* (starred review)

"An astounding piece of work, at once a portrait of Laudor made of countless fine brush strokes, a tender memoir of adolescence and young adulthood and, above all, a forensic, unflinching exploration of the factors that led to Laudor's public rise and bloody fall." —Ben Machell, *The Times*

"A moving evocation of childhood friendship that morphs into a devastating evocation of mental illness. Rosen is persistently judicious and precise. The result is a harrowing tour de force."

—Peter D. Kramer, author of *Death of the Great Man* and
Listening to Prozac

"This is that rare book that deftly works on several levels at once while remaining a compulsive read: as a narrative of a complex friendship; a cautionary tale about the price of intellectual ambition; and a clash between the unholy alliance of psychoanalytic and literary theory and the grim vicissitudes of reality. Jonathan Rosen writes with searing intelligence and admirable candor about his role in what is ultimately a heartrending story. As unobtrusively researched as it is deeply reflective, informed by a humane and comprehending voice, *The Best Minds* delivers on its own vaulting ambition. It is nothing short of a contemporary masterpiece."

—Daphne Merkin, author of *22 Minutes of Unconditional Love* and
This Close to Happy

"I am not sure when I last read a nonfiction book as satisfying as *The Best Minds*. It's a memoir, a medical mystery, the story of a close male friendship, a clear-eyed look at the criminal justice system, and, in a weird way, an academic satire, revealing Ivy League foibles that would make you laugh if they didn't make you tear your hair out, painfully. Jonathan Rosen has written a long book that felt too short; I wanted it to keep going and going."

—Mark Oppenheimer, author of *Squirrel Hill*

"*The Best Minds* is one of the best books about mental illness I have ever read. Its grand sweep takes in the nuanced cultural history of ideas and policies regarding people with severe illness. Andrew Solomon's *The Noonday Demon* did this for depression, and Scott Stossel's *My Age of Anxiety* for anxiety. Those books, both superb, are grounded in memoir as well, but the specific horror of Rosen's makes it especially unforgettable."

—Sally Satel, *Commentary Magazine*

"*The Best Minds* is a carefully crafted and beautifully written tale illustrating the failure of our mental illness treatment system. The irony of the title is that the 'best minds' did not understand that paranoid schizophrenia is a brain disease, not a behavioral choice. On any given day 40 percent of the 9 million Americans with serious psychiatric disorders are receiving no treatment. The Laudor story, with elements of the Ivy League and Hollywood, was high-profile but other tragedies quietly occur in the US every day."

—E. Fuller Torrey, MD, author of *American Psychosis: How the Federal Government Destroyed the Mental Illness Treatment System*

"I was gripped from the start by Jonathan Rosen's skill as a novelist as he tells the story of two boys, both alike in dignity and gifts, and the tragic impact of severe mental illness on their different life trajectories. The book is a kind of lighthouse, pointing out the dangers ahead if we don't pay attention to those small number of people with severe mental illness who pose a risk to others, and who need long term care from professionals, not from desperate families and partners. It is a must-read for those who are interested in mental health services, and should be required for those in government who have any influence on mental health policy. *The Best Minds* has its own strange and terrible beauty, and despite the tragedy described therein, it is also a tribute to human love and hope for better things."

—Gwen Adshead, forensic psychiatrist and author of
The Devil You Know

"A work of intimacy, scope and sweeping power, this epic book reads like a classic American novel. Both a heartrending tragedy and a story of love and companionship, *The Best Minds* is utterly compelling."

—Seán Hewitt, author of *All Down Darkness Wide*

"As a primer to the cultural and political concerns that emerged from the sixties, it is second to none. . . . Like all great American texts it is the detail and the flow of ideas that gives it power. This is social and intellectual history of the most powerful sort." —Brian Morton, *Tablet Magazine*

"Incredibly moving and panoramic work . . . Rosen's writing can break your heart . . . A worthy and incisive read." —*New York Journal of Books*

"Deeply personal, by turns sad, angry, empathetic, and, yes, funny, *The Best Minds* is a must-read account of the manifestations and mysteries of psychosis and the failures of our nation's mental health institutions."

—*Pittsburgh Post-Gazette*

"This devastating memoir will break your heart . . . In *The Best Minds*, Rosen breaks his silence, and the heart of any empathetic reader. It is a wrenching double memoir about converging and violently diverging lives."

—The Forward

"To say that this is a memoir, a case study, or a book about schizophrenia is to dramatically undersell it. Though Rosen's lens is particular, his view is panoptic. This is a magisterial work, as much a sociological study of late twentieth-century America as it is a book about madness. It is also a book about childhood and friendship, the long shadow of the Second World War and its unexpected intellectual legacy, about ambition and delusion and the danger of stories."

—David Shariatmadari, *The Guardian*

The Best Minds

A STORY OF FRIENDSHIP, MADNESS,
AND THE TRAGEDY OF GOOD INTENTIONS

*

Jonathan Rosen

PENGUIN BOOKS

PENGUIN BOOKS
An imprint of Penguin Random House LLC
penguinrandomhouse.com

First published in the United States of America by Penguin Press,
an imprint of Penguin Random House LLC, 2023
Published in Penguin Books 2024

ISBN 9780143132899 (paperback)

THE LIBRARY OF CONGRESS HAS CATALOGED THE
HARDCOVER EDITION AS FOLLOWS:

Names: Rosen, Jonathan, 1963– author.
Title: The best minds : a story of friendship, madness,
and the tragedy of good intentions / Jonathan Rosen.
Description: New York : Penguin Press, 2023. |
Includes bibliographical references and index.
Identifiers: LCCN 2022038816 (print) |
LCCN 2022038817 (ebook) | ISBN 9781594206573 (hardcover) |
ISBN 9780698196520 (ebook)
Subjects: LCSH: Laudor, Michael. | Schizophrenia—Patients—
United States—Biography. | Rosen, Jonathan, 1963—Friends and associates. |
Male friendship—United States. | New York (State)—Biography.
Classification: LCC RC514 .R6467 2023 (print) |
LCC RC514 (ebook) | DDC 616.89/80092 [B]—dc23/eng/20230106
LC record available at https://lccn.loc.gov/2022038816
LC ebook record available at https://lccn.loc.gov/2022038817

Printed in the United States of America
1st Printing

Designed by Amanda Dewey

In memory of Robert and Norma Rosen
May their memory be a blessing

זכרונם לברכה

And for Anna Rosen
sister, savior, friend

I call to the mysterious one who yet
Shall walk the wet sands by the edge of the stream
And look most like me, being indeed my double,
And prove of all imaginable things
The most unlike, being my anti-self

—WILLIAM BUTLER YEATS,
"Ego Dominus Tuus"

CONTENTS

�

Part III. The House of Law

Part IV. The House of Dreams

Part I

The House on Mereland Road

It is an illusion that we were ever alive,
Lived in the houses of mothers, arranged ourselves
By our own motions in a freedom of air.

—WALLACE STEVENS, *The Rock*

I am going back fifty years. Before the lurid headlines, the Hollywood deal, the publishing contract, and The New York Times profile of the role model genius who finished Yale Law School against all odds. Before delusions mistaken for stories, and stories mistaken for life. Before the fancy clothes you bought for management consulting and wore into the hospital, the halfway house, and the Gatsby House you guarded with a baseball bat against enemies disguised as friends and family, guarded in turn by beloved neighbors.

I am going back to the time before you graduated from Yale summa cum laude, which I always thought of as summa cum Laudor, since you achieved in three years what I failed to accomplish in four. Before high school, where you ran while I was beaten, and the horror twenty years later when it was my turn to run.

I am on a road racing backward out of a tragic sorrow whose circles radiate in all directions. Forgive me. I know there is no road and it isn't racing backward. Or forward. I know there is no going back.

But here I am on a short street in New Rochelle. There is a green-and-white colonial house at the top of the hill and a brown-and-white Tudor house at the bottom. There are two ten-year-old boys who live in those houses. Even now. They're just illusions but they're also real. And they're where I've got to start.

CHAPTER ONE

THE SUITABLE PLAYMATE

> When you were a small boy, the aim of the
> suitable playmate could not have been more
> perfectly fulfilled: across the street was
> Michael Laudor, the ideal friend. A
> brilliant peer.
>
> —CYNTHIA OZICK, letter to the author

My family moved to New Rochelle in 1973. There were good schools, green lawns, and quaint signs painted in the 1920s bearing legends like ONLY FORTY-FIVE MINUTES FROM BROADWAY and CITY OF HOMES, CHURCHES AND SCHOOLS, though there were four synagogues and Metro North got you to Manhattan—the rock around which all life revolved—in thirty-three minutes. But the real reason we moved to New Rochelle was so that I could meet Michael.

That, at least, is what my mother's best friend, the writer Cynthia Ozick, told me:

> I heard much of Michael Laudor when you were growing up. And in a way even before you knew of his existence, in this sense: that Michael, or someone like him, was always the goal in choosing where to buy a house.

Michael, in other words, was inevitable. I was destined to meet him, or at least someone like him, because friendship cannot actually be foretold any more than madness or the day of your death. Can it?

I met Michael soon after we moved in, as I was examining a heap of junk that the previous owners had left in a neat pile at the edge of our lawn. I was looking for relics of the three athletic boys who had lived there, and wondering if a small aquarium was worth salvaging, when a boy with shaggy red-brown hair and large tinted aviator glasses walked over to welcome me to the neighborhood.

He was taller even than I was, gawky but with a lilting stride that was oddly purposeful for a kid our age, as if he actually had someplace to go. His habit of launching himself up and forward with every step, gathering height in order to achieve distance, was so distinctive that it earned him the nickname Toes.

I didn't learn he was called Toes until fifth grade started, when I learned he was also called Big. The shortest kid in class was called Small, and when they lined us up in height order, Big and Small were bookends. Sensitive teachers sometimes let the short kids go first, which I'm sure did wonders for their self-esteem.

Big is less imaginative than Toes, but how many kids get two nicknames? And Michael *was* big. Not big like Hal, who appeared to be attending fifth grade on the GI bill, but through some subtle combination of height, intelligence, posture, and willpower.

In Brookline—the Boston suburb where my family had lived for three years before moving to New Rochelle—I'd been taller than all my friends, but nobody would have called me Big. I settled too easily at the bottom of myself in a shy sediment. Michael was only an inch or two taller than me, and just as skinny, but he seemed to enjoy taking up space, however awkwardly he filled it.

Even standing still he had a habit of rocking forward and rising up on the balls of his feet, trying to meet his growth spurt halfway. He stood beside me on Mereland Road in that unsteady but self-assured posture, rising and falling like a wave. He was socially effective the same way he was good at basketball—through uncowed persistence.

I often heard in later years that people found him intimidating, but for me it was the opposite. Despite my shyness—or because of it—Michael's self-confidence put me at ease. Perhaps because I was conscious of the awkwardness that he overcame, or simply refused to recognize, I fed off his belief in himself.

Besides, being shy is not the same as being modest. The same expectation shaping his life was shaping mine; the belief that your brain is your rocket ship and that simply as a matter of course you are going to climb inside and blast off. Propelled by some mysterious process—never specified, almost mystical and yet entirely real—we would outsoar the shadow of ordinary existence and *think* our way into stratospheric success.

Michael told me his name and my name, too, which he shortened to Jon. He liked to give the answer before the question, and offered his opinion that if the former owners had thrown out the fish tank, it probably leaked even if it didn't look cracked. I've never liked having my name abbreviated but I didn't correct him.

It's possible his mother had sent him. Ruth Laudor was a neighborly woman who came over herself at some point to welcome us—and sometimes came over to escape the roar of her own household—but Michael's geniality and supreme self-confidence were his own. Even then, he seemed like the ambassador of his own country.

It was Michael who pointed out that while my house was first on the block, it was number 11 not number 1, something I'd never have wondered about because numbers were always unpredictable, even without the "new math" that had been introduced in the sixties so we could win the Cold War. I didn't know it was called new math, only that having been shown a decimal point in fourth grade, I was going to spend the rest of my life trying to figure out where to put it.

Michael knew, and played me a song by Tom Lehrer called "New Math," one of many songs and records we spent hours listening to in his living room. The joke of "New Math" was that it was so simple "that only a child can do it," which is to say it was a song for adults, which was part of its special pleasure. Michael never believed in the line separating children from adults, or many other lines either.

The Tom Lehrer album was ten years old but new to me, full of names and concepts Michael cheerfully glossed—the Vatican; Wernher von Braun—that gave it an archaic but cutting-edge quality, like the Doc Savage mysteries he also introduced me to.

Michael often seemed like someone who had lived a full span already and was just slumming it in childhood, or living backward like Benjamin Button or Merlin. My parents were amused by the speed with which he took to calling them Bob and Norma, and the unabashed way he looked them in the eye as he cursed the bombing of Cambodia or discussed the Watergate scandal while I waited for him to finish so we could play Mille Bornes or go outside. I knew the president was a crook, but Michael knew who Liddy, Haldeman, and Ehrlichman were, and what they had done, matters he expounded as if Deep Throat had whispered to him personally in the schoolyard just behind his house.

Theodore Roosevelt Elementary School was so close, Michael told me, I could wake up fifteen minutes before the bell, eat breakfast, and still get to class on time. Michael treated the schoolyard, which had outdoor basketball hoops, like an extension of his backyard.

I could see the roof of the school building from the window of my mother's attic office, its ornate cupola suggesting a fancy barn or a village church. I could see Michael's roof from my own window, screened by branches. There were only six or seven houses on the whole street. The Laudors, number 28, were diagonally across and down; a knight's move away on a chessboard.

Michael gave me a tour of the Wykagyl shopping center, two blocks from my house, where there was a store called Big Top that sold toys in the back and candy in the front, an A&P, a pizza place, and a pet shop where I could get a new aquarium. Guppies cost ten cents apiece.

Michael was the sort of guide who didn't just point out George's Hair Fort, he told you the names of all four Italian brothers who cut hair there. I could only ever remember Rosario, who cut my hair. He cut my father's hair, too, and called out, *Professore!* when he walked in. He called Michael's father professore too.

That was something else we had in common. Our fathers were college professors, though my father taught German literature and Michael's father taught economics. Also, my father was bald on top, with wings of white hair on either side of his head; Michael's father had a dark pompadour combed dramatically back, like the greasers he'd grown up with on the Brooklyn waterfront.

The following year, Mr. Summa—who had given up working at the 7-Up bottling plant to become our sixth-grade teacher—started calling Michael "professor" after overhearing him use the word "epiglottis" to tell a joke about hiccups, thus giving him a third nickname.

Michael might have been the reason my parents chose Mereland Road, but my mother's friend Cynthia was the reason they'd chosen New Rochelle. Cynthia and my mother were both writers, with an all-consuming devotion to literature, a shared commitment to feminism, and a dark awareness of the Holocaust, the black backing of the mirror they held up to reality that made the reflected world visible. They talked on the phone every day. When they got off the phone, they wrote long letters, and when they received each other's letters, they called, because there could never be too many words, though the written word was the only medium that truly mattered.

Cynthia lived in New Rochelle's south end, which had been settled in the seventeenth century by Huguenots—French Protestants fleeing the persecution of Louis XIV. Her house was in walking distance to the train station, the Long Island Sound, and a Victorian house in Sutton Manor that my mother had fallen in love with. But the neighborhood, and my mother's dream house, were "quickly dismissed," Cynthia told me, "because of the absence of any Jewish ambiance." This objection came from my father. "The chief reason was to live in an area where there would be children appropriate for befriending."

Appropriate children lived in the north end, where Jews had been settling since the postwar boom. Rob Petrie—the fictional comedy writer played by dapper Dick Van Dyke—lived in a generic suburb called New Rochelle. Carl Reiner—the bald Jew who based *The Dick Van Dyke Show* on his own life but wasn't allowed to play himself— lived in the north end of New Rochelle.

So did Jerry Bock and Joe Stein, the composer and book writer of *Fiddler on the Roof*, a musical about a poor Jew who dreams about being a rich Jew, which was beloved by rich Jews who dreamed about being poor Jews, or at least remembered their grandparents who'd been poor Jews once themselves. The musical had closed on Broadway only two years before, after becoming a movie. Even my parents had the cast album, though my father considered it a Jewish minstrel show and my mother dismissed it as middlebrow schlock.

Jews had moved to New Rochelle to escape New York City, then moved to the north end to escape the troubled parts of New Rochelle, which wasn't a true suburb but a small city in its own right. There were housing projects as well as golf courses, and a once-thriving downtown killed by the departure of a department store whose arrival had also killed it, which was more than I could follow but was the sort of thing they talked about with knowing assurance in Michael's house.

The big Conservative synagogue my father wanted us to join, Beth El, had relocated from downtown to the leafier north end and opened its new sanctuary in 1970. Between my mother's dream house in the south and Beth El in the north lay a patchwork of old Irish and Italian working-class neighborhoods, fancy developments, integrated middle-class neighborhoods, a moribund Main Street, and a highway-fractured zone that like the housing projects were largely Black.

And so instead of streets with opulent and evocative names like Sutton Manor and Echo Avenue, we moved to Mereland Road. The "mere" in Mereland must once have denoted a body of water, but for my mother the "mere" had devolved into its pedestrian homonym: *nothing more.*

There was no view of the water, only the blind exterior of Beth El looming over North Avenue. Designed by a disciple of Frank Lloyd Wright, the building was windowless as a power station or a mausoleum but a comfort to my father, who was making peace with the Jewish observance he'd abandoned in retaliation for God's abandonment of his parents thirty years before, when they were murdered along with one out of every three Jews in the world.

Our neighborhood was called Wykagyl. The word is believed to be a corruption of an Algonquin name used by the Lenape, though it sounded vaguely Yiddish as pronounced by my father, who had erased a good deal of his accent but who still said his *w*'s like *v*'s. If you never understood why the Marx Brothers thought "viaduct" could be mistaken for "why a duck," then you never heard my father say Wykagyl.

Our next-door neighbor, Mr. Fruhling, a refugee from Germany who made me squeeze his eighty-year-old bicep (rock hard, he used dumbbells), also said his *w*'s like *v*'s. So did his tough, tiny sister, who lived in the house with him. So did Harry Gingold, a Holocaust survivor from Poland who lived one street over and gave out the honors at Beth El during Sabbath services, sidling up to congregants and murmuring furtively when it was time to open the ark, as if he were giving a tip on a horse.

To my sister and me he was a comic figure, but to my father he was part of the invisible fellowship of refugees it was his soul's secret work to gather up. My father could pinpoint an accent and locate the sorrow behind it the way Sherlock Holmes could spot a limp and account for the accident that caused it at a glance.

Once, in a coffee shop, while Michael and I played tabletop soccer with three pennies and sugar packet goalposts, my father divined the wartime history of a waitress—Romania, Paris, the Pyrenees, Spain, Palestine, the Bronx—between the ordering of dessert and the bringing of the check. Even allowing for the brewing of a fresh pot of decaf—my father's one constant demand in life—it was an impressive performance, especially because the information wasn't journalistically extracted but offered in telegraphic exchanges sparked by mutual recognition. As we were leaving, my father murmured, "Her whole family. Auschwitz."

Michael was fascinated by such displays, and in his way had a similar impulse. Friends might notice my father had an accent, but Michael asked where he was from and how he'd gotten out of Vienna, and incorporated the information into his way of referring to my father and perhaps me. He incorporated my father's accent, too, which he began imitating almost immediately; not with malice, but more the way you might commit someone's telephone number to memory.

He did the same thing in high school when he worked for Sam and Stella, the elderly Jewish couple who owned Stellar Gifts and like my father had fled Germany after Kristallnacht. You had to be at home with the alien strangeness of such things to find it darkly amusing, as we did, that Sam and Stella sold crystal. Michael would come to see the neighborhood's survivors as an unseen collective of righteous protectors, with a mystical aura born of suffering that made them a bulwark against evil.

Nothing seemed further from the Manichaean struggles of the twentieth century than Mereland Road, even if Betty Friedan called suburban houses "comfortable concentration camps" in *The Feminine Mystique*, where she warned that housewives "are in as much danger as the millions who walked to their own death in the concentration camps."

Surely such hyperbole was an indicator of how far America was from actual concentration camps, like the one where my grandfather was murdered, if it could appear in a bestselling book that came into the world the same year Michael and I did. The book lived comfortably on a family bookshelf where I peeked into it with adolescent curiosity, misled by the title.

Was Michael bouncing a basketball the day I met him? He often had one with him the way you might take a dog out for a walk. I'd hear the ball halfway down the block, knocking before he knocked.

Even today when I hear the taut report of a basketball on an empty street, the muffled echo thrown back a split second later like the after-pulse of a heartbeat, I have a visceral memory of Michael coming to fetch me for one-on-one or H-O-R-S-E, or simply to shoot around if we were too deep in conversation for a game or I was tired of losing.

If you saw Michael in the air, legs splayed, elbows out, you might not think he was going to score, but he had a sort of will to power over the ball that sent it booming off the all-weather backboard and sifting through the chain mail net that hung from the rim in rusted tatters. It took me time to realize this was actually the result of hard work. He shot baskets in the rain and when there was snow on the court and his hands were raw with cold.

I can't remember if Michael had a basketball with him the day he introduced himself to me. He might just as easily have had a book. He often had several tucked under one arm that he would dump unceremoniously at the base of the steel pole holding up the schoolyard basket nearest the stairs. It was always an eclectic pile: Ray Bradbury, Hermann Hesse, Zane Gray westerns. Some were "assigned" by his father, he told me, like *To Kill a Mockingbird*, *Gideon's Trumpet*, or a prose translation of *Beowulf*, but they were part of the general jumble stirred in with the *Dune* trilogy and Doc Savage adventures.

Thanks to Michael, I became a big fan of Doc Savage, originally published in pulp fiction magazines in the 1930s but reissued as cheap paperbacks in the '70s. We joked about the archaic language and dated futurisms—long-distance phone calls!—but Doc Savage, charged with righteous adrenaline, formed an important part of the occult archive of manly virtues that I received secondhand from Michael, who got them wholesale from his father, grandfathers, old movies, and assorted dime novels.

Michael read many more volumes than I did, but he was a great summarizer of plots and situations, which were all essentially the same, and it was the characters that were so appealing. We spent hours talking about Clark Savage Jr., the golden-eyed "Man of Bronze" known as Doc because he was a surgeon, though he was essentially a mortal superman trained from birth by a team of scientists who were not only "the five greatest brains ever assembled in one group" but badass characters in their own right, handpicked by Doc's philanthropist father to raise his remarkable son.

Doc was the strongest, smartest, bravest, best-educated, and most dangerous man in the world. He was also so good—the books called him "Christlike," a usage Michael explained—that rather than throwing bad guys into prison to rot, he used his surgical skills to perform

a "delicate brain operation" on them, eliminating their criminal in-
clinations and erasing all memory of their past evil so they could return
to normal life.

I needed Doc Savage like a vitamin supplement, starved as I was
by high culture and the unintended fallout of my mother's feminism,
developed for use against an entrenched patriarchy but collaterally
persuading me not simply that women were equal to men—which
between my sister and mother was patently self-evident—but that male
nature was itself a piggy corollary to a brutish, chauvinistic world, and
that I would do well to keep aspects of my biological self, or at least
my adolescence, hidden like a shameful secret. Tennis player Bobby
Riggs might cheerfully call himself a male chauvinist pig—despite
losing his "battle of the sexes" match to Billie Jean King in front of
50 million people the year we moved to New Rochelle—but he was
the product of a different time and place. Besides, we kept kosher.
Michael's mother mysteriously kept a jar of bacon fat on the stove.

Michael and I both had book-filled houses, but Michael, who
liked to quantify, spoke of thousands of volumes. So many, he told
me, that books were used to prop up his house, which was sinking
like Venice. To prove it, he took me down into his cluttered basement and showed me the makeshift columns his father had contrived
using stacks of books and what appeared to be car jacks.

The book piles rose like stalagmites from tables, chairs, and the
floor itself. They served as pedestals for the jacks, which could be ratch-
eted up to increase the tension against the sagging ceiling and door-
frames. Michael laughed at this Rube Goldberg system, but he was
proud of the fact that books were literally holding up his house, and
that his ingenious father's library was slowing its journey to the center
of the earth.

My father sometimes took us into Manhattan and turned us
loose in the giant Barnes & Noble warehouse store on Fifth Avenue
and Eighteenth Street, around the corner from his office at Baruch

College. Barnes & Noble was just becoming a national retail chain, but the Fifth Avenue store sold used books and was so vast it was in *The Guinness Book of World Records*.

There were miles of shelves and bins filled with paperbacks, some pristine, others missing covers and sold for the price of a guppy. There were tables of hardcovers in mint condition marked down to a dollar or two that my mother eyed with sorrow, as if I'd raided a tomb rather than found a bargain. "Remaindered" books did not earn royalties but were sold off to make room for newer and more successful arrivals. The next stop was getting "pulped," like the horse in *Animal Farm* they turned into glue, literally worth less than the paper they were printed on.

Michael and I threw volumes haphazardly into our carts, though I concentrated on classics since I wasn't going to read most of them anyway. That was my secret. I treated the volumes more as emblems of aspiration, placeholders shelved for future consumption that meanwhile propped up my metaphorical house. Michael, on the other hand, started reading in the bookstore and continued on the train ride home.

Entering Michael's house, I was greeted by a round-breasted Indian dancer framed in the vestibule, and by a signature combination of odors—detergent, heating oil, hamburgers. Mail was piled on chairs and tabletops along with books, folded laundry, and unfolded sections of *The New York Times*, a familiar stew but stirred with a bigger stick.

I often heard the Laudors before I saw them. It was hard to tell even with practice if someone was shouting in anger or simply shouting rather than climbing the stairs or turning down the stereo just to make a point. And someone was always making a point.

There were three contentious brothers, each bigger than the one before, like the Billy Goats Gruff. Michael, who was the youngest, may have been Big at school, but at home he was most likely to get butted off the bridge.

One of the first stories Michael told me was how his brothers had dressed him up in a Superman costume when he was little and thrown him off the roof of their old house to see if he could fly. In another version, he was already wearing the outfit and was merely persuaded to jump. Both versions ended with a broken arm, but either way he was the hero of the story—abused, perhaps, but still Superman.

Michael celebrated his brothers along with his ability to survive them. He talked about his family with tattling amusement shot through with pride, exposing and mythologizing them all at once.

His mother, Ruth, who had a lovely voice, sometimes sang in the house, unheard, or laughed incongruously when her husband and sons hollered. What else could she do?

I'd been raised to think of brain versus brawn, but Michael's father was an intellectual who participated in the rough household energy. Even his name, Chuck, was a verb. Michael told me about the time his father was cutting vegetables in the kitchen when he saw a man through the window letting his dog go on the lawn. Forgetting the large knife in his hand, Chuck ran to the front door and flung it open, waving his arms and cursing. Man and dog fled.

Unlike my father, who favored muted Harris Tweed sport coats from Brooks Brothers, Chuck sported a black leather bomber jacket. He walked with the bouncing stride Michael had inherited, but angled for confrontation. Chuck charged at you head-on; my father preferred oblique approaches and swift exits. Even in movie theaters he liked to sit on the aisle in case he had to go to the bathroom or escape the Anschluss.

I found the violent energy of Michael's house thrilling. When my sister and I played Monopoly, she did not buy Park Place if I already owned Boardwalk. I left her the yellow properties because she liked them. In the Laudor house, the brothers wrote their names on items in the fridge, and someone was always shouting, "*That better be there when I come back!*" or "*Who drank my Dr Pepper?*" Michael was at the bottom of the food chain but could still threaten to piss in the orange juice to teach the others a lesson.

There was a thunderous roar at feeding time, a feeling of eat or be eaten. Out of necessity Michael ate voluminously and at great speed. He could inhale, as he liked to say, an entire pizza. I managed at most three slices but adopted Michael's habit of taking a bite immediately even though molten cheese adhered like napalm to the roof of my mouth and I was never sure if I was dislodging mozzarella from behind my braces or a small piece of my own seared flesh.

Michael was calmer when his house was empty. He enjoyed playing host in his quiet kitchen. He had a ceremonious way of dealing slices of white bread and squares of American cheese like double hands of blackjack when he made us open-faced grilled cheese in the toaster oven that to me was the height of technological innovation, though microwaves were starting to appear in the houses of the rich, along with other futuristic marvels like answering machines and the video game *Pong*.

We watched through the tiny glass door as the cheese blistered and rose into a blackened shell you cut away like the top of a soft-boiled egg, though we ate that too.

Michael had all four grandparents, something I'd seen only in *Charlie and the Chocolate Factory*. I was always a little jealous at this unexpected extravagance despite our roughly equivalent lives. My father's parents had been murdered in the Holocaust twenty years before I was born. My mother's father had died of a brain tumor when I was two. Only my mother's mother was left to spoil me.

Michael's grandparents did not all sleep in one bed, like Charlie's grandparents, or even in one house, but he saw a lot of them. Like the amber tint of his aviators, they imparted a geriatric aura to his precocity. Getting out of a chair, Michael would sometimes groan like an old Jewish man, a habit borrowed from his father's father, Max Lifshutz, who like his wife, Frieda, was born in Russia, and who ranked his days as one oy, two oy, or three oy.

He loved to contrast his old-world grandparents, drinking tea in a glass with a sugar cube between their teeth, with his mother's parents, assimilated Jews who had retired to a small Connecticut town where they lived like WASPs. I didn't know what a WASP was. White Anglo-Saxon Protestant, Michael told me, a phrase he unfurled like a battle flag.

His improbably named grandfather, Henry James Gediman, known as Jim, had been an "adman" for William Randolph Hearst in the hegemonic heyday of print journalism, something Michael had a real appreciation for. During the Great Depression, while Max and Frieda were having three-oy days in outermost Brooklyn, Henry James had dined at San Simeon and met Hearst's Hollywood mistress, Marion Davies.

I'd never heard of Hearst's California castle, his mistress, or Hearst himself, though his kidnapped granddaughter Patty was about to become famous. Michael referred to *Citizen Kane*, the movie Hearst's life had inspired, so often that even though I hadn't seen the movie I would murmur, "Rosebud," in imitation of Orson Welles. In reality I was imitating Michael impersonating Welles pretending to be Charles Foster Kane, a movie character modeled on a real tycoon his grandfather had met long ago.

Though Michael was devoted to the Russian-born Max and Frieda, he was grateful to his father for changing Lifshutz to Laudor before he was born. His grandparents had kept Lifshutz, and still lived in Brighton Beach, Brooklyn, where his father grew up and his grandmother Frieda stuffed money into a hole in the bathroom wall until a plumber came and stole it one day. Michael told stories about "crazy" Frieda with such amused affection that it was a shock when he told me, years later, that she had schizophrenia.

CHAPTER TWO

THE GOOD EARTH

But when Quinn the Eskimo gets here

Ev'rybody's gonna jump for joy

—BOB DYLAN, "Quinn the Eskimo"

I did not learn who Norman Rockwell was until Michael and I saw *Annie Hall* in junior high school and heard Woody Allen accuse Diane Keaton of growing up in a Norman Rockwell painting. It was the ultimate New York put-down of all the other places where all the unfortunate people had the bad luck to be born.

But Rockwell himself had been born in New York City, moved to New Rochelle as a teenager, and lived there for twenty-five years. He'd established his style and launched his career in New Rochelle, found models for his paintings among the boys playing in the street, bought a vacation cottage on the water in the south end, a house and studio in the north end, sent his son Jarvis to the Theodore Roosevelt Elementary School, and even painted one of the quaint signs welcoming visitors to New Rochelle.

In other words, Michael and I grew up in a Norman Rockwell painting. Every morning, once school started, I'd walk to the bottom of our one-block street, ring his bell, and wait for him to step groggily out from the household chaos. We'd hike up the hidden steps behind his house that led to the basketball court, climb a second flight of outdoor stairs, and slip in the building through a side door that felt like a private entrance.

One morning early in the fifth grade, Michael emerged from his house wearing a fedora and carrying a man's jacket draped over one shoulder. Clenched between his teeth was an old-fashioned cigarette holder. He looked pleased with himself, or maybe amused by me. I was wearing a black velvet vest over a ruffled white shirt and carrying a large white feather.

Our classroom had a festive costume-party feel when we arrived. Everyone was dressed for Biography Day, prepared to give clues and answer questions. Miss Waldman had baked brownies.

When it was Michael's turn, he commandeered Miss Waldman's swivel chair, which she cheerfully surrendered, sitting on her desk as I wheeled him around the room. He wore his jacket cape-like over his shoulders, doffed his fedora, and raised a hand, acknowledging the adulatory multitudes.

Lifting his chin defiantly, Michael clamped down on the cigarette holder so that it stuck up at a sharp angle, and declaimed, "Yesterday, December 7, 1941—a date which will live in *infamy*—the United States of America was suddenly and *deliberately* attacked by naval and air forces of the empire of Japan."

Michael looked around in triumph, untroubled by the blank expressions. He was the most powerful man in the free world, and had just declared war. It wasn't his problem that nobody knew who he was. Besides, Miss Waldman knew, and told the class about the president who had overcome polio and saved the country. Michael stood up stiffly, as if he really had been paralyzed, and gave Miss Waldman back her chair.

Nobody knew who I was either. Even I wasn't sure, but my mother had been so confident when she suggested Nathaniel Hawthorne, and reminded me we'd visited his house in Concord, Massachusetts, and gone to Salem, where his ancestors sent witches to the gallows, that I decided I did know. Besides, the black vest gave me an armored manly appearance, and the billowy shirt added a swashbuckling effect: a knightly pirate with a quill pen.

It was only when I was standing before the class trying to remember *The Blithedale Romance* and sprouting damp sideburns that I caught a whiff of something familiar rising from my collar, or perhaps the velvet vest, filling me with horror. Perfume! Darkness scribbled before my eyes and Miss Waldman stepped forward and asked me gently to tell the class who I was. She had no idea. How could she? I had gone to school dressed as my mother.

I learned a lot walking around New Rochelle with Michael, who liked narrating the histories of people and places. The Wykagyl Country Club, a grand plantation-like building across the street from Roosevelt, was not only famous for its golf course but according to Michael still restricted. I didn't know the word. "No Blacks or Jews allowed," he said.

I was shocked, but when I reported this to my father, he did not seem surprised. The whole country had been restricted; otherwise more of my relatives would be alive.

The thought that Wykagyl Country Club might not want us made sneaking onto the grounds in winter all the sweeter. The sledding was great, but even pissing into the snow was a political act, another phrase Michael taught me. He considered a lot of things political acts.

Whether or not the country club was still excluding Jews in 1973, the rest of Wykagyl had clearly unlocked its door. Even the stone church next to Roosevelt, with its tiny Huguenot burial ground, had become an Orthodox synagogue. Converted in the 1960s, the synagogue had retained the steeple above and the dead Huguenots below, lying under crooked tombstones in need of the orthodontic services of the Glideman brothers, the twins who took turns tightening my braces on Quaker Ridge Road.

Michael's family belonged to the Reform temple, which had also started out in central New Rochelle before migrating north "as the white person flies" toward Scarsdale. The Orthodox synagogue might *look* like a church, Michael told me, but the Reform temple *was* one. He referred to Temple Israel as "Our Lady of Pinebrook Boulevard."

Our parents had no interest in joining the country club even if it wanted them and they could afford it, which they couldn't. Michael told me, with more pride than regret, that his father was one of those economists who understood markets without ever managing to profit from them. My father had been a socialist in his youth and agreed with Balzac's assertion, which my mother also quoted, that behind every great fortune was a great crime, though my mother would not have minded belonging to one of the beach clubs in the south end. She loved the water, and she would have been near her friend Cynthia.

It was one more bond between Michael and me that a lot of our school friends had parents who drove Beamers and Benzes to second homes for long weekends, ate in restaurants even if it wasn't someone's birthday, and came back from winter vacations with Florida tans or ski tags dangling from the zippers of their parkas.

Michael and I lived in the modest section of Wykagyl and spent vacations hanging out in each other's houses. I felt sorry for kids who couldn't walk to the pizza place or the pet store, but apparently that wasn't how people in the suburbs thought, any more than they considered the apartment buildings a few blocks beyond our shopping center a touch of urban class, or believed, with my father, that public transportation was the big two-hearted river of civilization.

Ruth got an office job as soon as her kids were old enough to allow it, though she still did plenty of housework and always seemed to be running from one place to another. My mother was home during the day, but she was writing and would have murdered anyone calling her a homemaker.

She would never have called our house a "comfortable concentration camp," but was closer to accepting Betty Friedan's argument in *The Feminine Mystique* that trapped housewives not only become sick themselves but produce "atypical" offspring. Friedan had studied psychology and went so far as to suggest that women living blighted domestic lives were more likely to raise autistic and schizophrenic children, making feminism a matter of public health as well as justice.

I wanted my mother to be happy, and made my own lunch in the morning without knowing how high the stakes were for my sanity. I was very proud my mother was a writer, and loved the sound of her typing in the attic late into the night. "Everything exists to be put into a book," a French poet said, a line my mother quoted with approval. It was a big job. I lay in bed listening to the keys of her manual machine rapping on the paper like heavy rain falling on a tin roof.

The maroon Chevy Malibu rusting in front of my house rhymed with the ancient Plymouth Valiant rusting in front of Michael's. The Laudors also had a battered Ford station wagon lurking in the driveway like a wood-paneled hearse. Chuck drove it like a Ferrari, swearing and swerving and keeping an eye out for cops. He was always trying to shave a few seconds off his personal best no matter how local the driving. When he drove us to the YMCA, where Michael and I played racquetball, I usually needed a few minutes with my head down in the locker room before getting changed.

When my father drove us to the Y, Michael liked to draw his long legs up, circling his knees with his arms in mock preparation for impact. My father was, in fact, perfectly capable of forgetting he'd put the car in reverse before pulling out of a spot, or looking behind him while lurching forward. For years I thought it took a family of four to change lanes.

My parents had both learned to drive as adults, though that seems insufficient to explain why they canceled car trips because of snow, rain, fog, and darkness. In the suburbs this was like being a Hun with a horse allergy.

I'd never been inside houses like the ones our friends lived in. A hefty self-effacing boy nicknamed Bremer lived in an enormous Tudor house with a turret like the Museum of Natural History. We met there to play Diplomacy—a marathon board game that used the map of pre–World War I Europe. Henry Kissinger was said to love the game, which involved whispered alliances and savage betrayals conducted between rolls of the dice.

Bremer's house had empty rooms like Versailles where you could hammer out deals. You might find Michael murmuring in a corner of the solarium with Small, while I conspired with a boy we called Eggo, who had wavy *Tiger Beat* hair and a confident smile, and who, despite our pact, was going to invade Turkey and wipe out my army.

Eggo's own grand house was next to the house immortalized in *Ragtime* by E. L. Doctorow, who lived in it, and put it in his novel the way Norman Rockwell put local boys into his paintings.

Michael and I cherished the rumpled status of our small, book-rich houses. We were proud that the barbers shouted, *"Professore!"* when our fathers walked in, even though we were both familiar with

the phrase "a professor's salary" as an explanation for not getting something or going somewhere.

Professores had time if not money. Though our fathers had to teach
summer courses to pay for camp or braces, neither of us was ever sure
if they were teaching or on break. I knew a semester was over when
I found my father lying on the living room sofa, his body thatched
with the blue exam books he'd fallen asleep intending to grade.

At Michael's house it was often Chuck in an undershirt who flung
open the door and looked me over narrowly before letting me in. Michael's father was an explainer who put great faith in reason, economics, and shouting, with a "let me tell you" manner that suggested the
world was fixable, if only people would listen to him and be less stupid.
I couldn't help admiring his self-confident style, which had a rough
sort of American optimism.

My father shared Chuck's disgust at the state of the world, but
not his faith in solutions. *The New York Times* was the wound and
the bandage for both of them, but my father did not consider the world
rational, and tended to take refuge in literary quotation, Jewish jokes,
Jungian archetypes, and ambiguous evasion.

When they ran into each other on the street, my father began retreating as soon as Chuck advanced to make a point. Returning from
the schoolyard, Michael and I sometimes spotted our fathers waltz-
ing across Mereland, my father still clutching a bag of groceries from
the A&P, moving backward.

The Vietnam War was always there, at least on television, but Americans didn't go to it anymore, as Hemingway put it about a different war, and it wasn't on television as much as everyone said. There
wasn't that much television. Still, its effects were palpable. Small had
an older brother who had successfully starved himself to avoid the
draft, which made him a kind of war hero in our eyes.

We had no intention of going to war ourselves. Ever. The draft had ended, but if they brought it back, our parents would drive us to Canada themselves, though my parents would drive there slowly and Chuck would floor it.

I wasn't the only kid raised without G.I. Joes or cap guns, as if the war were sustained by the passions of boys rather than the cold calculations of Ivy League technocrats scheduling our deaths. My anti-war convictions were matched only by an illicit desire to get my hands on something that would make a bang. We grew up gunless in the golden age of revenge fantasies; everyone did Dirty Harry impressions and hoped the punk felt lucky so you could blow him away without guilt, like the avenging father in *Death Wish*.

Technically, Michael and I were among the seventy-six million Americans born between 1946 and 1964, known collectively as baby boomers. But we arrived at the tail end, born on the border that made us what astrologers and sociologists call "cuspers." Arriving just before closing time, we missed the feast but got there in time to split the bill. Still, we were nostalgic for the world they'd made, even if it hadn't turned out the way they'd hoped.

Along with nostalgia, access to drugs, and great record collections, the kids with big brothers and sisters old enough to have tasted the sixties had inherited a kind of anticipatory cynicism about the decade we were going to become teenagers in. It wasn't that all wars had already been fought but that they had already been protested.

Michael knew all the words to "I Feel Like I'm Fixin' to Die" by Country Joe and the Fish, which he sang with a sardonic grin:

> *So put down your books and pick up a gun*
> *We're gonna have a whole lotta fun.*

Michael found it hilarious that "the Fish" was actually Barry Melton from Brooklyn. In the sixties, even Jews could turn into animals! Michael had a cousin Peter from New Jersey who had discovered his own paw prints in the snow one day after eating a hallucinogenic cactus, changed his name to Coyote, and disappeared into the California counterculture. He'd return as a famous actor by the time we were in college, but for us the age of wonders was over.

Country Joe and the Fish had performed their Vietnam protest song at Woodstock just four years before I moved to New Rochelle, but Woodstock was already part of the mythic past. This wasn't simply because we were young, but because the distance between 1969 and 1973 was unbridgeable.

The Fish had parted ways with Country Joe in 1970, the same year the Beatles broke up, which was also the year Janis Joplin and Jimi Hendrix "choked on their own vomit," a fact we knew better than their music. Their deaths did not seem like the culmination of the sixties but its unjust termination, as if they'd been throttled by the jealous new decade.

There were always rumors about the Beatles getting back together, the way there were Elvis sightings a decade later. But Elvis was still alive, a fat man in a jumpsuit lumped in with the disappointing present, where Paul McCartney and Wings sang "Band on the Run," and John Lennon and Yoko Ono sang "Woman Is the Nigger of the World," for which they were honored by the National Organization for Women for their "strong profeminist statement."

But the idealism of the sixties lived on in our classrooms like time in Jim Croce's bottle. Our teachers were the products and protectors of its dreams, and we were their eager assistants—like Daniel Ellsberg's ten-year-old daughter, who had cut off the "top secret" stamp at the top and bottom of classified documents when Ellsberg was xeroxing the *Pentagon Papers* for *The New York Times*.

Ellsberg was a hero in Michael's house, where conspiracy, Vietnam, the ACLU, and journalism were much shouted about. Not long before I'd moved to New Rochelle, Ellsberg's espionage charges had been dismissed after the judge learned that White House operatives—wearing wigs and phony glasses!—had broken into the office of Ellsberg's psychiatrist to look for information that could discredit the Defense Department analyst who had discredited the Vietnam War.

We all knew about the Watergate break-in that Woodward and Bernstein made famous, but the goon squad known as the Plumbers—created to "plug leaks" like Ellsberg's—had opened the door to Watergate when they broke into the psychiatrist's office a full year before. This clownish failure was organized in part by an ex-CIA operative, E. Howard Hunt, inspired by members of the American Psychiatric Association who had "found out" about Barry Goldwater during the 1964 presidential election. The psychiatrists had labeled the candidate schizophrenic, manic-depressive, psychopathic, and psychotic in response to a survey sent out by *Fact* magazine, which published the results under a modified version of Goldwater's campaign slogan: "In your guts you know he's nuts." Unlike the nearly two thousand mental health professionals who had analyzed the candidate without meeting him, the Plumbers had resorted to a smash and grab to expose the contents of Ellsberg's character, which they hoped to find in a file cabinet containing what Hunt referred to as "the mother lode."

The battle for hearts and minds was as old as war, but the idea that you could crack the brain like a safe, and access or rearrange its contents, was a twentieth-century phenomenon. In the aftermath of Watergate, the Senate's Church Committee discovered five administrations' worth of spy agency malfeasance, including the revelation that the CIA had tested mind-altering drugs on American citizens without their knowledge, a veritable Bay of Guinea Pigs sparked by fears during the Korean War that Chinese and Soviet scientists were brainwashing captured American soldiers.

One former CIA agent testified that the illicit doping continued long after it was clear there were no mind-control chemicals, because the movie version of *The Manchurian Candidate* came out, and it "made something impossible look plausible." Michael and I were children of a time when a "thought experiment" meant something more than Einstein imagining a beam of light on a trolley. A movie about a foreign conspiracy to brainwash Americans and destroy the country had served as justification of a domestic conspiracy to brainwash Americans in order to save it.

Such things were remote from our lives, but the fringe had a way of moving to the middle, the way the weedy bottom of the Farm Camp Lowy lake rose to the surface midway through our summer. Meanwhile, central blunders migrated outward. LSD, a drug the CIA thought capable of enslaving the mind—and tested on prisoners, mental patients, and unconsenting barflies—became a mind-expanding elixir, celebrated by artists, intellectuals, and an eager generation seeking a cure for convention, who tested it on themselves.

The first antipsychotic medication was patented in the United States the same year that LSD was sent to psychiatric institutes gratis by its Swiss manufacturer. Psychiatrists had a drug for squelching hallucinations in one hand, and a drug for inducing them in the other. It was only a matter of time before things got mixed up and the symptoms of mental illness blurred into the promise of mind expansion. One generation's brainwashing was another generation's mental hygiene. This, too, shaped our world.

The psychiatrist's office ransacked in 1971, with its broken file cabinet (now in the Smithsonian), turns out to be a fitter symbol than the hotel burgled in 1972, not only of the decade's political fiascoes, and the years leading up to them, but of disasters yet to come whose seeds were already planted.

Perhaps it could not be otherwise, because so many things that had been overturned had truly needed toppling. We lived in the aftermath of optimistic inversions as well as cynical ones. The challenge was telling them apart.

About some things we were not in doubt. There was no federal holiday yet for Martin Luther King Jr., murdered just five years before I moved to New Rochelle, but our teachers played the record of his "I Have a Dream" speech for us with solemn formality, a sacred strangeness ringing into the classroom from beyond the grave and even farther, from the American South, where "the Negro is sadly crippled by the manacles of segregation." We were all bound to Dr. King's dream by the year of our birth, which he announced in his speech: "1963 is not an end, but a beginning."

But the beginning of what? The shackles had been struck off, but the dream felt faded rather than fulfilled. Or perhaps it had come and gone, like Apollo 11, which had landed at Tranquility Base and miraculously taken off again, leaving the flag behind, as if the prophetic future, like the terrible past, was one more thing we'd missed.

Nobody told us what came next, least of all Dr. King, who had been murdered by a white supremacist five years after delivering his electrifying speech. For our teachers, the grief was fresh and ongoing, but so was the promise of a time when we would all be free together.

Triumphs and tragedies still happened, but they often lacked the meaning they were supposed to have, which we craved. That summer—my first joining Michael at hippie Farm Camp Lowy—Martin Luther King Jr.'s mother was shot to death while playing the organ in the Atlanta church where her son had preached. Alberta King's killer was a twenty-three-year-old Black man, and a model student at Ohio State until he began exhibiting the strange beliefs and behavior that propelled him to Georgia with a gun and a list of Black ministers in his pocket he needed to kill.

No lawyer, Black or white, would defend him, except for a lone follower of the Nation of Islam, dismissed by the defendant, who was insulted by the suggestion he wasn't in his right mind. Permitted to represent himself, despite incoherent outbursts about God and Satan, he was swiftly convicted of murder. Sentenced to die in the electric chair, he laughed, mimicked the convulsions of electrocution, and blew kisses to the crowd before being hustled from the courtroom while his parents wept.

We did not learn much American history, or history of any kind, but devoted ourselves to an experimental curriculum called Man: A Course of Study, MACOS for short, developed in the sixties to combat racism and ethnocentrism by teaching us to look at ourselves and others with an anthropological eye as a way to appreciate our common humanity.

MACOS was the brainchild of a brilliant Harvard psychologist, one of the experts tasked with transforming American education after the Soviet Union sent Sputnik, the world's first satellite, into orbit on October 4, 1957. Reeling from the discovery that we were losing the space race, the US military turned to elite universities to come up with a plan to attack the cognitive deficits at the root of our national failure.

War was too important to be left to the generals, and the education of young people was too important to be left to elementary school teachers. Who better than topflight social scientists—especially research psychologists who knew how we thought and learned—to sharpen young minds like pencils pointed at the night sky?

MACOS was based on the belief that children of any age can learn about any subject, that animals and human beings are bound together in a single web of life, and that you can learn everything you need to know about being human by studying any human society because all societies are of equal value. We fought the Cold War in the corridor the conventional way, by crouching down and covering our heads, but in the classroom, we opened our minds. Starting with the life cycle of the salmon, the herring gull, and the baboon, we progressed up an evolutionary ladder of social complexity until we arrived in triumph at the Netsilik Eskimo of Pelly Bay.

We still said Eskimo instead of Inuit, "man" instead of "people," and Miss Waldman instead of Ms. Waldman, but our hearts were in the right place, and we loved the earth and were filled with sorrow and admiration for those who lived in harmony with it. On our classroom wall was a poster-sized reproduction of the beautiful "Blue Marble" photograph of our planet, taken the previous year from the window of the Apollo 17 spacecraft, the last manned moon landing. We were the first generation to know what the earth really looked like in all its blue-green glory, without people to obstruct the view.

The ethnographic films we watched offered in their own way an unobstructed view of the Netsilik Eskimo, who lived in round snowhouses and went about their timeless business in the far north. The films had no narration, a conscious attempt to avoid a Western voice of authority telling us what to think. There was just a woman with stiff braids and a half-moon knife neatly excising the eyeball of a salmon and handing it to a little boy who pops it into his mouth like a jelly bean. There was a man and woman lying together under caribou skins, their beaming faces lit by the smoky glow of a seal oil lamp, as a cherubic boy swims up for air out of the shadows between them.

Michael and I were indignant about the critics who protested the wife swapping, cannibalism, bestiality, infanticide, and killing of old people they claimed would compromise our moral education. We were no more encouraged to do those things than we were to eat eyeballs. Besides, the old people *wanted* to stay behind on the ice shelf once they began slowing the others down on the brutal winter journey to hunt seals. Though it was true that Old Kigtak still felt "life was sweet," and crawled across the frozen sea in pursuit of her family's vanishing sled.

We blamed religious fundamentalists for the congressional hearings the following year that terminated federal funding, which came from the National Science Foundation, putting an end to MACOS soon after. A flower of the sixties born at Harvard and nurtured in the frozen north couldn't survive the Florida town where a Baptist minister had gotten hold of his daughter's social studies curriculum. An irony we failed to appreciate at the time was that the Netsilik were themselves religious Christians. They'd converted to Catholicism forty years before; while we were learning about the angry witch they worshipped at the bottom of the sea, they were living in concrete houses and going to church.

As for the films, the Netsilik had gamely performed a reconstructed version of their ancestral selves, coached by the anthropologist who had trekked to Pelly Bay with a MACOS film crew in the midsixties hoping to capture the culture that the explorer Knud Rasmussen had found when he made first contact in the 1920s. The subjects of the films were also the actors, reaching back to childhood stories they'd heard from grandparents who had themselves been reaching back. Meanwhile the cameramen concealed cigarettes, rifles, crucifixes, and snowmobiles so that "student anthropologists" like Michael and me could have an unmediated encounter with an authentic culture.

The education revolution suited Michael and me in different ways. For me, the best thing about MACOS was that we spent so much time watching films, playing the caribou migration game, and tearing up paper seals to figure out who got the liver and who got the skin, that we did very little reading, memorizing, or writing. I was a fast talker but an easily distracted, painfully slow reader with a lousy memory for things that didn't interest me or rhyme. The emphasis on *how* we knew things, rather than on *what* we knew, was a godsend. I might not have learned much, but I didn't forget anything either.

Michael never forgot anything because, like Doc Savage, he had a photographic memory. He also read at breakneck speed, like John F. Kennedy, who read 1,200 words a minute, as we learned from someone who visited our class and gave us a crash course in the Evelyn Wood speed-reading method.

The space-age world was full of information, and if you couldn't read at rocket speed, where would you be? Instead of troubling over individual words, we were taught to run our finger down the middle of the page, taking in whole paragraphs, like JFK. Michael could do this without using his finger, "inhaling" a page the way he inhaled a pizza. For me, a long word was more like a sentence with a beginning, middle, and end that I read the way I mowed our lawn with the rusty rotary mower left in our garage; going over the same strip multiple times, I went from left to right and also from right to left. But I got good at moving my finger vertically down the page, nodding thoughtfully and trying not to overdo it as I flipped the pages.

The Cold War had paradoxically brought together two equal and opposite impulses: empirical precision and social-scientific vagary. Information was so important that books had been replaced by something called SRAs, which stood for Science Reading Associates; these were laminated cards featuring passages of fiction or non fiction—it didn't matter which as long as they were boring—filed like recipes in a box. The color-coded cards were organized in ascending order of difficulty that avoided the stigma of numbered levels by introducing the stigma of colored levels. Everyone knew that rose was for dummies and aqua was for smart kids.

I read at the bottom of the spectrum, though for honor's sake I liked to keep an olive or purple on my desk. The beauty of self-directed study was that I could fudge my way up the chart on the wall. Nobody expected you to cheat on the self-corrected assessments that would only lead to harder readings and more questions. Besides, why would Hawthorne *pretend* to be on aqua when his friend FDR had burned through the entire Reading Laboratory kit with such robotic swiftness that he was allowed to read whatever he wanted even during regular class time?

Michael took full advantage of this arrangement. He kept stacks of paperbacks on his desk, working his way through fresh piles every day. He didn't just read the books, he read them all *at the same time*, like Bobby Fischer playing chess with multiple opponents. After a few chapters in one, he'd reach for another and read for a while before grabbing a third without losing focus, as if they all contained pieces of a single connected story.

I was a direct beneficiary of all that reading. Michael seemed to have almost as much compulsion to tell me about the books he read as he did to read them. I paid him back in murmured comments or jokes he broadcast aloud without hesitation, getting laughs or praise for my words. But I acquired a phantom bookshelf entirely populated by twice-told tales I heard while we were shooting baskets, going for pizza, or walking around the neighborhood. Michael told me about *Lord of the Flies* in such excited detail that I half believed I'd read it in fifth grade myself, and traded initiate phrases—"Sucks to your assmar!" and "Kill the pig! Spill his blood"—like secret passwords.

Though I didn't get past Ralph the fair-haired boy blowing on a conch shell, after the puffing bespectacled Piggy tells him how, I knew, thanks to Michael, that Jack steals Piggy's glasses to make fire and that Simon talks to a pig's head stuck on a sharpened stick, and that the pig's head talks back to him. Above all I knew that Piggy got killed, something Michael often brought up.

The first time he talked about the book, he asked if I knew what "the red stuff" was on the rock ledge. I guessed blood but Michael shook his head gravely: *brains*. Piggy's head had cracked open! I felt him mastering and expunging the horror, rehearsing it for himself while catechizing me in his experience.

Michael read while Miss Waldman taught, and I sometimes saw her watching him read the way my grandmother watched me eat. When he raised his hand, he kept on reading, and only looked up after he was called on and carefully put a finger on his place. When he asked a question, Miss Waldman seemed palpably relieved if it was something she could answer.

Reading in class was a hard habit for Michael to break in the coming years. So was napping, as if one nighttime activity led to another. He liked to tell the story about the time Mr. Summa, after repeated warnings, overturned his desk while Michael was sleeping in the attached chair. He woke to find himself sprawled on the floor, his books scattered and his desk on its side like a tipped cow. Did that really happen or was it more like the MACOS movies, an emblematic reconstruction? He told the story at his own expense, but like the account of his brothers tossing him off the roof, it was still a superman story.

Two weeks before junior high school began, I was in the Roosevelt schoolyard with Michael, Eggo, Small, Bremer, and a few other kids playing touch football when a guy on a motorized dirt bike roared onto the field. He was a teenager making a lot of noise, and we ignored him or maybe envied him but kept on playing as he rode laps around the field.

At first, he gave us a wide berth, but he kept drawing closer with every pass until suddenly he drove right through the middle of our game so that we scattered like chickens. When he came around again, we stopped and watched as he took aim at a boy named Andy; we were shouting and swearing, but he kept coming until the last second, when he swerved or Andy sprang. We were high-fiving Andy and thinking maybe it was time to go home but not moving all that fast, a little hypnotized perhaps by the buzz of the bike, and before we knew it, he had come around again.

I looked up and he was gunning right for me. He was a white kid, no helmet, older than us but not that much older, with black hair and what I would have called a crazy grin. I couldn't remember if we'd worked out that it was better to stand still and let *him* move, or to jump away at the last moment. I was aware of the others shouting, but were they saying, "Run," "Jump," or "Freeze"? It's possible even the kid on the bike was yelling at me; he looked angry, and his scowling mouth was open.

The next thing I knew I was flying up into the air as if I had been tossed by a bull. Then I was on the ground, with Michael and the others breathlessly peering over me. I was not in the same spot and felt like a banana that had just shot out of its skin. It would not have surprised me if all my clothes were gone, like Charlie Brown after a line drive.

Everyone was marveling at the arc of my flight. Michael was claiming it was a record of some sort, and using the word "trajectory." I had a surprised sense of being all right, and pulled up my pants leg, more because my left leg itched than because it hurt. There was a pulpy bulge of red and purple like Piggy's brains, with something white at the center more alarming than the red, which made me instantly sick. Michael turned and sprinted off to his house to call the cops, my parents, an ambulance.

CHAPTER THREE

MEMORY GLASS

It is a joy to be hidden but disaster not
to be found.

—D. W. Winnicott

I began Albert Leonard Junior High School on crutches, sitting out
recess as the Roosevelt crowd reconstituted itself on a balding patch
of field for a touch football free-for-all. Michael sometimes joined
me, especially if he emerged from the school building after the football game had already begun.

He was often running late, though the term didn't really apply
because he operated according to his own schedule, expressing exaggerated disregard for external expectations. Kids told mythic stories
about Michael's father answering the phone when the school called
about missed classes. Chuck would ask about his son's grades, and if
they were good, as they invariably were, he would tell the caller to
leave his brilliant son alone. Michael was the source of these stories,
but I had no trouble imagining Chuck telling some hapless administrator to shove it.

Michael had begun dating a slender, dark-haired girl named Cybele who laughed easily but often seemed a little sad. Her parents
were Lebanese Christians, Michael reported with excitement, though
her father, a doctor, had grown up in Cairo: *Arabs!* Not that anybody
thought of Cybele as "an Arab," though Michael told me her big sister

was a supporter of the PLO, which he found disturbing and exhilarating. He loved heated political exchanges, especially if nobody threw a chair, and Cybele's parents were cultured intellectuals, warm and welcoming and always eager to feed him.

Cybele fell in easily with our Jewish crowd, and sat at the lunch table where Michael and I played hearts with the Roosevelt regulars plus a few add-ons from other schools. In the background, an occasional M-80 blew up inside a milk carton while greasers pierced each other's ears with a safety pin at a table hemmed in by girls in short skirts and snorkel jackets, hooded like Druids.

We brought our lunch, but if it was pizza day, you could buy a lunch ticket for a quarter from a kid who'd gotten it for free. My parents didn't want me to take food out of the mouths of the needy, but the sellers seemed to have rolls of tickets like carnival barkers and no signs of malnutrition.

Michael's relationship with Cybele did not last long, though I was never sure when it ended. Cybele still sat at our lunch table and Michael continued going to her house even if she wasn't there. Cybele would find him settled on the red couch in her living room, talking to her parents the way he talked to mine, as if auditioning for adoption. He loved other people's houses and had a knack for leaving himself on doorsteps waiting to be found, brought inside, and swaddled in hospitality.

I was never surprised to find Michael chatting with my mother while she gardened, or my sister while she did homework in the kitchen. Our house was a natural extension of his, but he colonized other houses too. He was a Goldilocks who didn't run off when the bears came home, but stayed for more porridge.

In class, Michael liked to sit in the last row, tip his chair back against the wall, and play hangman. Though we shared some classes, Michael placed into every honors class, while my educational career was more checkered. After I failed one algebra test too many, my mother went to school to ask if there was another class better suited to my "abilities."

My teacher explained that I was already in the lower of two classes, which left only the remedial class, where I must not go under any circumstances. Math had nothing to do with it, the teacher explained; I was quiet and bespectacled, and it was a matter of health and safety.

To my mother's surprise, the "tracking system" was more like the European system of train travel; you wanted to travel first class, you could survive in second, but you should avoid third at all costs. Remedial classes weren't for remediation, they were holding pens for kids who didn't want to learn, as well as for kids who wanted to learn but didn't. Whether they failed for social, behavioral, emotional, or neurological reasons, who could say? It didn't matter. Once they put the dangerous with the unlucky, the teacher said, only one outcome was possible. I would just have to pay better attention, work harder, and cheat. He didn't say the last part, but did he have to?

My parents had left New York City because the public schools had failed, but they'd moved to the suburbs with a middle-class expectation that, like a department store, a public school provided everything under one roof. Which is probably why, in addition to the expense, nobody talked about getting me a tutor, and why Michael and I considered SAT prep classes a luxury for the spoiled rich.

But here was proof that being "smart," if not quite a matter of life or death, was at least a matter of public safety. Luckily, I did well in humanities classes, which in my home were the ones that counted. Though still a slow reader who spelled like a five-year-old, I had compensatory verbal skills. I'd also discovered spoken word records at the New Rochelle Public Library, memorizing poems and speeches that gave me a portable library I could access in the dark.

Our Roosevelt friend Bremer, whose well-to-do parents actually had him tested, did disappear into the remedial world. I was vaguely aware that Michael treated him with teasing contempt, as though he were a poor relation who earned his keep by fetching our snacks even when we were in his house. I did not want to wind up like that.

My mother referred to me as a "late bloomer," which, if you think about it, literally means retarded, but I didn't think about it. "Late bloomer" was meant to suggest that I had not yet become extraordinary in the expected way, which was not the same as being ordinary or even, God forbid, something worse.

I put my faith in concealment, a strategy that bit me in the ass at my bar mitzvah, a date that would live in infamy. This was thrown into stark relief by Michael's triumphant passage into Jewish manhood, making our bar mitzvahs a good example of parallel lives running on divergent tracks.

Michael's arrogance tended to keep pace with his abilities. Both were enjoying a growth spurt, but they grew in public, which gave him a kind of integrity even though some kids thought he was a jerk. He seemed in tune with himself, whereas my expectations, though as grand, were hidden like my deficits far below the surface, where icebergs grow and anxieties proliferate.

Michael had tried to get me to read *The Godfather* on several occasions, and though I never did—the movie had already been on television—I took up a line he liked to quote: "The Don was a real man at the age of twelve." The phrase said a great deal about Michael, who was constantly testing himself despite acting like someone with nothing to prove. At camp, he was the only person in our bunk who had swum the lake, or even bothered to attempt the challenge; the rest of us watched him doggedly lifting and dropping his arms, as a lone rowboat accompanied him slowly around the outer reach of the far shore, until we lost interest and wandered away.

Vito Corleone might have been a real man at twelve, but put him in front of a Torah scroll, as Michael and I liked to say, and let's see how tough he is. Reading from the Torah wasn't a problem for Michael, who read Hebrew "like a machine," he told me, though without comprehension. I had no aptitude for foreign languages, as my French teacher pointed out in the middle of class—"What happened to you, Rosen? Your sister was so smart."—and the Hebrew in the Torah is unvowelled and unpunctuated. Nevertheless, my father wanted me to chant the entire Torah reading, which as bad luck would have it, was one of the longest readings in the annual cycle.

Over at Our Lady of Pinebrook, Michael told me almost apologetically, you read a few lines of the Torah, gave a speech in English, and collected your checks. His father might have wanted him to read *Beowulf,* but he had no beef with Temple Israel's low bar. My case was different. I was named for my murdered grandfather, just as my sister was named for our murdered grandmother. Our existence was not the fulfillment of our father's escape but a provisional commentary on the meaning of his survival, which could be determined only by future generations and their relationship to the past. In other words, my inability to learn the whole Torah reading would be my father's failure as well as my own, not to mention a big disappointment to martyred millions.

Michael had learned everything he needed to know by the time my bar mitzvah, which was scheduled first, came around. For once I was jealous of him for learning *less,* and wished my father had taken the advice of our cantor, who said it would be perfectly respectable for me to learn only a section or two of my portion.

The cantor was a small man with a large voice who had trained to be an opera singer and liked to throw the occasional Mozart aria into the liturgical mix. He had already annoyed my father, who loved his voice, by refusing to chant the prayer for departed souls during my bar mitzvah service, which my father had requested to honor his murdered parents. The cantor pointed out, reasonably enough, that a bar mitzvah is not a funeral. He won the argument, but the dead, as often happens, got the last word.

I would have given anything for Michael's photographic memory as I set about memorizing the whole "reading" as if it were an oral saga or the state secrets the guy in *The 39 Steps* carries around in his head until someone shoots him. I listened without comprehension to a cassette I played over and over on the portable machine I took to camp for mixtapes of the Rolling Stones and Cat Stevens. I half expected the congas and shouts of "Sympathy for the Devil," but instead of the suavely demonic Mick Jagger introducing himself, there was the tragic-voiced Reverend Friedler, a Holocaust survivor from Poland into whose musical care I had been committed.

When the day came, I dressed in the three-piece powder-blue Pierre Cardin suit purchased for the occasion, and climbed the steps to the elevated bimah that makes a synagogue resemble a theater. Looking out over the sea of friends, relatives, and familiar synagogue strangers, I realized that everything I'd memorized had vanished from my head, and that it had never really been there in the first place.

The last thing I heard before the big double doors banged shut behind me was my great-aunt Fay announcing in her outdoor voice, "He's going to throw up now, just like Martin!"

My father found me lying on the floor in the basement men's room with my feet sticking out of a stall. I had indeed thrown up, and my father assured me that I would now feel better. He coaxed me back upstairs, where I chanted a few more words, froze, and fled again. He coaxed me back; I fled once more. This time my father threw in the towel. I was allowed to remain on the tiled floor, curled like a college freshman around the base of the toilet while Reverend Friedler finished my portion in the sanctuary above me.

Michael's transition to Jewish manhood went more smoothly. Though he'd confided to me that he had no idea what the Hebrew meant, and that consequently it meant nothing, he flew through his portion with self-assured ease, and I had no doubt he could have memorized mine as well as his. He delivered his speech like a guy who enjoyed doing it, and who somehow had done it before. He wasn't just talking but was working the crowd and getting laughs.

It was that, more than his fluent reading or the reception at the Fountainhead—with its carpeted walls, dance floor, and the "memory glass" a few girls always made—that I envied most of all. I had secretly decided to become a stand-up comedian. This would be hard if I could not stand up.

School presentations became a problem. Not long after my bar mitzvah, I gave an oral report about circulation and the heart. My sister had done a wonderful job with the giant poster—ventricles, aorta, superior vena cava, blue and red blood—but I never got a chance to show it off.

Our science teacher Mr. Selleck was sympathetic about the asthma I pretended to have when I walked out. My parents would have backed me up with a note had one been needed. I had sicknesses for all seasons, and my family had done a good job attributing my bar mitzvah to the lingering effects of bronchitis.

The day after I'd left class midsentence, Michael, perhaps to take my mind off my embarrassment, informed me that our science teacher had a metal plate in his head. He often knew such things from his older brothers or his father, who had taught junior high before becoming a professor. Mr. Selleck did have a slightly abstracted manner and a crew cut embossed on one side with a round subcutaneous scar like a tiny crop circle.

From then on, we spent hours of class time waiting for him to lean too close to the powerful desktop magnet he used for demonstrations. Michael's theory was that one day Mr. Selleck's head would crash into the magnet like a planet falling into the sun. "Here it comes," he'd murmur, and though it never happened, I was grateful for the distraction.

CHAPTER FOUR

STRANGERS

We all have a face that we hide away forever.

—BILLY JOEL, "The Stranger"

I'd started junior high sitting out recess because I had to, then out of fear of reinjury, and finally out of habit, mingled with a vague disinclination that must already have been there and morphed imperceptibly into a larger pattern of withdrawal. I was becoming more of a spectator while Michael was becoming more of an actor. He dropped the cello and took up the guitar, that skeleton key that opens all teenage doors.

We still met at the Roosevelt schoolyard, where kids got together to shoot baskets, fungo baseballs, and bullshit, but if someone produced a little weed, Michael was quick to stride off in their direction, while I hung back. When some of the Roosevelt guys went to a Who concert, it was Michael who procured the suspiciously abundant bag of green stuff. He forgot rolling papers and nobody else remembered, not even Small, who'd been practicing with oregano for just such an occasion, but at the last minute they found a store near Madison Square Garden selling corncob pipes that actually worked. Nobody got high—childhood was not quite ready to let go—but a threshold had been crossed.

They'd worked out the mechanics by the time I joined them at Madison Square Garden to see Jethro Tull, but I didn't take the joint when it came my way. I was already at the edge of panic, squinting through the rainbow haze at the far-off band whose throbbing sound reached into my rib cage. Eggo exhaled pot smoke into my hair so I would at least *smell* high.

Not that anyone at home was checking my pupils or sniffing my jacket. It wasn't parental warnings but private fear that kept me from crossing the threshold. More than a failure of memory or nerve, my bar mitzvah fiasco and its aftermath humiliations felt like the symptom of some larger incapacity, an inborn fragility that drugs would only make worse. Failing to complete one rite of passage kept me from participating in others, compounding the feeling of ineptitude while Michael raced ahead, in tune with the spirit of the age even as he marched to his own drummer.

My return alive from Manhattan was all that mattered to my weary father, who waited up for me in his unraveling terry cloth bathrobe.

It amazes me that our parents let us go into New York City at all, even if Michael and I were taller than our fathers and went with a group. My mother had always believed that crowds made the city safe, especially if you knew where you were going. Michael always knew, even high—*the Don had a real sense of direction by the age of twelve*—but the city no longer seemed to honor its own rules.

My first-grade teacher had recently been stabbed to death in an Upper West Side subway station on her way to buy tickets for Lincoln Center. The headline NEW YORKERS WATCH MURDER meant that a crowd had failed to prevent the daytime killing. Adding to the horror, the victim had been stabbed repeatedly without being robbed. Her zipped pocketbook was found with her body and the long bloody knife. Who killed merely to kill?

As if to dramatize the inadequacy of old protections, a Barnard student walking in Forest Hills, Queens, had been shot in the face by a man walking toward her. Instinctively, she'd raised the textbook she was carrying, and the bullet passed through its pages before lodging in her brain, killing her.

What made the story such big news was that the police were able to match the bullet in her brain with a bullet from the shooting of two young women who'd been killed back in the summer of '76 after a night of dancing at a New Rochelle nightclub. They'd been shot in nearby Pelham Bay, and suddenly a series of random attacks scattered over nine months and two boroughs was revealed to be the work of a single murderer the police and tabloids called THE .44 CALIBER KILLER.

Panic spread through New York City and into the suburbs, where teenagers went to discos and sat in parked cars. Even my father, a newspaper snob who could fold and refold *The New York Times* into a pocket handkerchief while swaying in a crowded subway car, his briefcase trapped between his feet, brought home the *New York Post* if he found a late edition on the train.

The killer called himself the Son of Sam in notes left in the parked cars where he shot couples to death, and soon the tabloids called him that, too, printing every scrap of information real or speculative about the investigation. The *Post*, recently acquired by Rupert Murdoch, ran the Son of Sam up its front page every morning like a pirate flag.

Despite these alarms, my family still went to the Mostly Mozart Festival at Lincoln Center, and to Shakespeare in the Park. We sat on towels waiting for free tickets in Central Park while we kept an eye out for dope fiends and muggers. My beautiful sister sat like bait at a stakeout, her hair up because the Son of Sam preferred shooting victims with long dark hair.

Michael often joined my family for outings, especially in the summer. I'd let him know if we were going to Saxon Woods, the massive public pool in White Plains, or Jones Beach in Long Island. He loved the ocean, hurling himself into the waves and bodysurfing to shore until his chest and belly were streaked pink from the sand and his shoulders were pink from the sun. We ate gritty hard-boiled eggs while ogling the oiled women in string bikinis, the backs of their legs breaded with fine white sand, while my father recited "Dover Beach," stirred by the surf and the "turbid ebb and flow of human misery."

When my mother signed my family up for Transcendental Meditation lessons, Michael joined us with surprising seriousness, and none of the sardonic asides I expected about "yogic flying." TM had gone mainstream, but the Maharishi still claimed you could learn to defy gravity simply by "dictating to the laws of nature how they should behave." Michael sat with his back straight, hands on his thighs, while my sister and I giggled on either side of him.

The day we got our mantras, we went to a party at our friend Pat's house, where Michael abruptly announced, "Jon and I have to meditate," removed his glasses, and shut his eyes. I followed his example, embarrassed but excited: *Look at me, I'm invisible!* I didn't last long, afraid I'd been set up, but Michael was still there when I opened my eyes. His face, with its long ruddy lashes, looked peacefully composed, tilted upward like someone trying to get a tan.

Michael and I studied for honors biology together using practice tests my sister had devised when she was acing the class. We worked at Michael's dining room table, heaped ever higher with newspapers as if the Laudors ran a clipping service on the side. Michael finished in half the time it took me but never seemed to mind, plucking a book or two off his parents' shelf, or a newspaper off the pile, and reading while he waited.

I don't know how much he really needed our study sessions, but we laughed and talked a lot in the old way, and it helped sustain our friendship. He disappeared on the weekends, though we still went to parties together thrown by the lunch table crowd. We wore boldly patterned Qiana shirts, a slippery synthetic material that made you look like you'd showered with your clothes on but that John Travolta had worn to great effect in *Saturday Night Fever* when he wasn't wearing the white disco suit.

Michael had a habit of wedging himself between me and a girl I was trying to talk to, and saying, "Jon's a neurotic bundle of contradictory emotions," as if smoothing the social waters for me. The melancholy ache of Billy Joel's *The Stranger* set the musical mood, ripening you like a banana in a paper bag before the record was halfway through. I wished someone had to tell *me*, "Slow down, you crazy child," like in the song "Vienna," but a neurotic bundle wasn't the same as a crazy child.

Madness was in the air when Michael and I were growing up, and though it was hard to know whether it was a colloquial or clinical condition, the confusion itself shaped our world, which avoided nuclear destruction with a strategy called MAD. *One Flew Over the Cuckoo's Nest*, which won the Academy Award for Best Picture in 1976, was about a sane wiseass named McMurphy locked in a mental hospital by a crazy culture. Michael, who saw more R-rated movies than I did, explained that the hospital had tried drugging McMurphy into submission, and shocking his brain until his body writhed, until it finished him off with a lobotomy, all because he would not behave.

I'd never heard of a lobotomy, but Michael assured me it was real; they stuck an ice pick into your head and wiggled it until you went slack like a pithed frog, docile enough to be dissected alive. He told me a joke he attributed to Dean Martin: "I'd rather have a bottle in front of me than a frontal lobotomy."

Like a lot of things in the seventies, *Cuckoo's Nest* sent a mixed message, exposing the abuses of mental hospitals while justifying the killing of a mentally impaired person. Reduced to zombie helplessness, McMurphy gets smothered to death with a pillow by a giant Indian called Chief Bromden who escapes out a window so the other inmates will still have a hero to believe in. Like Dirty Harry pulling the trigger, Chief Bromden has no choice.

Dirty Harry was different from *One Flew Over the Cuckoo's Nest*, of course; the psychopathic killer in the first movie should never have been on the streets, and the ordinary guy in the second movie should never have been locked up, but the solution to the problem they posed was the same. Lobotomized by an evil institution, McMurphy became the subhuman creature the hospital had pretended he was all along. Killing his broken friend is a favor bestowed by the Indian, who euthanizes the Lone Ranger and carries his independent spirit into mythic immortality.

The shock word in the title of my Richard Pryor album, *That Nigger's Crazy*, wasn't "crazy"—but "crazy" was also a negative word that Pryor turned into a positive by defiant self-application. If Richard Pryor was crazy, we wanted to be, too, and "crazy" was a word everyone could say out loud.

I'd bought my stereo and eight-track player from Crazy Eddie, the discount electronics store whose pitchman practically stuck his head through the television set shouting, "His prices are *in*-sane!" So was buying an eight-track player, which is why I owned only three eight-track tapes; one of them was Paul Simon's *Still Crazy After All These Years*. The title song was a melancholy downer, but when Simon sang, "I'm not the kind of man who tends to socialize," it suggested world-weary hipness, not antisocial deviance. Even if he did "some damage one fine day," a jury of his peers wouldn't convict him because they were crazy, too, and if everyone is crazy, nobody is. I found this mysteriously comforting.

It turned out that even *One Flew Over the Cuckoo's Nest* had less to do with mental illness than with the CIA's secret drug testing project, which Ken Kesey had participated in while writing the novel that the movie was based on. Kesey liked the LSD he was given so much that he got a job on the psych ward of the veterans' hospital where the testing took place, helping himself to hallucinogenic samples while working as a janitor on the night shift. He mapped out his novel wandering the halls in a drugged-out spirit of sympathetic fellowship, encountering psychiatric patients who appeared, through a scrim of government-sponsored acid trips, like versions of himself in need only of liberation.

When the Son of Sam was finally nabbed in front of his apartment building in Yonkers, thanks to an outstanding parking ticket, he asked the arresting officers, "What took you so long?"

His name was David Berkowitz, to the horror of my family, who were in the habit of picking out Jewish names among Nobel Prize winners. With his curly hair, closed sensual mouth, and Elvis sideburns, he even looked vaguely familiar on the cover of the *Post* under the giant word CAUGHT! inked in red. "A pleasant looking slightly chubby young man," as the *Post* put it.

Berkowitz had referred to himself not only as the Son of Sam but as Monster, Beelzebub, and the Chubby Behemoth, which he spelled "Behemouth" in a letter the police had withheld from the public. Berkowitz corroborated its details and confessed to all the murders. The most disturbing part of his letter talked about a man who "loves to drink blood" named Sam, who had lived six thousand years ago and was now a devil inhabiting a black Labrador who compelled him to commit murder.

My father took brief comfort in the news that Berkowitz was

adopted, but it turned out that the killer's biological parents had also been Jewish. More promising was the news that Berkowitz had become an ardent Christian in the army, before joining a satanic cult.

Still, there was no escaping Berkowitz's insinuating familiarity. He'd grown up in the Bronx, where he had a bar mitzvah, and even lived in New Rochelle before the barking of a neighbor's dog drove him to Yonkers, where mass murderers were supposed to live, and where a different dog, possessed by a devil with the name of an old Jewish man, ordered him to keep killing.

Two court-appointed psychiatrists from Kings County Psychiatric Hospital found Berkowitz unfit for trial, despite an IQ indicating "superior intelligence." Though he appeared to understand everything, they explained, he filtered everything through an "elaborate paranoid delusional system" and understood nothing. Like the man who had killed Martin Luther King Jr.'s mother, Berkowitz had no interest in a legal defense; he wanted a trial because he wanted "to tell the world about the demons." Otherwise, the psychiatrists observed, he did not seem to care at all about the outcome of his case.

An assessment of "flamboyant madness" did not stop Berkowitz from sending a letter to the *Post* explaining the demons, the dog, and the orders to kill, or stop the *Post* from publishing it. Berkowitz's letter, with its warning about "other Sons out there, God help the world," sparked theories about devil-worshipping accomplices still at large. There were stories about flayed dogs turning up in city parks, with maps detailing locations where satanic cultists were said to congregate, not far from the shootings.

Perhaps because madness meant so many different things, or didn't exist at all, Berkowitz's interests dictated the story, rather than the psychiatrists' assessment of him. Satan was bigger than disco in the seventies. *The Exorcist* had opened the year I moved to New Rochelle and in some sense had never left. After *The Exorcist* came *The Omen*, which scared the shit out of me; how could you be sure you wouldn't find three sixes if you shaved your head? My father consoled me with the news that Jews don't believe in such nonsense; people were perfectly capable of doing evil all by themselves.

Michael had a rationalist's imperviousness to superstition, with the exception of the time at camp a girl from Long Island said she'd drawn a hex on his back while giving him a massage, and he rolled away, shouting, "Take it off, witch!" He talked about *Rosemary's Baby* with wry amusement, having heard it was the author Ira Levin's Jewish joke on Christianity. I didn't want to think about naked old people on the Upper West Side worshipping the devil in the Dakota and talking like my great-aunts: "He has his father's eyes."

Rosemary's Baby was the horror movie before *The Exorcist*, kept current by kids carrying around *Helter Skelter*, the bestseller about the Manson family murders that even nonreaders insisted on talking about in lurid detail. Everyone knew the killers said things like "I'm the Devil, here to do his business," and that Sharon Tate was nine months pregnant when they stabbed her to death, cut her open, and wrote "Pigs" on the door with her blood. She was married to Roman Polanski, the director of *Rosemary's Baby*, which was still in theaters when the slaughter took place in the summer of '69.

The culture had prepared us for David Berkowitz. Even if the exorcist he invited to collaborate with him on his memoirs turned him down, the tabloids loved the story. Devil worship was easier to talk about than mental illness or homicidal strangeness. When Iago is captured, Othello can't help hoping his destroyer has cloven hooves, a sign of supernatural evil that would be easier to accept than human deviance and his own self-deluding credulity as the cause of his tragedy: "I look down towards his feet, but that's a fable."

That's what it was like with the Son of Sam. People kept checking his feet instead of examining his head. After the arrest, one of the detectives sounded almost disappointed, telling *The New York Times*: "For more than a year I had been hoping for just one thing—a chance to talk to 'the Son of Sam,' a chance to ask him why?" Now that he had asked, he had been told in an uninflected voice, "It was a command."

This was a significant answer for the psychiatrists who found Berkowitz unfit to stand trial, but did nothing for the district attorney who was up for reelection. He didn't want to wait until someone who had murdered six people, wounded seven others, and held millions of New Yorkers hostage to fear was medicated into competence, if such a thing were even possible. Accordingly, the DA hired another psychiatrist, as was his right, a psychoanalyst named David Abrahamsen who had recently published a popular psychobiography, *Nixon vs. Nixon: An Emotional Tragedy.*

Dr. Abrahamsen dismissed the demonic dog as a red herring. His clues came from childhood, and after several meetings he decided it was "probable" that Berkowitz had witnessed his adoptive parents having sex. This repressed memory had been inflamed by the sight of a couple making out in a car, "another love scene" that evoked the primal one. Such commonplace processes were hardly evidence of insanity, according to the psychiatrist, unlike Nixon's "infantile oral and anal drives" which were the type found "in introverted schizoid and secretive people."

Though he'd never met Nixon, Dr. Abrahamsen had gotten hold of a letter the future president had sent his mother when he was ten years old, written in the voice of a dog. It began, "Dear Master," talked about biting people who were bad to him, and was signed, "Your good dog, Richard." If Nixon had been ideologically motivated as well as psychologically screwed up, the psychiatrist told *The New York Times*, he would have been "worse than Hitler."

Berkowitz had invented a talking dog but Nixon had actually been one. "In my professional view," Dr. Abrahamsen said of the president, "his behavior was abnormal." As for the Son of Sam, "the defendant is as normal as anyone else, maybe a little neurotic."

None of this could blot out Berkowitz's weeping Jewish father, Nathan, who had owned a hardware store before retiring to Florida, and appeared on television to apologize to the families of the dead and wounded. He did this against the advice of the lawyers he had hired for his son, but his heart was broken.

"I am so deeply saddened that nothing I can say really expresses my deep feeling and sorrow for all you parents," Nathan Berkowitz said before dissolving in tears. He seemed convinced of his son's guilt: "From what I read, my mind cannot deny what my heart accepts."

CHAPTER FIVE

AMERICAN PIE

We all got up to dance

Oh, but we never got the chance

—Don McLean, "American Pie"

New Rochelle High School looked like a French chateau with ornamented towers, Gothic dormers, and balustrades overlooking twin lakes on either side of a long walkway. The building opened its doors in 1926, expanded in the early 1930s, when New Rochelle was the third-richest city in the United States, and went up in flames in the spring of 1968. The palatial facade survived but the interior had been gutted and rebuilt with faceless functionality, giving the whole place the feel of a Hollywood back lot.

The only physical reminder of the blaze was a stopped clock outside the principal's office that told the time the fire reached one of the towers. Somewhere it was always 9:26 on a May morning in 1968. The fire was one of the secret meanings of "American Pie," the pop song Michael and I spent hours decoding with proprietary interest because Don McLean had grown up in New Rochelle.

Everyone knew the music died the day Buddy Holly's plane crashed, but locals knew McLean had learned about it from *The Standard-Star* he was delivering that cold February morning in 1959, and that there was a bar called the Levee across the street from Iona Prep, where the singer went to school. Even if he meant the levee in Mississippi where the bodies of three slain civil rights workers were hidden, it led back to New Rochelle High School, where the mother of Mickey Schwerner was a beloved biology teacher when her son was murdered by Klansmen along with James Chaney and Andrew Goodman during the Freedom Summer of 1964.

Whether our high school really was "the sacrificial rite" McLean had in mind when he sang that the "flames climbed high into the night," it was exciting to think our suburb was the key to a mythic song about the loss of innocence, and that a song might be the key to our suburb.

The 1968 headline in *The New York Times* that announced FIRE RUINS SCHOOL IN NEW ROCHELLE was followed by a subhead that addressed the fears of the moment: ARSON BELIEVED THE CAUSE BUT NO LINK TO RACIAL ANTAGONISM IS SEEN AT SCHOOL. A Black high school senior watching the blaze told the *Times* reporter, "Somebody just didn't want to go to school, understand? It had nothing to do with demands."

The "demands" had been made less than a month before, when Martin Luther King Jr. was murdered and Ossie Davis had rushed over to talk to students and prevent a riot. A celebrity actor, Black activist, and longtime New Rochelle resident, Davis and his regal wife, Ruby Dee, also famous, had spoken to us in junior high school about what they thrillingly called "the struggle." Davis turned up again in the paperback Michael gave me of *The Autobiography of Malcolm X*, where he called Malcolm "our living black manhood" in a eulogy published as an afterword, and explained that "white folks do not need anybody to remind them that they are men. We do!"

The student quoted by the *Times* was right; the fire had nothing to do with "demands." A white boy had set it. He was only sixteen but already a senior and according to classmates a "loner" who had not bothered to sit for a yearbook photo or supply any information about himself beyond his address. As the building burned, he had chatted calmly with a teacher, but began to suffer "extreme self-consciousness" as the fire spread, and was arrested a week later after a small fire broke out at Albert Leonard Junior High where classes were being held for displaced high school students.

A judge ordered the boy remanded to Grassland Hospital's Psychiatric Institute for observation. Newspapers reported that his mother was blind and that he had received psychiatric treatment in the past. His arrest was a great relief to the community; it wasn't race, only mental illness, and there was nothing anyone could do about that.

New Rochelle High School had reopened under the leadership of James R. Gaddy, the first Black principal of a Westchester high school, who was still there when Michael and I went to high school. He was a formidable figure with a brush mustache, dapper seventies suits, and the bearing of someone who had been to military academy, which was useful for running a school with three thousand students whose parents took turns demanding more AP classes, badgering him about Ivy League admission rates, and accusing him of supporting a racially biased tracking system and suspending a disproportionate number of Black students.

The school was divided far more by what Michael called "class" than race, which didn't make avoiding the bathroom for three years any more pleasant. Even if the Black kids you were afraid of came exclusively from the poorest public housing, your fears still felt racist; you avoided the subject along with the bathroom, a double shame. We knew Dr. Gaddy as a voice on the PA, like the Wizard of Oz, and saw more of his three assistant principals, who acted primarily as security guards. They clutched walkie-talkies as they patrolled the school and the outside area called "the Bridge," where the walkway widened into a sort of plaza where kids smoked and hung out before, during, and after classes.

Though the carved wooden community entrance lost in the fire was never replaced, the high school had a planetarium, tennis courts, an indoor swimming pool, and prestigious clubs like Model Congress, created by a history teacher at New Rochelle High School back in 1964 when Richard Nixon was a guest speaker. Michael and I joined the *Herald* newspaper, which rivaled Model Congress in nerd prestige.

Michael's brother Danny had been favored to become editor in chief the year we started school, but decided to skip senior year and flew off to California to become a stand-up comedian. College was nominally involved, but the sheer bravado of the move filled us with open-mouthed admiration.

He left behind a mock front page: LAUDOR FLIES TO CALIFORNIA: RUBIN WINS BY DEFAULT. Eric Rubin had been Danny's best friend and rival since childhood, and neighbor, too, before the Laudors moved to Mereland Road. They'd gone to lefty Camp Trywoodie—where they had Hiroshima Day but no Fourth of July—the way Michael and I went to Farm Camp Lowy. Eric was a smart, likable, nervously self-confident boy who made a terrific editor in chief, but the parting shot from his friend stung.

The high school had one thousand kids in each grade but was subdivided even more thoroughly than junior high. Somewhere vocational boys were learning to change spark plugs and girls were styling the hair of dummy heads, but auto body and cosmetology were in their own wings.

Michael and I basically moved in to the *Herald* office the first day. Only editors got keys but there was always someone to let you in; my sister was an editor and ate lunch there with a circle of friends, including Eric. I felt more at home in the first week than I had in three years of junior high.

Early in the second week, as Michael and I were cutting across the sweeping high school grounds on our way home, talking about classes and the usual bullshit, I noticed a group of Black guys up ahead on the bank of the lake to my left. They seemed about our age, or a few grades older, but did not look like they had spent the day in school. Several were lounging against the low, thick branch of a weeping willow; others were horsing around, tagging each other and darting out of range; and one or two were sitting on the ground.

Michael was lost in talk and seemed unaware of the scene that I took in peripherally. I couldn't have said what the scene was except that the energy changed as we drew near and one of the boys stood up. My heart beat faster, though it was important not to make assumptions, and I kept walking, perhaps even veering slightly toward the group that Michael may or may not have noticed.

It was a cool September day. I had an unzipped windbreaker on over a T-shirt; the kid who stood up was wearing what Michael later called a "Guinea tee." He nodded to me the way Michael liked to nod, the head tilted up first and then down, instead of the down-up nod I considered more conventional.

He asked me for the time, and though I felt certain that he did not want to know it, I looked at my watch—little hand, big hand, always a two-step process—and when I looked up again, he was on my left. Now we were walking together toward the group. He flung his heavy right arm over my shoulders in a confiding way that felt almost flattering even though I knew he wasn't confiding in me, just as I knew he didn't care what time it was.

Michael had stopped talking at last but was no longer visible. Another boy had taken his place on my right. A third boy was standing directly in front of me, and I stopped walking. The heavy arm behind my neck bent and tightened, and a forearm under my chin locked me into place, pressing on my throat, unless it was my own choking fear.

Sounds were muffled inside the headlock, but I distinctly heard my own pleading voice filling me even then with deep disgust—"*Hey, guys, cut it out come on cutitout*"—until a fist slammed into my face so hard I discovered you really do see stars. I felt my head jump back but it was held in place, a stroke of luck it seemed to me at the time, otherwise it might have detached or popped up like a Rock'em Sock'em Robot. I was still getting punched, a blow landed on my nose like a hammer, and thunder the color of lightning exploded in my brain.

Somehow, I was on the ground, knees drawn up, face hidden but still getting hit, which seemed strange until it came to me that I was also getting kicked. A detached inner voice kept saying things like *I'm getting beaten up that's what this is I can't believe it* simultaneously translating my ass whipping for the dimmer parts of my understanding amid the blows and shouts—*whiteshitmotherfucker*—narrating the experience like Marv Albert covering a game: *That crack you heard was your nose.*

My body was on its own, shielding nuts guts face, resisting the smothering weight that I had not realized was pressing down on me like a lid until it was lifted and I was up like steam before I even knew I was up, shocked by my own vitality and running toward Michael, who was standing and watching me not far away but still requiring a run to reach. He was blurry; I wasn't wearing glasses, though there was a great concentrated pressure on my face as if I were wearing more than glasses.

Michael's face was twisted in pain when I stopped in front of him, and I understood that his expression was connected to my face and that he had not been beaten up too. This disappointed me, frankly, and amplified an intense feeling of loneliness that should have been the least of my problems, but my thoughts were not clear, and Michael was telling me in an uncharacteristically hurried manner how he had broken free, but then he stopped talking, because a gigantic Black kid was standing next to me.

I recognized him blurrily from the junior high bus, where he'd once brought his big fist down on the head of my sister's friend with the casual indifference of someone franking a stamp. But he was holding out the mangled remnant of my glasses almost apologetically and cursing the guys who had beaten me up. His contempt for them was palpable, which I found reassuring. "You have to get to the nurse," he said, and the three of us started walking toward the side entrance of the high school, the big kid's free hand gripping my left arm and steering me, which was a good thing because the burst of adrenaline that had gotten me off the ground was gone and I was afraid I might faint.

A woman half in and half out of the side entrance was watching us, and Michael sprinted to her. The big kid released my arm and murmured something about trouble and not going farther. He was businesslike all of a sudden, brusque as he forced my glasses into my hand, turning away unceremoniously as the woman who had been in the doorway came hurrying forward with Michael.

The nurse gasped when she saw me, and then I was on the daybed with no memory of lying down. Michael informed me that my nose was sideways, which made sense, because my whole face hurt and I was breathing only through my mouth, but the pain was not as sharp as I expected. It had clotted into heaviness, whereas my chest was killing me, and I wondered briefly if I was having a heart attack. When I looked down, I saw, along with blood splattering the red writing on my T-shirt, the patterned whorls of overlapping sneaker treads and one big dusty print in the middle of my chest like a footprint on the moon.

The nurse was fussing but not with me, making phone calls and chasing away the kids who poked their heads in, saw my cubist face, said, "Oh shit!" and came back with other kids. Michael had vanished. The nurse told me my mother was meeting me at the hospital, which seemed odd because I was at school.

Michael came back with my backpack, burst like a piñata, its contents strewn, but he or someone—I thought about that big kid—had collected my books and various crumpled pages. Michael reported that his Adidas bag had been hurled with all his books into the lake, which even at the time was funny. I felt things turning into a story I would never tell because I did not like my part.

The EMS guys transferred me to a wheeled stretcher, and as they belted me in, I felt, more acutely than broken ribs, a profound sense of shame that got worse as they rolled me out of the nurse's office and into the fluorescent hall, which was full of kids staring down at me. "Oh, smack, they fucked him *up!*" Didn't anyone go home after school?

Michael followed as far as the main entrance, as if he were seeing me to the door of his house. The gurney did not fit through a single door; both had to be opened and held by students. The EMS guys angled the gurney down the few front steps and set it on the Bridge, where more kids were milling around making comments, but I had shut my eyes and was pretending I wasn't there.

I felt myself rolling down the long walkway between the lakes that had once been a single lake that supplied blocks of ice in the days E. L. Doctorow wrote about in *Ragtime*. The ice harvest was over and I was gliding toward North Avenue in 1978, where an ambulance was waiting.

This is what they should do," Chuck Laudor was telling my father. "Get some guys together, some lead pipes and take care of it! That's how we did it."

Michael and I were leaning against my parents' maroon Chevy, which was parked in front of our house, collecting maple leaves on the windshield like unpaid parking tickets. We were watching our fathers talk. On this occasion, my father actually turned around and walked up a few of our front steps with Chuck stalking after him shouting about how it was done in Brooklyn.

"You take *care* of it!"

Personally, I thought Chuck's suggestion was the best idea I'd ever heard in my life. I couldn't imagine the Diplomacy crowd in a rumble, and there was no question of lead pipes, but the mere fact that someone thought such a thing might be possible did me more good than all the therapy in the world. Not that anybody was offering therapy.

I'd spent the night in the hospital for "observation" and would have to go back for surgical reconstruction of my nose, which had been hammered into a new shape but was still too swollen to repair. The ribs would heal by themselves. So would the black eyes and the long red impression the temple piece of my glasses had seared into one side of my head.

My father was pained and sorrowful; my mother was outraged. Her anger extended to our rabbi, who had visited me in the hospital and murmured, "It's always something." At a special session of the PTA devoted to my ass kicking, my mother read a long letter demanding guards on the high school grounds. When she was finished, Chuck stood up and declared that my mother's letter did not speak for him. She came home seething.

A sympathetic African American cop with the cheerful name of Detective Flowers interviewed me at home. He'd already spoken to Michael. Neither of us had known our attackers, who had said some racial things, but was that proof of a motive or mere improvisation? Richard Pryor had a routine about guys who insisted on talking to you while they beat you up. I took comfort in our overlapping experience, but if I wasn't beaten for the color of my skin *or* the content of my character, what was my offense?

When I was back in school, I was summoned to Dr. Gaddy's office and shown pictures of various boys, all of them Black, none of them wearing a white muscle tee. Dr. Gaddy had already told my parents he'd figured out who they were, though he did not say how. Two had been expelled the year before, but the others could still be punished, once I identified them. He made it clear that these were the guys, and that my agonized uncertainty was of no value, but identifying Black kids I couldn't recognize felt even more racist than not recognizing them in the first place.

Whether he thought I was a dumbass or just another bureaucratic obstacle, he needed my corroboration. Here was a man from the Jim Crow South who had to talk Italians out of Catholic school, Jews out of moving to Scarsdale, and me into identifying Black kids he knew had beaten me up. I felt him running out of patience.

I was trying to hold on to my status as a blameless victim even though I suspected that my need to be blameless was a crime all its own, like saying, "Cut it out," at the start of a beatdown, instead of using my fists or at least my feet like Michael.

After surgery, I went to school with a white cast on my nose held in place by white tape radiating outward like cat whiskers, perhaps believing I was invisible. I lasted one day, announced I was done until college, and was allowed to stay home until my cast came off. Michael stopped by regularly after school to fill me in on what I'd missed but mainly to hang out. It was a warm fall and we spent a lot of time in reclining beach chairs on the patio.

We never talked about what had happened beyond the generic story we shared with classmates about getting jumped. Michael would explain how he shoved the guys closing in on him, spun away, and sprinted off, as if he'd executed a shake-and-bake basketball move.

When he realized I wasn't with him, he'd stopped running and turned around in time to see me leap up off the ground, a generous suggestion that I had defeated gravity if not my attackers with a burst of power, though I was aware of a hurried awkwardness to that part of his telling.

I didn't ask why he hadn't gone for help or come back to help me but had waited outside the circle of my thrashing, watching until I was released. I was under no illusions that he could have helped me fight, especially because I wasn't fighting myself. And for all it felt like an eternity, my beating would have been over by the time he'd run to North Avenue to flag down a car or back to the high school. But the fact that I had found him spectating hung over us both, and our different fates and fortunes divided us.

I wasn't sure if he was embarrassed about his own behavior or about mine—my lack of street smarts, my bad luck. I know I was embarrassed. He was a canny survivor; I was a victim. It was possible he was avoiding the subject for my sake as much as his. In any event, we had reached the same conclusion: the less we said about it the better. At the same time, we were welded together by what had happened and, in some sense, closer than ever, at least in everyone else's minds.

Eventually the cast on my face came off and I went back to school. I caught up in my classes with the help of Michael and my sister, and though I still took personal days, I did establish a school rhythm. Michael and I hung out in the *Herald* office, where we bantered like vaudevillians and vied for assignments and attention. We competed in complementary ways—I was more alley and he was more oop—and were considered a duo.

When Michael lifted a bottle of booze from the liquor cabinet at our friend Pat's sweet sixteen party and got privately drunk in the upstairs bathroom, I was the one he asked for through the locked door. He'd been in there a long time throwing up; nothing was left of his face but the freckles. It wasn't a party where kids were drinking, and he was embarrassed. He didn't want Pat's mother to find out, though she was the one who had told me to take him home. Michael seemed to think we were slipping out of the house as he lurched down the stairs with Frankensteinian dignity. He needed propping up the whole way.

We were both devoted to our European history teacher, Greg Morrison, who smoked in class, treated us like adults, and carried the living aura of the sixties with him. Greg read faster than Michael, and knew everything about art and music. He had lived in a Brooklyn commune and a village in Biafra, where a flesh-eating ant had chewed into his ear as he rode his weaving motorcycle howling to the hut of a missionary who poured in molten Vaseline, killing the ant and half his hearing.

He'd been in Africa with the Peace Corps, and had put on a production of *Macbeth* with his students, translating witches and kings into wizards and tribal elders. Something terrible had happened to his village and changed his life, which he alluded to indirectly. He lived in Harlem now, the only place he felt comfortable after Biafra, which no longer existed. It was clear we were the beneficiaries of some unknown calamity that had altered the future he'd mapped out for himself years before.

He was the only person to talk to me about getting beaten up, and who listened nonjudgmentally to how I felt about it. He'd asked my sister, who was in his AP class, "How's his head?" and stopped her in the middle of her account, laughing. It was sixties slang; he meant how was the *inside* of my head?

Though he revered high culture, Greg brought in a portable record player because Donna Summer's cover of "MacArthur Park" was topping the charts and he wanted us to hear the mournful original, written about a breakup but pregnant with the deaths of Martin Luther King Jr. and Bobby Kennedy in 1968, when the dreams of a generation dissolved like a cake left out in the rain. This too was a history lesson: first time tragedy, second time disco.

Both Michael and I adopted Greg as a mentor. Sometimes we waited together for him and started talking at the same time when he opened the smoky door of the supply closet he used as an office so that neither of us got the individual meeting we wanted.

It was Michael's idea for us to go to the review class Greg taught after school for seniors in his AP European History course, even though we were tenth graders. Michael's goal was to take the AP test without taking the course. My sister and her friends were in the class; I loved hanging out with them, and when the weather was good, Greg would leave a note on the door of his classroom: "Beside the lake, beneath the trees."

We gathered not far from where I was beaten up, the only time I allowed myself near the spot. That alone made the study sessions worthwhile, even if I forgot the Peace of Westphalia. Michael was in it to win it, and eager to show up his elders with competitive zeal. I didn't take the AP test in the end; Michael aced it. So did my sister, who was valedictorian that year and gave a speech telling one thousand graduating seniors to resist being the me generation. Though she cringed at the memory, I was incredibly proud of her.

Junior year began well, which is to say I didn't go to the hospital. I had my *Herald* key, and there were kids waiting outside the office like hungry puppies when I got there in the morning, just as I had waited eagerly for shelter and attention.

My sister and Eric had both gone to Yale. Michael became news editor; I became features editor. We both visited Greg, though he was no longer our teacher. He got me to read books like *The Sound and the Fury*, which rewarded my slow style. The novel, Greg said, was about the same thing all Greek tragedies were about; did I know what that was? When I shook my head, he shouted, "Fucked-up families!"

Once I ran into Michael coming out of Greg's office with his own copy of *The Sound and the Fury* and couldn't help feeling a pang. I was aware of an aura of awkward secrecy, as if we were seeing the same shrink.

One day Greg strolled by as Michael and I were entertaining a group of kids, bantering in our customary way. Greg told me later that I was good at making people laugh but that I seemed to do it mainly by making fun of myself. I explained that's how the comedians Michael and I admired did it, but Greg shook his head.

"That's not what Michael is doing," he told me.

For some reason I did not tell Michael that I was applying to a program called Telluride, an all-expenses-paid nerd camp that met for six weeks in the summer, which my sister had learned about from two Yale friends who told her the experience had changed their lives. Her friends "knew about me" and thought it would be a great place for me too. But Telluride took only forty-five kids, and wanted five essays, recommendations, an annotated list of all the books I had read, and, if I made it that far, an interview with a roomful of intimidating people.

Prodded and coached by my sister and Greg—who wrote me a recommendation, read drafts of my essays, and insisted I not give up— I worked into the winter on the application. Telluride was offering three seminars that summer, one on literature and revolution, one on the life of the American city, and the third on sociobiology, a subject I had never even heard of. Literature was my first choice, but I wrote about Lincoln Steffens's *The Shame of the Cities*, a book that Greg had

given me, and about getting beaten up. I expressed a wish to understand the urban poverty and dysfunction that lay behind the lives of
my attackers, keeping to myself the part about wanting to beat them
senseless with a lead pipe.

I was called for an interview. The intimidating questioners, crammed
into a small Manhattan office, turned out to be mostly college and
graduate students whose adversarial Socratic manner was not unfamiliar to me.

"Isn't trying to understand your attackers a cliché?" asked one intense interviewer.

"What about 'All men are created equal,'" I asked him back. "Isn't
that a cliché?"

Lucky for me, times had changed since the elitist founder of Telluride, Lucien Lucius Nunn, had spoken of "the bitter dissatisfaction which our educational system, with its teaching that 'All men
are created equal,' is plunging the nation into."

When I opened my acceptance letter one late spring day, I was
so beside myself that I grabbed a basketball and dribbled it down
Mereland. I needed to discharge some energy at the schoolyard—or
was I half hoping to meet Michael? I almost rang his bell but realized
that would be gloating.

I did not cut through Michael's backyard but took the longer route
past his house before making a left. It occurred to me that it was fear
that had kept me from telling him about the program. I did not want
him ruining my chances; they weren't going to take two people from
the same street. I was not proud of this realization, and after twenty
minutes of shooting baskets, I was still elated but feeling vaguely guilty.

As if to torment my conscience further, Michael was coming out
of his house as I was going home. We stood in the street messing
with the ball. Almost as if he suspected something, Michael asked
me what I was doing that summer. I took a breath and told him about

Telluride, making it sound as though the whole thing had been done at the last minute and not over the course of months.

Michael nodded with unhurried amusement.

"I'm doing that too," he said.

Dumfounded, I asked how he had learned about it. He shrugged nonchalantly.

"An application showed up in the mail," he said. "I must have checked one of those little boxes on the PSATs."

Michael had gotten into the literature program and was going to be living at Telluride House, a sprawling mansion on the campus of Cornell built by the eccentric founder of the Telluride Association. I would be studying urban decay and rebirth at Johns Hopkins University in Baltimore.

Greg was thrilled. He had helped us both.

CHAPTER SIX

FREEDOM SUMMER

Do I dare

Disturb the universe?

—T. S. Eliot, "The Love Song of J. Alfred Prufrock"

As summer approached, the *Herald* office grew crowded with seniors who had learned where they were going to college and consequently did nothing but sprawl on top of the tables and each other like sea lions in the sun. Michael and I were the presumptive heirs of this windowless fluorescent kingdom, waiting to learn which one of us would be next year's editor in chief and which one managing editor.

Our fate was in the hands of the *Herald*'s faculty adviser, a heavyset history teacher named Frank Agresta who had grown up in New Rochelle in the 1930s, loved journalism, and had once coached football. He moved through the halls with slow power on bad knees, though in 1968 he had charged up the high school stairs toward the blaze to make sure everyone got out. He was also a carpenter on whose strong hands a heavy ring with a red gemstone looked like something you got for winning the Super Bowl in the days of leather helmets. You noticed his hands when he clamped you on the shoulder, pointed to a headline on a page proof, and said, "Change that."

Mr. Agresta came into the *Herald* office looking for Michael and me.

"You first," he said to me.

I followed him into an empty classroom where he told me to sit down, squeezed into the desk next to mine, and said he had a tough decision to make. I nodded and asked if Michael and I could share the job.

"I don't want to do that," he said sharply. He needed someone to be editor in chief who could make decisions, carry them out, work hard, get along with people, and get along with him. Could I do that?

Yes, I could.

Could I work with Michael as my managing editor?

Absolutely.

What if he made Michael editor in chief? Would I accept managing editor and help him get out the paper?

Of course. We were friends.

Michael looked unhappy when he came back from his audience with Mr. Agresta, and I tried without success to catch his eye. I wondered if he'd heard something he didn't want to share, but Mr. Agresta said he'd make up his mind before Regents Week, still several days away.

Michael was subdued as we walked home. I told him I'd suggested co-editors. If we both pushed, perhaps Agresta would go for it. But Michael was shaking his head.

"That's not possible."

I didn't ask why, only what had happened in his meeting. Michael gave me a quick account. Mr. Agresta had put the same questions to him that he'd put to me, but Michael had not answered the same way. He'd told Mr. Agresta that if he wasn't made editor in chief, he would quit the paper.

I laughed but Michael wasn't joking. He was looking down, lips compressed, chin sharp. I was stunned. When I asked him why, he spoke quietly but with a determination that ended the conversation: "It should be me."

Well, I thought, that's that. If Mr. Agresta gave the top job to Michael, the paper would get us both. If he offered it to me, he'd lose Michael. The math was simple and Mr. Agresta was no dummy. Running the paper together had been the thing that was going to make it fun. Even with that illusion gone, I didn't want to lose the *Herald*. If Michael got tapped, I knew I'd stay on. So did Mr. Agresta. Michael knew it too.

From the Diplomacy point of view, he'd made a brilliant move. The problem was that I didn't think it was a move.

"Congratulations," Mr. Agresta called out as he barreled toward me in the hall. "You're editor in chief."

He was grinning broadly. I thanked him in the somber voice I used for good news, hiding my elation behind superstitious decorum. Before I could ask about Michael, Mr. Agresta said, "He knows and he's quit."

My family toasted Mr. Agresta, a man who could not be bullied.

"Don't feel sorry for Michael," my sister told me. "He'll land on his feet."

"Or somebody else's," my mother said.

But I wasn't feeling sorry for Michael; I was feeling sorry for myself. I'd spent so long assuming we would run the *Herald* together that it was hard to give up the dream, even if I was no longer sure how much the dream grew out of friendship and how much out of my dependency. Either way, it was a lonely victory.

Michael and I did not discuss his quitting. The fatalistic shrug of inevitability he gave me suggested that he was simply doing what he had to do, like Martin Luther, as Greg Morrison had taught us: *Here I stand, I can do no other.* The only explanation Michael gave—

not to me, but I heard it—was that managing editor wasn't "worth it" since he would be doing the work of editor in chief anyway without getting credit.

I didn't expect an apology, but I did want him to acknowledge that he was bailing on me. At some point, though, it dawned on me that Michael considered himself the aggrieved party, wronged not merely by Mr. Agresta but also by me. That might explain the weary stoicism he seemed to exhibit around me, as if he were trying to ignore my behavior for the sake of our friendship.

I was feeling this only dimly when my father came home furious from the A&P. He had bumped into Chuck Laudor, who had told him flatly that Frank Agresta had made a terrible mistake, and that Michael had been passed over only because he was strong-willed and independent minded. Surely my father could see this? My father could not. Nor did he appreciate Chuck's suggestion that if I had any honor, I would step down so Michael could assume his rightful place.

My father fumed, but I couldn't help marveling at Chuck's chutzpah. It was like opening the front door to get the newspaper and finding a meteorite on your lawn. I wondered if Mr. Agresta felt that way when Michael had issued his ultimatum, a flying chip off the old block that forced Mr. Agresta to take a step back but must have impressed him and was perhaps the reason it had taken him so long to make up his mind.

I wanted to believe that Mr. Agresta had been so persuaded that I was the best man for the job that he was willing to risk losing Michael, but what if he'd considered me only after Michael's ultimatum? In that case, Michael's behavior—not my worth—was responsible for my selection. I would never know why I had been chosen, and the possibility that I owed my position to Michael helped taint my triumph. Without leaving town, he'd managed to do what his brother had accomplished only by dropping out of high school and flying to California. **Rosen Wins by Default.**

At the end of June, Michael went north to Ithaca to learn about failed revolutions, and I went south to Baltimore to learn about failed American cities. I lived in a house on the campus of Johns Hopkins University with sixteen book-obsessed adolescent misfits.

My mother had predicted that at Telluride I would finally be with kids as serious as I was and could get down at last to serious things, but something much better happened. I could finally stop being serious. I went to a toga party, made out with a girl, and delivered a presentation without leaving the room. I came home with new confidence, new friends, new music, and a Telluride T-shirt with the words "Disturb the universe!"

We'd voted on the motto, which turned J. Alfred Prufrock's self-doubting question into a call to arms. Michael's Telluride T-shirt, which he was wearing the day I ran into him, had the cryptic words "Furious sheep!" He laughed when I asked him about it. The phrase came from the journal of Alexis de Tocqueville, who had encountered a group of rifle-toting young men during the winter of 1848 and marveled at the way gentle artisans had been transformed into blood-thirsty killers overnight.

"Furious sheep" was a running joke at Michael's TASP, along with the pronunciation of Flaubert's name so that it rhymed with "cow dirt." This didn't prevent Michael from learning a lot about the novelist, who'd had a mental breakdown to avoid law school, and about Tocqueville, Karl Marx, "The Eighteenth Brumaire," the proletariat, and the revolution of 1848, which he talked about as if he had personally manned a burning barricade in the streets of Paris.

He also talked about his summer girlfriend, who had a beautiful Irish name like something elfin out of *The Lord of the Rings*. She lived in Maine and he missed her. He missed Collegetown, where he went on late-night raids with friends for pizza and beer and was taken for a Cornell grad student and never carded. Collegetown was just south of the campus; all you had to do was cross a stone bridge spanning one of the deep gorges students were famous for flinging themselves into. This was called "gorging out."

We both laughed, not at suicide but the incongruous language. It was like "furious sheep" or saying, "It's only a flesh wound!" when your limbs have been lopped off, like the knight in the Monty Python skit Michael often quoted.

The *Herald* still hung over us. Even if Michael changed his mind, I'd already given the managing editor job to Lynelle. Not that Michael gave any indication of regretting his decision. If anything, there was wariness in the way he regarded me. Strains diffusely present in the past seemed concentrated now, an undertow of mockery or skepticism beneath the familiar rush of talk. I was aware in myself of a competitive resentment waking up, born perhaps of new confidence and new friends.

So it was good to laugh with Michael in the old way, and renew the solidarity of friends who in spite of everything kept meeting up on the same side of a magic bridge. Who else in New Rochelle knew that TASP stood for Telluride Association Summer Program, or that factotum was the pretentious name for our counselors?

We could laugh at the elitist language of the founder, L. L. Nunn—an electricity tycoon who spoke of the elect he hoped to cultivate as "the Children of Light"—and enjoy our taste of Ivy League destiny while still in high school. You didn't have to believe it was a "fact of social evolution," as Nunn put it in 1920, that "spiritual leadership is the work of the few" to feel rightfully singled out.

Michael still worked at Stellar Gifts, but we no longer walked to our jobs together or met up in the parking lot. I had been working at the grocery store Gristedes but had been fired for pricing every six-pack of Heineken at $0.38 instead of $3.80. The store was obligated to honor incorrect prices if they were lower than the original price, and some guy had discovered my mistake and cleaned us out. The manager could not even persuade him it was $0.38 cents for a single bottle rather than for a six-pack because, with my love of the price gun, I had not only stamped the top of each bottle but plastered the sides of every six-pack with price stickers.

The manager wasn't a bad guy, and I felt he meant it in a kind way when he told me, "You don't really want to be here." If I wasn't flipping off the store, he reasoned, it must have been self-sabotage for a college-bound kid to screw up like that. The truth was that I'd simply failed to "add up the sum," as my math teacher used to say when I wrote "minus three miles" without thinking, "That's a funny distance for Johnny to travel."

It's true I didn't love the job, but I did want the money. If I was too incompetent for ordinary work, I would have to do something extraordinary or face destruction. This unwholesome approach to life, simultaneously grandiose and abject, was hard to shake. Michael, meanwhile, talked about the old couple at the gift shop as if they were ready to draw up adoption papers.

M y stomach still seized a little when Michael and I walked to the entrance of New Rochelle High School, more with remembered vulnerability than present fear, not that I could always tell the difference. We were both above six feet tall. Michael was a few inches taller, bouncing beside me with reassuring familiarity. We had been going to school together for eight years, which is why it felt almost natural for him to accompany me to the door of the *Herald* office and follow me inside. And why it didn't really surprise me to find him there during free periods and lunchtime despite his having quit in protest.

Staffers and their friends were welcome in the office, and I often let in random kids seeking lunchtime asylum. But Michael was in a category of his own. He behaved as though the *Herald* had quit *him*, but he refused to abandon his post, loyally keeping faith with the tables and chairs and with the kids he knew. He was so matter-of-fact in his disregard for any awkwardness this might cause me, or himself, that it was easier to pretend he was supposed to be there.

Another reason I didn't object was that I had discovered how much I liked running the paper. Michael hadn't rejected my authority for my sake, but I couldn't help feeling I'd picked up something he'd dropped.

My habit of consulting people, which exasperated Michael, might have grown out of self-doubt, but I genuinely liked collaborating with people, and the origins of the impulse no longer mattered, any more than it mattered that being a slow reader had made me a careful editor.

It was fun working with Lynelle, who was cheerful, organized, upper middle class, and Black. She often came to meetings in her purple cheerleading uniform, with its short pleated skirt, and knew everyone on the football team, which came in handy for covering "the Purple Crush." She was planning to become a doctor, like her father. Seemingly so different from Michael and me, she made it easier for me to enjoy being myself.

Whenever Mr. Agresta lumbered into my fluorescent kingdom, he would stare for an extra beat at the spot where Michael was holding forth or, conversely, bent over a notebook cramming a week's worth of homework into half an hour of concentrated scribbling. Sometimes Mr. Agresta would draw closer without saying a word and wait for the contagious bloom of silence to catch Michael's attention. This could take a while.

Michael had an extraordinary ability to ignore distractions, especially if he was writing. He never wrote in script but printed in speedy block letters, his large hand moving the pen with stop-and-go fury like a cabdriver driving with the brake on, his body rocking slightly with the effort. When Michael did look up at last, it was never entirely clear at what point he had become aware of being watched. Mr. Agresta would smile blandly, as if to say, "Please, don't let me interrupt you." Michael would smile back with equal and opposite irony: "Don't worry, I won't."

Michael had not lost his talent for napping in public no matter how noisy the room. Occasionally I'd find him stretched on a table with his jacket over his head; more commonly he'd be leaning back against the wall, his face tilted up at the ceiling as if he were sunning himself. When he woke, he'd give a few stork-like flaps to repossess his body, squint at the wall clock, and look unhurriedly around the room. If he noticed someone watching, he'd shrug, sheepish but unashamed.

We sometimes got a ride home from an obliging junior named Dylan with sheepdog hair, Birkenstock sandals, and the anxious, peaceable vibe of someone who had escaped a hippie commune. He drove a battered station wagon with a bumper sticker that read "And on the eighth day God created the Doors." He had a younger brother named Guthrie, born the night his folkie father took Dylan to a Pete Seeger concert in Manhattan he never got to hear because Seeger walked out and announced that Dylan's mother had gone into labor.

Six months after the concert, Dylan's father walked out on his family, leaving five-year-old Dylan, baby Guthrie, and two other siblings in the care of their erratic mother, a child psychiatrist whose suicidal behavior and self-medicating excess often drove Dylan out of the house. He found refuge at the home of his friend Josh Ferber, who lived in a state of mysterious freedom in a grand seaside house with a giant turret and a private stretch of beach.

Michael, who spent a lot of time there too, called it the Gatsby House. Josh's parents were both community psychiatrists, and the mansion served as an informal meeting place for a wide circle of idealistic colleagues and friends who had come of age at a time when community was itself a word potent with healing power. Michael was deeply devoted to Josh's mother, Jane Ferber, a person of rare curiosity and compassion, who ran a community mental health center in downtown New Rochelle that her husband had helped her create. Their shared dream of shutting down state hospitals, and caring for distressed people in the community, had not worked out as planned. The marriage had not worked out as planned either.

In the seventies, if a mental health professional took off his clothes, got on the floor with his patients, or dressed only in sunrise colors, it wasn't entirely clear if he was having a breakdown, making a political statement, or trying out a new technique he'd picked up at the Esalen Institute. Still, life had grown tumultuous after Josh's father had donned orange clothes, hung a mala around his neck, and run off to Poona, India, where he was learning to let go of the things of this world, including his wife and children.

Michael spoke about Andy Ferber with a kind of appalled fascination. A brilliant family psychiatrist, he played electric bass in a band called the Nocturnal Emissions—formed with colleagues from Bronx State Hospital—but refused to read music, despite being a classically trained musician, because he didn't want to inhibit his playing. Like many of his generation, he was tired of following the rules. Though he'd become the director of Family Studies at the Albert Einstein College of Medicine while still in his twenties, he only found peace "digging ditches and planting mushrooms," as Michael put it, for the Bhagwan Shree Rajneesh.

Known to his followers simply as Bhagwan, which Michael said meant "God," the guru offered middle-class professionals a way out of the dulling bonds of sexual, spiritual, and economic convention, asking only for their assets and total obedience in return.

Michael was keenly aware of the chaos caused when Josh's father came home for visits, dressed in orange clothing and calling himself

Bodhicitta. Dr. Ferber was still torn between family life and the transcendent community calling to him a world away.

Lately, he'd been in the Pacific Northwest, where the Bhagwan and his followers were establishing a utopian community called Rajneeshpuram. There the former Dr. Ferber stood among the faithful showering love on their spiritual master as he drove down the central street in one of his ninety-four Rolls Royces that, like his vast collection of gold Rolex watches, was an ironic commentary on the corruption of materialist values. Andy Ferber's family still hoped their husband and father might choose home.

Meanwhile, his big circular meditation room in the attic became the place where Michael, Josh, Dylan, and their friends partied, played music, and talked until dawn. Michael spoke of these gatherings rhapsodically, without ever suggesting that I come along. Not that I ever asked. We both understood that I was unlikely to go.

The children of divorce often had a jilted, defiant aura I envied. They'd learned from warring, unfaithful, self-actualizing mothers and fathers to grab what they could, combining middle-aged desperation and adolescent impulse. Their boldness propelled them toward experiences everyone wanted, even as it set them apart, and you could never be entirely sure whether they were pursuing pleasure or self-destruction. The confusion was part of the fascination.

Michael was often among them, but returned to his strangely old-fashioned two-parent home with its high-decibel suppertime arguments and even higher expectations. Every nuclear family is nuclear in its own way. Michael still sought out houses like mine the way people went to double features in the days when movie theaters were the only places with air-conditioning. But he was at home with a different crowd. I admired the way they tended to each other in attics and basements, choosing the music and the drugs, and driving the sexual tempo of teenage life. A lot of the kids who hung out at the Ferber house at night were *Herald* editors who hung out in the office during the day. I had daytime custody of the inhabitants of Michael's night world.

The Ferber crowd didn't really conform to my fantasies. Wry, melancholy Dylan—a gifted writer who would succeed me as editor, only to give it up when he fled his mother's house senior year—was just trying to survive his childhood, despite a father who'd walked out when he was five and a mother who'd vanished into a psychiatric hospital shortly afterward for one of many spells. At other times, as Dylan recalled in a memoir, she told him not to be surprised if he found her dead on the bathroom floor when he got home from school. No wonder he tried a couple of his mother's Valium at age thirteen, after his friend Josh—who "was more pharmaceutically conversant"—surveyed his mother's formidable medicine cabinet and identified the benzodiazepines.

In later years, I was forced to recognize that in high school I was the one with a drug problem: I wasn't taking any. Michael accepted the fact with such nonjudgmental equanimity that it felt like a judgment. Here was one more symptom of my developmental delay about which nothing could be done.

In light of later experience, I can say that the drugs available in high school would not have helped me, and might well have done me harm. But if I could go back to visit my younger self, as therapists sometimes advise, I would hand myself a prescription for Prozac. I'd gotten dizzy on a date at the Metropolitan Museum of Art, sinking down behind a glass case filled with surprisingly small Rodin horses, and had actually lost consciousness during my Harvard interview, suavely telling the interviewer, whose cigar wasn't helping, "I'm sorry, I seem to have stopped breathing," before going into a dolphin dive on his couch.

In those days, psychopharmacology was not equipped for people like me, though in coming decades "the worried well" would inherit the profession, along with many of the community mental health centers created for people suffering from far more serious illnesses. That wasn't the reason they'd failed, but it certainly hadn't helped.

Even if there had been something chemically available, my parents were psychoanalytically oriented. They'd both been in analysis themselves and would have sent me to a talk therapist if they sent me anywhere.

I think Michael understood that my real problem was fear, and that beyond the law or my parents' hearts, I was afraid of breaking my brain, like Piggy landing on the rock. Just imagining myself smoking pot, I felt a surge of panicked claustrophobia. What if my altered state never went back to normal and I wound up in a loop of eternal confusion?

Michael considered such neurotic fretting a throwback to the days of *Reefer Madness*, a movie made in the 1930s to scare the youth of America. It had become a cult classic in the '70s to remind us of the paranoid style of our elders, like the rants from *Dr. Strangelove* Michael loved about fluoride and precious bodily fluids: "Have you ever seen a Commie drink a glass of water?"

Michael's attitude was much more practical. He might have stolen a bottle of booze from Pat's family and gotten drunk, but he was businesslike when he came over with a six-pack of beer so he could "practice" for college. He explained his plan to my mother without embarrassment, as if it were a strategy for taking the SAT, and brought his own can opener in case my parents didn't have one. My mother found this absurd. Not the beer—the drinking age was eighteen—but the can opener dangling from his belt when she let him in.

It did not trouble Michael that I sipped from a single can while he drank the other five. On the contrary, he'd told me in advance that I should get my own six-pack if I wanted to drink. Weren't they practically giving them away at Gristedes?

Michael didn't need a drinking companion, just someone to sit with while he drank, more like a witness, which was how I felt. As he drank, he got a little slower but remained essentially, almost stoically, the same. When he got up to take a leak, his gangly body rocked ever so slightly, like a wasp flying into cold weather.

Though my mother found his behavior odd, it was, in a way, a Doc Savage thing to do. He was building up his stamina so he could drink with people *without* getting drunk. In a similar spirit, perhaps, I'd bought a weight bench and barbells in the aftermath of my beat-down and was secretly building up my strength. I'd sent away for a weightlifting course that came each month like pornography in unmarked envelopes. My family had considered that strange, too, though my father dutifully spotted me so I didn't smash my face with a barbell.

Michael was dating a tall, slender girl with a wide Carly Simon smile who was crazy about him, as Michael himself told me with the disavowing shrug he used to neutralize his own boasts. As far as I was concerned, to have a girlfriend like that was to be fine. She wanted to take baths with him, he said, give him massages, and basically do whatever she could think of to please him.

Michael and I both got into Yale. For the ninth year in a row, we would be going to the same school. It was now our turn to lounge like bored sea lions on the tabletops in the *Herald* office.

I got contact lenses, passed my driver's test at last, and was miraculously given a car to use until college began. My benefactor was a family friend, an English professor named Avi. The car was a 1968 Volvo, which Avi and his beautiful wife, Muriel, also an English professor, had driven to New Rochelle from Berkeley, California.

The car had a stick shift, and Avi took me to Roosevelt field so I could learn to drive it. He wasn't afraid I would strip the gears and let me buck around in the heavy whale-shaped car until I could handle the clutch and two-footed shifting with relative ease. I drove my

Volvo over the spot where the motorcycle had hit me, and over the bones of bad memories, in triumph.

Our elementary school was being converted into fancy condominiums. The baby boom tap had been turned off, and redrawn districts, along with changes in the neighborhood school policy, had made Roosevelt redundant. But the basketball courts and the field were preserved for community use. That summer, Michael and I and many of the old gang turned up there, sharing an impulse to return as we were about to say goodbye.

A lot of things had come to an end, including the seventies, but our conventional world was still green, however watered with subterranean streams of music, conspiracy theory, and our dreams of radical liberation. The election of Ronald Reagan shocked and horrified us. We were certain he'd bring us to nuclear annihilation, though he was humanized, a little, when he got shot by an unmedicated mentally ill man obsessed with Jodie Foster, the actress and Yale freshman, and with *The Catcher in the Rye*, a novel narrated by a young man in a mental hospital obsessed with "phonies."

The shooter had also been inspired by the murder of John Lennon just a few months before. Lennon was killed by an unmedicated mentally ill man who had taken more LSD trips than you could count and was arrested in front of the Dakota holding a copy of *The Catcher in the Rye*. That was the day *our* music died. Pete Hamill in *New York* magazine described the stunned doctors and nurses in the hospital: "Behind them, in a refrigerator, lay the sixties." Oddly, the sixties had also pulled the trigger.

My father was upset when he heard I was going to the senior prom with a girl whose last name was Murphy; there were Baumwalds and Levis all over the place; couldn't I have chosen one of them? Not that he didn't understand the appeal of "golden-haired

Margarete." That wasn't her name, but a phrase from "Death Fugue" by Paul Celan, a Jewish poet born in Romania who survived the Holocaust, wrote in German, lived in Paris, and drowned himself in the Seine in 1970. *Your golden hair Margarete. Your ashen hair Shulamite.* I was supposed to date Shulamite.

Along with a few translated lines of "Todesfuge," my father quoted his favorite passage from the Bible: "Choose life," a wonderfully plastic expression that was often used to instill pride or banish anxious self-doubt. "Choose life" was the Deuteronomic equivalent of the prime directive in *Star Trek*. It could even mean "You're killing me."

Still, he went with me to rent my tuxedo, and paid for it. My date wore an antique dress covered with pale beads, her yellow hair piled high on her head. She got sick in the course of the evening, thus saving me the trouble. Michael meanwhile didn't go to the prom at all because by then he'd become obsessed with a dark-haired, openhearted girl named Jo-Ann. He'd poured out his love for her on a full page of her high school yearbook for all to see, but Jo-Ann had already made plans, and Michael, stung by this non-rejection, stayed home.

The summer before college I found myself filled with optimism. I was surprised when Michael told me one late summer afternoon, as we chatted on the patio, that he did not think we would see much of each other at Yale. When I asked him why, he told me that I was simply too slow.

CHAPTER SEVEN

MESSAGE IN A BOTTLE

For the great enemy of truth is very often not
the lie—deliberate, contrived, and dishonest—
but the myth—persistent, persuasive, and
unrealistic.

—JOHN F. KENNEDY,
Yale commencement address, 1962

Freshmen at Yale live on Old Campus, a leafy quad with a real
colonial building from 1750, a fake colonial building that looks
just like the real one, and a statue of Nathan Hale, class of 1773,
flipping off the British with his eyes because his hands are tied behind his back. These four acres of neat lawn, crisscrossed paths, and
remnant elm trees are surrounded by neo-Gothic dormitories whose
stone backsides keep the city of New Haven at bay so a thousand
lucky teenagers can study, panic, and party in the green lap of Ivy
League privilege.

My father responded to campus with the same wary, embarrassed
pride I recognized from two years before when we dropped off my
sister, now a junior. I wasn't sure if I was intercepting "How will I
pay for this?" or "Were my parents murdered by Nazis so my child
could spend four years in a country club?" He also felt guilty that I
had the maximum in student loans and, despite a work-study job,
would graduate in debt.

It was a relief when my father, after telling me to remember where I came from—which didn't mean New Rochelle but the ancient civilization from which the Puritan founders had borrowed Yale's Hebrew motto—kissed me once more and got into the car. My mother was already behind the wheel crying.

The one time I'd caught a glimpse of Michael, he was walking a few steps behind his father, who looked like General MacArthur returning to the Philippines.

I ran into four TASPers my first day on Old Campus, and walked past a girl wearing the same Mostly Mozart T-shirt as the one I had on. We turned around at the same moment and doubled back, amused. I had the distinct impression we had both decided to become different people in college, changed our minds at the last minute, but found we were different after all. I only felt a little dizzy when I discovered that I was pointing at her breasts as well as the musical logo on her red shirt and grinning.

The drinking age, like the voting age, had outlived the military draft that had justified lowering it to eighteen. ROTC and Students for a Democratic Society had disappeared from campus, but the Social Activities Committee sponsored boisterous outdoor "SAC parties" where prep school kids who knew how to drink, and public school kids who knew how to throw up, clustered around giant kegs of beer and card tables wobbly with bottles of booze. By morning, plastic cups and a handful of undergraduates were strewn on the expensive grass.

After a night or two coiled around a toilet bowl, I went back to "nursing a beer," in my father's unmanly but practical phrase. I had not come to college to relive my bar mitzvah, and there were other forms of liberation.

At a mixer under a striped tent, I ate an unkosher hot dog while standing near a girl with green eyes who groaned when "Message in a Bottle" by the Police came on. Turning to me, she asked what I thought of the song but before I could answer told me it expressed exactly what she was feeling: "Like I'm sending an SOS to the world? And I don't know if someone will get my message?"

Her musical voice turned assertions into questions; even her groan had been more of an invitation than a warning. Everything felt like that, softer and sharper at the same time. The thick Gothic buildings standing guard, like the bullies Bremer made friends with in remedial class, were on my side.

That fall, a freshman in the dorm next to mine drank himself into a stupor at a SAC party, was carried to his room to sleep things off, but failed to wake up the next day. His death stunned us, sparked furious debates, and led to official talk of banning alcohol and SAC parties altogether. At some point, though, the official statements stopped and the parties resumed. Still, the national mood was shifting, and by senior year the drinking age was twenty-one.

Michael didn't live on Old Campus but in his residential college, which made my running into him less likely. Modeled on Oxford and Cambridge, Yale's residential college system is the pride and organizing principle of undergraduate life. There were twelve colleges at the time, each with its own quad, library, dining hall, and living quarters. Only two housed freshmen, and Michael was in one of these.

His college, Silliman, was the biggest and one of the farthest from Old Campus. Assignments were random, unless you were a legacy, but vaulting over the freshman nursery to live and eat among upperclassmen suited Michael.

Each residential college had graduate fellows who ate with undergraduates in the dining hall. Michael made friends early on with a PhD student in economics named Linus who was working with

James Tobin, that year's winner of the Nobel Prize in Economic Sciences. Linus had never met a freshman who knew as much as Michael about economists and economics, though he discovered that Michael's conceptual grasp was much greater than his technical skills when he stayed up all night helping him with an assignment for an advanced economics class.

A graduate of MIT, Linus was used to reckoning intelligence in terms of mathematical prowess, and it was a new experience to work with someone whose mind was arranged so differently from his own. I'd always assumed that Michael was as good with numbers as he was with words, but though far less imbalanced than I was, in his own way he also leaned on the verbal to get by.

Like all first-year students, I'd been assigned a residential college and given a key to its heavy gate. I got invitations to Master's Teas, could hang out in the courtyard, study in the little library, and eat at designated times in the dining hall, but I would not live there until sophomore year. This was fine with me, determined as I was to get in on the ground floor of my deferred adolescence.

Except for the two colleges that included freshman, and the two "new" ones built in the 1960s—ugly, architecturally important, and air-conditioned—the residential colleges had been built in the '30s. Designed to look centuries older, they were Hogwarts fantasies long before Harry Potter, with gargoyles, hidden rooms, leaded glass that had been broken and mended for authenticity, and stairways to nowhere. Like Hollywood movies of the same vintage, they were a vision of wealth, power, and elegance, but instead of borrowing it for two hours, you got to keep the illusion for four years—and maybe the rest of your life.

Paradoxically, the gated, clubby elegance of the residential colleges had contributed to a more egalitarian spirit by competing with the exclusive Yale societies that had previously siphoned the superrich away from undergraduate life. By the time a public school meritocracy arrived in the sixties, the colleges were the place to be.

My college, Davenport, was Gothic on the outside and Georgian on the inside, like a dual-purpose movie set. The architectural incongruity, like the faux heraldic coat of arms stamped on the heavy china, did nothing to diminish the grandeur of the dining hall with its oak-paneled walls and Waterford chandelier. Only working in the kitchen did that, scraping other people's food off the embossed plates and loading them into an industrial dishwasher that steamed my glasses and made even my socks soggy.

Despite being named for the Puritan minister who founded New Haven in 1637, Davenport was known as the "white buck" college back in the day. That was the day when students were judged by the contents of their bank accounts, and white bucks were the favored footwear of Yale's elite denizens.

It was easy to feel contempt for all that, just as it was fun to laugh at the black-and-white photos of humorless Yale athletes from the 1920s, with their Hitler Youth haircuts and Ozymandias thighs, and feel that children of the meritocracy were the rightful heirs of an ill-gotten fortune. What a strange satisfaction it was to dismiss the builders and stewards as unwanted guests—a taste, perhaps, of what it felt like to have a new testament that let you disavow the old one while quoting from it freely.

You could take secret pride in knowing that Vice President George H. W. Bush had been in Davenport while laughing at him in *Doonesbury*, where he was represented as a disembodied speech bubble too insubstantial to be seen with the naked eye. The vice president's father, Senator Prescott Bush, had also been in Davenport, and so had his son George W., who was still an unknown baby boomer with a drinking problem.

More impressive was knowing that the cartoonist Garry Trudeau had created *Doonesbury* while an undergraduate living in Davenport in the sixties, where it began as a strip about his classmates and himself. In some sense it still was. Trudeau had overlapped with George W. Bush, mocked him in his campus cartoon when he was a cheerleader and frat boy, and would mock him again when it was his turn to become president.

Trudeau and Bush weren't accidental neighbors at Yale, any more than Michael and I were on Mereland. Their fathers had both served in World War II, lived in Davenport before them, and inhabited intersecting social circles in the outside world. They were the WASPs Michael was always talking about, raised with money and a tradition of public service, though for the Bushes that meant being president and for Trudeau it meant making fun of the Bushes. Satire, for Michael and me, was the nobler calling.

But Michael believed in the power of the WASP establishment. The first time I ran into him on Old Campus, the bells of Battell Chapel were ringing, and he gestured sardonically at that mighty fortress of Congregational Christianity as if it were summoning us to mandatory Sunday worship. In fact, Battell was hosting Yom Kippur services, Yale's president was Italian American, and the student body was something like 30 percent Jewish. *The Official Preppy Handbook*, a current bestseller, was turning the khaki-wearing scions of the superannuated ruling class into J.Crew fashion models, shrinking even William F. Buckley Jr. to the sum of his pants.

Buckley wasn't actually a WASP but an upstart Catholic who'd gone to Yale when there was a 10 percent quota for Catholics, same as for Jews. But he'd lived in Davenport, talked like Thurston Howell III on *Gilligan's Island*, and lamented the loss of Yale's religious traditions in a famous book published in the 1950s that Michael referred to in unflattering terms.

Michael was the least intimidated person I knew, but he liked having an opposing force as a focal point for his striving. He often talked as though we'd grown up in our fathers' neighborhoods, though my father wasn't afraid the gate would be slammed in my face. He was afraid that I would fail to realize it had been flung wide open, and that I'd sail out an open window on the far side of my ambition, like the cat in a Tom and Jerry cartoon, and wake up in a dumpster with amnesia.

Michael was raised to be a gate-crasher, but it was more fun crashing the gate if there was someone on the other side leaning against it. Unfortunately, it was hard to find a WASP like Tom Buchanan, the Yale man from *The Great Gatsby*, with his polo ponies and "cruel body," waving a copy of *The Rise of the Coloured Empires*. The best Michael could do was Mike Curtis, who lived one floor below him in Silliman and was more like Oliver Barrett IV, the hockey-playing golden boy from *Love Story* who learns to cry.

Mike Curtis didn't have a III or IV after his name, but he'd been captain of the hockey team at Groton, his father and older brother had gone to Yale, his great-grandfather had run Chase Bank's English operations, and a great-uncle had been a cavalry officer in British-ruled Palestine. Better yet, Mike's mother was descended from German nobility, men who wore monocles and had "von" in their names. Joachim von Ribbentrop, negotiator of the Hitler-Stalin pact, was a distant cousin. Nazis!

In reality, Mike tutored underprivileged New Haven kids at Dwight Hall, and confessed his Nazi connections to Michael with deep shame. Listening gravely, Michael told his new friend he must not carry the burden of the past like a curse. By the power vested in him as a New York Jew, he offered Mike full absolution, though he continued to refer to him as "the WASP," and sometimes "the Golden Boy."

Michael's fondness for ethnic taxonomy—one roommate was "the intense Chinese guy," another "the guilt-ridden Irish Catholic"—owed something to all those comedians we'd grown up listening to. Freddy

Prinze, the star of *Chico and the Man* and a stand-up prodigy, called himself a Hungarican, and did Hispanic, Black, and Asian American characters on his album, *Looking Good*, though we dropped it from the rotation after Prinze shot himself in the head when he was just twenty-two. We still had George Carlin—"I used to be Irish Catholic, now I'm an American"—and of course Richard Pryor, explaining why *The Exorcist* would be over in eleven minutes if it had Black people in it.

Michael's political philosophy seemed to merge seventies stand-up with nostalgia for his father's Brooklyn, where you didn't pretend sameness to achieve harmony but forged a camaraderie of confrontation, sticking it to Nazis abroad and the Man at home.

The first time I met Michael for lunch at Silliman, I had to drag him out of bed. I'd already waited outside the dining hall for more than half an hour, then wandered around the college, which had four entrances, before I found his suite. I was let in by one of his amused roommates, already back from eating. The kitchen was closed by the time Michael was up and dressed. I was furious, but he'd looked so astonished when I woke him—shaking his head as if he were his own incorrigible child—that I let it go.

His roommates were clearly familiar with this sort of thing. Sleeping through everything—like eating a whole pizza without getting full, or reading a book in one sitting without losing a word—was treated as one more prodigious ability, a view Michael cultivated. The bottomless well of exhaustion he carried inside only threw into sharper relief the self-confidence, encyclopedic recall, and verbal will to power that made him dangerous in an argument but fun to joke around with.

He got along especially well with Jim, a "lanky Virginian and washed-up high school lacrosse star," as Michael put it in his ornate way. Jim looked like the everyman hero of a Frank Capra movie, a judgment Michael delivered with the same archaic ease that allowed him to say "lanky Virginian." The Capra analogy was encouraged by Jim, who wanted to be a filmmaker and recited earnest movie lines in a laconic Gary Cooper drawl, though Michael reported that Jim was really a "guilt-ridden Irish Catholic" who went to mass every day and planned to make films "for the greater glory of God."

I assumed Michael was teasing his roommate, but Jim nodded and said he was planning to create a production company called Ad Maiorem Dei Gloriam, or AMDG Films for short. I had been the straight man in enough Laudorian vaudeville acts to wonder if *I* was being teased. But Jim spoke with earnest intensity, though his eyes were laughing, and I wasn't really surprised to discover as I got to know him better that everything he said was true.

Michael had finally found someone who knew as many lines from old movies as he did. If Michael said, "Liberty's too precious a thing to be buried in books, Miss Saunders," Jim knew it was Jimmy Stewart in *Mr. Smith Goes to Washington*. If Jim called himself the luckiest man-an-an on the face of the earth-erth-erth, Michael knew it was Gary Cooper playing Lou Gehrig, the pride of the Yankees—and of New Rochelle, where the Iron Horse had a house.

They played a game whose object was to take a sentence and make it sound like a line from a Frank Capra film by adding the phrase "just a man like any other" and saying it in the voice of Jimmy Stewart. *Odysseus is just a man like any other, trying to get home to his wife. Wittgenstein is just a man like any other, who believes that what can be shown cannot be said. Schrödinger's cat is just a man like any other, trying to think outside the box.*

Old movies were everywhere, a cheap form of campus entertainment you could see every night. One of my roommates, who had brought his own projector and showed movies for one of the film societies, showed them on our wall before shipping them back in their circular tins. I'd walk into our darkened common room to find Death playing chess with the knight in *The Seventh Seal* or Alex the droog strapped to a chair, having the violence tortured out of him in *A Clockwork Orange*. Most often, women with gigantic breasts were running around in the preview for *Faster, Pussycat! Kill! Kill!* that seemed to come with every film.

Jim had a theory about movie acting that I thought about long afterward because it had so much to do with Michael, not only as he was then but later. The great thing about golden age movie stars, he said, was that they didn't have to be good actors, and could even be bad, as long as they were consistent. Except that it wasn't being bad, or good, it was being themselves. Audiences expected to recognize the star inside the character; they went to see Cary Grant or Katharine Hepburn, not to see them become different people. Who remembered the names of the characters they played?

Everyone knew that Gary Cooper, who delivered his lines the same way in all his movies, was only pretending to be Lou Gehrig in *Pride of the Yankees*. It worked because the real Lou Gehrig pretended to be himself, too, and not always very well. Paradoxically, the stubborn immutability of the stars made the movies more believable.

Michael's mannered locutions did something similar. There was nothing natural about calling Jim a lanky Virginian, but he embraced the artifice with so much conviction that it came across as sincerity. Jim did something similar with his deadpan declarations of simple faith that at first seemed disingenuous, but the more you doubted him, the more implicated you felt in the cynical world he was casting off, which you compensated for by elevating him to an even higher plane of sincerity.

And Jim *was* a lanky Virginian, just like Michael had said. He *did* look like a Capra hero and really was an Irish Catholic lacrosse player obsessed with sex, guilt, and death. Michael's role was being the person who knew those things and said them aloud.

Michael introduced his roommates with the same language he used to talk about them privately, as if they were characters in a play he had written. He assumed their acquiescence in his descriptions, as if Ying also thought of himself as the intense Chinese guy who typed 120 words a minute and could do an infinity of push-ups, and Mel was a self-identified Hollywood princeling who resented his crowded dorm room because he'd grown up in a Brentwood mansion with a wing to himself.

According to Michael, Mel's father had come up with the tagline "Just when you thought it was safe to go back in the water," the phrase used to promote *Jaws 2*. It seemed to support his belief that Mel himself had the makings of a Hollywood shark, "a real-life Sammy Glick," as Michael put it, a reference to Budd Schulberg's 1941 novel *What Makes Sammy Run?* Michael was fascinated by the ruthlessly ambitious Sammy Glick, a Jew from the Lower East Side who lies, cheats, and backstabs his way to the top of the movie business, shtupping starlets and selling his soul more times than Bialystock and Bloom sell shares of *Springtime for Hitler*.

Michael's roommate did not embody any of these qualities. He was a small, genial kid with big glasses who owned a "microcomputer" that took up three quarters of his desk. I'd never seen a personal computer before, which was such a novelty that the *Yale Daily News* ran a story with a big photo of Mel posing with his machine. Michael put the cost of the computer at $10,000. Beyond his resentment of the price tag, and Mel's picture in the paper, what seemed to irritate Michael the most were the spreadsheets his roommate printed out on a screaming dot matrix printer that occupied what was left of his desk.

As far as I could tell, these were nerdy, innocuous compilations of data about courses, professors, and friends' telephone numbers, but Michael saw them as evidence of Sammy Glickishness and spoke about the spreadsheets with suspicious irritation. When I ran into Michael a few weeks after our lunch, he told me it had become necessary to stuff his roommate into a closet to teach him a lesson.

He said Jim had helped him, though why he needed a second athletic six-footer to put a kid half his size into a closet was as mysterious as why he felt he had to put him there in the first place. And Jim wasn't the sort of person who would do it. On the contrary, he was someone who stood up for the little guy, as his beloved movies put it. But then so was Michael.

The Hollywood princeling who shared Michael's bedroom moved out before the year was over. He found it impossible to sleep— not because, as Michael said, he was used to his own wing, but because Michael never put his reading light out no matter how often he was asked or how late it got. Though, as if by magic, the light was always off by morning when Mel, who had early classes, had to find his clothes in the dark and dress outside because Michael was finally asleep.

Mel moved into a spare room on the third floor of the Silliman master's house. All the colleges had spare rooms for just that purpose, which everyone called "psycho singles" no matter why you needed one. Michael, meanwhile, with what seemed to be characteristic good fortune, inherited a room of his own. If he brought a girl back to the suite, he could have privacy.

New Haven was a decaying and dangerous city in the early 1980s, and I was grateful for the barricading buildings that doubled as dorms and classrooms. The English Department was housed in a neo-Gothic hulk on Old Campus that was part of the fortress. I attended lectures in its creaky wooden auditorium by day and saw movies there at night, part of the self-contained pleasure Michael described as rolling in and out of bed.

One movie that made a deep impression was called *King of Hearts*, an anti-war film made in the midsixties whose real theme was the madness of society and the wisdom of retreat. It was set during the First World War and starred Alan Bates as a British soldier sent to a French village to defuse explosives left by the retreating German army. The villagers have fled, leaving the unguarded inhabitants of the local insane asylum to take over the town dressed in scavenged finery.

The clueless young soldier, who carries a homing pigeon around in a cage as he explores the booby-trapped village, is so beguiled by these otherworldly innocents—especially the beautiful and childlike Coquelicot—that when they retreat to their asylum, locking the gate behind them because they've had enough of the mad world, you know he is going to follow. Ordered to blow up a German town, he pulls off his uniform and stands naked at the asylum gate, holding his birdcage and waiting to be admitted. He has discovered that insanity, as the Scottish psychiatrist R. D. Laing announced at the dawn of the sixties, is "a perfectly rational adjustment to an insane world."

I had never felt so protected and so free, and wanted to prolong both feelings as long as possible. Still, rumors of our own vulnerability reached us, like the boy who died of alcohol poisoning in the fall. That winter, a junior in Michael's college fell to her death from the top of the Art and Architecture Building. Snow had dusted campus the night before, and at first it seemed possible that the young woman, who wanted to be a painter, had simply lost her footing. Her friends admired her free and fearless spirit, and still talked about the time she had walked into the Silliman dining hall one bitter cold day wearing only a slip.

It was soon determined, however, that she had jumped. She'd been growing more withdrawn as well as more erratic, and her grieving friends were left to wonder how they'd continued to see in her behavior an artistic soul's brave resistance to conformity. It was terrible to learn that her hands were still in her pockets when she hit the ground.

Our first semester, Michael published a long letter in *The New York Times* defending the use of mandatory busing to achieve racial balance in public schools. Recalling the time "massive waves of immigration struck our shores," his letter celebrated diversity and attacked a Harvard professor who had proposed letting Black parents decide for themselves whether their kids got bused to majority-white schools or stayed close to home where, Michael warned, they would "suffer the loss of an integrated environment."

One of our friends heard about Michael's letter from his parents, who read it to him over the phone with a tone of admiration that instantly released in him a corresponding sense of inadequacy. He was at an Ivy League college, but like most of us he was still figuring out where to put his tray in the dining hall while Michael sat down in the faculty lounge and picked a fight with a Harvard sociologist and public policy expert, Nathan Glazer, whose work I'd been assigned in my urban studies TASP.

My parents owned a copy of *Beyond the Melting Pot*, Glazer's seminal study of ethnic groups written with Daniel Patrick Moynihan and published the year Michael and I were born. Michael's ability to take on a Harvard professor who thought about education, poverty, and housing for a living was impressive. So was his willingness to dive into a thorny debate over busing at a time when Blacks as well as whites were rejecting it as a remedy for the de facto segregation that remained entrenched nearly thirty years after *Brown v. Board of Education*.

A lot had happened since federal marshals had escorted six-year-old Ruby Bridges to an all-white school in New Orleans in 1960, which Norman Rockwell turned into an iconic painting, *The Problem We All Live With*, and *Look* magazine printed in 1964.

There was no equivalent image for the complicated reality a decade later, when a Boston judge from upper-crust Wellesley ordered Black kids from run-down majority-Black schools in working-class South Boston neighborhoods bused to run-down majority-white schools in working-class South Boston neighborhoods, and vice versa, leaving the upper-middle-class suburbs untouched, until all the schools were 50 percent Black and 50 percent white. This had not gone well.

Glazer was one of those experience-tempered liberals trying, after the idealism of the sixties and the policy failures of the seventies, to achieve a pragmatic balance between individual liberty and community responsibility.

Like Michael, I preferred the picture of Ruby Bridges. Still, it took a lot of chutzpah to accuse a Harvard sociologist of ignoring "moral and social considerations," and even more for a white teenager to argue that Black parents should be forced to send their kids to white schools even if they wanted to keep them close. He did not ask if there might be reasons besides ignorance or prejudice for Black parents to want their kids close to home, or vote for a state law, as many had, barring mandatory busing. It was "simply a posited, moral assumption" that diversity made you better, and everything followed from that.

I heard an echo of his father's voice speaking with righteous social science certitude. He was also invoking the social scientific wisdom that had helped persuade the Supreme Court unanimously to strike down school segregation. At Roosevelt, Michael and I had learned about the famous doll experiments conducted by psychologists Kenneth and Mamie Clark, demonstrating a preference, among Black children in segregated schools, for white dolls otherwise identical to Black ones. The experiment, by demonstrating the toll segregation took on the self-esteem of Black children, helped Thurgood Marshall persuade the court that separate could never be equal.

It did more than that. Psychology, which made hidden things manifest, came of age in that court case, not simply as a tool in a legal battle, but as an aspect of what the battle was all about. The Clarks' evidence for the irreparable psychological damage that Black children suffered in segregated schools didn't just uphold equal protection under the law; it introduced psychological well-being as a way of measuring equality.

Thurgood Marshall's earlier courtroom strategy had been to prove the fallacy of "separate but equal" by demonstrating how inadequate educational facilities were in all-Black schools. By introducing psychic damage as evidence of inequality, rather than deficient facilities or quality teaching, Marshall had a way to argue that separate was always unequal. Integration was the only solution because anything else caused psychological harm. As the court wrote in the famous footnote referring to the doll experiments, "Whatever may have been the extent of psychological knowledge at the time of *Plessy v. Ferguson*, this finding is amply supported by modern authority."

Instead of using psychology to support the equal application of the law, the law would support a psychological measure of equality. This was the power of social science as a modern authority. Its prominent role in *Brown v. Board of Education* made giving psychologists a role in all aspects of our education after Sputnik even more logical. Who else could dip into the unconscious life of students and take soundings to figure out what was really going on?

Like his father, who had investigated early childhood intervention programs for the Department of Education, Michael was planning to study economics and political science. He was already translating his New Rochelle childhood into public policy recommendations.

Life at Yale could feel as symbolic as "American Pie." This was not only because we were teenagers who thought everything was about us but because the Puritan founders—who designed the New Haven Green to hold the 144,000 survivors of the Second Coming—thought everything was about *them*. Yale was established in 1701 as an extension of allegorical dreams mapped out in 1624. Three hundred and sixty years later, the dreams were still allegorical, even if the world had turned upside down. There were homeless people living on the New Haven Green, but across the street stood Phelps Gate, the main entrance to Old Campus, home of the secular elect.

Discovering that *Doonesbury* was not only the brainchild of a precocious undergraduate but also *about* Yale was part of the experience of being at Yale. All Trudeau had to do to turn his semi-autobiographical strip into a national one, when it was picked up for syndication in 1970, was replace the *Y* on B. D.'s football helmet with a star, and change the name Yale to Walden, which also became the name of the commune where his characters live after graduation.

There was even a perverse campus pride that John Hinckley Jr. had claimed he shot President Reagan to impress a Yale freshman, the actress Jodie Foster, who was taking the year off to avoid publicity. Though the trial would not begin until the spring, newspapers speculated that Hinckley's lawyers were planning an insanity defense.

Ironically, the new *Doonesbury* collection, *In Search of Reagan's Brain*, featured a cover drawing of a TV reporter aiming his flashlight at a tangle of frayed presidential synapses. The cartoons had run in newspapers before Reagan was elected, mocking the candidate's competence by tracing his policies to damaged regions of his cerebral cortex, fancifully turning his political views into symptoms of mental deterioration.

It was ironic that the president whose cartoon brain *Doonesbury* pathologized had been shot by a man suffering from an untreated brain disease, who had also shot Reagan's press secretary, James Brady, in the head, administering with a bullet the barbaric equivalent of a lobotomy, the treatment of last resort from the darkest days of state hospitals that had come to symbolize the institutions themselves and to justify shutting them down.

There were many ironies when it came to brains. "We are best equipped to be our brother's thinker," Yale's patrician president Kingman Brewster—immortalized in *Doonesbury* as President King— boasted in 1968, flush with excitement about Yale's role in the transformation of New Haven. Thanks to Yale brains, the answer to the question asked by a 1965 headline in *The New York Times*, WILL NEW HAVEN BE THE FIRST AMERICAN CITY TO ELIMINATE POVERTY? was a resounding yes. Additional help came from half a billion dollars in government funding, and millions more from the Ford Foundation, headed by McGeorge Bundy, a brilliant Yalie who had helped plan the Vietnam War before turning his attention to the War on Poverty.

"For Yale," Brewster declared, "New Haven is the laboratory for study and experimentation with better ways of evaluating physical renewal and human renewal problems." By the time Michael and I got there, one third of the city had been plowed under in a great spasm of utopian optimism, a quarter of the population had been displaced into housing projects, and New Haven had gone from being the thirty-eighth poorest city in the country to the seventh poorest.

That year, too, Oriental Masonic Gardens—a low-income highrise habitat for the elderly designed by Paul Rudolph, the former chairman of Yale's architecture department—was torn down. The unrepentant architect, whose Brutalist community mental health center in Boston—an experiment in "the psychology of space"—was so disorienting that psychiatrists were afraid to send patients there, blamed the poor people of New Haven for failing to understand his innovative use of raw concrete modules. "Psychologically," he told the *Times*, "the good folk who inhabited these dwellings thought that they were beneath them." Because the building had begun sinking into the ground almost as soon as it opened, this, too, was ironic.

CHAPTER EIGHT

MISREADING

I'm in love with Jacques Derrida
Read a page and I know I need ta
Take apart my baby's heart tonight.

—GREEN GARTSIDE (SCRITTI POLITTI),
"Jacques Derrida"

My encounters with Michael were usually unplanned. His roommate Jim was in my Chaucer class, and sometimes we'd wander back to Silliman and have lunch with Michael, who listened to us joke about our professor's obsession with Heidegger, indulgent and amused because he wasn't studying such nonsense.

Sometimes we saw each other at crowded events where famous names became flesh. Norman Mailer looking shorter, angrier, and more like David Ben-Gurion than I expected, paced the stage, impressively unprepared—almost incoherent at times—prophesying doom if we did not become more democratic, for which he recommended "the tool of sacrilege." When someone asked him about the killer Jack Henry Abbott, who had been released from prison after Mailer vouched for his literary talent, and stabbed a young man to death two weeks later, Mailer began to shout.

This was a far cry from hearing Elie Wiesel inaugurate Yale's Video Archive for Holocaust Testimonies, his voice rising with passion as he reminded the audience that it took the Nazis longer to crush the Warsaw Ghetto uprising than it took them to conquer France.

Sometimes we ran into each other on Metro-North, headed back to New Rochelle for one long weekend or another. In the language of "Lycidas," we were nursed upon the selfsame hill, and though I felt our paths diverging, even chance encounters felt primary, stirring up the old warmth and the old instinct of competition. We carried the world of each other's childhood in our pockets like a kryptonite pebble, a fragment of the home planet.

Despite his phlegmatic manner, Michael did a frenetic number of things, even if he made them all sound like the accidental accomplishments of Ferdinand the Bull. All he wanted was to smell the flowers, but as soon as he sat down under a cork tree, a beautiful girl came over, or somebody signed him up for the Social Activities Committee.

He played intramural volleyball, practiced guitar, jammed in the courtyard, ran the SAC committee and went to its parties—no small commitment—while reading Telluride applications and serving on the committee that interviewed finalists from area high schools, helping to choose TASPers for the program that had meant so much to us. All the while, he got excellent grades in a double major despite an accelerated course load and a mysterious habit of spending whole days in his room with the lights out. Mike Curtis, who had become his roommate, was never sure if he was noiselessly practicing the guitar, meditating, or indulging in long hibernatory sleeps.

I read too slowly, lost focus too easily, and fled numbers too completely to major in something unfamiliar and exciting, as I'd hoped. English literature saved me, despite the reading it required. Somehow when the world was turned into stories, or set to meter, my ear and some instinct for associative logic allowed me to absorb its meaning and return fire. *Paradise Lost* was a long poem, but it was only one volume, and had been dictated by a blind man in rolling phrases that became portable with repetition. *So lively shines in them Divine Resemblance.*

It helped that I'd grown up inside a great books course. Now perhaps, however slowly, I would fill in the contours of a map that had always been on the wall. Still, I was afraid of running out of time.

When Michael had given me a tour of Silliman, he extolled the virtues of a world where everything was in reach of his long arms. He could roll out of bed and into the dining hall, and if the dining hall was closed, he could get hamburgers and milkshakes in the Silliman buttery. He could play foosball in the Silliman basement and ultimate Frisbee in the courtyard, which was large enough for full-bore games. He didn't even mention classes, though he took a lot of them.

In high school, I'd stayed home if I had a book to read or a long assignment to complete. Now, school was home; what Michael considered luxurious convenience was for me an infinite source of distraction. When one of my English professors said that anyone who memorized all 193 lines of "Lycidas" would get out of writing a paper, I taped Milton's elegy for his drowned friend to the metal flank of the industrial dishwasher in the Davenport dining hall it was my job to empty, load, and fill with soap whenever a buzzer sounded.

The word "multitasking" hadn't crossed over from computers to people yet, but the goal certainly existed. I'd been memorizing poetry for years, but "Lycidas" was long, the kitchen was noisy, and my glasses fogged every time I opened the giant machine. When I got back to my dorm, soggy with self-pity and a food smell in my nose that reminded me of the high school cafeteria I'd studiously avoided, I usually felt too tired or demoralized to study. Michael could concentrate surrounded by chaos, like Harold Bloom, the son of a garment worker, who had plowed through volumes sitting at a kitchen table in the Bronx and who claimed to read one thousand pages an hour.

I was surprised that Michael didn't have a college job. He shrugged evasively when I asked him about it, almost embarrassed. I imagined his adman grandfather had come through, though I also wondered if he'd received a scholarship of some sort instead of a work-study package.

Dining hall jobs paid the most, and I was lucky to have mine, but I marveled at the kids who did their jobs with a matter-of-fact cheer that made the work seem almost enviable. When they were servers, they tied bandannas over their heads, slid roast beef onto extended plates, and asked without irony, "Au jus?" They did not find it necessary to call the breaded fish "cod pieces" so that everyone knew which side of the counter they belonged on.

My father had worked during the day and gone to school at night, as he often told me, beginning with high school and ending with his PhD. I saw nothing shameful in my job, or so I told myself, and yet I did feel shame, mingled with fear. It wasn't clear to me that I would be able to organize my brain to do what it would have to do if I was going to make my living using my head instead of an industrial dishwasher.

I bitterly resented the kids who couldn't be bothered to scrape their plates, drop silverware into its proper holes, and turn drinking glasses and coffee cups upside down into square racks, but just shoved the whole jangling heap across the countertop that divided workers from eaters. I banged the food-heavy plates against the interior of the food bucket that I dreamed of emptying over their heads, the way Michael and I had poured the slops on the gargantuan pig Big Nuts at Farm Camp Lowy.

But I failed at class rage, and succeeded only in hating the hardworking manager of the dining hall, who wasn't a Yale student but a blue-collar adult who didn't care whether I learned "Lycidas." He cared that I refilled the "Hi-C product" when the dispenser ran low and made sure that "the chocolate milk product" was agitating in its plastic tank. He was guilty only of expecting me to do my job, and of knowing that I wasn't too good for the job but not good enough.

My mother's father had manufactured coats for large ladies, known in the business as "fancy fats." The term was used for both the coats and the ladies, my mother told me, laughing at the crass world she'd escaped. That was business; it made people and products interchangeable. But it was thanks to fancy fats that my sister and I were able to go to Yale. It was thanks to my grandfather, who had dropped out of school at the age of thirteen to push a clothing rack through lower Broadway, and who died when I was two. And it was thanks to my grandmother, a high school dropout who invested carefully and made up the shortfall in our tuition.

I wasn't afraid of being a product; I was afraid of being priced too low, like the beer I'd mislabeled in Gristedes. I'd taped "Lycidas" to the dishwasher more to remind myself I had a higher calling than to learn the words. Every time the soap buzzer went off, I felt like a game show contestant who had run out of time. Instead of identifying with the poet, I found myself identifying with his drowned friend:

> Look homeward Angel now, and melt with ruth;
> And, O ye dolphins, waft the hapless youth.

Things improved when I switched to a job in the Language Lab, where I worked behind a large plate glass window hooking up headphoned students to conversational German or beginning Sanskrit. One day I discovered that I had access to a vast library of recorded literature that almost nobody requested but that I could copy onto cassettes and listen to on my Walkman. Suddenly I felt like a sighted blind man. This was before iPods, CDs, or the internet; I became a voracious listener, with a private portal in my head fed by Shakespeare plays, *Paradise Lost*, romantic poetry, and lectures on every imaginable subject.

That summer I started dating the girl with green eyes who said she was sending an SOS to the world. I had a summer job in Midtown Manhattan; she lived on the Upper East Side, and I went to see her every day after work. She did not need to earn money but volunteered as a candy striper at a local hospital. Sometimes she was still wearing her uniform, a red-and-white-striped pinafore so innocent it looked pornographic.

We went to restaurants with her childhood friends who thought nothing of spending in an hour what I earned in eight. Often, we were alone in her parents' apartment. On the living room sofa, and in the bedroom where she had blasted French pop records bought in Paris when she was a teenager, I got a second chance at high school, sailing into the late twentieth century on her narrow bed. Riding to Grand Central to catch a late train, I stared out the bus window in a state of transported euphoria that felt almost like illness.

I got dumped at the end of sophomore year, and though briefly convinced that I was actually going to die, I began dating a comp-lit student who spent the summer in New Haven so she could keep seeing her psychoanalyst. I moved in with friends who had a sweltering New Haven apartment where the odds were good you would spoon a cockroach into the coffee filter along with the ground beans, and I worked in the freezing subbasement of Sterling Library organizing file cards for the Islamic collection while listening to books on tape. When August came and I learned that all psychiatrists went away, and so did my girlfriend and everyone else, I discovered it was possible to live alone in a city, even though I felt a shadow of the old doubt whenever I crossed the New Haven Green.

Michael told me, with the marveling matter-of-factness that made his modesty so much like boasting, about the fling he'd had with a beautiful junior whose dorm room overlooked the spot in the

Silliman courtyard where he liked to sit on a stone bench under a silver-barked beech tree. *She* had noticed *him* and gone down to introduce herself, because even silent and alone he was eloquent and magnetic.

Michael described this as a sociological adventure as well as an erotic one. Robin was an African American, midwestern premed student, Christian by background but secular, while he described himself as a lower-middle-class New York Jew. Despite their differences, or because of them, they had been passionately connected. Their three-week affair was coda to his argument in the *Times* that a student's education should be measured in "what a student gains from a school both as a member of a community of scholars and as a person in a socializing community."

When Michael found himself in Robin's suite, her petite, athletic roommate began practicing splits on the floor, trying without words to get Michael's attention. She was a yoga enthusiast, played intramural soccer, and studied tae kwon do, a transfer student who had gotten into Yale but gone to Middlebury only to drop out, spend a year at home, and transfer to her original choice. Her splits irritated Robin but seemed to have no effect on Michael, at least at the time, though the situation spoke to his schematic imagination. Twin archetypes vying for his attention: the brassy African American woman who'd found him in the courtyard; the shy blond roommate, delicate but determined. Her name was Caroline Costello, but everybody called her Carrie.

When Robin first met Michael, it was his religious nature that struck her. They talked about his faith, and about the nature of intelligence and truth. Robin found Michael's faith fascinating. I would have found it fascinating too; for as long as I'd known him, he'd defined himself as a person of doubt with a deep, ironic skepticism.

But Michael was changing. My reference points were associations fixed at an earlier time in our friendship, when "faith" and "religious affiliation" were old-world attributes ascribed to my father

and extended less flatteringly to me. His own family was knowingly
new-world, tempered in the crucible that melted Lifshutz into Laudor,
though they retained immigrant toughness even as they worshipped
at Our Lady of Pinebrook Boulevard.

Michael had grown more contemplative. He had become a volunteer for Walden Peer Counseling, a major commitment not only of
time but psychic energy. Walden had been created by students in the
early 1970s, a time when Thoreau's misanthropic manifesto of self-
reliance was transformed into a byword for community concern.

Michael spent evenings on Old Campus waiting until 1:00 a.m.
in the basement of Welch Hall for drop-ins needing an empathetic
ear. After that, there was an all-night hotline staffed by volunteers
working in pairs. His sleep habits were well suited to crisis counseling. Still, it wasn't something you could do in the accidental way he
liked to describe his activities.

The peer-counseling program had a rigorous application process—
essays and interviews—followed by intensive training for those who
got past the screening. Michael had always been a charismatic listener, with a way of nodding as if to a piece of music. He knew how
to attend to people with sympathetic gravity when they came to him
with problems.

Peer counselors were not supposed to resolve problems, only listen
with nonjudgmental sympathy. If students showed deeper signs of
distress, the volunteer's job was to nudge them gently toward the
professionals in the Mental Hygiene department of University Health
Services. You had to know who was panicking over calculus and who
was suffering from something more insidiously rooted. This was not
simply about divining who needed mathematical help and who needed
a psychological solution; it was about having the confidence to make
the right call.

As often as I thought about the boy who drank himself to death
at a SAC party, I thought about the medical student who'd been in-

formally consulted that night by the unconscious freshman's alarmed roommates. The med student, a Davenport graduate fellow I'd gotten to know, had suggested letting the boy sleep it off. Ninety-nine percent of the time that might have worked out, but a 1 percent chance of calamity had claimed all of the boy's life, and an untold portion of the med student's, who bore no culpability but nevertheless looked afflicted whenever I saw him in the dining hall.

In addition to talking to Robin about faith, Michael told her stories about the golem, the monster fashioned out of earth by a wonder-working rabbi who animates the creature and commands it to save the Jews of Prague. Michael had read golem legends on my father's bookshelf; all of them ended badly. After a strong start, the golem inevitably runs amok and has to be unmade by its creator, who hides the clay man in the synagogue attic, where it waits for the day it will be called back to life.

I never asked myself if Michael was drawn to Walden Peer Counseling because he wanted to receive counseling as well as give it. When he told me he was going to graduate in three years, I assumed it was his future he heard calling out to him, and Time's winged chariot that he heard at his back, as always hurrying near. I took it for granted that Michael told golem stories to the girl who'd come on to him in the courtyard because he identified with the monster's maker and master. It never occurred to me that he might see himself as the man of clay.

Yale was an extension of my intellectual homelife as well as an inversion of it. One of my professors was a Wordsworth scholar with the same accent, love of puns, white beard, and bald spot as my father, and had even fled Nazi Germany on a Kindertransport, the same youth rescue operation that had gotten my father out of Austria. But he seemed to have gotten out at a different stop.

He was a member of "the Hermeneutic Mafia," as even the *Times* called the brilliant circle of Yale literary critics who dabbled in the dark arts of deconstruction. The designation was tongue in cheek, but it bestowed celebrity status on a handful of literature professors. They were stirred by "post-structuralist" ideas blowing out of postwar France, and obsessed with the indeterminacy of language that gave literary theory the abstract air of quantum physics and the geeky cool of highbrow punk.

The godfather of the Hermeneutic Mafia was Paul de Man, Yale's deconstructionist man of mystery, who had fled Europe *after* the war, worked at the same Doubleday bookstore as my father, and risen to become the chairman of the comparative literature department. He was famous for killer close readings that zeroed in on two equally plausible but mutually exclusive understandings of a passage. These divergent meanings often depended on a single word sounding like another word, though de Man's murmurous multilingual accent made most words sound like other words.

Whether you knew what was going on or not, the swirling excitement that put literature professors on the cover of *The New York Times Magazine*—with the headline "The Tyranny of the Yale Critics"—contributed to the feeling that literary theory, not to be confused with literature, could refashion the world as much as economic theory, though into what nobody said.

I knew next to nothing of post-structuralism, or its intellectual predecessor, structuralism—which took a more anthropological approach to erasing the individual—but it was so different from the dusty, well-wrought urn of poetic appreciation, and so much more glamorous, that it was impossible to ignore.

Jacques Derrida, the dashing silver-haired enfant terrible from the Sorbonne, who had bottled deconstruction for overseas distribution, visited Yale every year for a few charismatic weeks of seminars and lectures. It wasn't a philosophy you explained so much as demonstrated, choosing a text like a volunteer at a magic show willing to be sawed in half—except that the volunteer really *was* sawed in half, and usually into a lot more pieces than that, before being sewn back together again. Derrida's real trick was persuading the audience that the volunteer had never been whole to begin with, which he accomplished with seductive phrases like "writing under erasure" and "absent presence" that sounded even better in French.

Derrida's arrival made sober graduate students tremble like teenage girls waiting for Ed Sullivan to introduce the Beatles in 1964. And though it was true that 40 percent of the country had tuned in to watch the Beatles, and even Richard Nixon's fifteen-year-old daughter was in the studio audience, while most Americans didn't give a crap about deconstruction, it was also true that the people who did give a crap would be teaching the children of those who did not for years to come.

Illuminating the impossibility of meaning was a far cry from the beautiful dream of putting the world into words, but the magical inverting power of postmodernism was still fresh. The word "discourse" somehow made technical things sound as sexy as the word "intercourse" made sexy things sound technical.

The word "text," another term of art, sounded smaller than "poem" or "novel" but was actually larger. As the deconstructionists liked to say, "Everything is text." This meant that *Hamlet*, graffiti, *On the Origin of Species*, the phone book, and even your thoughts were "texts," linguistic constructions that fell under the jurisdiction of post-structuralist ideas about language and its limitations.

Derrida's theories lingered in corridors and classrooms; even if you didn't speak French, or go to his seminars, you could absorb a lot just by inhaling deeply. I also got a tutorial from my sister's boyfriend, a hip philosophy PhD student who helped me understand the famous gap between "the signifier" and "the signified," which is to say between the word we use for a thing and the thing itself.

As a result of this central semiotic problem, of which I'd been unaware, there would always be an unbridgeable distance between the word "glass," for example, and the transparent receptacle for liquid in your hand arbitrarily *called* a glass. This seemed like the sort of problem that could be overcome just by asking for a glass of water, but I had never studied philosophy.

The reason for the gap, I learned, was that words could only be understood by referring to other words. This was easily demonstrated by opening a dictionary, where you could see that a word was defined not by what it *is* but by what it *isn't*. A synonym isn't the word you want, but only *like* the word you want, and a definition is just a space carved around a word by other words that also aren't the word you want. Those words are themselves just spaces carved out by still other merely approximating words, piling tiny gaps on the backs of other tiny gaps, and so ad infinitum, until the fabric of meaning was riddled with more holes than substance.

Thirsty schlubs might ask for a glass of water, and even get one, but at the university level, once you knew how the gaps ramified, you understood that meaning itself was an illusion. Indeterminacy ruled our language, and because language was all there was, it ruled our lives as well.

Accepting this dark knowledge with equanimity made Paul de Man a moral as well as an intellectual force. His close reading of Rousseau's *Confessions* did not flinch from concluding that we can never distinguish between "fictional discourse and empirical event," a predicament that "makes it possible to excuse the bleakest of crimes."

Deconstruction, which made "knowing" anything impossible, contained a dark but exculpatory promise, like the insanity defense. Because everything hinged on linguistic constructs, and language was infinitely contingent, it erased the line between reality and illusion. If meaning was just a metaphor, there could be no line drawn be-

tween truth and falsehood, madness and sanity, and ultimately between right and wrong.

After it was discovered that de Man was a liar, a bigamist, a thief,
and a Nazi collaborator who had prospered during the German oc-
cupation of Belgium, some looked back on his insights and wondered
if perhaps he'd woven a cloak of interpretive ambiguity only so he
could hide behind it. His defenders, however, could console themselves that the essays he'd published for the Nazis—in one, he called
Jews "a pollutant"—were themselves subject to the infinite ambiguity
that made individual understanding just another text written on water as it swirled into what deconstructionists liked to call "the abyss
of meaning."

The de Man debacle was still a few years off, and deconstruction
was still tied to the study of literature like a virus in a lab living
inside an egg. It was hard to imagine the abyss of meaning tunneling
its way under the walls of the ivory tower into the wider culture,
devouring distinctions like a sinkhole swallowing cars.

Part of the playful pleasure of postmodern theory was pretending
that a flaw in a poem was evidence of a crack in society, and that
verbal constructs held true for three-dimensional life, like a pin stuck
in a voodoo doll that made a real person scream. What would happen
if such fanciful borrowings from the realm of magic and mental illness began seeping into law, public policy, or political culture, turning
everything into a text that meant only what the interpreter believed
it meant?

I took classes with Harold Bloom, who had lost patience with deconstruction; his own theories required writers to have a self that
could make distinctions between the world and words, as well as
between the words of one poem and the words of another. Bloom

had spoken only Yiddish in his Bronx apartment until the age of six, but had mastered the Western canon so intimately that he called the author of *Paradise Lost* "Uncle Milty," and the author of *The Interpretation of Dreams* "Rabbi Solomon Freud." I often watched him making his solitary way across Old Campus, a large but diffuse presence, talking softly to himself and staggering slightly as he forded the river of his own genius.

His most famous book, *The Anxiety of Influence*, treated the literary tradition as an extended, unhappy family whose members were locked in a Darwinian struggle raging across space and time. Having grown up in a world of writers, I found this titanic battle for creative supremacy compelling. What did it take to find your own voice, tell an original story, or leave a mark on the written world?

The story Bloom told was about "strong writers," Oedipal monsters who ate their parents and grandparents, along with their own young, in order to give birth to themselves. They achieved dominance by willfully misreading the great writers they revered and wanted to replace, an act Bloom called "misprision." Strong writers used "savagery and misrepresentation" to make their predecessors sound like imitators, and their successors appear like shadows cast by their own supreme imagination.

Around the time Michael had published his letter, my mother had begun publishing a series of short essays in *The New York Times* for a feature called Hers, showcasing women writers. One of her essays, "Sons and Mothers," was about the time I was "run down," as my mother put it, by a boy on a motorcycle. Michael was impressed to find me flying through the air once more, this time on the *Times* Jumbotron. But I did not want to be the boy on crutches hobbling around New Rochelle like Tiny Tim, asking, "Why would anybody do a thing like that for no reason? Why?"

"He's sick," my mother quoted herself telling me, adding that the boy's mother "must feel so terrible."

One reason Michael retained his hold on my imagination even as we drifted was the way he seemed to resist absorption into anyone else's script. Battling fiercely independent brothers had taught him to carve his own name into the world tree. He was the author of a piece in the *Times*, while I was the subject, or perhaps the object, of one.

Bloom considered Freud a strong writer but a lousy doctor, and though he talked about anxiety as a motivation for great poetry, he veered away from the psychotic reasoning that served as the secret spring of post-structuralist theory. Perhaps he knew too much about the devastating effect of real madness on individual lives to embrace a metaphorical version of it.

When my mother's friend Cynthia debated Bloom, and he saw the speech she was planning to read, he had begged for mercy in advance, telling her he had a sick child. The speech, which she read anyway, accused Bloom of turning literature into an idol, a closed system "indifferent to the world and to humanity," and of turning himself into the indispensable mediator of a cruel and sacrificial system.

Unlike the story of Cynthia asking Norman Mailer what color ink he dipped his balls in, the Bloom story baffled me. Mailer had bragged that he wrote with his balls, and when confronted by Cynthia, laughed and said yellow, "for lack of a better answer." Why should Bloom, with his formidable intellect, find being called an idol maker who "schemes to invent a substitute for the Creator" a reason to invoke the specter of a sick child?

At the time, nobody wondered what it meant for Bloom to have a sick child. He wasn't asking for pity; he was telling Cynthia that he had reasons for thinking about God and literature as he did, even if he did not wish to discuss them. Bloom later wrote that while "a nature that contains schizophrenia is acceptable to the monotheistic orthodox," it was not acceptable to *him*.

He felt the same way about the Holocaust, which had killed many of his relatives.

He could not countenance a divine order that permitted "schizophrenia and death camps," and wrote that he refused to justify it with "the mystery of faith." Bloom didn't want to turn literature into an idol, but Cynthia had been half-right; he did want to smash God for allowing "a cosmos this obscene."

Madness calls literature's bluff by going beyond it and falling short of it at the same time. When Bloom wrote that "schizophrenia is bad poetry, for the schizophrenic has lost the strength of perverse, wilful, misprision," he meant that in order to read something "wrong," there had to be a way to read it right. There had to be truth, whether or not you acknowledged it, instead of mere illusion.

Bloom contrasted literary misprision with the misperceptions caused by mental illness; in order to become a writer, you had to distinguish between what was real and what was imaginary. You had to bend reality to yourself and give it back to the world in your own voice. Art can't be the lie that tells the truth in a world that cannot recognize lies.

Michael informed me that he had decided to become rich, as if it were something you could declare like a major. I had no reason to doubt him. Even the way he conducted SAC business in the dining hall seemed like an extension of his new resolve. Tipped back in his chair, he received a parade of jocks like someone cutting deals and bestowing favors, trading fist bumps and jokes about drinking to oblivion as a pile of cash accumulated at his elbow like poker winnings.

Financial wizardry was hardly required to plan the Silliman Saloon, but confidence was an economic as well as a social asset, Michael explained. That was why he had been recruited by a Boston-based management consulting firm called Bain & Company. His life was about to change.

In the 1980s, the financial world was rewarding brains and brass balls as never before. Knowing how to fix a car was a skill, persuading someone you had a skill was a talent, and convincing someone with a talent that you could teach him how to do it even better and at scale was called management consulting. This lucrative service, Michael said, was provided to corporations, banks, hospitals, and pretty much any other business.

We had grown up laughing at the word "plastics," the advice Dustin Hoffman gets from a jaded grown-up in *The Graduate*, but "plastics" was a punch line without a joke, a comic obscenity like "product" or "fancy fats." "Management consulting," a term I'd never heard before, had an intellectual ring, like "logical positivism." Michael spoke with something other than irony about the sharp-dressed recruiters who came to campus to offer fat salaries to cocksure undergraduates who possessed nothing but a talent for persuasion.

I had never heard of Bain & Company, but learned about its special mystique from Michael. It was a place where the supersmart became the superrich, though they paid for it with blood. Michael mentioned the "hundred-hour work week" that did not seem physically possible, or legal. Even if it was pure hyperbole, I doubted his meetings could be scheduled, like his classes, to begin after lunch.

Michael was boastful and ironic about the company, which sounded like "brain" and "bane" combined, and was referred to by envious rivals as the KGB of consulting firms. His mood was elated and elegiac at the same time, as if he were going off to war in the days when there was more glory than gunpowder and no PTSD. He admired Bain's brilliant and enigmatic founder, a "Tennessee gentleman" whose name really was Bain. The tone suggested personal acquaintance as if they had sipped juleps on the porch together, discussing the terms of Michael's employment and the rise of the yen.

For all his jokes about the bane of his existence, Michael was exultant. He mentioned the "ridiculous" amounts of money they were "throwing at him," shaking his head at the wasteful extravagance.

The interview process had gone on forever but he had enjoyed it, unlike a lot of the aspirants, who had been shattered. "Bainies" had come to his room and sat on his bed, giving him home-court advantage. I pictured him lying there like the Sun King while immaculately tailored courtiers in monogrammed shirts fired questions at him. He had not only talked his way into the job, the job *was* talking.

Bainies was an ironic allusion to Moonies, the soul-snatching cult whose leader, the Reverend Sun Myung Moon, had recently married off two thousand couples at one shot in Madison Square Garden, strangers he'd matched like partners at a square dance before joining them for life. *Forbes* wrote that Bainies were like "religious zealots" for whom business "is a holy war that the client must win and the competition must lose."

A master of squaring the circle, Michael wanted me to know that he was not abandoning intellectual or artistic aspirations by pursuing money, but had found a way to achieve both: his plan was to spend a decade making bricks for Pharaoh—gold bricks, to be sure, but still bricks—after which he would buy his freedom and become a writer. He was spotting me ten years, though I would have to get a job and pay off my student loans. Still I was impressed by his ability to take the long view, a sprinter embarking on a marathon.

Only once did he seem genuinely regretful, and that was when he introduced me to a Sillimander named Debra who had gotten a full scholarship to the Iowa Writers' Workshop. Debra was going to be a writer. Michael spoke with unguarded admiration; every young writer in America, he said, wanted to go to Iowa.

"You should apply," he told me, with sudden magnanimity. Because we had always disdained writing programs—nobody could *make* you a writer—and because he had also said Iowa had "more pigs than people," I wondered what he meant by it. If it was such a great thing to do, why hadn't he applied? But then I saw that he had, and that perhaps for the only time in his life, he failed to gain admission to something he wanted to do.

Once when I ran into Michael, he asked me to join him on a shopping excursion. He'd been doing a lot of shopping for "the uniform"—power suits, tailored shirts with French cuffs, a red silk tie, a blue trench coat. He needed fancy dress shoes, a painstaking and expensive ordeal. For some reason I agreed to go, and though I feared I was there to witness his triumph, it was friendly in the old way and I had the feeling he genuinely wanted my company.

I sat next to him as the kneeling clerk laced up a pair of handmade leather English oxfords. He grew wistful. His college life was ending after three years. I was having the time of my life and wondered if four years would be enough. I'd taken to wearing an absurd, oversize tweed coat with wide shoulders from the 1940s I'd bought at a thrift shop called Alice Underground on a visit to my sister, who was living in Manhattan. Michael was buying grown-up clothes of a different sort.

The last time I saw him before he departed for his new life was on Mereland Road. I was visiting my parents. He had a barbered look and was already cultivating a style that belonged to a world beyond the one we shared.

Josh Ferber was going to drive him to Boston, where Bain had "well-appointed" offices in Copley Square. It also had offices in San Francisco, London, Paris, Munich, and Tokyo. Who could say where Bain would send him? He'd never been on an airplane before and seemed apprehensive. If he regretted his decision, he did not tell me.

He'd been spending time at the Ferbers' house in Maine, and had baked a legendary batch of marijuana brownies so potent that everyone who tried them fell into an enchanted fairy-tale sleep. Finding it impossible to rouse Josh, and eager to get back to New Rochelle, Michael and another groggy friend had left him sleeping.

Josh was furious when he woke up alone but felt lucky when he learned that Michael, speeding down I-95, had a blowout that sent his car careening across the highway toward the divider and back to the shoulder, nearly ending his career before it began. Somehow, Michael and his traveling companion had both emerged unscathed, which had seemed like one more smile of fortune from the universe.

Part II

✳

The House of Psychiatry

I sometimes think that the world will either be saved by psychologists—in the very broadest sense—or else it will not be saved at all.

—Abraham Maslow,
Towards a Psychology of Being

Anyone who is in any way connected with gestalt therapy, psychoanalysis, group movement is doing my work. They awaken a thirst that only I can satisfy.

—The Bhagwan Shree Rajneesh
to Andy Ferber

At the south end of New Rochelle, on the largest deeded beach in Westchester County, a grand house with a high turret looked out over Long Island Sound, a scattering of sailboats, and a distant glimpse of Connecticut. On the top floor of the turret, in the year of our bicentennial, a shirtless man, barefoot and bearded, could sometimes be found jumping up and down. Behind him were floor-to-ceiling bookshelves holding three generations of medical texts: his grandfather's, his father's, and his own. His wife's medical books were there, too, along with her mother's medical books, her father's law books, and a healthy supply of Western literature, history, philosophy, science, and psychology.

The jumping man, who was a psychiatrist, had turned his back to all this. He faced the large curved windows that looked out over the dark water and bright sky. Around his neck, a small framed picture of a bearded man with enormous, laughing eyes hung from a necklace of 108 wooden beads. The mala jumped when he jumped.

The mansion on Wildcliff Road stood at the end of a winding three-hundred-foot driveway. It might have drifted west from the more glamorous parts of the north fork of Long Island, or torn itself loose from the pages of an F. Scott Fitzgerald novel. Michael called it "the Gatsby House" and claimed, when he lived there in the fateful year 1986, that he could see a green light glinting far out on the water as he sat up late, writing stories and staring into the night. He wanted to be Fitzgerald and Gatsby both, the dreamer and the dream. Didn't we all?

The house was itself a vision of integrated elements, like the hotel in *Tender Is the Night* where the dashing psychiatrist Dick Diver and his beautiful, mentally ill wife, Nicole—modeled on Fitzgerald's own mentally ill wife, Zelda—live at the start of the novel: "The hotel and its bright tan prayer rug of a beach were one."

When Michael and I were growing up, two psychiatrists owned the house on Wildcliff Road, Andrew and Jane Ferber, who were as glamorous in their way as Dick and Nicole Diver, even if they spent their time with the destitute mentally ill of downtown New Rochelle. They and their friends had answered President Kennedy's call to replace the "cold mercy" of mental hospitals with "the open warmth of community concern and capability." They devoted themselves to a new kind of psychiatry that took place outside of institutions, and made the mind itself a new frontier.

The stories Michael told me about the house and its inhabitants had a shimmering, dreamlike quality. The house itself had once belonged to D. W. Griffith in the early years of the twentieth century, when Westchester was a hub of the movie industry. Griffith, whose racist masterpiece *Birth of a Nation* was screened at the White House by a racist president, built his movie studio in nearby Mamaroneck on a spit of land called Satan's Toe, jutting into Long Island Sound. There, he re-created eighteenth-century Paris with two hundred local extras for *Orphans of the Storm*, starring Lillian and Dorothy Gish, who lived in a Spanish-style house with red ridge tiles that became the Huguenot Yacht Club after the original yacht club burned to the ground, as so many things did, in the 1960s.

But the mansion on Wildcliff that would prove so central to Michael's life stood as it had on its private beach, still in its way a dream factory. Instead of Charlie Chaplin, Mary Pickford, Rudolph Valentino, and the Gish sisters, the Ferbers hosted community psychiatrists,

Freudian analysts, TV producers, self-actualizing "hug therapists," a Nobel Prize–winning quantum physicist, and even a few Black Panthers sticking it to the ghost of D. W. Griffith.

Up in the turret, a pioneering family psychiatrist, brilliant and charismatic, jumped and chanted. He had finally awakened to the truth of a passage he often shared with his patients, written by R. D. Laing, the Scottish psychiatrist who saw schizophrenia as a form of resistance to a mad world. "Any attempt to wake up before our time," Laing explained, "is heavily punished, especially by those who love us most. Because they, bless them, are asleep. They think anyone who wakes up, or who, still asleep, realizes that what is taken to be real is a 'dream,' is going crazy."

The first time he saw Bhagwan, Dr. Ferber felt he had known him forever. He crawled across the floor and touched his foot, a traditional gesture of respect.

"I've been waiting for you, Bodhicitta," the Bhagwan said, calling his sannyasin by his new name. Then he reached down and touched the place of the third eye; Andy—Bodhicitta—saw inside himself three explosions of light. He realized that all he thought he knew of love before had been only a thimbleful in the ocean of this man's love.

Back in New Rochelle, it wasn't easy to explain what had happened, or what he had to do. The only people who seemed to recognize at once that he had been transformed were the people with schizophrenia at the Huguenot Center, which he affectionately called the "hug a nut center." Andy found himself spending most of his time with patients as he prepared to return to the man in the picture hanging from his neck, himself a great healer. The guru had given Andy Ferber a new name, wisdom beyond the medical books behind him, and love surpassing anything he'd found in his family. He looked out at the water that rose and fell as he leapt. On a clear day you could see Poona, India.

CHAPTER NINE

THE SHADOW KNOWS

The forces of Evil have begun their decisive
offensive. You can feel their pressure, yet your
screens and publications are full of prescribed
smiles and raised glasses. What is the
joy about?

—ALEXANDER SOLZHENITSYN,
Harvard commencement address, 1978

I decided to go to the University of California, Berkeley, to get a
PhD in English literature. The English Department was excellent
but the real reason was the 1968 Volvo that had set me free for a
summer, and the brilliant Shakespeare professor who had loaned me
the car. He'd gotten his PhD at Berkeley and lived in the Bay Area
when the car and the world were new. I visited the campus in winter
when the brown hills were fuzzed with green and the streets smelled
like flowers. Even quadriplegic students in Sproul Plaza seemed daring and fit, flying past in motorized wheelchairs designed by the
Berkeley engineering department and operated by breath in a straw.

Along with my acceptance letter I received an impersonal xeroxed
disclaimer on a half piece of paper, like a warning from the surgeon
general, informing me that the job market in the humanities was grim
and would remain so for the foreseeable future. Apparently, baby boomers who had changed the world in every way except for the ways they
wanted had taken all the jobs and planned to live forever.

I wasn't deterred, in part because I was ambivalent about winding up in academia and because I had an entirely unrealistic sense of the economy. I lacked the skill set that allowed Michael his ten-year plan of corporate consulting and early retirement, but I'd gotten Berkeley's highest fellowship—free tuition and $8,000 a year. Michael earned that in about six weeks but it felt like a princely sum. In any event, it was enough to make me self-supporting, and as long as I stayed in graduate school, I would not have to pay off my college loans.

The hardest part of going to California was that I'd fallen in love with a sophomore a few months before graduation. Her name was Mychal and she was from Brookline, Massachusetts, where my family had been exiled before escaping to New Rochelle. She'd been in a Hebrew class I took, laughably because she spoke Hebrew and even had a guttural biblical name. Her parents had spelled it with a *y* to avoid confusion with Michele, so telemarketers pronounced it Michael.

The first time I asked her out, Mychal didn't even realize I'd intended a date and did not sit next to me at the lecture by Noam Chomsky I had pretended to care about because I'd heard her mention it to someone else. But afterward we went to Atticus, the campus bookstore café, and talked until the chairs around us were turned upside down and the vacuum darting under our table bruised our heels.

I lost track of Michael during his first year at Bain, though once or twice I'd hear my name on Mereland while home for a visit. Turning, I'd see him loping up the hill, grinning as if we were still fifth graders and his fancy coat was just a costume.

He approved of my decision to get a PhD. Someone has to carry on the tradition, he said, though it was unclear if he meant the Western intellectual tradition, the professorial life, or chronic job dissatisfaction and an old car. He was ironic about his own choice and the young upwardly mobile Philistines the media had taken to calling yuppies, whose folkways he described like an anthropologist who had started out observing headhunters and ended up inducted into the tribe.

They wore business clothes day and night, he told me, as he himself seemed to do. They were always working, even when they gathered in well-appointed watering holes where they talked for hours about the hours they worked, the money they made, the fancy restaurants where they met clients, and the bars where they met each other to drink and talk about restaurants, work, and money. If a woman in this crowd was impressed by the company name on the front of his business card, Michael said, she would return it with her name and phone number written on the back. He shook his head at the shallowness of it all, boastful and abashed.

I hadn't seen him for some time when someone in New Rochelle threw a college graduation party that doubled as an informal reunion. The party was in one of those mammoth New Rochelle houses that intimidated on Halloween even if there was a skeleton taped to the distant door to let you know there'd be candy. The wide terrace in the back was full of friendly, half-familiar faces that already seemed to belong to another world. The mood was generous and faintly elegiac. Our childhood addresses were still on our driver's licenses, and we still came home for holidays, but we shared an expectation that soon we would be scattered beyond easy recall.

Several people asked me about Michael as if we'd remained a team. I didn't know if he was coming, but I'd been hearing that he was having a rough time. He found the pressure to perform constant, and had begun complaining that his heart raced and his digestion was bad. He saw doctors who agreed that stress was taking a toll and that the relentless pace meant he could never catch up on sleep.

When he did turn up, he seemed much the same. He still had the bearing of someone called Big, though nobody called him that anymore. He still stood on tiptoe to make a point, holding forth with veteran authority about the cutthroat camaraderie of the business world, though he spoke with a muted formality that gave his words a rehearsed quality.

I'd heard before how his case team got a week to master an entire industry, how he stayed up for two straight nights studying company reports and figuring out the best way to tell clients who'd spent more years building their business than Michael had been alive what they were doing wrong. He did not like to think people could lose their jobs because of his conclusions, but such was the power of Bain, the Ivy League, and his own golden-tongued articulations.

It was hard to imagine that anyone so junior could have that sort of impact, but his concern seemed genuine, and its intensity enhanced the credibility of the boast. The corollary to Michael's sense that his words could cost people their jobs was his worry that other people's words could cost him his. He had begun to suspect that Machiavellian higher-ups were "out to get him," which seemed unlikely even for the KGB of the consulting world. But what had once been part of Bain's alluring mystique seemed increasingly to fill Michael with dark foreboding.

Boston was also getting to him. The drivers really were crazy, he said, and after a close encounter with a reckless taxi, he'd "gone New Rochelle High School." Striding after the offending cab when it stopped at a light, Michael had banged on the roof and glass, shouting, "You want some of me, motherfucker?"

The "taxi incident," as it became known to friends, was a comic piece of performance art. He had attacked a car, not a driver, and the picture he drew was a cartoon: a bullfighter taking on a mechanical bull. But Michael's disavowing laughter was not so disavowing that it erased the cabbie's culpability or his own righteous fury.

His father liked to look from face to face when holding forth, whether on Reaganomics or lead pipes, taking a quick straw poll while he spoke. Michael had the same habit, and it felt rude not to laugh or nod even if you weren't entirely sure what you were assenting to, or the story wasn't entirely funny.

The real takeaway from the taxi incident was that Michael needed a new environment. The problem, Michael explained, was that although he was only an associate consultant, he was so good at his job, and Bain had invested so much in him already, that they would never let him go. At least not without a fight.

Much of what I knew about "business" came from Michael, the two *Godfather* movies (you try to get out, they drag you back), and a book I'd borrowed from my sister, *The Age of Desire: Reflections of a Radical Psychoanalyst*. The author, a Marxist psychiatrist named Joel Kovel, offered case histories of unhappy investment bankers whose emotional detachment, workaholism, and general misery were rewarded with ever-increasing salaries, praise, and promotions by employers who literally paid workers to stay sick in the head because the system itself was sick. This made perfect sense to me.

Michael spoke wistfully about those of us just starting out, as if his single year carried the weight of the ten he'd planned to spend. Even the kids going to business school—a newly popular choice in part because of places like Bain—would get to hold on a little longer to the calendar that had ruled our lives for so long before they were dropped into the fiscal year that was chewing him up.

Michael and I both recalled Greg Morrison telling us that in France even grown-ups got the whole summer off, no matter their profession, because the French valued slow time, slow food, and timeless art—though Greg added that the French were also "whores" who would sell their mothers to keep German bombs off the Arc de Triomphe, the Louvre, and Les Deux Magots. This didn't dim the allure of Paris, where Michael and I had talked about going "to write" ever since we'd read *The Sun Also Rises*, though only Michael had described a girl in tenth grade having curves like the hull of a racing yacht, which sounded much less sexy off the page.

The key to Paris, and to writing, seemed to be avoiding certain things that everyone wanted you to do, so you could do other things that nobody wanted you to do. Even the British, Michael told me, had an unofficial arts program called "the dole," their answer to the long French vacation.

The dream of writing still bound us with the old competitive glue even if neither of us was actually writing. It was what we listened for when we ran into each other, curious how far the other had gotten. Even present misery, understood as fodder for future literary transformation, took on a more hopeful color.

I believed Michael when he talked about his plans to get rich, but at some level I'd always thought of his job as a head fake; soon he would double back down the road he'd only pretended to leave behind. Claiming that Bain wouldn't let him leave seemed a way to save face.

Flaubert had suffered seizures to get out of law school so he could hole up in his mother's house and write. Sickness as a reprieve, and even a roundabout road to health, had been the unwholesome but not entirely unsuccessful bargain of my childhood. Perhaps attacking a taxi was a kind of seizure, the unexplained spasm that would allow a strategic retreat back to the Gatsby House that was in its way a kind of Paris.

Michael's old flame Jo-Ann turned up at the graduation party, speaking in her frank, enthusiastic way about playing the clarinet. She was finishing a five-year program that combined conservatory study with a liberal arts degree, and wanted to become a professional musician, which was no small commitment. Michael listened to her with an admiring glow.

Whatever bitterness he'd felt at the end of high school, when he'd astonished Jo-Ann by declaring his love in her yearbook, seemed behind him. In college he'd had a poster on his wall of a slender blond ballerina bending her gamine form backward in an impossible arc. Jo-Ann was the opposite of that image, all loose black hair and earthy forward-flowing energy.

I remember them dancing to Chaka Khan's "I Feel for You." Michael seemed to be dancing *at* her as much as with her, and somehow also around her. His long arms, flung out to full wingspan, lifted stiffly to the beat as his lower half made wide-stance pelvic thrusts in the proto hip-hop style of the day. Jo-Ann was giggling with flattered surprise, beaming genially up at Michael, who stared with impassive composure, his jaw set though his body moved with an exuberance bordering on frenzy. *Chaka Khan let me rock you it's all I wanna do, Chaka Khan let me rock you cause I—unh unh—feel for you.*

CHAPTER TEN

REVOLVING DOOR

There's no such thing as schizophrenia, there's
only mental telepathy.

—SYLVIA FRUMKIN, quoted in Susan Sheehan's
Is There No Place on Earth for Me?

Michael quit Bain, returned to Mereland Road, and began writing
in earnest. The ten-year plan had become a one-year plan. I ran
into him when I flew home (ninety-nine dollars on the now defunct
People Express, which sounded like Berkeley's own airline). He wore
remnants of his management consulting duds in a mix-and-match
dress-down manner that made his navy-blue suit pants resemble the
uniform he'd worn the summer he'd worked as a Burns security guard.

He still had savings from Bain, lived cheaply, and earned extra
money working for his uncle as a telemarketer. It was the first time
I'd heard the word "telemarketing," which Michael deployed like one
of the pseudo-futurisms from the science fiction he liked, suggesting
a world beyond my ken. His uncle paid him generously, and the flexible hours left him plenty of time to write and play the guitar, which
he'd gotten quite serious about.

He'd discovered a bookstore that opened its doors to folk musicians on Monday evenings, and went there to jam. The bookstore
was called Riverrun, a name plucked from *Finnegans Wake*, and

was in Hastings-on-Hudson, an artsy river town eleven miles to the north.

According to my mother, Ruth Laudor was unhappy about the "hootenannies" at Riverrun. Michael called them "jam sessions," or sometimes "just fooling around." I assumed Ruth's disapproval was more about the family's mounting impatience with his absence from the labor force. Chuck, who now talked to my father, complained about sons coming home to roost.

Despite the flexible hours, the telemarketing became a burden for Michael, who wanted to devote more time and energy to writing and music. Also, he thought his phone was being tapped. This was the outcome he'd feared at the time of his departure from Bain & Company.

Michael had been certain the company would never respect his desire to cultivate an inner life or release him simply for the sake of his health. They would instead offer him a raise and insist that he stay. He was convinced that the only way to get out was to speak to them in the only language they understood, which was the language of money. Accordingly, he set about inventing a job offer that would pay him so much more than he was making that Bain would never even try to match it.

He decided on a venture capital firm; to make it believable Michael invented the company as well as the offer, which was no small task. Already exhausted by his work at Bain, he began to feel like he really was doing two jobs even though one was imaginary. But the ruse worked and Bain had let him go, or so it had seemed. Now he realized it had been too good to be true. Bill Bain, like Pharaoh, had changed his mind and wanted his wage slave back.

Michael thought the Bainies were spying on him, and shared his suspicions with his mother, who was more inclined to think it was actual Moonies or the Hare Krishna. That was why she didn't like the hootenannies; Michael had reported that some of the musicians were following him home and *they* didn't work for Bain. His own behavior was often secretive and at times inexplicable, and though Ruth thought he was too smart for easy entrapment, she worried he might have gotten himself into some kind of trouble.

Chuck, focused on getting Danny to move out of the house, was more annoyed that his youngest son had also wound up back at his front door. But cults were a real danger; everyone read stories in the *Times* and heard rumors about stressed-out Ivy Leaguers lured by friendly young people into a temple or whatever they called it. Behind-the-scenes puppet masters slipped drugs into the vegetarian food and turned them into foot soldiers for a brainwashed army, sending them out to sell peanuts and pull in new recruits, a pyramid scheme of lost souls.

Though the mass murder-suicide of Jonestown had receded, the Bhagwan and his followers had recently been front-page news when their Oregon commune collapsed into paranoia, bioterrorism, charges of conspiracy to commit murder, and frantic flight. Josh Ferber's father had been in Rajneeshpuram with the Bhagwan, a believer to the end, and *he* was a psychiatrist.

I wish I could remember if Michael intimated his fears at the time, or only told me later about the clicks on the telephone and the need for evasive maneuvers driving home from his Hastings hootenannies. I can't say it would have seemed so improbable. For one thing, I was used to being schooled by his authority. I'd also been warned plenty about cults myself. As for Bain, he'd always described the whole industry as a kind of confidence game, and his account of landing the job had sounded almost as hyperbolic as his difficulties giving it up.

It didn't seem out of the question that Bain hadn't wanted to lose its investment in Michael. In any event, I was too busy thinking how lucky he was to be writing, playing the guitar, and hanging out at the Gatsby mansion where the door was always open and where Jane Ferber had a great talent for gathering in people who needed gathering.

When Josh's friend Dylan had quit his house during senior year of high school to get away from his mother, a child psychiatrist who'd thrown a butcher knife at him, Jane Ferber had taken him in. Dylan's mother had told him for years that he was mentally ill, but this time she'd added that in her professional opinion he was likely to end up in a mental institution, or dead by his own hand.

The extremity of the pronouncement, not to mention the butcher knife, broke the spell for Dylan, and so did the kindness of Jane Ferber, who actually worked at a mental institution. Her private and professional opinion, like her accepting nature and open-door policy, was the healing antidote to Dylan's abusive mother. The Ferber house was where people went to recover their equilibrium—except for Jane's husband, who had gone to Nepal after the collapse of Rajneeshpuram to study the Bardos.

It was Michael's turn to be gathered in by the Ferbers. Though he was still living on Mereland, there was a seat for him and a beautifully wrapped gift at the elegant Christmas dinner Jane Ferber made in the old German-Jewish manner that impressed and amused Michael. He also attended the grand New Year's Eve party Jane hosted at a fancy Manhattan hotel on the east side.

He fit in easily with the maverick academics and mental health professionals who passed in and out of the mansion. They referred to themselves as "the Network," an overlapping personal and professional designation for the collection of old friends who had been drawn together by their experience in community psychiatry, a sincere desire to leave the world better than they found it, and gratitude for Jane's overawing generosity and the elegance she brought to social gatherings without any apparent betrayal of her commitment to social justice, which was itself an absolving gift given to them all.

Most had met in the sixties, when friendship and work and common cause converged, and the country had shared their dedication to liberating the mentally ill from state institutions exposed in the postwar years as little better than prisons and frequently worse. Their dreams were energized by the Community Mental Health Act, which President Kennedy signed on October 31, 1963, the last ceremonial signing of a major piece of legislation before his assassination.

With the same spirit that had declared our determination to go to the moon, the president promised that "emphasis on prevention, treatment and rehabilitation will be substituted for a desultory interest in confining patients in an institution to wither away." It was the institution's turn to wither away, replaced by the sort of communal care offered by the Huguenot Center, which Jane had run in downtown New Rochelle.

At the signing of the Mental Retardation and Community Mental Health Centers Construction Act of 1963, to use its full name, President Kennedy gave the first of several pens to his crusading sister Eunice, who had written a groundbreaking article in *The Saturday Evening Post* about their sister Rosemary, whose mild retardation, as it was then called, had inspired Eunice to create what would become the Special Olympics. Eunice disliked psychiatry, which she felt ignored people like her sister and the condition her article had helped bring out of the shadows.

Left in the shadows was Rosemary's lobotomy in 1941, on orders from her father. At twenty-one, Rosemary had been exhibiting mood swings, verbal confusion, and violent outbursts, frightening Joseph Kennedy with the specter of madness, shame, stigma, and thwarted family ambition. Rosemary had been escaping from the convent outside London where her family had placed her, eluding her private attendant, and returning with her clothing disturbed and leaves in her hair. Joseph Kennedy, who was President Roosevelt's ambassador to the Court of St. James's, summoned Dr. Walter Freeman, pioneer of the ice pick lobotomy, who called his procedure "soul surgery" even though it involved grinding out a small portion of the brain.

Some stigmas were worse than others. Eunice made no mention

of the lobotomy, or the possibility that her sister had been developing mental illness, in her article in *The Saturday Evening Post*, where she wrote that "there are important differences between the mentally retarded and the mentally ill. The vast majority of the mentally retarded are not emotionally disturbed. They do not 'go berserk.'"

Eunice and her brother John had been devastated when they discovered that their vivacious sister had been reduced by lobotomy to a barely responsive shadow of herself. The experience informed the president's pledge to Congress that the "reliance on the cold mercy of custodial isolation will be supplanted by the open warmth of community concern and capability."

Ironically, Dr. Freeman had been motivated by the same desire when he broadened his use of lobotomy after reading "Bedlam 1946," a harrowing photo spread in *Life* magazine about filthy, overcrowded state hospitals. In the days before antipsychotic medication, lobotomy seemed to him a quick and humane way to get patients back to the warmth of their families.

Daniel Patrick Moynihan, who had served on President Kennedy's mental health task force as a young assistant secretary of labor, had also received a pen at the signing of the bill, which he'd helped draft. Years later, as a senator from New York, he looked back at that moment with deep regret. In a letter to the *Times*, written in a city "filled with homeless, deranged people," he wondered what would have happened if someone had told President Kennedy, "Before you sign the bill you should know that we are not going to build anything like the number of community centers we will need. One in five in New York City. The hospitals will empty out, but there will be no place for the patients to be cared for in their communities." If the president had known, Moynihan wrote, "would he not have put down his pen?"

But the president did not know. He was killed less than a month later, and the Community Mental Health Act was championed by the Johnson administration as part of the JFK legacy and folded into the Great Society. Though predicated on the promise of cures that did not exist, preventions that remained elusive, and treatments that only worked for those who were able to comply, its broad mandate for community transformation, and fluid notions of mental health—broadened far beyond the exigencies of the severely ill—dovetailed for a time with the war on poverty run by Eunice Kennedy's husband, Sargent Shriver, who used the Office of Economic Opportunity to fund some of the first community mental health centers.

In his letter to the *Times*, Senator Moynihan claimed that the members of President Kennedy's task force had "no thought of getting rid of mental illness." On the contrary, having recognized that "schizophrenia was basically a genetic affliction with a more or less constant incidence in a large population," they merely wanted to establish a way of "caring for mental patients in more humane and therapeutic settings."

But there were competing concepts of psychiatry, and the president had been guided by experts like Robert Felix, the director of the National Institute of Mental Health who, like most psychiatrists at the time, did not work with people suffering from severe mental illness. A psychiatrist with psychoanalytic training and a degree in public health, Dr. Felix had created NIMH in the 1940s, before the advent of antipsychotic medication. Though modeled on the National Cancer Institute, the agency jettisoned "Neuropsychiatric" from its working title in favor of "Mental Health," adopting the well-being of the entire country as its mandate, instead of a narrow focus on a handful of intractable mental disorders, about which little was understood, and the small but significant percentage of the population they affected.

Even without knowing the details, everyone saw what Senator Moynihan saw on the streets, and knew something had gone terribly wrong. My mother had come home one day as if she'd seen a ghost and announced that Mattie, our neighbor when we lived on the Upper West Side, was now "a bag lady" roaming the city completely out of her mind.

She'd had a son my age; we'd stood on the roof of our building trying to watch the solar eclipse of 1970 without going blind. The trick was to coax the sun through a tiny hole in a square of cardboard and onto a piece of paper so we could watch it get swallowed by the moon, where men had walked just the year before. Where was he now?

We always looked for Mattie when we were in the city, though we had no plan if we found her. What plan could there be? There were laws like the Lanterman-Petris-Short Act, passed in California with support from right-wing members of the John Birch Society, who thought psychiatry was a Communist plot to lock up conservatives, and from left-wing civil libertarians, who subscribed to Thomas Szasz's theory that mental illness was a myth, and had read Erving Goffman's *Asylums*, which viewed mental illness as the product of mental hospitals.

New York had adopted its own version of the California law in 1975, which made it all but impossible to require treatment for people suffering severe mental illness, no matter how terrified and disorganized their life on the street became, unless they were an "imminent danger to themselves or others." Psychosis was not grounds for even short-term commitment, and Mattie was free to refuse the treatment that might help her disordered thinking, even if she was too confused to know that her thinking was disordered.

Only if she were observed pushing someone into Broadway traffic or causing herself immediate harm could she be hospitalized, at which point it would be too late.

In exchange for federal funding, community mental health centers had promised to provide "day hospitals"—open wards with drop-in psychiatric services—as well as beds waiting in the wings, but by the seventies only six percent had day hospitals and these tended to shun the population they were funded to help. Some CMHCs became addiction centers, or offered services for the "worried well." For many, the community itself was the real patient.

Looking back at his time running Baltimore's community mental health services in the late 1960s, psychologist Roger R. Burt describes how his young idealistic staff were careful to avoid the most disturbed members of society. Focused on "counteracting harmful policies, situations, and circumstances before they can produce mental illness," they were afraid their community program "might simply become an outpatient arm for chronically ill state patients."

"It wasn't that we weren't interested in dealing with difficult cases," writes Burt, in *Whatever Happened to Community Mental Health?* The problem was that their community center only had a handful of beds: "To blindly accept 'dumping' would have bled the staff of time and taken services away from people who would benefit from it."

As for helping severely ill patients in acute need, who also lived in those damaged environments, the only recourse for their families was to call the police, who would arrest them "often in a spectacular event." The police, Burt writes, "found the task thoroughly distasteful," and who can blame them? They did not sign up to be caretakers of people with severe mental illness, a job you would think the staff at the Baltimore community mental health center *had* signed up for. Meanwhile, the most vulnerable members of the community were being criminalized.

Having gone around smashing things up like Tom and Daisy, the experts retreated back into private practice, government agencies, or wherever it was they had tenure. Hard enough to find in state hospitals, psychiatrists in the 1970s began disappearing from community mental health centers. The number of psychologists working in CMHCs nearly doubled, but it was psychiatrists, and the medications they could prescribe, that had been central to the argument for community care in the first place. The thinking was that if pills could eliminate the stubborn, costly needs of people with schizophrenia, then even the severely ill could be assimilated back into the mainstream of mental health.

The Network had stuck together through the twilight of the community mental health movement, when Jane's large heart and quiet, stabilizing strength were all the more appreciated. Several members had worked with her and her husband at the Huguenot Center, and several worked with her now at Creedmoor Psychiatric Center in Queens. Creedmoor was no longer the vast fortress swallowing patients for indefinite stays but a rump institution where patients cycled in and out for short chaotic visits followed by release, breakdown, and readmission in what had come to be known as the revolving door.

The failure of the CMHCs, paradoxically, helped ensure the survival of state hospitals. Not all—twelve shut their doors between 1970 and 1973—but others, like Creedmoor, in some ways provided care closer to community psychiatry than the psychiatry practiced in the community. This didn't make state hospitals places people wanted to go, but it made them places that would not go away so long as they still accepted people in the grip of severe psychosis nobody else would take, even if they did not keep them long.

It turned out that going to the moon was easier than curing, preventing, or even providing adequate treatment for illnesses that doctors, not so long before, had referred to as lunacy, a name that would survive in federal statutes until the Obama administration.

Elizabeth Ferber had vivid memories of her father bringing her, when she was very young, into the appalling "board and care" houses of the mentally ill that had begun to replace the appalling state hospitals. Elizabeth was still haunted by the dim, squalid rooms her father had led her into, reeking of cat piss, rotting food, and human waste, the terror of people smoking and pacing in the shadows or huddling inert on unclean beds, murmurously silent or rantingly loud, sometimes both in the same visit. Her father related to even the sickest with uncanny, sympathetic understanding and, despite his well-earned reputation for rudeness, treated them all with natural unsentimental respect.

In some unspoken way Elizabeth understood that Michael was helping to fill the void left by the charismatic and egotistical man who had lived in the house, leapt in the attic, and swum in Long Island Sound, where, brooding over a report on overpopulation and global collapse, he was overcome in the water by the terror of death, and ran off to India in search of a cure.

When Jane went to India herself to try joining what she could not beat, she left her beloved children behind in the care of friends, and they held the rope for her, handing it back when she returned months later brokenhearted. It was on that trip that Jane had asked Bhagwan how she could overcome four suicides on her mother's side of the family, including her grandmother, and how to combat this "perversion of death which runs as a theme through the family." To which the guru, much like R. D. Laing, had replied that for the sensitive and intelligent person living in a crazy world, the choices were madness, suicide, or becoming a sannyasin, a follower of his teaching.

Jane had rejected those choices. She wore orange for a time but, like the Sanskrit name she had received from the Bhagwan, gradually gave it up. She had come home, but the tug-of-war had continued for years until the line went slack at last and Jane's friends watched with sorrow and relief as her brilliant, impossible, orange-clad husband slipped the bonds of space and time and passed at last beyond the reach of obligation and regret.

In his landmark *The Book of Family Therapy*, Dr. Andrew Ferber had written, "We go on for the future of our children." But Bodhicitta had said goodbye to Dr. Ferber along with his wife and children. Elizabeth was sixteen when her father told her, "You are old enough to take care of yourself and you're no longer a priority in my life."

When Elizabeth, now an undergraduate at Barnard, came home to the seaside mansion for a visit, she wasn't surprised to find Michael making a snack for himself in the kitchen, playing guitar on the terrace, or hanging out in the attic with her brother Josh, who was between colleges and living at home trying to get his own head together. Michael had a special rapport with Jane, and had been adopted as well by the women who huddled in her kitchen, old friends, primarily psychologists and social workers in the Network, who had received Jane's extraordinary generosity and stood by her when her husband was thousands of miles from home.

To the cachet of being her big brother's brilliant friend, Michael had added breezing through Yale in three years, landing a high-flying job, and the greater glamour of turning his back on it in order to pursue his literary dreams. He spent late nights in the Ferber turret perched over the desktop computer that Elizabeth's mother had bought for Josh but that Michael commandeered to write stories.

Elizabeth and her brother agreed that Michael's stories were the only thing he put his hand to that did not bear the stamp of his brilliance or bring automatic success, but his aura of achievement remained undimmed. To Elizabeth he was an outsize presence rising out of an outsize station wagon, slamming the door with unapologetic force and loping down the hill to join them on the expanse of beach that flowed from the edge of their backyard into Long Island Sound.

Tall and ruddy in the white cable-knit fishing sweater her mother had given him for Christmas, its collar thick as an Elizabethan ruff, Michael arrived like someone carrying gifts even though his arms were empty. His confidence was itself an offering, though his arrogance was exasperating when he waved away the women poets Elizabeth was reading for a class at Barnard, blithely informing her that women did not write as well as men.

And yet he was charming. He laughed apologetically after he said something outrageous, and sometimes *while* he was saying it, shrugging contrapuntally as if to add that he did not make the rules and could not be faulted for telling the truth.

CHAPTER ELEVEN

GOING SANE

The only people for me are the mad ones.

—JACK KEROUAC, *On the Road*

At Berkeley, I bought a used ten-speed bike, went to the gym, and swam in an outdoor pool at Strawberry Canyon, a mountain gorge crossed with trails and streams. My stamina increased slowly like someone recovering after a long illness, and though I never became one of those skinny guys in shiny clothes peddling madly over the Berkeley Hills, I made it to Berkeley Lab, where there were sweeping views and occasional protests against the military-academic complex.

The real demonstrations were thirty miles away at Lawrence Livermore National Laboratory. That's where physicists worked on President Reagan's Strategic Defense Initiative, popularly known as Star Wars, in case the Esalen Institute's exchange program with New Age Soviet bureaucrats, popularly known as "hot tub diplomacy," failed to bring about nuclear disarmament.

I got to know a few physics grad students at International House, where I was living. They disapproved of Star Wars and doubted it could ever work, but they were a merry bunch, and it was clear nobody had sent them a warning about dim employment prospects. On the contrary, the government money was flowing.

Having figured out how to blow up the world after patient centuries exploring matter and energy, physicists had restored to science the alchemical glow and terror confiscated by the age of reason. Biologists, too, had gone from studying life to engineering it, fulfilling the old Frankenstein fantasy and making a fortune while they were at it. Even computer geeks had become as gods, especially in the Bay Area, where the acid-dropping nerd hippies who built the first PCs in their garages became local heroes before taking over the world.

Perhaps to compensate for their marginal status, literature students talked about interrogating, dismantling, disrupting, and destroying more than Defense Department contractors or the CIA. Some even pretended that a paper on patriarchal structures of dominance in *Lady Chatterley's Lover* was a space-based laser threatening hegemonic Western neo-imperialism. This did nothing for the balance of literary power. It was more like violence prescribed by Frantz Fanon's *The Wretched of the Earth*, which "frees the native from his inferiority complex" and "restores his self-respect."

I made good friends at Berkeley, had modest adventures, touched trees as old as the Bible, and traveled down twisty Highway 1 along the Pacific coast to Big Sur. The drive was an overload of vertiginous beauty: high cliffs and billowing ocean weighted down by giant boulders frilled with white in the blue expanse. At a highway lookout I stood in the oceanic updraft feeling what Jack Kerouac called "end of the continent sadness." I was with friends, three thousand miles from home, and happy.

The Beat writers had come to Big Sur to find themselves and obliterate themselves, often at the same time. Chanting into the waves, drawing Japan closer, they passed through the doors of perception opened by Aldous Huxley, the old man who gave the sixties drugs, stripping off their clothes to soak in the hot springs where Henry Miller, the old man who gave the sixties sex, did his washing.

Not that it occurred to me then that the youth revolution I'd pined for in my geriatric adolescence had been created by old men rebelling against the limits of time and mortality. Any more than I understood that the revolution in consciousness I hoped would free my mind so my ass could follow came at the expense of people whose mental pain I could not begin to fathom. That would come.

Huxley had visited Big Sur in 1962, the year before he died. A tall patrician expatriate with gray combed-back hair, he walked by the water, if not on it, counseling two young men who wanted to turn his ideas about "human potentialities" into a way of life. The Human Potential Movement became the house philosophy of the Esalen Institute that Michael Murphy and Dick Price were also creating, which would transform the Big Sur hot springs into the hippie Lourdes, incubator of a counterculture so successful it was simply culture by the time I got to California.

Murphy and Price had studied psychology at Stanford ten years before, and shared an attachment to Eastern mysticism, a hunger for transcendence, and a reverence for the author of *Brave New World*. A novelist, screenwriter, journalist, and public intellectual, Huxley had won a new audience as a popularizer of Eastern religion and the mystical promise of chemically altered states. He wrote about the magic of mescaline with the same erudite authority he used to warn Mike Wallace about the dangers of overpopulation in a somber CBS sit-down.

Perhaps because his grandfather had been the eminent Victorian zoologist T. H. Huxley—whose fearsome defense of evolution had earned him the nickname Darwin's Bulldog—Aldous Huxley could claim that staring into the sun had improved his eyesight without dimming his reputation as a serious public intellectual. Price and Murphy had chosen the name Human Potential from a lecture Huxley delivered about "the non-verbal humanities" that discussed human intellectual limitation as a frontier of unlimited possibility. Huxley emphasized that "neurologists have shown us that no human being has ever made use of as much as ten percent of all the neurons in his brain." Though this made everyone a mental underperformer, it made our brains a veritable Alaska of unmined "human potentialities."

When Michael and I were growing up, teachers were always telling us the 10 percent statistic, which we were always repeating to each other. It helped explain why we felt so much smarter than we were. Nobody ever suggested that working harder or studying more would give us access to the whole thing because the fault was not in our heads but in our hearts. Cowed by convention, alienated from our true abilities by fear and habit, we would change the way we thought only by changing the way we lived.

Dale Carnegie mentioned our 10 percent brain use in *How to Win Friends and Influence People*, one of the books Michael knew from his adman grandfather. Michael had always seemed conscious of his invisible 90 percent, borrowing against it like accounts receivable, having intuited that self-confidence and faith were aspects of intelligence.

According to our teachers, Albert Einstein had used slightly more than 10 percent of *his* brain, and even that small difference had been enough to make him a genius. Once we figured out how to use all of our brains, we'd be *smarter* than Einstein, who used only *some* of his—like the tailor in a joke my father told who insisted he'd be richer than Rothschild if he had the banker's money because he could still make pants on the side.

Huxley thought the brain worked as a "reducing valve," and if we could find a way to open wide the narrow portal of perception, through either the addition of activating ingredients or the removal of blocks, we would emancipate ourselves from the mind-forged manacles that made us miserable. That was why he had written to the British psychiatrist Humphry Osmond and offered himself as a test subject for mescaline.

It was widely believed that mescaline was a "psychomimetic" drug capable of creating a "model psychosis." Osmond had been using mescaline to train psychiatrists, convinced that "no one is really competent to treat schizophrenia unless he has experienced the schizophrenic world himself."

Dr. Osmond later admitted he'd been reluctant to help Huxley for fear of being known as the doctor who drove the author of *Brave New World* over the edge, but when he went to Los Angeles for the 1953 meeting of the American Psychiatric Association, he made a house call and gave Huxley four tenths of a gram of mescaline in pill form. It turned out that a little schizophrenia was just what the doctor ordered. Blind in one eye and dimly sighted in the other, Huxley found he could see even with his eyes closed. When he opened them, the one-eyed man was king. The crease in his pants was "a labyrinth of endlessly significant complexity." If this was how people with schizophrenia saw the world, they, too, were on the royal road to cosmic consciousness.

Looking at a vase of flowers, Huxley understood that he "was seeing what Adam had seen on the morning of his creation—the miracle, moment by moment, of naked existence." The grandson of Darwin's Bulldog, who had famously told Bishop Wilberforce that he would rather be descended from an ape than a clergyman, was back in the Garden of Eden that his grandfather had rolled up like a carpet.

In *The Doors of Perception*, which Huxley wrote in a month, the only shadow in his garden was the fleeting fear that too much of a good thing would drive him mad: "It was inexpressibly wonderful, wonderful to the point, almost, of being terrifying. And suddenly I had an inkling of what it must feel like to be mad." This surfeit of wonderful sensations raised the possibility that the model psychosis theory was wrong—as indeed it was—and simultaneously suggested that psychosis itself might be better than anything previously imagined.

Huxley told his readers that "most takers of mescaline experience only the heavenly part of schizophrenia." Still, he decided to find a new label for hallucinogenic drugs so as not to tarnish mescaline's reputation. "It will give that elixir a bad name," Huxley argued, "if it continues to be associated, in the public mind, with schizophrenia symptoms. People will think they are going mad, when in fact they are beginning, when they take it, to go sane."

After watching Huxley turn his model psychosis into a spiritual journey, Dr. Osmond agreed that hallucinatory distortions were in fact something more than mere symptoms. With Huxley's assistance, he came up with the word "psychedelic," which means "mind manifesting." The psychiatrist introduced the term at a meeting of the Academy of Sciences in New York in 1957, explaining that "these are not escapes from but enlargements, burgeonings of reality." This wasn't entirely scientific because it was the mind of the beholder, not reality, that did the burgeoning, but it was scientific enough for an intellectual revolution inspired by a thought disorder.

Huxley need not have worried about unwelcome associations with schizophrenia because schizophrenia itself would be reimagined as a mind-manifesting condition in the coming decade, a psychedelic rather than a psychiatric disorder and even a form of enlightenment. The heavenly part would become its essential element, if not for the people who suffered from the illness, then for those hoping to borrow it to help them go sane.

Before the creation of Esalen, cofounder Dick Price had suffered a psychotic breakdown and consulted his old Stanford professor, the eminent anthropologist Gregory Bateson, father of the famous "double bind" theory of schizophrenia devised while studying LSD at the Menlo Park Veterans Administration Hospital, where Ken Kesey had first tried the drug that inspired *Cuckoo's Nest*. Bateson sent Price to Allen Ginsberg's psychiatrist, who introduced Price to LSD. When Bateson was dying of cancer in the late 1970s, Price invited him to live in the round stone house overlooking the Pacific that had been built for Fritz Perls, the father of gestalt therapy, who had helped put

Esalen on the map with his motto "Lose your mind to come to your senses."

This was more than a metaphor for Dick Price, who remained bitterly resentful of the year he had spent medicated in a psychiatric hospital. He remained convinced that his parents and doctors had gotten everything backward; what they called psychosis was the healing reversal of a soul-sickness caused by a toxic society that mistook sickness for health. His "treatment" had not only interrupted his self-healing but cut short his evolution toward enlightenment.

That was the real break. Esalen had been created to be the opposite of the psychiatric hospital where Price had suffered, which is why Michael Murphy called it "Dick Price's revenge on mental hospitals."

I'd heard so often that we were ten-percenters that by the time I finally learned that the neurological findings about the unused 90 percent of our brains had no basis in fact, it was too late to shake the feeling I'd lost something precious that I'd never owned. If I'd been using a whole loaf all along, it meant that there were other reasons I felt so often starved of understanding, limited, and in the dark. Perhaps it wasn't that I used too little of my brain but too much. That, too, was why I had come to Berkeley; to learn how not to think.

But I still expected to illuminate the dark side of my brain, and half believed California was itself the thing that would open my eyes to a larger reality, even if I woke inside a larger dream. When I told my Berkeley therapist that I was having panic attacks in the elevator of International House, he asked me why, as if they were voluntary. He cut me off before I could point the finger at childhood beatings, the Holocaust, or the Freudian saga of the dwarf cherry tree from Cooper's Nursery that turned out to be full-size, outraging my mother, who had me lop the top off every fall.

"*Here's* why," he said, tapping the eraser of his pencil against the dome of his conveniently shaven head, high above his eyes. "They're called frontal lobes."

I laughed but he did not. It was a simple fact, he said, that the brain had evolved in stages and the parts fit together badly. Thinking caused anxiety the way walking upright caused backaches. Our ability to remember the past, imagine the future, and use language, all recent acquisitions, did not mesh well with ancient regions of the brain that had guarded us for eons, knew only the present, and did not distinguish between imaginary fears and real trouble.

Fair enough, but why was it my frontal lobes' fault if the primitive portion of my brain was too drunk on limbic moonshine to distinguish between real and imaginary monsters?

Because, he told me, there *is* no difference between real and imaginary monsters, just as there is no difference between the past and the future: neither exists. Unless I wanted to spend the rest of my life on the elevator floor, I had better realize that the brain isn't an intellectual, any more than the stomach is a gourmet. The brain *is* the body, and the body *lives in the present*, which is all there is.

The good news was that he wasn't recommending a lobotomy, just biofeedback, which was covered by the Berkeley health plan. I would have plenty of cerebral cortex left over.

He sent me to a friendly, white-haired woman in sandals and knee-high pantyhose who attached my left hand to wires connected to a machine connected to more wires attached to my head. My job was to warm my hands with my thoughts, which was like trying to levitate an elephant. Plugged into myself I was a closed circuit pitting my brain waves against my heartbeat, which was visible on the monitor along with my body temperature. I felt like a human game of *Pong* that always lost.

The white-haired woman advised me to lay aside such negative thoughts; there was no winning or losing. She taught me to breathe "through my stomach" and talked me through relaxation techniques. Her soothing, authoritative voice directed warming rays of imaginary sunlight onto my head, outward toward the tips of my fingers and down to my toes.

I loved the visualizations; had I known that the secret of the here and now was pretending to be someplace else, I might have become present a lot sooner. I'd come in thinking of Buddhism as prophylactic death, and mind-emptying meditation as premature evacuation, but I began to feel filled up instead. Maybe I *would* visit the San Francisco Zen Center for morning zazen, as she recommended.

A small reverberation of the body-mind revolution was reaching me at last, tamed and diluted by bourgeois culture. How many pilgrimages had been made to the East, marriages broken up, children abandoned, bad acid trips taken, and humiliating sessions endured in the hot seat of an Esalen encounter group just so I could picture myself in a happy place with sunlight on my hair? I didn't inquire, any more than I thought about the people who died during trials of the Salk and Sabine vaccines or Paul Ehrlich's magic bullet for syphilis.

I dusted off my old mantra from the Scarsdale TM center and practiced visualizations and hand warming in my tiny room in International House, with its tiny but inspiring view of the San Francisco Bay and the Golden Gate Bridge. Progress was slow, to say the least, but the less I tried to browbeat my pulse into unconditional surrender the better I felt. And perhaps I really was edging closer, by imperceptible degrees, to the shadow possibility that slowly, over time, the elephant of my anxiety might become a balloon, and that someday, when I least expected it, I would lift it with a warm breath.

The tide of revolution had gone out at Berkeley long before I got there. It left behind a shaggy guitarist on every corner playing "Mr. Tambourine Man," a guy who slept in a tree above the heads of jewelry vendors on Telegraph Avenue, and a Rump Parliament of protesters on Sproul Plaza where, I learned, the rabbi's wife had once picketed her own son's circumcision.

The Grateful Dead were still alive and playing, but when the tie-dyed families went back to Brigadoon after a concert, you were surrounded by resurgent fraternities and sororities, a football stadium that fired off a cannon every time Cal scored, and thirty thousand undergraduates who would all need jobs and looked like they were going to find them.

Still, I couldn't stop looking for remnants of the fantasy Berkeley that flashed into view like those unexpected glimpses of Alcatraz winking from the bay. I bought my coffee at Caffe Mediterraneum, where Allen Ginsberg had finished "Howl," the poem he recited to great acclaim in San Francisco in 1955. The Mediterraneum had only opened in 1956, but so what? It had been a hangout for writers, hipsters, and Black Panthers less than a decade before I got there.

Once, I went to Wheeler Hall to see Allen Ginsberg give a poetry reading with Peter Orlovsky, his sometime lover and longtime companion from the fifties. Ginsberg played a wheezing hand-pump harmonium, chanting Tibetan mantras, the poetry of William Blake, and his own recent poems while Orlovsky played the finger cymbals and danced with spastic abandon, his long gray hair flying. Occasionally he emitted a strange cry full of pathos that left me vaguely embarrassed, as if he were on display like a dancing bear and I shouldn't be watching.

Ginsberg was on display, too, but he was displaying himself, and perhaps Orlovsky. He was sixty, and in his blue blazer, trimmed beard, and owl glasses, he looked like the accountant he might have become, there to audit the world he'd made. It was hard to believe that forty years before he'd spent a year in Columbia Presbyterian Hospital's Psychiatric Institute.

After the hospital, and before "Howl," Ginsberg had worked as a market researcher on the fifty-second floor of the Empire State Building, where he spent his time trying to figure out whether "glamorous" or "sparkling" sold more toothpaste. He was in his thirties by the time he found the courage, with the help of a psychiatrist, to quit his job, move to San Francisco, live an openly gay life, and write about how he saw "the best minds of my generation destroyed by madness, starving hysterical naked." Most Beat writers had hatched out of asylums, and it was never clear to me if they were the best minds before that happened or because of it.

Ginsberg was in his forties when the 1960s hit their stride, and though hysterical and naked himself at times, also famous and well-fed. When I saw him, he was on the verge of eminence, recently featured in *The New York Times Magazine*, where he recalled the importance of his marketing years in his gray-suited twenties learning how "hand-tooled phrases" could manipulate mass opinion. This confused my expectations of the writer's journey, represented by Jack Kerouac in *On the Road* plowing the darkness at a hundred miles an hour with the cosmic chauffeur Dean Moriarty behind his "raving wheel."

Dean Moriarty—half James Dean and half Professor Moriarty— was really Neal Cassady, the prison-bred car thief and manic philosopher beloved by the Beats, who wrote about each other and themselves. Ginsberg celebrated Cassady's horse-powered libido in "Howl," and Kerouac, who put him in *On the Road*, put Ginsberg there too. He calls him Carlo Marx, the "poetic con man" who rushes down the street with Moriarty, "the holy con man," while Sal Paradise, Kerouac's thinly veiled narrator, "shambled after as I've been doing all my life after people who interest me, because the only people for me are the mad ones."

The Beats released madness like a fox at a hunt, then rushed after—not to help or heal but to see where it led, and to feel more alive while the chase was on. This was a radical thing to do in the fifties, before it became universal practice and public policy.

Ginsberg had grown up with his mother's screaming paranoia, schizophrenic pain, slashed wrists, and naked attempts to seduce him in the midst of wild delirium. As a young man he granted permission for her lobotomy, a desperate last-ditch effort to relieve the suffering he'd been witness to in the days before antipsychotic medication, and spent the rest of his life atoning for it.

He did more than atone. With a genius for merging life and art that rivaled Hemingway's, he made his mother's illness the fixed point around which the world revolved. Like one of those light bulb jokes about turning the room instead of the bulb, he spun the surrounding culture into alignment with his mother's psychosis.

It isn't unusual for a poet to make childhood pain into a clock telling Greenwich mean time for everyone else. What is remarkable is how much help he got from the surrounding culture; not just writers and artists but psychiatrists, psychologists, philosophers, literary critics, social scientists, filmmakers, lawmakers, and ordinary citizens who put their shoulders to the wall and helped turn the room.

In the summer of 1968, the year of my Volvo, the Esalen Institute in Big Sur sponsored seven events under the general heading "The Value of the Psychotic Experience." Ginsberg, flanked by psychiatrists and psychologists, appeared on a panel called "The Poetry of Psychosis," where he announced to general acclamation, "What has been called all along 'madness' or 'psychotic experience' is an experience of the great planetary consciousness, which is like common, so common among us today, that it is ridiculous to talk in the old psychiatric terms, this is what Laing has been saying all along."

I was in no hurry as I waited for Ginsberg to read from "Howl," dedicated to Carl Solomon, the friend he made during his hospitalization at the New York State Psychiatric Institute—though in the poem he speaks of "Pilgrim State's Rockland's and Greystone's foetid halls," ending with his mythic tribute to Solomon:

> I'm with you in Rockland
> in my dreams you walk dripping from a sea-
>   journey on the highway across America in tears
>   to the door of my cottage in the Western night

I didn't know that Carl Solomon was still alive, thirty years after Ginsberg's poem was published, and that when he wasn't incapacitated in a hospital, he worked as a walking messenger in New York City, just like my cousin, who also had schizophrenia and struggled heroically with the help of his heroic mother and sister through each medicated and delusional day, punctuated by outbursts and hospitalizations nobody ever spoke about, just as they never used the word "schizophrenia."

Carl Solomon, making his rounds as a messenger, would call Ginsberg from every corner pay phone and scream at Ginsberg's long-suffering assistant, Bob Rosenthal, "He ruined my life!" and then call from another pay phone and say, "Aw, it's okay."

Of course, I didn't know that then, or know that the year before I went to Berkeley, Peter Orlovsky tried to stab Rosenthal in the crotch with a pair of scissors while Ginsberg was touring in China. Rosenthal had worked for Ginsberg since the 1970s and helped care for Orlovsky, who had been in and out of psychiatric hospitals for years. Rosenthal endured the open window in winter, the pigeons eating and shitting in the apartment, and the drugs and alcohol and all manner of screaming freak-outs. But Rosenthal was no longer the young poet he had been when he began working for Ginsberg, and this time Orlovsky had not only tried to stab him but threatened to kill his children. Rosenthal called the cops.

"I loved him, I loved that guy—until he threatened my children," Rosenthal recalled in a memoir of his own. "And when he threatened my children, all the love just flowed right out of me like toothpaste out of a tube. I had never experienced any taboo like that but all of a sudden I never felt the same again." Orlovsky was naked and waving a machete in the air when Rosenthal called the cops. The police grabbed him, strapped him to a chair, and carried him down the stairs while he howled at the top of his lungs.

Rosenthal was acutely aware that one week before, Eleanor Bumpurs, a mentally ill Black woman living alone in the Bronx, had been shot dead by the police. She, too, was large, naked, and waving a big knife, but she did not have someone like Rosenthal, who had acted as go-between with the police, and had fetched a local Zen priest to persuade Orlovsky, when he barricaded himself into a bedroom, to open the door a crack for a bottle of sake, allowing the police to barrel in and overpower him.

Bumpurs had refused to pay her rent because people were coming through the walls and floors to rip her off. Her daughter, who later sued the city, advised her by phone to keep her door locked. A psychiatrist determined she was psychotic after maintenance men responding to her complaints found nothing broken but noticed feces in her bathtub, which she blamed on "Reagan and his people." A social service supervisor decided that evicting her was the best way to get her into a hospital, and the cops were called after agents from the New York City Housing Authority were driven away by threats of boiling lye. Despite the presence of an NYPD emergency unit specially trained to deal with mentally disturbed people, an officer shot and killed the naked 260-pound woman when she lunged at his partner with a ten-inch butcher knife.

Rosenthal knew all this—it had been front-page news every day—but he had called the police anyway because his children had been threatened. After Orlovsky was in Bellevue, where he had spent time before, Rosenthal wrote to Ginsberg in China, telling him with trepidation what he had done, only to find that "Allen loved it all because it reminded him of his mother's old episodes."

It dawned on him that whenever Orlovsky started drinking and drugging his way toward a psychotic episode, Ginsberg watched, in no hurry to intervene. "He always kept files on Peter. So he was really the enabler to that kind of crazy behavior and he got a special glow going." The glow faded as the outbursts and hospitalizations increased. Eventually, Ginsberg would apply for an order of protection against Orlovsky, by all accounts the gentlest of men when he was not in the grip of psychosis.

Memoirs have a way of ruining things. I was there to hear "Howl" and to fortify my own defenses by reminding myself how a cruel culture betrays its best minds and drives them into conformity and madness.

Ginsberg never did read from "Howl." His new poems sounded made up on the spot, though some were written down and read with remembered spontaneity in a deep, sonorous voice. Still, there he was in Berkeley. And there I was, watching Ginsberg play the harmonium while Peter Orlovsky, playing the finger cymbals, danced.

CHAPTER TWELVE

STORIES

We longed to be real people in a real
community, not anonymous shadows, which is
what we were in New Rochelle.

—MARK RUDD, *Underground:*
My Life with SDS and the Weathermen

After finishing the fifth year of her combined degree, Jo-Ann returned to New Rochelle and moved into her parents' house determined to become a musician. She practiced the clarinet for hours, played with any ensemble that would have her, and studied with a master teacher in Manhattan—doing her best to catch up to the single-minded musicians who'd skipped college, gone straight to conservatory, and already launched musical careers.

A year had passed since the graduation party, and Jo-Ann, if anything, was surprised by the attention Michael paid her. He'd been an exalted presence even in high school, with an aura of destiny that had only grown in brightness since Yale and Bain. It wasn't just Michael's intellect but a sort of moral grandeur he brought to discussions that impressed her. And he seemed to see fascinating things in her. She was flattered. He stared into her eyes with an unabashed desire to read her and to be read by her. His whole soul was at her service, which made her feel, she had to admit, like a princess.

And yet something cautioned her to hang back. Instinctively she understood that she would never catch up to his racing mind or match his peculiar way of seeing the world. His brain inhabited a different sphere that she admired but felt, without putting it into words, was a place she was prohibited from entering and didn't quite want to go.

Jo-Ann had only recently ended a serious long-term relationship with a man several years her senior who had been ready for a commitment she wasn't prepared to make. But she also wasn't prepared for what Michael wanted, which she began to realize was, for him, already there. It began to dawn on Jo-Ann that time had not passed for him in the same way it had passed for her. For Michael, their time together was the extension of a relationship already underway in his mind.

Determined to keep things with Michael low-key, she parried evening invitations by suggesting daytime walks. Michael was a wonderful person to wander with, but sometimes when Michael looked at her in his deep way, Jo-Ann felt frightened. Not for her safety; Michael was not only a gentleman but a gentle man. It was her sense of self, which she had been working so hard to cultivate and protect, that felt threatened. What unsettled Jo-Ann when Michael looked into her eyes was the dawning realization that she wasn't there, and that Michael was gazing at someone entirely separate from her.

Jo-Ann's dreams started to coalesce. She was admitted to a master's program in Yale's Department of Music, and before moving to New Haven was going to spend six weeks in the far north of Germany, where she'd won a seat in the prestigious Schleswig-Holstein Musik Festival. She would be sleeping in a real castle and performing in elegant manor houses, converted barns, and historic churches with musicians from around the world, conducted by Leonard Bernstein and Justus Frantz, the German concert pianist and creator of the festival.

She was talking more and more to her old boyfriend. Their time apart had been clarifying for both of them; what had begun as a permanent break was becoming the prelude to something new. Michael saw the writing on the wall, and as the summer approached and Jo-Ann withdrew into preparations, Michael withdrew into himself.

His writing stalled and his mood sank. He called Mike Curtis and asked if he could spend time with Mike's parents in Switzerland. He thought Europe might restore his spirits and help his writing, he said. He wanted to see London and Paris, and above all spend time in the idyllic alpine village he'd heard Mike talk about, where his parents kept a chalet.

Not long before, Mike had arranged for Michael to house-sit for his grandparents on Cape Cod, only to have Michael call with a week remaining to say he was leaving. Mike drove hours, and devoted hours more to cleaning up an astonishing accumulation of garbage for so short a time: beer bottles, soda cans, filthy toilets, and a stovetop mysteriously enameled with a dark brown substance that had to be chipped off with surgical care.

But Mike was compassionate, loyal, and enormously fond of Michael. He put Cape Cod behind him and quickly made arrangements. The kindness of other people's parents had always sustained Michael.

In addition to London, Paris, and the Swiss village, Michael decided to stop in Kiel, Germany. A strategic supply center on the Diplomacy board, Kiel was also the Schleswig-Holstein town where Jo-Ann was sleeping in a schloss with views of the Baltic Sea and the Kiel Fjord.

Abandoned cowsheds and stone barns, part of the rural life of the region for hundreds of years, had been renovated to serve as musical venues. Ticket prices were kept low so that locals could afford to come, and the grain barn could seat a thousand people. Jo-Ann loved rehearsing with the orchestra in the cool stone barn, which had wonderful acoustics and smelled faintly of bread and earth. The festival had been going on for less than two weeks when someone informed her that she had a visitor waiting for her. She could not imagine who it might be, but made her way to the back of the empty barn. There, sitting in the last row, was Michael. He got up grinning sheepishly and flung his arms wide in greeting.

Astonished, Jo-Ann hugged him. She did not know what else to do.

"I know you didn't invite me," Michael said, coming to the point right way. "And I'm not here to take up any of your time." But he was experiencing some writer's block and explained that if only he could be near her, he felt he would be able to write.

He was polite, reasonable, respectful as always; nevertheless, his presence contradicted his apologetic protestations. Jo-Ann had been quite clear that things were over. It was a stretch to say that they had ever begun, and she felt again the strange sensation of being misaligned with his perception of her, and consequently with the world around him, so different from the one she saw.

She tried to stress how entirely taken up with the festival she was and would be, how obligated to the people around her, and how she had been given this tiny golden window of time and needed to make the most of the opportunity. Michael nodded, understanding everything. He had no intention of disrupting her schedule.

Freaky as she found his extravagance, she could hardly refuse to see a friend who seemed to have flown four thousand miles to see her. He'd already rented a room in a nearby inn, and secured a bicycle, which was how everybody there got around. Jo-Ann agreed to see his room, which had a splendid view of the water.

Michael invited Jo-Ann to set the parameters of his visit; would it be all right if he came to some rehearsals? She told him that would be fine, but she could not eat meals with him or anything like that. She had to be with the group.

Michael accepted all her conditions. Sometimes when Jo-Ann lifted her eyes during rehearsal, she saw him sitting in a distant row of the cavernous barn, and it was easy to imagine him in the dimness even when he wasn't there. Jo-Ann was aware that he wanted a different sort of reunion, a deeper connection, and she needed to remind herself that she had always been honest with him.

Jo-Ann was haunted by a memory of something that had happened once when they were lying together on Michael's bed. Their relationship had hardly been physical, but on this occasion they had been holding each other, kissing mostly. Her arms were still around him when a sudden convulsive shudder swept through him. Jo-Ann had never witnessed anything like that before: a full-body shiver, as if a strong current had passed through him. She asked Michael if he was all right, and he had waved the whole thing away.

Jo-Ann had no idea if this was something that had happened to him before or if it was the first time, only that Michael clearly had no wish to talk about it. He assured her tersely that he was fine; nothing in fact had happened. Except that it had. Jo-Ann had been holding him and knew. At the same time, she had an intuition that he was telling the truth; it wasn't physical, at least not in origin. She could not shake the notion that the trembling that overtook him was the product of some strong passion, as if Michael were battling himself on the inside, or some difficult thought had swept through him with the force of a physical calamity.

From Germany, Michael fled to Switzerland. Though he'd skipped out on the Cape Cod house, Mike Curtis had covered for him, and when Michael showed up at the Curtis family farmhouse, he was welcomed with open arms. The house was in a valley at the foot of a cluster of mountains called the Wildstrubel massif, exhilarating just to say. There were alpine views, glaciated peaks, kittens, cocoa, strong coffee, excellent cheese, and an assortment of lightweight walking sticks you grabbed on the way outside.

Switzerland was restorative. Michael wrote and hiked. He tramped to the Simmenfälle, a rushing cataract where he thought about Sherlock Holmes "grappling with Moriarty, poised above the flood," as he put it in the farmhouse guestbook. Holmes and his nemesis had actually fought their death match at Reichenbach Falls an hour and a half away, but the Simmenfälle was sufficient to remind Michael of the "The Final Problem," the story in which Arthur Conan Doyle tried to rid himself of his great detective, though Holmes had proven too popular to kill off, returning for more adventures despite the evil professor and the wishes of his creator.

The spy novel Michael was writing was filled with villains who were themselves proving uncannily resistant to death. He thought he had glimpsed one of them in the village, a sandy-haired young man who kept a hand in his jacket pocket.

Michael was working intensely on the book, driven by the sense that he was falling behind. He had just turned twenty-four, and though he had never needed the allotted time to do anything, time and money were running out. Mike Curtis had already completed two years of medical school at Case Western and was still seeing his college girl-friend, Anne Calabresi—though everyone called her Nina—who went there too.

Jo-Ann would be in New Haven when Michael got back to New Rochelle where a growing pile of rejection letters from little maga-zines was waiting for him. He had promised to take the LSATs and had sent away for law school applications but hoped there was another way. He was planning to move in permanently with the Ferbers; his father wanted him out of the house, but he was already thinking about returning to Switzerland.

My father had been diagnosed with Parkinson's disease my first year at Berkeley. Whenever I came home to visit, the tremor in his left hand, which he tried to conceal by covering it with his right, was more pronounced, and one foot seemed heavier than the other when he walked. Most distressing was that he kept forgetting things despite his excellent memory. He seemed both vigilant and resigned, as if he'd already said or done something and was keeping an eye out for the authorities even if he wasn't sure why.

This was not like his old absentmindedness. I'd barely managed to pull the cellophane-tipped toothpick out of his tuna sandwich before he took his first bite as we sat across from each other at the Friendly's where my sister had waited tables in high school.

He asked me if I was writing, the way you might ask a drug addict if he was using. I'd started to think about a dissertation but I knew that wasn't what he meant. In fact, I'd discovered I could get a master of fine arts on my way to a PhD if I completed a collection of stories I was already working on. My father in his uncanny way had somehow intuited this. He leaned forward and lowered his voice almost conspiratorially. "It destroys everything," he said.

His own long-deferred literary ambitions, like the ancient Greek alphabet he'd taped above his desk to keep his mind nimble, had become entangled with his mental condition, which my parents never called dementia and was eventually identified as Lewy body disease. Whatever it was called, my father understood that it made for a bad story, and perhaps spelled the end of stories altogether.

I didn't tell Michael about my stories when he came over unexpectedly with his own stories for me to read. They were rolled up and held fast with one of the wide rubber bands that the delivery people used to make *The New York Times* easier to toss.

Michael told me that he'd been having trouble "placing" them. As always, I was impressed by his ability to admit setbacks in a way that assumed his listener would understand that an injustice had been done to him. Still, he wanted a second opinion. In spite of myself, I felt flattered. Not that I wanted to read his stories. I was afraid I wouldn't like them and just as afraid that I would. I didn't want them in my head now that I was finally trying to find my own "voice," but I accepted the scrolled manuscript, which he handed me like a diploma.

We were still standing in the foyer of my parents' house. He seemed taller and more stooped, looking down expectantly as if he thought I would read them on the spot. He often asked about my classes, and I was often surprised by how interested, almost envious, he sounded. Now, though, he was shifting slightly from foot to foot in a rhythmically nervous manner my father referred to as shokeling, the Yiddish word for what Orthodox Jews do when they pray and sway.

He asked if I would give his stories to my mother when I was finished, and if I could please ask her to pass them along to her friend Cynthia. If that wasn't convenient, I could give him Cynthia's address, which he hadn't been able to find, and he would deliver them himself. I understood suddenly that he hadn't known I was visiting but had come over expecting to find my mother. That would explain the mixture of hesitation and impatience killing off casual conversation and keeping me from asking him if he wanted to come in.

Michael's stories were strange, violent, and surreal. One was set in a Mexican border town where a girl had been brutally raped. The local community caught the attacker vigilante-style and brought him stripped and bound to a field in the dead of night. The women of the town formed a ring around the terrified rapist, holding red-hooded flashlights that glowed luridly in the darkness like "members engorged with blood." The mother of the violated girl stepped forward out of the circle, knife raised high, ready to strike.

I didn't *like* the story but I admired its intensity. The engorged flashlights were absurd and unforgettable. The anticipation of violence gave it an expectant energy, unless it was my own urgent wish to get to the end. I wanted resolution, not of the story but of my own nagging uncertainty.

My judgment around Michael's stories was like a compass near a magnet. Were they terrible? Were they great? Impossible to say. What

I felt and envied was the power of their conviction. Even stories set in a Polish shtetl and written in the manner of I. B. Singer were recognizably his, no matter if they were about a young woman pouring wine over her naked thighs to make a potion, or a dybbuk—a spirit of the dead—taking possession of a body.

Michael's stories were pure pastiche, but there was an uncanny current running through them, like the voice of a dybbuk speaking out of a borrowed body, that felt weirdly original. This had to do, I thought, with his powers of *persistence*; he'd always managed to keep the deadpan going after I'd started laughing, swim the lake whether or not anyone was watching, invent a source *and actually put it into the footnotes*. That was it, I thought; Michael's stories *believed* in themselves, like Michael himself.

My mother called me after I was back in California to report that Michael had recognized Cynthia in Grand Central Station and joined her on the train. When they got to New Rochelle, he asked if she would read his stories, and Cynthia had given him her address.

My mother sounded irritated, as if I'd put him up to it. I hadn't given Michael's stories to my mother, who hadn't wanted them, or given them back to Michael, but left them under my detached bunk bed in New Rochelle and tried to put them out of my mind. I'd failed to do what I promised but still felt he'd taken something that was mine.

When I'd graduated from college, Cynthia had given me a pen with a note suggesting I might use it for "the Sacred Purpose." Writing was always the goal of goals, though Cynthia added that "it requires an obsessive and idiosyncratic instrument of one's own obsessive and idiosyncratic choice," because "the Sacred Purpose has its own laws." So the gift was like the hilt of a sword I still had to pull out of a stone. I didn't want someone else getting to it first, and made a pledge to redouble my own efforts.

I assumed that Michael was living the life he wanted. I definitely thought he was living the life *I* wanted. I saw him as he described himself, perched over the keyboard of a computer in a tower room wallpapered with rejection letters, dreaming and daring and looking out at Long Island Sound.

I'd thought of his trip to Europe as he had described it to me: a quest for a girl, a literary pilgrimage, an assertion of freedom. He had flown off on a whim but was always drawing nearer to the finish line of our shared ambitions. It was Michael who had introduced me to *The Hero with a Thousand Faces*, an old book on my parents' shelf, newly in vogue, with Joseph Campbell's alluring "mono-myth" of adversity and triumph and the wound that made you stronger. Even a broken heart or a rejected manuscript could feed a writer's soul.

It did not occur to me that in Switzerland he'd glimpsed enemy agents escaped from his own imagination, or that those figments made flesh had followed him home, where others were waiting for him, like the secret members of a murderous cult pretending to be musicians at Riverrun.

It did not occur to me that Cynthia had been struck by how "estranged" Michael seemed on the train: "An oddball loner," she later recalled. Michael was so diffident that it surprised her when he began to speak about his writing and the seriousness and devotion that he brought to it. As for his stories, she had no memory of them whatsoever.

Nazis were abroad in New Rochelle. Even if they were imaginary, they ran Michael off the road when he was driving and tried to run him down when he was walking. They stalked him in daylight and hounded him at night. He stayed awake like the prey in one of those horror movies I vowed never to see, where a monster slips inside your dreams and kills you for real if you drift off for only a second.

He blamed the novel he'd been writing, and himself for writing it. The tormentors it had released into the world were alive in the night, drawing close to the Ferbers' house. That was why he brought a baseball bat into bed with him.

Even without the bat, Michael's behavior alarmed Josh Ferber, who worried about his friend's worsening state of mind. Michael was morbidly fixated on Jo-Ann, who was back with her old boyfriend. His broken heart had not made him more whole. Michael phoned her obsessively in New Haven until a man picked up one day and told him in a stern voice that he must never call again.

Josh was having troubles of his own. Prone to depression, he'd been sinking to depths of frigid darkness, numbed and terrified by turns. Sharing the attic with a man who slept with a baseball bat wasn't helping. Michael often prowled until dawn. Josh was afraid that if Michael didn't smash him first, his own mental pain would undo him. He didn't know how much longer he could hold out, or if he wanted to.

Michael went to bed with a baseball bat; Josh went to bed with a noose. Eventually it came to sound like a comedy routine—Josh had also been raised on Richard Pryor—but at the time it wasn't funny at all. Josh really did keep a noose under his bed, or under his pillow; it was a measure of his pain that he found it comforting, like a rope ladder that helps a child afraid of fire fall asleep, even if the ladder is too short to reach the ground.

Josh's mother was growing concerned. She had rejected the Bhagwan's choices—madness, suicide, or discipleship—as the answer to the "perversion of death" haunting her family, but she was still struggling to find a fourth way as she tried to keep the young men under her roof safe. Between her job at Creedmoor and her private practice in New Rochelle, this was not easy.

Josh was glad to have a friend to talk to, party with, and teach him John Prine's "Paradise" on the guitar, but he did not especially like having to share his computer, the attic, or his mother—who was also his psychiatrist—at a time of deepening depression and increasingly suicidal thoughts. That was why he'd come home in the first place.

Michael was an overshadowing presence at the best of times who easily held his own with the psychiatrists, psychologists, social workers, academics, and radical originals who spent time in the Ferber home. He liked to shine, and Jane and her friends in the Network took a sort of communal pride in him, as if they all owned shares in his ego.

Michael taped the rejection letters he got from magazines and literary journals to the curved turret wall of the Ferber attic with as much defiance as defeat, at least at the beginning. If anyone could stitch rejection letters into a victory flag, it would be Michael. His very openness about rejection robbed the letters of their power.

Jane had first begun to suspect that something was wrong with Michael when she noticed the taped-up letters. Michael had come back from Europe in worse shape than when he'd gone, though he still had a great capacity for articulate conversation, humor, and the courtly solicitousness that had so moved Jo-Ann.

With Josh suffering in the attic, it made sense for Michael to go back to his parents' house, but Jane found him a psychiatrist, an old friend and colleague Michael knew as Murray from Jane's gatherings, where he was a regular. Michael went home but remained inside the Network's extended family, which spread its protective umbrella over him even on Mereland Road.

Murray had trained as a ballet dancer, and still had a dancer's carriage and dramatic flair, tempered by a thoughtful intellectual manner that Jane knew appealed to Michael. He'd decided to become a psychiatrist after reading Erving Goffman's *Asylums* at Stanford medical school, where the father of the double bind theory of schizophrenia—"the great Gregory Bateson," as Murray called him in later life—was affiliated with the department of psychiatry.

He'd gotten his start in community psychiatry working with Andy Ferber at Bronx State Hospital in the optimistic early 1960s, and with Jane at the Huguenot Center in New Rochelle. Like Jane, he worked at Creedmoor Psychiatric Center in Queens, last of the state behemoths. He also had offices on the Upper West Side of Manhattan, where Michael saw him, and remained devoted to the Network's values, well expressed in *Crisis: A Handbook for Systemic Intervention*, which Jane and a colleague had published in the late seventies, where the enemy wasn't mental illness but mental institutions.

Jane's co-author, John Schoonbeck—a journalist turned psychologist who drummed for the Nocturnal Emissions when Andy Ferber played bass—wrote in the manual that he had learned with crisis work "not to accept the idea that anyone is crazy." He had learned, in fact, "not to believe in psychosis as a state," merely as a behavior dependent on circumstances.

One of the manual's case histories described an elderly Jewish woman with "regressive psychosis" who had been wandering the halls of her Upper West Side rooming house naked. Jane's team was called in to help get the woman into a nursing home; instead, they coached her "on how to avoid being committed." They gave her tips like "wear your clothes at all times" and "evacuate in the toilet instead of the floor," and they reminded her to smile at the nurse "no matter what."

Keeping people out of the hospital was the hospital's policy, too, even if it had more to do with legal constraints and available beds than a faith in community care. This was true even in the case of Mrs. Cruz, a thirty-five-year-old woman who had walked into Bronx State Hospital and announced that she was going to kill her five-

year-old son. The doctor on call had diagnosed her with paranoid
schizophrenia and sent her home with "a bottle of Thorazine" and
instructions to come back if the medication didn't help.

Jane and her team were called in the next day by an alarmed therapist who wanted to get Mrs. Cruz's child out of the house. One challenge was figuring out "whether or not Mrs. Cruz would kill her son,
and who would be responsible if she did." It was not an easy decision:
"Anyone who has been a parent, or a child, must, at some time, have
felt like killing somebody in their family," the authors wrote. "However most women have not stabbed and seriously wounded their husbands."

Mrs. Cruz *had* stabbed her husband, who had survived but moved
out. Jane and her team found that there was "substantial risk of homicide or homicide-suicide." Nevertheless, they decided to give Mrs.
Cruz a choice; she could go to a hospital until the crisis passed, allow
the team to find a temporary placement for her son, or agree to a
contract, pledging "not to kill herself, or her son, between then and
the next day." She chose the contract, promising to call the crisis
team or the police if she changed her mind.

Jane's crisis intervention guide was endorsed by none other than
Joel Kovel, the Marxist psychiatrist I'd found so persuasive, who served
as director of residency training at the Albert Einstein College of Medicine, where his friend Andy Ferber had taught psychiatry. *Crisis* was
addressed to mental health professionals who "feel in some way oppressed by the existence of mental hospitals, jails, reform schools,
hierarchical corporations or governments of covert nepotism." Its
techniques were offered to those who "derive some personal pleasure
from seeing people change without being inducted by such institutions."

CHAPTER THIRTEEN

CHOOSING

Reason is the ultimate language of madness.

—Michel Foucault

Reason is but choosing.

—John Milton

I finished my coursework in two years, which left me a third year of funding with nothing to do but study for my orals and think about my dissertation. I decided to spend it in New York City, where a friend from International House had an apartment on the Upper West Side that she was letting me live in for minimal rent. My father's illness had been getting worse, but the main reason I went back was to be with Mychal, who was moving to Manhattan to start rabbinical school.

If I was honest with myself, which happened very little in those days, I'd wanted to be near Mychal since our first night having coffee after our non-date spent not listening to Noam Chomsky in the middle of my senior year. Having persuaded her she wasn't a senior fling, and followed her to Jerusalem, where she was studying Arabic, I'd flown off to California at summer's end to keep my rendezvous with destiny. Since then, I'd pushed our separation to the limit and was afraid that if we did not spend time together now, too many things would grow around us and make it impossible.

Being at Berkeley had involved me in an emotional sleight of hand whose hypocrisy I'd done my failing best to deny. I'd even allowed myself to believe that falling in love with Mychal was a remnant of the dependent nature I'd gone to California to reform, and that the braver I got, and the freer I felt, the easier it would be to say goodbye. Instead, I'd discovered the opposite was true. The stronger and more self-reliant I became, the more I wanted to be with her.

I was also growing alienated from the intellectual atmosphere of academia. One of the things I'd always liked about literature was that it wasn't philosophy or history or social science but its own thing that helped me think about the world and my place in it.

I understood that theory was a tool of my new profession, but at Berkeley the handle was bigger than the pot. It was also more exciting.

In those days, you felt the unsettling charisma of Derrida, Foucault, and the other Frenchmen of the Apocalypse whose ideas you absorbed in classes taught by the rising stars of the department I was ambitious enough to want to impress. I spent a lot of energy trying to get my head around post-structuralist theory, and even more dodging it like a bullet. Neither effort was entirely successful.

The hotshots who brought luster to the department didn't seem to like literature very much, but the defenders of traditional values, in whose classes I sought refuge, engendered a vague feeling of irrelevance.

The long allusive march of literary representation that grew richer the more you knew had come to an end, and even gone past the end, like those cartoon characters that run out a window but don't fall until they look down. Still, you were expected to recognize the chalk outlines under your feet. My advantage was that I was conversant with the pale shadows populating what was still called "the Tradition," while brilliant students who thought nothing of plowing through Lacan's "The Agency of the Letter in the Unconscious or Reason since Freud" put off reading *Paradise Lost*, which was a requirement, from one year to the next.

I'd come to *Paradise Lost* out of necessity, but stayed with it for the simplest of reasons. I liked it. Not all of it, but there were parts I listened to over and over like a piece of music, which is how its blind author had dictated it each morning after dreaming it in the night. I'd been drawn to the poem ever since an English professor my freshman year in college told our class that instead of wedding vows, he'd recited the words that Adam speaks to Eve after she's eaten the forbidden fruit. Adam is still unfallen but determined to share Eve's fate. The professor, a shy man with large glasses, who had sailed to America from Hong Kong as a child, began to speak Adam's words aloud, his soft voice barely above a whisper:

> How can I live without thee, how forego
> Thy sweet converse, and love so dearly joined
> To live again in these wild woods forlorn?

It was for such simplicities, as much as the charismatic complexity of Satan, that I'd been considering a dissertation on *Paradise Lost*. Perhaps, too, I hoped to restore something I felt I was losing, which is one of the worst reasons to choose a dissertation topic.

I knew so little about ideas when I arrived that I'd assumed "postmodernism" was just the movement that came after modernism, replacing Virginia Woolf and William Faulkner, say, with self-referential writers whose avant-garde winks at the reader were considered novel enough to let them get on with the old-fashioned business of writing. It dawned on me slowly that modernism meant the whole modern show—including the Enlightenment, empirical science, and rational thought—and postmodernism, which was sometimes called poststructuralism, was its refutation and replacement.

If the old dispensation was the age of reason, the new one was the age of unreason. That would explain why Michel Foucault's *Mad-*

ness and Civilization was one of the touchstone texts always lurking in the background. It didn't matter that its author rejected the postmodern label, because postmodernists like Foucault rejected all fixed meanings. That was the whole point.

There was no truth in this new world, only "truth"—sometimes called "knowledge"—which lived inside quotation marks whether you noticed them or not. Truth wasn't established with empirical evidence but talked into existence with a kind of rhetorical magic called "discourse" that made something so because of how you expressed it.

Truth was the "product" of discourse, not the other way around. It was manufactured like a salami in a metaphorical meaning factory operated by unseen systems of authority whose interests it ultimately served and whose only purpose was maintaining power. Accordingly, the madness in *Madness and Civilization* wasn't a medical diagnosis but a "social construct," devised in the seventeenth century to enforce the rule of reason by demonizing anyone who strayed beyond the boundaries of convention. "Madness" turned nonconformists into "the other" so they could be locked away. Like madness, invented to serve as reason's defining opposite, the asylum was the indispensable foil of freedom, making forced confinement not just the dark side of the Enlightenment but its raison d'être.

Foucault's true theme was power, the only thing that was really real. There was something seductive about seeing everything in terms of its secret relationship to power, and the critic as someone trained to unmask it. It made the intellectual a kind of superhero, freeing people from the structures of oppression embedded inside institutions, social systems, and works of art. The suffering of people imprisoned by a poem might not be great, but the person exposing it was a liberator. And wasn't I trying to liberate myself, at least a little, from false constructions, so I could live inside the story of my own unfolding?

The beauty of postmodernism was that it erased the world with one hand while rewriting it with the other, allowing you to inherit the authority you discredited like a spoil of war. But there was something arbitrary about it, too, that left me feeling falsified in ways I lacked the clarity to put my finger on. Foucault's obsession with hidden power engendered a low-level paranoia that took the place of thought while making you feel smart.

The hyperrational aspects of the Enlightenment *did* have a dark underside, and those with power *were* constantly drawing arbitrary lines they pushed the powerless across, but did the Enlightenment really destroy an age of freedom and use reason only to suppress its enemies? Having banished medical causes, all that remained to explain madness in *Madness and Civilization* was a social construct creating a supply of demonized "others" leading to a demand for asylums that in turn increased the supply of madmen in a widening spiral of expanding categories and segregating spaces culminating in "the great confinement."

Foucault even considered AIDS a social construct, waving away the warning he received from the writer Edmund White in the early 1980s when he was teaching at Berkeley. "You American puritans, you're always inventing diseases," Foucault told White, though people were already dying of AIDS, most conspicuously gay men like Foucault himself, who had plunged into San Francisco's bathhouse scene in the orgiastic seventies and remained passionately devoted to anonymous drug-fueled sadomasochistic sex. Still, he preferred to see the disease, which killed him the year before I got to graduate school, as an imaginary disorder, "and one that singles out blacks, drug users and gays—how perfect!"

One reason, I sometimes thought, literature grew pale beside the reigning theories was that they already operated according to the laws of fiction. Even when they appeared to address history or science, postmodern intellectuals saw the world as symbolic. Having stripped literature for parts, they had no further need of it, and invited you to feel the same.

But using something wasn't the same as enjoying it. Something else I'd always liked about literature was that I'd always liked it, which was harder to assert when all forms of culture were seen as servants of the unjust power they were created to conceal. Liking literature, instead of exposing it, was like kissing the boot stomping your face, or someone else's.

These were the sort of dark ideas that started to make me second-guess my own instincts. Foucault claimed that the mental hospital was structured on the modern family, treating those it called mad like children, and turning doctors and nurses into medical mothers and fathers doling out discipline. He also claimed that the reverse was true; the family was structured on the mental hospital, a stronghold of state power engineered by capitalist culture to indoctrinate its tender charges with the punitive logic of bourgeois power.

A version of this idea was at the center of *Capitalism and Schizophrenia*, published with a preface by Foucault, which saw the family not only as the incubator of mental illness but as the symptom of a sick society. One of the book's co-authors, the radical therapist Félix Guattari, had worked with mentally ill patients at an experimental clinic where he organized "erotic kamikazes" tasked with destroying relationships among the staff by seducing one or another of the partners. Smashing the bourgeois family, and the monogamy that helped sustain it, was a blow against the oppressive hierarchies that *Capitalism and Schizophrenia* was written to explode.

I'd wanted to get away from my family, not rid the world of "the family," much as I'd wanted to step outside the long shadow of my parents' library, not banish literature or the possibility of meaning. My father's family had been smashed as part of a plan to wipe out an entire people, including my sister and me, before we were born. My father had only survived because he was sent as a child into exile. His father was stolen from his family, enslaved in a concentration camp, and killed by murderous conditions even before the death factories began to operate.

That early in the war, the Nazis still sent their victims' ashes home from the crematoria. My grandmother buried her husband's ashes but was so focused on life and family that she asked the young tombstone cutter she hired to come to her apartment for the last payment so she could introduce him to her daughter, my father's sister Fanny. They were married six weeks later and escaped via an arduous route through Russia, leaving my grandmother, at her insistence, to find another way out. She did not find another way, and my aunt never forgave herself for her mother's murder.

In other words, I knew the family wasn't a bourgeois impediment to progress, or a tool of capitalist oppression, but a life raft of resistance in a sea of state tyranny. It was how you preserved and passed on values worth dying for, and was itself one of those values. My grandparents had died trying to save what my father and mother had created for my sister and me, who were named for our father's parents.

Oddly, I felt something similar about *Paradise Lost*, with its taproot deep in biblical soil. If it turned out stories really did write me, instead of the other way around, let me at least choose the ones that spoke to my soul. Was I a child to find so much comfort in the words of a fictional Adam, swearing allegiance to an imaginary Eve, read aloud by a professor the first time I left home? It felt like an age had passed since then, but Adam's declaration of love in the garden still stirred me:

> Should God create another Eve, and I
> another rib afford, yet loss of thee
> Would never from my heart . . .

CHAPTER FOURTEEN

THE BREAK

Listen while I talk on

against time.

It will not be

for long.

—WILLIAM CARLOS WILLIAMS, "Asphodel,
That Greeny Flower"

One cold winter morning my father saw Michael in the flapping remnant of his fancy trench coat walking distractedly up Mereland Road like someone with no place to go in a hurry. My father was waiting outside our house for his ride to the train station. The closer Michael got the worse he looked, and my father asked him what was wrong.

I haven't been well, Michael told him, uncharacteristically uncommunicative. He seemed to struggle for words but managed to add that he was seeing two doctors. Psychiatrists.

My father was often wary of Michael, as well as amused and impressed by him, but he was deeply affected by Michael's drawn and distracted features, his haunted air, and almost palpable aura of affliction. My father wanted to stay and talk more, but his neighbor and synagogue buddy, David Friedman, pulled up in the old Plymouth that had once driven Michael and me to New Rochelle High School. They still called this the carpool, though to the relief of everyone my father no longer took his turn. He got in the car with the feeling he was abandoning someone in crisis.

A few days later my father ran into Chuck on Mereland and learned that Michael was in the neuropsychiatric unit of Columbia Presbyterian.

My parents called to deliver the news. I was living in Manhattan by then and knew something was wrong because both my parents were on the phone. This was unusual unless it was my birthday, and they'd already called and sung to me when I turned twenty-five a few weeks before. They sounded so grave and strange that I thought my grandmother must have died or that something had happened to my sister, but my father said they were calling about Michael Laudor. The formal use of his full name was a portent of bad news, as well as an acknowledgment of how far we'd drifted, though some childhood portion of myself was always listening for news of Michael.

Evasive at the best of times, my father had grown increasingly elliptical. He said "break" without "psychotic," and Columbia Presbyterian without adding that it was the neuropsychiatric unit, though he dropped his voice meaningfully, as if the tragedy involved Presbyterians.

It was my mother who said, "It's a psychiatric hospital."

She also told me that Michael thought his parents were Nazis, and that he'd been patrolling his house with a kitchen knife. The break was not orthopedic. Ruth had been unable to persuade Michael she was his mother and not a Nazi, locked herself in the bedroom, and called the police.

Somewhere in the course of the conversation, my father told the story of meeting Michael on Mereland. His guilt was such that the climax of the story was his getting into David Friedman's car to catch a train, implying that if only he'd stayed a little longer he might have saved Michael from his fate, though what his fate was remained unclear.

My father's voice was full of sorrow—for the world and the bad news in it, for Michael, for me, for himself and the neurological disorder that hung over him like a question mark. My mother was as upset as my father but she'd heard Michael's story from Ruth, who'd given her a glimpse of the terrible nature of his psychosis. The cooling note of restraint in my mother's voice wasn't a lack of sympathy for Michael; it was sympathy for his mother.

My mother had always found Ruth's incongruous coping laughter unnerving. Now she identified with her, and saw her as a figure of female vulnerability. My mother never stayed alone in our house or any house at night, afraid the killers from *In Cold Blood* would find her. The idea that someone could behave like an intruder in his own home—or mistake his own mother for an alien invader—was a whole new order of terror. Once, years before, Ruth had taken refuge on our patio after her husband had thrown a kitchen knife at one or another of the boys. The incident had not made much of an impression on my mother at the time, but now she was haunted by the memory of it, and by the image of a mother barricaded in her bedroom afraid of her own son, the gentlest man in the house.

My head was reeling when I got off the phone. I had to remind myself that Michael had not been in a car crash, though a feeling of physical calamity remained. I was unclear about what precisely had happened and even more uncertain about what it meant. My parents hadn't used scientific names, only called it a break, and hadn't mentioned a prognosis. Was it like the "19th Nervous Breakdown" the Rolling Stones sang about, which didn't sound so bad if only because eighteen breakdowns had come before it and more might lie ahead? Was it permanent like a broken back or could it heal like a broken arm, and wind up stronger at the break?

As soon as I got off the phone, I called the Laudors. I still knew the number by heart, though it had been years since I'd dialed it. Chuck answered in his booming way. I'd barely spoken to him since he'd informed my father that I'd robbed Michael of his editorial birthright and ought to resign the post, but he greeted me with gruff warmth and I felt a surge of affection for him.

Chuck told me that being at home had been hard for Michael with his brother back and Chuck himself on sabbatical wanting everyone out of the house. Michael had helped Danny move out, he said, but "couldn't manage it himself." Chuck had "hinted now was the time to vacate the premises." Michael, who'd already vacated the Ferbers' attic, didn't take the hint.

I appreciated Chuck's blunt manner but sensed he was holding something back. He was clearly heartbroken, though he didn't sound guilty or apologetic about his efforts at eviction, saying only, "Somehow this was a pressure on Michael."

The rejection letters Michael accumulated were also a pressure, Chuck said, adding with a flash of the old boastfulness that Michael had gotten personalized letters from editors and encouraging notes too. Still, they depressed Michael, who became increasingly paranoid. His delusions "included the family."

Chuck said "there was something else" he would tell me if we spoke again. Meanwhile, he encouraged me to call Michael, who was at Columbia Presbyterian in Washington Heights up on 168th Street in a locked ward. This was the first time I'd heard that terrible phrase. No phones in the rooms, just a pay phone in the corridor. Chuck gave me the number but told me not to call on Saturdays because Michael "might not answer the phone on Shabbat."

Since when did Michael observe the Sabbath? Chuck sighed and explained that Michael was experiencing growing "religiosity." Apparently a psychotic break could make you an observant Jew, a joke Michael would have appreciated had he not been its victim. Chuck sounded irritated and told me to steer clear of religious subjects altogether. Still, he hoped I would call.

Sometimes, Chuck said, the doctors gave Michael special drugs, and if he was "tuned-in," he would talk. The notion affected me almost as much as "locked ward." Michael had always been able to talk; the idea that he needed to be "tuned-in" was hard to imagine.

I dialed the number Chuck gave me, and was surprised to hear Michael's groggy voice, as if he'd been waiting by the pay phone and fallen asleep. I was afraid he wouldn't recognize me or want to talk—I'd been afraid he wouldn't be *able* to talk—but he knew me right away and sounded pleased in a weary way that I was on the phone. His voice was leaden and far off, but I felt the muffled intensity of his familiar presence.

"I've never been in prison before," he said ruefully when I asked how he was doing. The "day room" was full of noise and cigarette smoke, the TV on all the time. "I don't like smoky rooms with televisions," he told me, "but they say if you want to leave, you have to go there and interact."

It sounded bleak. Was there nothing else to do?

"Eight a.m. breakfast. Twelve p.m. lunch. Five p.m. dinner."

It was only after I'd laughed that I realized this wasn't deadpan humor, just deadpan delivery. Or *probably* just deadpan delivery. Disconcertingly, I wasn't sure.

Michael hadn't lost his old way of saying things, and I was still listening with ingrained expectations, even if his meaning was different. Could he still be ironic? Could he still tell a joke?

I wanted to apologize for laughing but didn't. I felt Michael's need to talk, to tell me things more than to converse. He was "tuned in," as Chuck put it, though to a different frequency from the one I was used to.

"Dr. Ferber says I have a delicate brain," he told me with a hint of pride that only enhanced the pathos of his abject situation. He didn't offer medical explanations so much as spiritual ones, infusing everything with the language of sin and repentance. His mannered, aphoristic style was repurposed for confession.

"I was greedy and arrogant," he said slowly, "and now I'm paranoid and not particularly up to mental par."

Michael wanted out of his prison but he also wanted to confess his crimes. He'd been "riding high on a certain presentation of myself," he said. Living at home, he'd entered into his parents' relationship too much. Along with "sponging off" his parents he'd "looted" his Brooklyn grandmother's apartment and expected his Connecticut grandparents to pay for law school.

I didn't ask about the looting, which seemed improbable, though Michael's uninflected, almost robotic tone seemed incapable of inventing anything. He sounded like someone who'd been given truth serum, or tortured into a confession. I could feel how hard he had to work to put sentences together as he alluded to "bizarre fears" and "not bizarre guilts."

"I've moved far from what was good in myself," Michael said, but added that he was now "in a slow process of healing."

It had all been what Michael called "a roller coaster ride." I caught myself thinking that he would never have used a cliché like that before, and was instantly embarrassed by the thought. Life wasn't a writing seminar. Maybe clichés were more valuable than original formulations, despite what I'd been raised to believe.

"You have to have a positive attitude," Michael said.

I agreed.

The novel he'd once talked about with such optimism he now described as a repository of wicked thoughts and bad words. He'd written 160 pages "before coming here," he told me, loaded with "stuff I thought would sell, stuff I'd held my nose at before." The plot involved the CIA, the Mossad, pederasty, a "seamy underworld" of French homosexuals, the torture of children, and Holocaust survivors working as secret agents.

The book was "a desecration of language, of survivors," he told me. Writing it was a sinful act requiring atonement; he'd burned it in the driveway of his parents' house. I could picture him bending over a smoking trash can the way he'd bent over the hood of his Fiat Spider, the tiny car he'd bought that never ran, squirting in lighter fluid and somberly stirring the sparks with a stick.

"I feel good I burned it," he said.

He didn't sound like he felt good, but his self-recriminating litany suggested there was something providential or at least logical about his suffering. His words had a gloomy hopefulness, as if by fitting into a larger pattern, his sins had a role to play. For the time being he wasn't supposed to write, but he'd been reading "the scriptures" a lot—Genesis, Exodus, *Sayings of the Fathers*. He wanted to dedicate himself to "making valuable words." This humble aspiration felt paradoxically boastful, the way his confession of arrogance seemed oddly like an assertion of the very thing he was renouncing.

"I want my words to be good," he told me. "Maybe even important."

It occurred to me that his confession over the phone was already part of his effort to make his words matter, and that he'd rehearsed it in his mind expecting me to call. He had more to say, and the last item was the most painful—at least for me.

"In the sixth or seventh grade," Michael said, "you and Cybele sat me on the stairs and told me I was chameleonlike."

"Oh God, Michael, I hope that hasn't risen to haunt you."

"No," he said, with painful sincerity, "it's risen to help me, to heal me. It's true. I have to find out who I really am."

I felt sick imagining that my adolescent indictment had stayed in his head all these years, feeding his guilt and playing a role, however small, in his unraveling. He sounded like his old self once removed, distant and intensified at the same time. Everything had a denatured familiarity, surreal and recognizable. My own speech, as in a dream, felt overheard not spoken, as if I were listening in on our conversation even though I was part of it.

But then Michael asked, as if we were having a perfectly ordinary conversation, what I was up to. Given all he was going through, I was touched that he would think to ask. I spared him my grad school limbo and told him about teaching English as a second language to Russian immigrants, which I was doing to supplement my fellowship, which did not go far enough in New York.

"I'm back where we started from," I said, meaning immigrant origins, huddled masses, *The Education of Hyman Kaplan*, which Michael had read aloud from in the *Herald* office.

"Good," he said. "That's very good."

He approved, the way he approved of my having a girlfriend who was studying to be a rabbi. I was being admitted into the sanctioned realm illness had carved out around him, just as I'd been admitted into his world when I moved to New Rochelle. Our common childhood was itself a sacred element arguing for my inclusion, even though his parents were barred by a flaming sword of paranoia.

The sight of his parents could still send him into a kung fu crouch in the hospital, arms raised for combat. Meanwhile my father, for all his guilt about abandoning Michael on Mereland, was one of the watchmen invisibly guarding him in the night.

I'd called half hoping Michael wouldn't come to the phone but heard myself asking if he wanted a visit. He was eager for one. When

I asked if there was anything I could bring him, he said, "I'm thinking of asking for tefillin but I don't know if that's because I'm really
discovering something or if it's just fake protection."

Tefillin are small black boxes with leather straps that traditional
Jews bind to the arm and position on the forehead between the eyes
during morning prayers. They contain passages of scripture on parch-
ment. I'd gotten a pair for my bar mitzvah and had put them on for
a brief while.

They're called "phylacteries" in English, a Greek word Michael
and I turned into "prophylacteries"—spiritual condoms—which we
found hilarious. Michael wasn't joking now; he was poised between
his old self and a new desire, uncertain if what he wanted was real.
This was my first glimpse of how hard he had to struggle to distinguish perceptions from symptoms in disguise. I'd often resented his
brash certitude, but his guileless insecurity was heartbreaking, like a
child handing over his money and asking, "What can I buy with this?"

Remembering Chuck's injunction to avoid religion, I suggested
holding off on the tefillin. I was also thinking about the dangerous
potential of long leather straps. Michael let it go but said, "I feel Judaism is mine. It's making me feel better. I only wish I knew more."

For years he'd teased me about my "old-world" proclivities and
pious devotions. This was no vindication. I regretted the loss of his
skeptical spirit and felt a creeping fear that we were becoming more
alike at the very moment I wanted our fates to remain as far apart
as possible. At the same time, I felt a strong familial pull as if we
were brothers and I had no choice.

We agreed I'd visit on the coming Tuesday. Michael recited the
visiting hours, which he knew by heart. I copied them into my notebook: one to five and six to eight. I gave him my phone number in
Manhattan and had to repeat each number very slowly.

"It's hard to work the pen right now," he said.

CHAPTER FIFTEEN

ENTANGLEMENT

I became terrified of him, for him, of the
nightmare which was becoming reality for
him. What would happen to Michael, and
would something similar happen to me, too?

—OLIVER SACKS, writing about his brother's
schizophrenia in *On the Move: A Life*

I still knew nothing about Michael's illness, which nobody had yet named and which was discussed more as an event than a disorder: something had happened and the police had been called. Michael himself spoke of being in prison, not a hospital.

He had referred to himself as paranoid, but wasn't everyone? "Just because you're paranoid doesn't mean they aren't after you" was a line from *Catch-22* I'd first heard from Michael but everyone said it, the way everyone said, "Don't trust anyone over thirty," even if they didn't say why. In high school, we'd read "The Paranoid Style in American Politics," by a historian who adapted a term from psychiatry to explain how "more or less normal people" deployed the language of conspiratorial fantasy.

Michael described his own paranoia as a punishment, but his explanations still had a way of sounding rational, or at least internally coherent, just as formerly his references to paranoia had been part of a generally knowing air.

At the same time, I knew something terrible had happened to

him. Your mother doesn't call the cops because you have a paranoid style or have fallen below "mental par."

For years I'd been unclear about what if anything remained of my friendship with Michael. The binding sympathy I'd felt on the phone had little to do with the current state of our friendship. It was the product of an essential attachment that overwhelmed me with emotion, though afterward doubt and competitiveness crept back in, mingling with affection and pity.

Michael had been the hare to my tortoise for so long that part of me still attributed to him all his old powers and motivations. Even now I half assumed he'd only stretched out for a nap and would be up and running again soon. He'd shake off whatever was bothering him, like Jack Nicholson in *Cuckoo's Nest* when he staggers onto the ward after his first bout with electroconvulsive therapy, pretending he's been zombified to fool his fellow patients before breaking into a broad grin.

On a separate page of my journal, I made a list of a few of the parallels of our lives, as if writing down the junior high newspaper (which he edited) and the high school paper (which I edited), the names of our cats, and our twinned acceptances (Telluride, Yale), would answer some essential question. For some reason, I used "him" and "me" instead of our names.

Was I laying out the overlapping aspects of our lives to remind myself of the connection, despite our drifting friendship, and strengthen my resolve to see him? Or was I trying to prove the opposite: that I wasn't like him, owed him nothing, and could walk away without guilt? Though the less I was like him, the more easily I could visit him without worrying I would contract his contagious fate.

The list wasn't chronological but ended back at the first week of high school: *tenth grade beaten up—flight*. The beating was mine; the flight was his. Now, however, Michael was down, and I promised myself I wouldn't fly. Under the place where I'd written down the visiting hours, I pledged to stand by him, to visit him and help him if I could.

His amorphous world of literary aspiration, rejection letters, and filler jobs had been a disaster. He'd already burned his first novel. Feeling the heat from his parents, he'd applied to law school but it was too late. Posters on our classroom walls had told us that castles in the air were fine places to live—all you had to do was put foundations under them—but neither Thoreau nor our teachers had told us how much harder it was to build down than up.

I still had a place in graduate school, but my academic identity was wearing as thin as Michael's power suits. The clock on my fellowship was winding down, and I'd already needed an outside job just to make up below-market rent. I shared his literary aspirations, and had come east partly to catch up. But catch up to what?

My mother warned me about getting drawn back into Michael's life merely out of guilt or pity. My sister, quoting her thesis adviser, said that anyone can have a psychotic break. But the later you had your break, the better the odds that your brain might regain some of its normal functioning and keep what it had learned.

It had not occurred to me that anything would be lost. I'd thought "break" was a euphemism. Now it sounded as accurate as a hammer-blow. But Michael was also lucky; he was almost twenty-five.

I called Michael to confirm my visit. An unfamiliar voice answered and vanished abruptly before I could give my name. I heard the voice shouting for Michael down the hallway with mirthless energy like a kid in a family of strangers. I waited and was about to hang up, when Michael came on the line sounding like a familiar record played at slow speed.

Michael formed his words carefully as he gave me the hospital address, which I was surprised he knew. Each word had a little space around it, but he seemed completely lucid. He made no mention of tefillin when I asked if there was anything I could bring, but he spoke with somber urgency about needing a camera, a tape recorder, and *The Literary Guide to the Bible* by Robert Alter and Frank Kermode.

Along with his familiar confidence, there was an unfamiliar undertow of agitation pulling everything he said in the opposite direction. He was assertive in the old way but diffident, too, full of solicitous regard to the point of apology for burdening me with his needs or even having them.

I wrote things down and said I'd try. After we hung up, I hunted for my portable cassette player and old instamatic camera, then went to Shakespeare & Co. on Broadway and bought *The Literary Guide to the Bible*, which was out in paperback.

It was only when I was describing to Mychal that evening how I would have to wrap the book in a brown paper bag inside my backpack to get it past the guards, and saw her expression change from sympathy to confusion to suppressed amusement, that I realized with mortification I'd been inside another person's delusion.

I couldn't even remember the reasons for the camera or the tape recorder, only vague intimations of danger and his need to document— what? In the moment it had all made a kind of sense. Michael's urgent, confiding tone was persuasive, and so were the specificity of his instructions, the brown paper bag, and above all the need for secrecy. Gullibility and Good Samaritan vanity (*I'm being so helpful!*) had done the rest, along with a lifetime of deferring to Michael's authority.

In the end I brought only the book. Mychal assured me that Chuck would not consider *The Literary Guide to the Bible* an inflammatory work, and neither would the security guard in the lobby. I knew that very well, and still I'd been prepared to mule a tranquilizing work of academic scholarship across the border like heroin. What did it say about me that I'd been so quick to believe "they" didn't want Bible scholarship on the premises?

Mychal dismissed my fears; I'd wanted to help a friend in crisis and had gotten caught up. She did wonder if I'd ever told Michael I'd taken a tutorial in the Hebrew Bible with Robert Alter, who taught at Berkeley and had asked me to index the very book Michael wanted.

I must have. Michael often grilled me about my classes, and the Bible study had been a bright spot. I'd sat with the professor in his office taking turns reading Genesis aloud, translating one sentence at a time, something even I could do because I knew the stories and the English was on the opposite page. It had even filled my ancient language requirement. But the index would have been a nightmare. Confronted with hundreds of manuscript pages to read, annotate, reread, and distill onto three-by-five cards organized by single-word categories, I realized it would take me a lifetime or longer. It was the sort of thing Michael would have done in a long night of NoDoz, but I'd turned it down, reinforcing my fear that I was unsuited for scholarship of any kind. Which is no doubt why I had told him I'd been asked, leaving out the rest. I felt like the butt of a practical joke I'd played on myself.

What was significant for Mychal was that Michael wanted something associated with me. I was thinking something else. I'd assumed madness was an overt abandonment of reason and logic, and though it was terrifying to contemplate, there was a satisfying clarity to this black-and-white simplicity. Either two plus two equaled four and you were sane, or it equaled five and you were nuts. But what about someone who was sane *some of the time*? What if it equaled four on some days and five on others? Or four and a half?

Was participating in someone else's madness also madness? Closing your eyes and taking ten steps on the sidewalk was not the same as being blind. But while I'd been thinking about how to smuggle *The Literary Guide to the Bible* into a psychiatric hospital, my eyes had been closed without my knowing it.

Mike Curtis had discovered the intermediate zone when Michael called to tell him he was in the hospital. Mike was in medical school in Cleveland and accustomed to getting depressed phone calls from New Rochelle late at night. Nobody had caller ID in those days, but if the phone rang after 11:00 p.m., he knew it would be Michael's exaggerated, mock-stoner drawl: "Heyyy, Mike, how's it going?"

The voice was never too gloomy for irony, or so ironic that you could dismiss the gloom, though it was tempting. Mike always responded with his own "Heyyy, Mike, I'm fine." Designated the cheerful one, he listened patiently as Michael unfurled his long Eeyore lament, which could take hours.

The night Michael phoned from the hospital, it was only after the "Heyyy, Mike" call-and-response that Michael said, "I'm on the tenth floor of Columbia Presbyterian. I'm on a locked ward." And still the conversation felt remarkably similar to all their other conversations, except that from time to time Michael would add, "But I know they're trying to kill me. I've got to get out of here."

Mike flew to New York the next day and found Michael in the neuropsychiatric unit where, despite the abnormal setting, he again sounded like his old self, until Michael informed his friend that the doctors were planning to operate on him without anesthesia to remove a portion of his brain.

No appeal Mike made to reason or logic had any influence on this delusion. Michael had always been dazzlingly logical and he still *almost* was, except that his formidable intellect was in the employ of an irrational idea. Mike flew back to medical school, his former roommate still convinced that he was going to be gruesomely lobotomized.

Michael had taken AP Physics in high school, a subject I'd managed to avoid altogether. In college I'd attempted Physics for Poets, but physics by any other name was still math. I'd withdrawn to avoid getting an F but came away with a few metaphorically memorable concepts, including the bizarre proposition that two particles could become "entangled" at the quantum level in such a way that anything you did to one particle would happen to the other. Even if they were banished to opposite ends of the universe, they behaved like reciprocating voodoo dolls or invisibly conjoined twins bound to each other's fate despite billions of light-years between them.

Quantum entanglement was so weird that Einstein called it "spooky actions at a distance," which sounded like a concept Philip K. Dick would have abbreviated as SAD in one of the science fiction stories Michael used to tell me that unraveled time, space, free will, and the mind. Of course, particles aren't people, they're not even Schrödinger's cat, another memorable concept, but quantum entanglement was supposed to be science. I couldn't help feeling, or fearing, that Michael and I were spookily attached.

The night before my visit, I had a nightmare and woke up gasping. The only part I remembered was that Michael and I were fighting. I was trying to get away, but Michael, hanging on, sank his teeth into my leg.

CHAPTER SIXTEEN

LOCKED WARD

Oh, do not ask, "What is it?"

Let us go and make our visit.

—T. S. Eliot, "The Love Song of J. Alfred Prufrock"

A taciturn attendant with a Caribbean accent and keys on a ring like a jailer in a movie unlocked the heavy door of Michael's ward. The door had a small thick window at head height for peering through. The attendant locked the door behind us, and I felt a clinch of claustrophobia. "Locked ward" was not a metaphor; someone with a key would have to let me out.

I followed the attendant. A woman was sobbing in Spanish, filling the whole corridor with a mood of lamentation. I saw her when I peered into a room as we passed, and a young woman, perhaps her daughter, who was being given oxygen, for what reason I couldn't imagine.

Michael was sitting rigidly on his bed, trancelike, the way he used to look meditating. There were several beds, but only Michael and his parents were in the room. The Laudors, sitting in chairs near the bed, leapt up when I came in. Ruth hugged me hard. Chuck shook my hand, explained that only two visitors were allowed in a patient's room at a time, and went out.

I sat down next to Ruth. Michael had opened his eyes and put on his glasses carefully but crookedly. His legs were drawn up, his

sneakers resting on the blanket. He looked thin and angular, all elbows, knees, and chin. He gave me a weary smile, and for once his
old man sigh fit his circumstances.

He sat up very straight like Buddha but he had a black cloth kippah on his head, of the type worn by Orthodox Jews. It floated on
his reddish hair as if it had been dropped there without his knowledge, softly dented and rising to an awkward point.

I unzipped my backpack and held out *The Literary Guide to the
Bible*. I hoped he wouldn't mind getting it so overtly or wonder where
the other items were. He took the book in his big hand with no hint
of our conversation from the day before.

"I have my checkbook here," was all he said.

As if speaking to a small child, Ruth said to Michael, "People
sometimes bring presents to hospitals when they visit."

Michael added the book to his night table, where there was a
King James Bible and several prayer books in Hebrew and English,
along with the remains of a braided loaf of challah in a bag.

Ruth excused herself to give us a chance to visit, she said. Michael
seemed marginally more relaxed with his parents out of the room,
but was apparently past thinking they were imposters. He was shifting uncomfortably on the bed, an occasional tremor running through
his body.

They were giving him drugs, he told me, but barely treating him
therapeutically. He felt like a television set with bad reception; nobody knew what to do except move the antenna around and bang on
one side and then the other hoping the picture would improve.

I felt or imagined the powerful medication trapping madness and
sanity together, masking and freeing him, in what proportion I could
not know. I was grateful for the small sane voice that made its way
out of the mask. Denatured as he sounded, there was something reassuring in the familiar way he had of narrating himself as if he'd always been an object of study.

Before he wound up in the hospital, he had applied to the top seven law schools in the country. They'd all accepted him, he said, though by then he was in the hospital and in no condition to do anything with the news. He asked Danny to reject all of them except Yale Law School, which he had his brother defer for a year.

It was, in a way, a typical Michael story. An embarrassment of riches; he had rejected the law schools, not the other way around. Except for the lost way he confessed that "at some level maybe I don't want to go. Subconsciously." Maybe, he said, "that's a reason I'm here."

I didn't ask what else he wanted to do. I didn't know what else he *could* do.

Michael, who had been shifting uncomfortably, said it was easier to walk than to sit. He worked his way carefully off the bed, and we went out into the corridor and walked up and down together. He moved slowly but talked more easily once we were in motion. He spoke again about his ill-fated attempt to nestle back inside his family and to become an artistic spirit free from "trapping identities."

He spoke again about balance, which was physical as well as psychological. He reminded me a little of my father, both the way he moved and what he said. His schoolyard bounce was gone; he seemed almost inanimate as he passed along the corridor, like a heavy sled hauled over snow. He carried himself with effortful stillness, cautiously erect as if his cloth kippah might blow off, or there was a whole stack of hats on his head, like the man in the children's book we'd grown up with who walks around yelling, "Caps for sale!" until he discovers that monkeys have stolen his wares.

When we came to a water fountain, Michael put his hand slowly on his head. It took energy and concentration for him to bend down and drink.

At one point he led me to a barred window that looked out over fire escapes, water towers, the windowless back ends of buildings exposed by demolition, things not meant to be seen.

"Look what's become of me," he said pitiably as if he were the view.

Even without bars it would have been a sad scene, despite the river and a cathedral of pale copper green that was really a power station. The strewn buildings and tangled highways had the random uncreated look of something shaken out of a Lego box.

Michael gazed out at the urban jumble, unless he was only seeing the bars, like the panther in the Rilke poem my father recited, and beyond the bars, no world. Keine Welt.

We resumed our walk. Whenever Michael got tired, we went back to his room and he'd climb onto his bed and stretch out his long legs without taking off his sneakers. One time, a nurse came in with a pill, something to control the side effects of the medication. Michael took it dutifully, tipping his head back like a long-necked bird swallowing a fish.

His birthday was about six weeks away, and I wondered if he would still be in the hospital, and if not, where would he be? Would Chuck let him come home? I didn't ask such questions, but Michael volunteered that he could leave whenever he wanted because he'd signed himself in. This ʃurprised me not only because he hated being there but also because of the dramatic story I'd heard about his arrival.

I knew nothing about commitment laws. It would not have occurred to me that someone marching around with a kitchen knife might *not* be considered a danger to himself or others. The psychiatrist Michael had been seeing on the Upper West Side before his hospitalization did not consider him violent. Michael had carried a knife, and slept with a baseball bat, because he thought his parents had been replaced by surgically altered Nazis who had murdered them and wanted to kill him. His psychiatrist considered that defensive behavior, not aggressive.

The doctors at Columbia Presbyterian believed he ought to be there. The longer they could keep him, the more time he would have to receive treatment and to heal, a process much slower than the temporary abatement of florid symptoms that medication provided. And he had been persuaded to stay, or was at least afraid to leave.

Michael told me he was worried that he wouldn't be able to pass a seventy-two-hour observation period, in which case he *would* wind up committed. Choosing to be in a place he did not want to be offered at least the illusion of freedom, which was preferable to the total loss of freedom he risked if he bolted and was committed against his will—even if he wound up in the same place he was in now. And he might wind up in a worse place, because Columbia Presbyterian was a private hospital that cost, he murmured, more than Yale.

Once when Michael and I went back to his room, a heavyset young man with pale hair was pacing in the middle of it. I was aware of a faint fecal odor mingled with cigarette smoke. Michael climbed onto his bed without acknowledging his roommate, who had stopped pacing and was watching us with a look of inner amusement and external affliction. The young man pointed abruptly at the rump of braided challah on Michael's bedside table and said with an odd laugh, "Give me some of that Jew bread."

Michael merely blinked at him.

When at last I had to go, Michael stood up laboriously and shook my hand. His formality, like his ineffectual grip, felt like an aspect of his altered state, but there was also something deeply familiar, an almost concentrated presence. I promised to come back soon. We decided that next time I came we'd study the Bible together.

"I'd like to think I'm learning something in here," Michael said.

I felt a great wave of heartache and raw relief when the door of the ward was locked behind me. Odysseus in the underworld, I thought, and instantly recoiled from my literary impulse.

Michael, his pacing roommate, and the patients I'd glimpsed in the smoky dayroom weren't ghosts, any more than I was Odysseus. The locked ward wasn't Hades or Ken Kesey's cuckoo's nest. It certainly wasn't the French village in *King of Hearts*, where war turned madness into sanity, or Frantz Fanon's Algeria, where war turned sanity into madness. It wasn't the attic in *Jane Eyre*, where Mr. Rochester shuts up his violent wife, a feminist symbol of sexuality, intelligence, and freedom punished by Victorian culture in *The Madwoman in the Attic*, even though she burns down the house.

Never had my education felt so inadequate. Metaphors wouldn't help me, and they sure as hell weren't helping Michael, who had burned his own novel in the driveway. The woman who brought him pills wasn't Nurse Ratched, and he wasn't Randle McMurphy, locked up for being a wiseass. He was in a hospital because he was ill.

Still, Michael wove himself symbolically into my thoughts. I saw him with his head religiously covered, walking through the corridor with slow rigidity, carrying himself like a glass of water full to the brim. And I saw him as he'd appeared in my dream, wild with fury. I tried to see him only as he was, but he was an image glimpsed in a dark mirror: a consequence, a warning, a danger.

Michael's mind had been a touchstone of high mental functioning and the measure of my own mind for a long time. He read faster, remembered more, and processed information more quickly. If Michael had cancer, I'm sure my own body would have felt more vulnerable, but easy identification with his illness would have been harder. Aberrant cells caused cancer; the causes of mental illness were murkier. Eminent researchers had attributed schizophrenia to parents, vitamin deficiency, and chemical imbalance all within the same short span.

At least "delicate brain," Jane Ferber's phrase, referred to a physical organ. But nobody said Michael had "brain disease." They said he had "mental illness," which stretched from claustrophobia to schizophrenia, blurring thought, language, and biology. It was, in the words of Rod Serling, whose hyper-enunciating narration Michael had mimicked with the same voice he used for Carl Sagan in *Cosmos* and Reform rabbis, "a dimension not only of *sight* and *sound* but of *mind*." How you escaped was anyone's guess, but the entrance was never far: "That's the signpost up ahead—your next stop, the Twilight Zone!"

Psychiatrists, insurance companies, the courts, and the culture all had their own definitions of mental illness. Freud began as a neurologist and detoured through hypnosis, nasal surgery, and cocaine before deciding that the brain worked symbolically and that talking was the key. His heirs forgot about the brain altogether, the way artists in the Middle Ages "forgot" what the body looked like until the Renaissance dug up enough naked statues to remind them. Remembering the brain was a slow business; neurologists led the charge—with an ice pick. Thorazine, discovered by a surgeon, came along just in time, but the contrast between crude instruments and delicate brains remained.

Michael had gotten sick amid the ruins of a demolished system. The wall dividing many things—including the asylum and the street—had come down while we were growing up. So had the distinction between severe mental illness and what Freud called "the psychopathology of everyday life." Psychiatry had been piecing itself together, but was Humpty-Dumpty sufficiently healed to put Michael together again too?

Michael phoned me from the hospital hallway with a request: he wanted me to take him outside the next time I came. He hated being confined indoors. All I had to do was phone up one of the psychiatrists at the hospital and arrange for a day pass. They didn't really want him leaving, he said, but if I agreed to accompany him off the premises, and bring him back, they couldn't refuse.

I could only imagine how cooped up Michael must feel, and how nice it would be to get out of the spectral hallway and overheated room he shared with Jew Bread, as I thought of his roommate, who seemed to have been selected by a psychiatric matching service with a sinister sense of humor. But whether it was my embarrassed memory of colluding with his paranoia the first time, or the heavy locked door and barred windows—obviously there for a reason—I hesitated.

Was the neighborhood even safe, especially for someone who, stiff with medication, moved geriatrically? Washington Heights was the crack capital of New York City; on the short walk from the subway to the hospital I'd seen "crews," as the newspapers called the kids in puffy coats clustered on side streets selling drugs. Michael was dismissive of any concerns about the neighborhood, which was home to old German Jewish refugees, Dominican immigrants, and doctors and nurses in training who lived near the hospital in high-rise beige monstrosities. Maybe he suspected me of pinning my fears of him on the crack epidemic, or my fears of the crack epidemic on him. I felt his irritation through his medication, illness, and the pay phone crackle, and promised to make the call.

The psychiatrist had just one question for me: If I took Michael outside and he bolted, would I feel comfortable calling the cops?

It hadn't occurred to me that Michael might run—or that he could. He seemed brittle to the point of breakable, not that I was going to tackle him even if I could catch him. Calling the cops in those days meant finding a phone booth and a quarter, or shouting, and by then Michael, who could hail a taxi even if he couldn't run, would be long gone.

Why would I have to call the cops anyway, why not the hospital or Michael's parents? Though I was beginning to realize that the police were used as a sort of unofficial armored ambulance service, I felt the doctor implying something more ominous. Michael "bolting" might not be the only danger.

I told the psychiatrist that I would not feel comfortable calling the cops.

In that case, he informed me, there was nothing more to say. I didn't argue.

Perhaps that was how Michael had been persuaded to sign himself in voluntarily, despite narrowed commitment laws that weren't likely to justify holding him, especially after he'd been stabilized with initial medication that, legally, he might also have refused.

Michael later admitted that he had already attempted to run away, determined to make it to the Iowa Writers' Workshop. He didn't say what he was planning to do when he got there, just that he'd managed to slip out the fire door and down the stairs, past the security desk and onto the street, where he had it in his head that he would be met by someone who would help him the rest of the way. It was a bitter cold day with snow still on the ground; he had no money, no friend appeared, and he did not get far before deciding to turn back. I wasn't sure if his escape was actual or itself a delusion, though he told it with a look of pained recollection.

I didn't need to know about the escape attempt to recognize that the doctor wanted to scare me away from taking Michael off hospital grounds. I didn't need scaring, and was feeling enmeshed in unwelcome ways.

I only hoped Michael wouldn't hold it against me. Perhaps he'd even forget, the way he forgot about the camera and the tape recorder, or at least never brought them up again. And we'd already arranged to study. I was bringing my fat Hebrew-English bible that I'd bought in Jerusalem and used at Berkeley.

I was looking forward to studying with Michael. His need for meaning wasn't literary or intellectual but urgent and electric. This was precisely why Chuck had warned me away from anything that might feed his "religiosity," but Michael had been "poring over scripture" on his own, and I had to think it would only be healthier for him to study with another person. It would give the visit a focus and might even feel familiar in that alien place.

Michael looked much as he had the last time I saw him, legs drawn up on the bed, angular, spiderlike. Chuck was with him; as before, he greeted me and said goodbye with the same handshake. Ruth wasn't there but Michael already had a visitor, a voluble classmate I'd never met who'd become a management consultant after graduation, like Michael, and was now in business school. He kept joking about making piles of money. Michael sat unblinking on the bed like a night animal waiting for night.

The money talk was somehow lewd, as it often was in the 1980s, and completely incongruous. The guy was addressing the Michael of a few years before, but he was so good-natured and eager to cheer Michael up that I had a hard time resenting him. He'd traveled out of his way to be there, and all his shoptalk was obviously intended to make Michael feel that his former world was waiting for him as soon as he got back on his feet. How could he know that Michael had seen the Bain secretary turn into a monster with long claws and vampire teeth? He obviously admired Michael and, when he heard we were planning to study, cut his own visit short so we'd have time.

I was pleased Michael remembered our plan. He also remembered his request to go outside, and was crestfallen when I told him I hadn't gotten the pass. I was vague about what had transpired on the phone, saying only that the doctor didn't think it was a good idea right now.

Michael said very little but I felt him withdrawing deeper into himself. When he did bring it up, it wasn't to reproach me, merely to lament his plight. But I was aware of the masked irritation I'd felt on the phone, which seemed to increase as the visit wore on.

He'd always had contempt for my inability to stand up to authority. Was that it?

Chuck, who had not been pleased when he saw my Bible, returned once Michael's classmate was gone. He seemed to feel about
our study plans the way I'd felt about the money talk; I'd brought a
red flag to wave at his son. I explained that we were just going to
read aloud from Genesis as I'd done in one of my classes. Michael
was wearing the kippah he'd had on when I visited the last time; I'd
brought my own and clipped it on, which seemed to annoy Chuck
even more.

He was a distressed father with a son who had fallen ill in a terrible and mysterious way. That it was not entirely mysterious may have
been even more distressing. It never occurred to me to associate Michael's illness with the stories he told about his grandmother, but there
was a history of psychotic disorders on Chuck's side of the family.
Chuck must have worried about how stacked the genetic deck was
against his son. Even if he did not discuss his mother's schizophrenia,
he had been raised by it.

Chuck had wandered off again by the time Michael and I had
set ourselves up in chairs with the Bible before us on the bed, which
we were using as a desk. It was Michael's Bible. He'd wanted to use
the King James Version he kept on his night table. I suggested we
begin at the beginning, but Michael shook his head. He wanted to
read Cain and Abel.

We took turns, reading a verse at a time out loud. It's always a
surprise how fast things happen in the Bible. We started with Adam
knowing his wife Eve, who "conceived, and bare Cain." In one of the
odder descriptions of motherhood, Eve said, "I have gotten a man
from the Lord."

We'd once have laughed at the somber-comic King James locutions the way we'd laughed at the instructions for the Holy
Hand Grenade—"three is the number thou shalt count, and the
number of the counting shall be three"—read aloud from Armaments,

chapter 2, in *Monty Python and the Holy Grail*. "Four thou shalt not count."

But Michael read soberly, without irony:

> And in process of time it came to pass, that Cain brought of the fruit of the ground an offering unto the Lord.
> And Abel, he also brought of the firstlings of his flock and of the fat thereof. And the Lord had respect unto Abel and to his offering.
> But unto Cain and to his offering he had not respect. And Cain was very wroth, and his countenance fell.

Michael had complained about the deterioration of his reading skills. I couldn't tell if he was reading slowly or just *speaking* slowly, which wasn't the same thing. We were sharing the book, and neither of us saw well enough to read without holding it up to our faces.

Michael asked the first question: "Why is Cain's sacrifice rejected?"

I knew he was going to ask that, because it is unanswerable and because I was thinking about it myself. I had little to offer beyond the banal basics; maybe Cain's fruits weren't the best, like Abel's "firstlings." Maybe the test wasn't his sacrifice but how he reacted to its rejection.

> And the Lord said unto Cain, Why art thou wroth? and why is thy countenance fallen?
> If thou doest well, shalt thou not be accepted? and if thou doest not well, sin lieth at the door. And unto thee shall be his desire and thou shalt rule over him.

Michael was stirred by this passage. It occurred to me that he had been studying it on his own. He talked about "the evil urge" and sin, sentiments that had surprised me the first time I'd called him. He was gripped by the concept of sin lying at the door, the coiled enemy. It wasn't what we were reading or saying but some larger force under the current of words that he was grasping for that I found moving and alarming.

Chuck came back after only ten minutes or so. Michael tried to get him to go out again. There were still days Michael wasn't persuaded that his parents were his parents; I didn't think this was one of them, but Michael spoke to his father with elaborate, burdensome considerateness, indirect to the point of meaninglessness and yet perfectly clear. Chuck was immune to his son's ornate importuning. He sat on the end of the bed and listened disapprovingly.

The story was quickly finished. I was struck by how sympathetic God was to Cain after he protests, "My punishment is greater than I can bear." Had I even understood that the "mark of Cain" was to protect Cain, not to punish him?

I had never identified with Cain before. But when God said, "The voice of thy brother's blood crieth unto me from the ground," I took it personally. Maybe it was Chuck's glowering disapproval, or Michael's disappointment about the day pass. The questioning from the psychiatrist had unsettled me. *Would* I call the cops if I had to? And if there were no cops?

I didn't want to be my brother's keeper. Even before I said goodbye, part of me was already on the far side of the heavy door, racing for home.

CHAPTER SEVENTEEN

MAKING ILLNESS A WEAPON

"France was once the name of a country: be
careful lest it become the name of a neurosis
in 1961."

—Jean-Paul Sartre, preface to Frantz Fanon's
The Wretched of the Earth

While I was at Berkeley, I hadn't really wondered why literary theories borrowed so heavily from the metaphors of mental illness, any more than I asked why ideas bottled in the bitter aftermath of France's Vichy collaboration, and flung like cobblestones in 1968 Paris, were humming through the air in the late 1980s. . . .

But after I visited Michael and saw his transformation for myself, it was no more possible to pretend that he was suffering from a "social construct" than it was to believe that his confusion and pain were the products of "discourse." I disliked the hospital, but even with its heavy locked door, I knew it wasn't a branch of the "carceral state" devised by a power-mad society to torment him, though that is what Michael thought when he was still in the grip of his illness.

Somehow, mental illness had become the indispensable elixir of literary theory, not just the vermouth but the gin, the olive, and the glass. *Madness and Civilization*, *The Anxiety of Influence*, *The Madwoman in the Attic*, and volume two of *Capitalism and Schizophrenia*, which appeared in English while I was at Berkeley and was the long-awaited companion to *Anti-Oedipus*—which had been translated in the late 1970s with a glowing preface by Foucault, who praised its recommendation that we "learn from the psychotic how to shake off the Oedipal yoke and the effects of power."

Was it because of Michael that I began to wonder why a literature seminar should sound like a public health conference conducted on the far side of the looking glass, and what effect that might have on public health as well as literature? At some point it became impossible to ignore the way a metaphorical version of mental illness had been institutionalized in academic life at the same moment that people who suffered from actual psychotic disorders were being released from hospitals and forgotten, as if the university and the asylum had organized a sort of exchange program.

Félix Guattari, co-author of *Capitalism and Schizophrenia*, had attempted to bring psychotic patients from his experimental clinic to Paris so they could take part in the violence of the 1968 strikes, and though he failed, students carrying placards that read SCHIZOPHRENICS ARE THE PROLETARIAT stormed the offices of Jean Delay, pioneer of the antipsychotic medication that, in its rough way, was helping Michael recover his life.

The real scandal at Guattari's experimental clinic—where he devised his theory that schizophrenia was a disease of capitalist culture and also an instrument of liberation that could bring it down—was the news that the clinic used antipsychotic medication and electroconvulsive therapy to complement its radically open and inclusive policies. For the metaphorical schizophrenia to do its theoretical job, the organic illness needed to remain quiet.

Frantz Fanon, who actually was a psychiatrist, described violence as a "cleansing force" with a healing property that "rids the colonized of their inferiority complex, of their passive despairing attitude." In

The Wretched of the Earth, he prescribed this violence not merely as a practical necessity in the fight for Algerian independence but an antidote to the psychic derangements of colonialism: "Such madness alone can deliver them from colonial oppression." Conventional psychiatry—designed to help people adapt to their environment—was not only impossible but undesirable, because "colonization in its very essence" creates psychiatric hospitals, and fills them with those it has driven mad.

But that was Fanon the intellectual theorist. Fanon the psychiatrist had trained at a progressive psychiatric hospital in central France that had served as a hub of the Resistance and subversively cared for its patients during the war at a time when French doctors, collaborating with the Nazis, viewed mentally ill patients as "life unworthy of life," a policy that led to forty thousand deaths. Fanon, himself a hero of the Resistance, brought that humane spirit to Algeria, where he served as the director of a psychiatric hospital that cared for both colonial settlers and native Algerians. He limited the use of restraints, created social clubs, and allowed stabilized patients to sleep at home, thanks to the antipsychotic medication recently discovered in France, and the electroconvulsive therapy developed in Italy during the war, therapies he continued to use even after he'd fled to Tunisia to continue fighting for Algerian independence.

Fanon left that psychiatry out of his book, the way the sociologist Erving Goffman left out the reforms that would have complicated his contention in *Asylums* that mental hospitals caused the illnesses they'd been created to alleviate. Published the same year as *The Wretched of the Earth*, Goffman's *Asylums* ignored the patient-edited publications, dances, and sports activities he himself organized as assistant athletic director, the cover he adopted for his research at St. Elizabeths Hospital in the 1950s, when he worked for the National Institute of Mental Health. If you identify psychiatric hospitals as "total institutions," like prisons and concentration camps, it made sense to leave out the tennis lesson you gave, not to mention the association of former patients created to help a growing population of discharged patients transition to life outside the hospital.

For the same reason, perhaps, Foucault turned the eighteenth-century psychiatrist Philippe Pinel—a liberal reformer who struck the chains from the mental patients he cared for at the Salpêtrière hospital in Paris—into a villain in *Madness and Civilization*. For Foucault, improving conditions was a sinister act, extending the life of the hospital, the concept of mental illness, and the authority of the doctor whose liberalizing gesture, the very symbol of humane psychiatry, only made it harder to tear down the whole structure.

What hope was there for Michael in this inverted world where causes were cures, madness bestowed mental health, and murder restored innocence? In his anointing preface to *The Wretched of the Earth*, Jean-Paul Sartre sounded like one more psychiatrist discussing the progress of a repressed patient, who happened to be the world. Because "murderous rampage is the collective unconscious of the colonized," Sartre explained, bloody revolution would have the effect of a successful psychoanalysis: "Once their rage explodes, they recover their lost coherence, they experience self-knowledge through reconstruction of themselves."

Thanks to Freud, the sick man of Europe *was* Europe; thanks to Marx, the cure was revolution. According to Sartre, only when Europeans became like Algerians—trampled, humiliated, self-hating, and sufficiently deranged to "finally unleash this new violence" on their own society—would they decolonize themselves from the inside out and find peace.

The curse of Greek tragedy, "whom the gods would destroy, they first make mad," was erased. Now, madness was the first step to recovery, even if it sounded more like philosopher-assisted suicide.

Michael had taught me what I knew about Sartre's existentialism: that there was no God, life was meaningless, death was absurd, but you were still free "to act," and the more you acted, the freer you were as long as you took responsibility for your actions. Sartre was as obsessed with authenticity as Holden Caulfield was with "phonies," but I was unclear how you could tell what was real and what was phony if the world was "completely absurd." For Michael, who used the word "absurd" the way he shrugged, as a kind of hat tip to the universe, existentialism was a consoling philosophy that encouraged a manly morality, like the poem he recited about being "the master of my fate."

He'd excavated the small trove of existentialist classics on my father's shelf—his father had a similar collection—and recommended *Nausea*, which he wryly noted was my area of expertise. I never read *Nausea*, but I did keep a copy of *No Exit* next to my bed and would occasionally say, "Hell is other people," in a knowing voice, although I was intensely lonely and didn't mean it.

At Michael's urging, I'd read Camus's *The Stranger*, which he'd written about for his Telluride application, and felt only blank anxiety briefly relieved by the erotic splashing of the deadpan narrator and his girlfriend, and the perverse release of the murder once it came.

But Camus had decided that the absurdity of life paled in the face of radical evil and devoted himself to the French Resistance, though limited by tuberculosis to a supporting role. Sartre, his co-editor at *Combat*, was uncomfortable with a supporting role in the great moral conflict and redefined resistance to make talking and writing its primary expression: "Our job was to tell all the French, we will not be ruled by Germans. That was the job of the resistance, not just a few more trains or bridges blown up here or there."

This was discourse at its finest. Although the French *were* ruled by Germans and Sartre accepted a teaching position vacated by a deported Jew, and spent a lot of time flattering the Nazi officials who stamped *No Exit* with the swastika of approval, he was still, in his way, a hero of the Resistance. Sartre had written *No Exit*, about how being locked up in the afterlife with people you can't stand, including yourself, is a fate worse than death, at the very moment members of the French Resistance were being physically tortured.

French thought, which was universal thought—or at least university thought—was born to handle the contradictions of collaboration and a great deal more. Milton's Satan might claim that "the mind is its own place, and in itself can make a Heaven of Hell, a Hell of Heaven," but even he knows that's a lie: "Which way I fly is Hell; myself am Hell." Sartre's dialectical powers somehow made cafe society a hell worse than Nazi torture and simultaneously a form of brave resistance.

A decade after introducing Europe to *The Wretched of the Earth*, Sartre wrote the preface to a booklet called *Turn Illness into a Weapon*, far less famous than Fanon's book but even more prophetic. The authors were members of the Socialist Patients' Collective, whose slogans were "Kill, kill, kill for inner peace" and "Bomb, bomb, bomb for mental health." Sartre's preface was written in the form of a letter addressed to the collective: "Dear Comrades! Make illness a weapon!"

The group's founder, a German psychiatrist named Wolfgang Huber, believed that capitalism was making his patients ill and that the only cure was revolution. His motto was "Crazies, to arms!"

Huber, described as a "psychiatrist guru" by Jane Kramer in *Europeans*, as well as "a kind of Leninist R. D. Laing," created the collective while working at the University of Heidelberg's psychiatric-neurological clinic in 1970. When the university fired him, his student-patients occupied a portion of the university and threatened both mass suicide and violence, a persuasive tactic in those days.

The university reinstated Dr. Huber, giving him extra space in the university clinic. To group therapy, hashish, and the study of dialectical materialism, Huber added workshops in martial arts and explosives. When one of his patients jumped to her death because she "did not get along with Marx and Lenin," as she wrote in her suicide note, Dr. Huber blamed the university and declared all-out war.

The members of the collective had read *The Wretched of the Earth* as a mental health handbook and referenced it in their manifesto, exaggerating its claims about the salutary benefits of violence: "Not only did psychiatric symptoms clear up for the freedom fighters but also seemingly chronic physical ailments disappeared, such as spinal disc disease, gastric ulcers, muscle spasms, etc."

By the time *Turn Illness into a Weapon* was published in 1972, Wolfgang Huber and several members of his collective had been arrested for acts of terrorism. But Sartre urged the members of the Patients' Collective not to be deterred by "silly arrest charges," and many were not. They joined the terrorist group known as the Red Army Faction, also called the Baader-Meinhof Group, whose cofounder, Ulrike Meinhof, had started out as a radical journalist and anti-psychiatry advocate. When the Popular Front for the Liberation of Palestine hijacked Lufthansa Flight 181 in 1977, they demanded the release of imprisoned members of the Red Army Faction, though by then Ulrike Meinhof had committed suicide in prison.

I watched the Lufthansa hijacking unfold live in 1977 because it kept interrupting the Yankees' World Series against the Los Angeles Dodgers. My fourteen-year-old self would have been amazed to learn that although the hijackers were killed by German commandos, I would meet their ghosts in graduate school, where illness would remain a weapon even for those who did not understand that was how they were treating it or why.

Following the hijacking, Sartre, Deleuze, Guattari, Foucault, and other intellectuals tried to prevent the extradition to Germany of a member of the Red Army Faction from France.

If someone had read aloud Wolfgang Huber's observation: "For the patient there is only one programmatic way to combat their illness—namely the dissolution of our pathogenic, corporate-based, patriarchal society," and told me it was the remark of a critical theorist, I would not have batted an eye.

CHAPTER EIGHTEEN

UNDERCLASS

When you see the suffering it brings, you
have to be mad, blind or a coward to resign
yourself to the plague.

—ALBERT CAMUS, *The Plague*

Michael spent eight months in the locked ward at Columbia Presbyterian. If his family hadn't coerced him into signing himself in of his own volition, because they understood that his volition was not his own, he might have been released long before—assuming he'd been admitted in the first place. His long stay had given his doctors time to find the least incapacitating dose of the powerful drugs that were supposed to have eliminated mental hospitals years before. Though nobody had figured out in the thirty years since antipsychotic medication had been introduced precisely how or why they worked, their effects, which could differ wildly from person to person, were easily observed.

Michael still likened psychiatric intervention to whacking a TV set to fix a fuzzy picture, but his clumsy medication had been calibrated carefully enough that he was no longer convinced Mengele was preparing to remove his brain without anesthesia. He had his suspicions, but had stopped trying to bash his skull against the sink in a preemptive effort to destroy his brain before Nazi doctors strapped him down and did it for him. Now when hallucinations came calling,

Michael could often recognize them for what they were and "change the channel," as he put it, or at least split the screen as if he really were a television set.

Mainstream psychiatry had awakened from its long psychoanalytic slumber and accepted the biological dimension of schizophrenia, even if nobody could point to it on a map. This didn't make emotional factors irrelevant, but it was no longer respectable to say that bad parents *caused* the disease. There had never been any evidence for that conclusion, only expert consensus, but now that had broken down. Still, it was one thing to know that schizophrenia was an organic brain disease, something else entirely to understand where it came from or how to make it go away.

The same might be said for psychiatric institutions. It was one thing to recognize the terrible toll they could take on the people inside them, and that, thanks in part to new medications, a majority of people with schizophrenia no longer needed to live there. It was something else to know what could replace the state system without destroying the idea of asylum that had given rise to it in the first place, or harming the people the system had been created to help. Hardest of all was to realize that the answers of a moment could not substitute for the slow, hard, complicated, and imperfect work of providing daily practical care for patients whose rights had finally been recognized but whose illness could itself seem like a violation of their reason and will.

In addition to my solo visits, I'd gone with Greg Morrison, who had driven us in his tiny red teacher's car to hilly Washington Heights to visit Michael. Greg had shaved off his Reagan protest beard. The Ray Gun, who had terrified us in high school, had not destroyed the country or the world.

He had, however, done less than nothing for people with schizophrenia. Left and right often met at the gates of the asylum. As governor of California in the 1960s, Reagan had tried to close all the state hospitals to save money, while utopian optimists rode roughshod

over the reality of mental illness, its victims, and the system that cared
for them. In the 1980s, rugged individualists backed up an SUV over
what remained. Michael left the hospital to live among the ruins of
multiple systems.

Books had begun appearing in the '80s not only to reckon with
the consequences of what was widely known as deinstitutionalization
but to help families like Michael's care for relatives released from the
system. One of the earliest guides was *Surviving Schizophrenia: A Family Manual*, first published in 1983 by the psychiatrist E. Fuller Torrey, who had been an undergraduate at Princeton in the late 1950s
when his mother called to say that his younger sister was lying in the
front yard shouting that the British were coming. He had decided to
become a psychiatrist while sitting beside his mother, listening to a
specialist at Massachusetts General explain that his sister's schizophrenia had been caused by the death of his father. Others blamed
it on his mother's parenting style.

Surviving Schizophrenia helped readers separate the myths and
facts of an illness about which a great deal remained unknown and
nothing was simple, including the fact that it runs in families but is
not inherited.

Having a close relative with schizophrenia was a risk factor, but
just one of many. While emphasizing how little predictive power the
numbers had, Torrey did provide a chart showing that having a mother
with schizophrenia had increased the odds of Michael's father getting the disease to somewhere between 9 and 13 percent. The odds
of getting the disease were slightly lower if your father had it, which
meant, among other things, that Michael might yet have children
without undue fear.

It was generally agreed that an average person has a 1 percent chance
of getting the disease—a figure grotesquely affirmed in postwar Germany where, despite the extermination of the hospitalized schizo-

phrenic population, the percentage of people with schizophrenia once again matched the prewar percentage.

Even if both your parents had schizophrenia, the increased risk of getting the disease was estimated at 36 percent, which gave you a better than 60 percent chance of *not* getting it. As the son of an economist, and as an economics major himself, Michael knew how easily distorted statistics could be, so while you could say that smoking pot doubled your chances of getting schizophrenia, you could also say that it moved you from a 1 percent chance of getting the disease to a 2 percent chance, all things being equal, though for Michael all things had not been equal. You could also say that having a grandmother with schizophrenia quadrupled Michael's chances of getting the disease, or that it had given him a 4 percent chance. And yet Michael did have schizophrenia.

There was no known cure, but 25 percent of people diagnosed with schizophrenia recovered completely within the first two years, a surprising and hopeful statistic often drowned out by the dread sound of the diagnosis. And though the percentage of people achieving a full recovery went down in studies that included only people whose symptoms lasted six months or longer—because short-term psychosis can mimic schizophrenia—a sizable percentage of people fitting the narrowest definition of the disease still experienced total remission. Unfortunately, that population did not share its secrets.

Those who recover completely, according to Torrey, get better "whether they are treated with antipsychotic medication, wheat germ oil, Tibetan psychic healing, psychoanalysis, or yellow jellybeans." No wonder so many bogus remedies were mistaken for successful ones in the past. Perhaps 25 percent of patients twirled at sickening speed in the spinning chair of Benjamin Rush, a founding father of American psychiatry, as well as a signer of the Declaration of Independence, went home praising the miracle of modern science. In reality, neither the chair nor the explosive emetic the doctor called "Rush's Thunderbolts" worked any better than discussions of buried sexual conflict two hundred years later.

Michael was in the hospital for eight months, and if you included the murky "prodromal" phase he'd spent in the narrowing vortex of expanding delusions, he'd been sick a lot longer. How long, nobody could say. Warning a fellow TASPer at seventeen to be careful his girlfriend didn't eat him might have been an adolescent joke however somberly delivered; and the story Michael had written in high school about a precocious boy murdered by a malignant darkness hiding in the wind might have been an innocent stab at science fiction. But four years had passed since Michael had watched the Bain secretary reach for him with clawed hands and bloody teeth. He'd been fighting a secret war for years.

Though Michael's break had not been sudden, he was twenty-four when it finally came, which, according to Michael, who also read about his illness, had given his brain plenty of time to bank knowledge and experiences that he could draw on now, like a federally insured savings account.

Michael would have to continue taking antipsychotic medication, which cured no one but helped many, though 15 percent of people with schizophrenia were, according to Torrey, "treatment-resistant." This meant that medication did not help them, not that they resisted taking it. *That* percentage was much higher than 15 percent, in part because the conviction you weren't sick was often an aspect of the illness, especially at times of acute psychosis. Torrey referred to this "not knowing" as anosognosia.

I'd never seen Michael in the full throes of psychosis, but it wasn't hard to see how anosognosia had made his illness an artfully knotted rope binding him tighter the more he struggled against it. It was easy to say that Michael had lost his mind, but his mind was the only instrument he had for locating what he'd lost. Knowing and not knowing were gray areas to begin with, shot through with ignorance and denial. My father said he would only join a support group for people who *might* have Parkinson's disease, a joke he was perfectly serious about—though he did take the medication that helped raise the dopamine that his body no longer produced in sufficient amounts.

Before Michael's psychotic break tipped the balance one way, and medication tipped it back the other, he had seemed to know and not know what was happening to him—a state strangely mirrored by those around him, who had also recognized and ignored his illness by turns. I'd experienced for myself how rational his reasoning manner made unreasonable things appear. Ruth and Chuck had helped Michael install debugging devices on his phone, and by the time they realized they'd been played by his delusions, he'd reclassified them as double agents. His outlandish conclusions rhymed so logically in his mind with his suspicions that the thought of plastic surgery for replacement people seemed irrefutable. He was like someone using beautiful penmanship to write gibberish and deciding that anyone who couldn't read it must be illiterate.

And yet Jane Ferber had been able to tell Michael that the things he was talking about in her house were not real, and because he admired and trusted her, and was not yet in the grip of full-blown psychosis, he had gone to the psychiatrist she recommended and moved back home. And though home is where he decided his parents had been replaced by murderous counterfeits, the counterfeit Chuck had managed to persuade his son—by showing him his appendix scar, according to Michael—that he *was* his real father, at least for a time. Chuck had even persuaded Michael that his best chance of freedom was in the hospital that Michael called a prison.

Paradox was as much an aspect of his recovery as it had been of his descent into illness. Despite grand delusions and paranoid terror, Michael had submitted to a locked facility where every doctor was a potential Nazi, and every orderly with a key, and even the janitor mopping the floor, seemed to know who he was better than he knew himself. He swallowed denaturing drugs to keep denaturing delusions at bay, slowly getting better by feeling worse. His reward for all this obedience was a dawning awareness of how changed he was from the person he'd been, and a growing fear that he might never go back to being himself again.

Michael's madness, woven out of fragments of sanity, had a weird vitality; his recovery, on the other hand, seemed full of the pain of sickness. The fragile sanity he left the hospital with felt like an aspect of his illness, a force running counter to the main valence of his mind. The more his head cleared, the more alienated he appeared to be not only from psychosis but from his natural self, so that I sometimes felt his medicated lucidity was just a guest inside his schizophrenia, which had not, after all, gone away. Everyone said insight was the key, but the more insight Michael got, the sadder and lonelier and angrier he became.

It was easier to visit him in the hospital at the height of his illness than to encounter him on the street struggling through this intermediate existence. I wanted to think of illness and recovery as two clear, diametrically opposed states. Michael challenged that. Perhaps that was why *Surviving Schizophrenia* encouraged an unsentimental recognition of all that was known of the disease, beginning with the fact that it *was* a disease. For Torrey, this was the road to sympathy and support: "As we come to understand it, the face of madness slowly changes before us from one of terror to one of sadness. For the sufferer, this is a significant change."

I felt that sadness when I saw Michael. His slowed speech, stiff formality, and dark suit, a hand-me-down from his former self, made me think of an undertaker in an old movie. I must have understood at some level that he was really a mourner, grieving for the part of himself that had been his greatest pride, a loss so vast that I did my best to ignore it. I felt sympathy, aversion, affection, and fear in unfamiliar and shifting combinations. His collar was half-up and half-down. I wanted to smooth it all down for him, or lift up the other half, but did neither.

He was poor, he told me. Not bohemian poor or artist poor, just poor. He had no job and no prospects, though now that he was out of the hospital, he qualified for public assistance. That in fact is what made him feel poor. He received something called Supplemental Security Income for the Aged, Blind, and Disabled, commonly referred to as SSI, a modification of Roosevelt's Social Security Act of 1935. The original Social Security Act had been amended twenty years after its passage to include physically disabled people fifty and older; that had been amended under Nixon to allow people of any age to receive Social Security if they were unable to work for any reason, including mental disability.

Michael's SSI payments in turn qualified him for Medicaid, an emendation of the Social Security Act in the 1960s that provided healthcare for the poor. Roosevelt, Eisenhower, Johnson, and Nixon had all contributed to his support, though as governor of California, Reagan had denounced the "faceless mass waiting for a handout" and as president had tried to thin the disability rolls when he first came into office, hoping to save the country a projected $3.5 billion by 1985. An outcry had reversed his decision.

Michael felt not only poor but invisible. Bureaucratically he was bundled in with children, pregnant women, the old, the blind, the poor, the mentally impaired, and the unemployed. Technically, he was not on welfare but a modified form of Social Security, a point of pride though he talked with horror about going to the welfare office in downtown White Plains to fix some small clerical screwup and waiting on long lines with the down-and-out who tried to bum cigarettes off him.

The welfare office made the DMV look like a Swiss bank, and though he might once have savored this glimpse of the bottom, it wasn't a glimpse, and it wasn't the bottom but the floor below. He was really there among "the underclass" we'd heard about at our dinner tables, a somber euphemism for people who would never climb out of poverty and dispossession, who were the most abused and the most dangerous, the most in need of help and the hardest to reach.

Michael hated the welfare office, which epitomized everything he felt had gone wrong with his life. He had to navigate its stygian labyrinths just to fix an insignificant clerical error requiring a form that could only be obtained by waiting on a *different* line from the one he'd been directed to, unless he'd misheard the directions through what he called the cotton wool of medication padding his brain, as sometimes happened. The woman behind the teller's window was immune to his charm, perhaps because he'd lost it or because he was poor or white or mentally ill, he didn't know. He didn't blame her, he said with condemning sympathy; he knew she was underpaid and overwhelmed. His bitterness came from having to rely on underpaid, overwhelmed people who didn't care that he had gone to Yale or worked at Bain and who, like everyone else, had power over him. When he saw her lips moving on the far side of the glass, even if she was only telling him the code of the correct form, or which line to wait on to get it, what he heard was "fuck you please die, fuck you please die" over and over.

He had awakened from a nightmare of illness only to find himself standing with people he would instinctively have championed, but he was not there as a champion and it was too close for comfort, too wounding and disorienting to be on the wrong line. And it had to be the wrong line. He needed there to be something separating him from them, just as I needed there to be something separating him from me.

CHAPTER NINETEEN

HALFWAY

What could Limbo have been, man?

—George Carlin, *Class Clown*

I sometimes saw Michael on Mereland Road, even though he wasn't living there but was visiting like me. He had moved into a halfway house in White Plains called Futura House. I wasn't sure what a halfway house was, though my father said it in a hushed tone as if protecting someone in earshot from shame.

Suburbs didn't like halfway houses or group homes, and New York suburbs had been very successful at excluding them. It was only after the passage of a 1978 law sponsored by New York state senator Frank Padavan, a Republican whose Queens district included Creedmoor Psychiatric Center, that things began to change. The Padavan Law, passed on its third try, made it harder to exploit zoning laws to exclude small groups of people whose modest needs and common struggles brought them together under one roof even though they weren't a single family.

For Michael, Futura House was like Limbo in the George Carlin routine we loved as kids, the place the church used to store the souls of unbaptized babies too young to be blamed but still not allowed to see God: "Whip 'em into *Limbo*!"

We'd congratulated ourselves that "our" afterlife didn't have a punitive tracking system like those sorry Catholic kids who blamed us for killing Christ, as we knew from Lenny Bruce. In addition to hell, they had to worry about purgatory—"as bad as hell but you knew you were going home, man"—and even this celestial ministorage for babies. Michael pronounced it the way Carlin did, a spooky echo bouncing off distant rocks: *Limb*-b-o-o-o.

Everything Michael found funny about Limbo he hated about the halfway house, starting with the fact that he had to be there at all. He was like someone bumped back to the starting square of a board game he'd been close to winning; he could not get excited about rolling double sixes when his turn came around at last.

Futura House wasn't even a house; it was two apartments, one for men and one for women, on two floors of a building in a nondescript residential neighborhood in White Plains. Each apartment had room for ten residents, who slept two or three to a bedroom and shared the living and dining area and the communal kitchen. Every night a different resident, with help from a counselor, prepared dinner for the whole group, which was eaten communally at a long table. Social workers were present twenty-four hours a day. Each resident was assigned a counselor who served as a troubleshooter, confidant, mentor, and minder.

Michael's mother, who worked at the state Office of Mental Retardation and Developmental Disabilities, said Michael had been lucky to get into a halfway house, where there were far fewer places than people, and the intake process was tougher than Yale or Bain.

Futura House was not like home where—as my mother liked to say, quoting Robert Frost—when you have to go there, they have to take you in. Michael's hospital team had recommended him, and the director of Futura House had studied his unvarnished medical transcripts, along with his education and work history, after which he was interviewed alone, in a group, and with his family. He'd met the staff, toured the apartment, and eaten a meal with the residents, who discussed him afterward at one of their meetings, debating his compatibility.

All the residents had been hospitalized with severe mental illness; some were also battling addiction and faced a double challenge. They were all expected to avoid recreational drugs, take prescribed medication, and participate in regular meetings where, coached by counselors, they offered encouragement or called on each other to account for hogging the television, neglecting chores, neglecting themselves, or engaging in insensitive or disruptive behavior that might be a sign of deeper trouble.

They were there to recover the confidence that illness had stolen, and cultivate the self-care and coping skills that would help them move on. Michael thought one or two looked like they might not make it out of the building if someone yelled "Fire," a minimum requirement for living in a group home.

He did, however, meet a shy, slender young woman he liked, with pale blond hair, who lived on the women's floor directly below him. She had suffered a psychotic break while at college and was hoping, eventually, to go back.

They went to the same day hospital, which was run by St. Vincent's Hospital in nearby Harrison. St. Vincent's had a locked ward for those who might need it, but the day hospital let you come and go for medication maintenance, multiple forms of therapy, and workshops devoted to vocational skills Michael felt were beneath him in middle school.

Most of Michael's Supplemental Security Income check went straight to the halfway house, leaving him with about seventy-two dollars a month for living expenses. But because individuals could collect SSI payments from the federal government only if they were *not* in a state hospital, and because state hospitals had been excluded from Medicaid, the law of unintended consequences had turned federal entitlements into an engine of deinstitutionalization that did more to empty hospitals than any lofty plan for community care, though they did nothing for creating an alternative system.

Federal benefits had been excluded from state hospitals in part to recognize the authority of the states but quickly became an incentive for states to off-load costly patients who would be eligible for federal funding only once they were outside asylum walls. The old went first, transferred en masse into private nursing homes where they qualified for Medicaid and Medicare. This wasn't deinstitutionalization, as is now understood, but reinstitutionalization, sometimes referred to as "trans-institutionalization."

Private nursing homes made a killing, filling beds with old people who were unlikely to recover and bring lawsuits or write accusatory memoirs, though their neglect did attract spectacular attention once conditions rivaling the worst of the state hospitals reached a critical mass.

Discovery could take a long time because the federal government paying reimbursements was far away, the homes were private, and the states, cut out of the loop, felt little responsibility to investigate. Still, I remember my father's outrage and shame in the 1970s when an Orthodox rabbi who owned what was called "a chain" of nursing homes, as if they were fried chicken franchises, was found guilty of Medicaid fraud, and stories of old people lying in piss and shit were aired on nightly news.

What Medicaid allowed with the destitute elderly, SSI payments allowed with everyone else. The squalid board-and-care homes that Elizabeth Ferber had visited with her father were privately operated by owners who took in former patients as boarders, like foster children but without oversight, in exchange for their SSI checks. Often therapy aides at state hospitals would take in the patients that the hospitals released, reconstituting for private profit a miniature version of the wards they had worked on.

Former patients might be undernourished, unmedicated, under-dressed, and left without heat in the winter, but they were also free citizens spending their money as they chose, as a former physical therapist from Creedmoor put it in the *New York Daily News*, refer-ring to three ex-patients who had come with her house when she bought it from a therapy aide. The residents, all unmedicated, turned over their Supplemental Security Income checks to her, and she no longer worked at Creedmoor.

Money had replaced community mental healthcare the way med-ication had replaced state hospitals. Medication did not go looking for those who resisted taking it, and money could not administer itself. Neither came with counseling or support. The SSI checks Michael received, and the Medicaid reimbursements he was eligible for, did not create a caring community or even an indifferent one. Neverthe-less, checks and pills were what remained of a grand promise, the ingredients of a mental healthcare system that had never been baked but were handed out like flour and yeast in separate packets to starv-ing people.

Unlike the early wave of released patients who had spent many months if not years in the hospital, and who transitioned more smoothly to homes of one sort or another, the present generation were often released quickly, before they had been stabilized. Futura House tried to fill this gap. Its directors worked overtime scouting apart-ments, sweet-talking landlords, fighting zoning laws, and fundrais-ing to make up shortfalls in the operating costs that remained even after grants, state money, and the residents' SSI checks. In an effort to make the White Plains apartments as much like a home as pos-sible, they bought matching dishes and silverware and urged residents to rearrange the furniture—after a discussion and vote—to person-alize the place. They emphasized the ceremonial importance of giving each new resident a key, which symbolized "the restoration of freedom and independence."

Michael found the whole place a shabby reminder that he was a prisoner of other people's taste, thrift, rules, and low expectations. With or without a front door key, he had to be out of the apartment from nine in the morning until four in the afternoon, a rule intended to encourage outside activity that made it impossible for him to sleep late. Someone was always watching.

He had always been fiercely self-reliant, but at twenty-five he was dependent on medications with geriatric side effects, on parents who had celebrated his precocity and encouraged his independence—which is why they'd been trying to get him out of the house shortly before his breakdown—and now on the staff of Futura House. He heaped scorn on the director, a middle-aged social worker named Sylvia he blamed for preventing him from sleeping with his girlfriend. This was not strictly the case, though in keeping with policy, he was encouraged to go elsewhere for "the physical part" of his relationship for the sake of residents prone to feelings of rejection and shame.

The final straw came when the residents of the men's and women's floors were brought together for a state-mandated demonstration of condom use. This seemed the height of hypocrisy to Michael, who asked at the demonstration if he had to wear a condom on his tongue since he wanted to go down on his girlfriend. Though his shy girlfriend had shrunk away in mortification, he looked back on the event with satisfaction as a heroic stand taken against tyranny.

When Michael was in the hospital, his illness had been omnipresent, even if he spoke about it as a form of religious penance, a soul reckoning imposed by a power larger than himself, rather than a biological or psychological disorder. When he talked about the halfway house, the fact that he was there because of an illness, whatever its causes, never really came up.

That he had put aside the burden of cosmic guilt felt like a sign of improving health, but when he complained of being imprisoned by a mindless bureaucracy whose administrators pathologized his personality as an instrument of control, he made Futura House sound like Foucault's description of an asylum or prison, despite the fact that he had applied to get in. But how could they watch him like the all-seeing eye of Sauron if they wanted everyone out of the house for most of the day?

Defying the staff and rejecting its rules was not, to his way of thinking, "oppositional behavior" but the sort of self-assertion that proved he was recovering. Thinking independently and standing up for his rights were signs of mental health. If he was sick, it was with what he called "the New York Jewish intellectual disease," whose primary symptom was a need to question and dispute authority. It wasn't in the *DSM*—the *Diagnostic and Statistical Manual of Mental Disorders*—but it ran in his family, thrived on Mereland Road, and could be found in universities across the country.

Michael was painfully aware of where he had been and where he ought to be. It wasn't sharing a run-down apartment with a quorum of mental patients, voting on whether to have spaghetti and meatballs or Shake 'n Bake chicken for dinner, or learning how to sanitize a bathroom. He had studied economics with a winner of the Nobel Prize and was being told how to make a budget and balance his checkbook. That he couldn't concentrate long enough to do either only made the assumption that he did not know how all the more painful.

Michael had dazzled his Bain interviewers by talking with authority even when he didn't know what he was talking about. That, in fact, was *why* they had hired him. Specialness was a job qualification that could dispense with all the others, as if brilliance, like a reverse disability, deserved its own accommodations.

I was familiar with this view, which I'd nurtured for the opposite reason; my only hope, I'd often thought, was to swing for the fences.

When I got fired from Gristedes for pricing the beer wrong, I found Michael's shrugging acceptance consoling. Punching a clock was for "wage slaves," he informed me, something neither of us was ever going to be, though I couldn't help thinking it was not the sort of mistake he would have made.

Brilliance was so highly prized in our world that it seemed to guarantee all the other brain functions. By the same token, to feel dumb or lost, forgetful or confused, was at times enough to make you think perhaps you were losing your mind.

Michael found the mundane aspects of his recovery, the mantra "small steps," the expectation that you could do only one thing, say one thing, and mean one thing more than insulting. It felt like an effort to pull him down into dumbness, or worse, the reason for his losses rather than part of a process leading him slowly back into the high-functioning world.

Michael had always been able to do the basic work if he had to, but it was easier to be brilliant than smart, and easier to be smart than competent. I'd always blamed my anxiety for my incompetence, but I was beginning to realize it might be the other way around: I was anxious *because* of my deficits. What I did well I did very well, but my accomplishments walked on shaky legs. Old fears returned as I wondered what I would do if I did not become a professor, where being "absentminded" covered a multitude of sins. My father's old joke—"Read it? I haven't even taught it!"—worked only in higher education, which assumed higher abilities. What other profession let you keep working with dementia?

Teaching idiomatic expressions to adult immigrants was a lot harder than talking about *Robinson Crusoe*, and yet they paid you by the hour, just like Gristedes. But leaving academia would be my choice; Michael had been yanked out of his life by illness, and his options were unknown.

He spoke of the blurring effects of medication, but *Surviving*

Schizophrenia also identified "four types of cognitive functioning especially impaired" by schizophrenia. The first three were short-term or "working" memory, executive functioning, and general attention. The fourth had to do with the ability to recognize your own illness.

Michael had always excelled at the first three. When we'd swapped our homemade practice tests for biology, he bent low over the questions my sister had drawn up, dispatching them robotically at high speed. Even if he was concentrating so he could get back to *not* concentrating, his intensity of application was uncanny. I'd hear him flip the page while I was still reading and rereading the first or second question, the way I looked at my watch and then looked at it again before I realized what I was doing and reminded myself to remember the time. To some extent, I already exhibited three of the four types of impairments, it's just that I'd always had them.

The fourth was different, and harder to measure. Michael might not have believed he was sick, at least not in the way they told him he was. Or he might just have been displaying the confidence that would ultimately get him through this.

Intelligence, attention, and reason were often taken for affirmations of sanity. I'd spent a lot of time in childhood at the fuzzy border between distraction and "distraction"—which Torrey pointed out was once a word for madness—wondering which side I was on. Michael had looked out the window as much as the next kid, but information stuck to him like pollen whether he was playing hangman in the last row or flitting from book to book piled on his desk.

It wasn't so much what Michael knew that I'd envied as the confidence that came from knowing that what he knew would be there when he wanted it, an assumption that still infused his personality. My childhood expectation that the bottom would fall out, as it had at my bar mitzvah, was always there.

Which is just to say how Michael could remain my intellectual mirror in the old inverted way. Even when I was moving fast, I felt like a tortoise in a taxi. Michael might be slow, but he was a hare stuck in traffic.

It did not sink in that his life had become one of perpetual evasion. In addition to contending with hallucinations and intrusive thoughts, masked imperfectly by medication, Michael was contending with an unfamiliar array of cognitive frustrations that he blamed on his medication but that might have been symptoms of his illness. Even without the encyclopedic swagger, his intellectual hauteur guarded his new reality from other people, and perhaps from himself.

Michael was part of the first generation that came of age after deinstitutionalization. Caught between dysfunctional systems, a higher percentage spent time with their families; life at home, even interrupted by hospitalization or wandering, was often an improvement over the sprawling neglect of declining state hospitals. But it was also a restless generation, raised to resist conformity and turned loose in an age of abundant street drugs.

We'd grown up with "Question authority" bumper stickers, a chief executive called Tricky Dick, and posters that praised marching to our own drummer. Michael's defiant spirit had served him well, but it must have been doubly difficult for someone who loved correcting his teachers and hated doing what he was told to hand over his autonomy like a passport with the vague promise that, eventually, he'd get it back.

If community mental health centers no longer helped people like Michael, and the state hospitals, which were frightening, did not let people stay even if they wanted to, where did they go? As part of its congressional testimony in the late 1980s about the crisis in community care, the National Institute of Mental Health prepared a chart that showed only 17 percent of adults with schizophrenia were getting outpatient care. Of the rest, 6 percent were living in state hospitals, 5 percent in nursing homes, and 14 percent in short-term inpatient facilities. This left a full 58 percent of the schizophrenic population that had simply vanished.

Would Michael wind up among the lost population? It seemed unthinkable, but then so did his illness. Where would he go if he needed to be hospitalized again and this time his family couldn't afford it?

Michael might refer to Futura House as Limbo, but the real trouble with halfway houses was that in addition to serving a fraction of the population, they were short-term solutions for people with long-term needs. Residents might do everything expected of them, take their medication, and follow all the rules, and still not be ready to move on after the one- or two-year limit. The arc of recovery did not always bend toward independent living—sometimes it didn't bend at all, or bent backward. Even if you had reached the outer limit of recovery, and the halfway house felt just right, you'd still have to get out like Goldilocks when the bears came home.

Some might graduate to other types of "supported housing" that offered less support and more independence, and from there perhaps find a place of their own. But that type of housing was even harder to find. More likely, residents might shuttle between transitional housing, a family home, a hospital, a short-term "hotel" on hospital grounds, a board-and-care facility, perhaps the home of a different relative, followed by another hospital, though never for long, with the process starting again but never in the same place or moving in a straight line as it followed the course of an illness that waxed and waned, and responded better or worse to medication at different times and to a host of poorly understood factors.

None of which solved the immediate need for housing, or made families able or willing to care for sick members who might not wish to be cared for or who hoped to live on their own but who could not manage a job or afford an apartment with SSI checks or find the sort of supported housing that hardly existed at the time.

Michael didn't like Futura House, but he still heard its loud clock ticking. Every few months there was a resident review where counselors talked about a "life plan" and "vocational readiness." Futura House and the day hospital had relationships with local businesses willing to work with people with disabilities. As always, the emphasis was on small steps, low stress, and a noncompetitive environment. Not necessarily forever, but definitely for now. One possibility, endorsed by the shrinks at St. Vincent's, was for Michael to work as a cashier at Macy's, a suggestion that fell like a hammerblow of humiliation.

Chuck had done a great deal to encourage Michael to keep himself signed in to Columbia Presbyterian, and to submit to his psychiatrists' directions, but this time around he shared Michael's indignation. The idea that Macy's was the best they could come up with for a brilliant young man was unfathomable. Still, he went with his son to see what life was like for a "checkout boy," a term I doubt the doctors used but that captured the insult they both felt.

Rather than go to the Macy's Mall in New Rochelle—the downtown Death Star that had killed off what was left of Main Street's shopping district, which was perhaps too close to home—they went to the flagship Macy's in Herald Square, THE WORLD'S BIGGEST DEPARTMENT STORE, as it said on the side of the massive building. After Chuck watched hapless clerks get pushed around by impatient customers, his verdict was clear: Yale Law School would be a lot less stressful. Law school would also solve, at least for a time, the housing problem that was even more daunting than the job market. Housing was getting worse by the second, thanks to changes going on in the real estate market.

The number of SROs in New York City, around fifty thousand or so in the 1970s, was down to eighteen thousand and falling as old buildings went co-op or were bulldozed to make way for high-rise apartments priced far out of reach of my parents, who wanted to move back to the city, let alone the former tenants. The SRO hotel on our old block was now a doorman building. Even in White Plains, Futura House would have to buy or abandon one of the units of supported housing it administered in addition to the halfway house because the building was going co-op, which meant even more money would have to be raised for already underfunded services.

That year, too, the Fair Housing Act—the landmark 1968 legislation outlawing housing discrimination on the basis of race, religion, national origin, or sex—had been emended on its twentieth anniversary to include people with mental and physical disabilities. Michael was being gathered retroactively into the civil rights movement, that mythic struggle from our childhood, though for reasons different from those that had loomed so large when we were kids. It wasn't religion or the color of his skin but the way his mind worked that earned him the government's special protection. Where did he belong now in the scheme of rights and exclusions?

His pride had always been in being among the facilitators of other people's civil rights, not the beneficiary of their advocacy. Our eyes were still on Schwerner and Goodman dying in Mississippi alongside Chaney. He put his faith in gate-crashing, which we could manage on our own, or so Michael had always told me.

The Fair Housing Act of 1968, with its open housing laws, provisions for affordable mortgages, and overall goal of integration, was intended as the remedy for racial segregation, but what was the redress for people suffering from mental illness? At the height of *Cuckoo's Nest* anti-psychiatry, it must have been easy to see the hospitalization of people with mental illness as the equivalent of segregating Black people for purely prejudicial reasons. Likewise, the call for community care was the call for integration. This had not been an especially helpful analogy for either group.

Michael of course had the right to live anywhere he wanted, but he also needed there to be housing that accommodated his particular needs, and that allowed him to acknowledge those needs without punishing him for them. As it happened, he didn't want to live in a place predicated on his being different, needing support, or having an illness that he was still struggling to define and accept.

I'd seen in Baltimore how the original Fair Housing Act, important as it was, had failed to undo discriminatory housing patterns that had been set in concrete by earlier federal programs with sweeping goals like "slum clearance" and "urban renewal." Federal funding had gone to local municipalities who bulldozed dilapidated housing stock and while they were at it tore down racially mixed "slums" as a way to reinforce and even intensify local segregation practices.

Deinstitutionalization had been in its way a sort of slum clearance and urban renewal for people with mental illness, a noble idea on paper disfigured by a sweeping centralized approach marred by local prejudice. Experts employed by the government justified the project with promises of prevention unsupported by medical evidence and cures that did not yet exist, relying on local implementation far from federal oversight to bring about the economic and political transformation of poor neighborhoods that would not merely mitigate mental illness but eliminate it.

The first step had been identifying mental hospitals as the institutional equivalent of "slums," which like weeds could be defined as any unwanted impediment to progress growing in your way. This time, though, the goal was integration. In eugenic America, Black people had been treated like people with a genetic disease; now, people with schizophrenia would be treated as if all differences were skin-deep, and the path to equality lay in simply knocking down walls, removing external impediments, and denying difference.

Nothing brought this tension home like a story filling the newspapers at the time, about a woman with schizophrenia named Joyce

Brown who had been hospitalized against her will as part of a new program to prevent people from dying on the streets. Though she slept on a sidewalk grate, ran into traffic, covered herself with her own excrement, screamed racial epithets at Black men (though she was Black herself), and tore up dollar bills, set them on fire, and urinated on them, a judge ordered her released, agreeing with her lawyers at the New York branch of the ACLU that her behavior was the result of homelessness, rather than its cause, and writing in his opinion that although burning money "may not satisfy a society increasingly oriented to profit-making and bottom-line pragmatism," Joyce's behavior was nevertheless "consistent with the independence and pride she vehemently insists on asserting."

Her four sisters, on the other hand, who had struggled to care for Joyce in their homes until psychosis, drug abuse, and violent behavior had made it impossible, came to a different conclusion. If the judge believed that a Black woman shrieking obscenities and lifting her skirt to show passersby her naked buttocks was living a life of "independence and pride," he must be a racist who thought such degradation was "good enough for her, not for him or his kind." Because if that were *his* sister on the street, they had no doubt, he "would not stand for it."

Lurking in the background was a distant hope. It lay beyond the bureaucratic mazes of housing and mental healthcare, separate from all the daily chores, incremental changes, and conversations about buying an alarm clock and how far from the bed to put it so that it forced you up without unduly irritating your roommate. The hope was not in White Plains or New Rochelle but in New Haven, at Yale Law School, which Michael had never turned down but merely asked his brother to defer.

Hallucinating at the time, he'd added that the monkeys were eating his brain. The waters of madness had closed over all that, but now his Yale acceptance, like a message in a bottle flung out by his former self, came floating slowly back to him.

The possibility hung on the horizon. He heard it like a distant bell, or an alarm clock placed out of reach that might yet get him out of bed.

In the hospital, he'd talked about the pressure to go to law school as a factor contributing to his crack-up. Writing fiction had been his dream, but his doctors had told him to give that up. The alternative was Macy's. Perhaps law school could help him heal.

It was unclear if going was still possible. He was living in a halfway house and reporting to a day hospital where everything the doctors and counselors suggested pointed in the opposite direction. Perhaps Guido Calabresi, the dean of Yale Law, would make him apply again, given the change in his circumstances. Would the dean even take someone with schizophrenia?

As it happened, Mike Curtis, who was going out with Guido's daughter, was in a position to ask him. When he next found himself in the Calabresis' Connecticut home, Mike talked to Guido, as everyone called him, about his brilliant friend and former roommate, who had been accepted to Yale Law School but had since fallen on hard times.

Guido, a famously liberal man, did not in fact need persuading. As far as he was concerned, the right and obvious thing for Yale Law School to do was to honor Michael's acceptance, just as it would honor the acceptance of anyone who had deferred, for any reason whatsoever, and to let him begin classes in the fall of 1989. To do otherwise would not only be unfair, it would be impractical. As Guido liked to say, if he paid too much attention to mental health, he could not run a top-notch law school.

Part III

The House of Law

We wanted psychiatry as well as
the criminal code.

—WILLIAM O. DOUGLAS,
Supreme Court justice

The question of the need for hospitalization
is a legal question, not a medical question.

—INES T. AUELL, principal lawyer for patients
at Pilgrim State Hospital, quoted in
The New York Times, November 7, 1988

When I was young, I had a book called *Legends of King David*; in the last story, the king has grown old and God sends the Angel of Death to retrieve his soul. David is playing his harp so sweetly that the Angel of Death, instead of collecting his soul, stops to listen. The king understands perfectly well what is happening, and walks through his palace playing his beautiful melodies without pause until God, taking pity on his angel, breaks a palace step under David's foot. The king stumbles, the music stops, and the Angel of Death carries off his soul at last.

Nobody told us that being smart would make us sane, successful, and maybe immortal; it went without saying. Just as it went without saying that Michael, plucking the strings of his intelligence, would keep the Angel of Madness from carrying him away. It went without saying, though Michael said it anyway: "I may be crazy, but I'm not stupid." Which actually meant he was neither. It also went without saying that Macy's would destroy him and Yale Law School would set him free.

I believed it. My parents and Michael's parents believed it. So did Guido Calabresi and the professors who became Michael's mentors.

CHAPTER TWENTY

BRAINS

The Brain—is wider than the Sky—

—EMILY DICKINSON

Michael may have thought the monkeys were eating his brain when he told his brother to accept Yale Law School, but he had chosen well. For one thing, grades had been abolished in 1968 and had never come back. For another, the school accepted fewer than two hundred applicants a year, and the entering class, one third the size of Harvard's, was subdivided into small groups of sixteen or so students who spent the first semester taking all their classes together. This included a "small-group seminar" in one of four required areas—contracts, torts, civil procedure, or constitutional law—that gave the "1Ls" a taste of the Socratic intimacy for which the school was famous, and provided a ready-made social circle, emotional support system, and study group.

For Michael, the small group provided a great deal more than that. Several of its members read to him, took dictation, edited, proofread, typed, and retyped his work. This was especially impressive because they had no idea, in the beginning, that he had schizophrenia. To most, he spoke obscurely of trouble with his eyes, intermittent blindness, and vague motor difficulties that made it hard for him to read and write.

In those days, someone was always asking you the difference

between a lawyer and a vampire (one's a soulless bloodsucking monster, the other one turns into a bat) but Michael, who was often the one asking, was overwhelmed by the kindness of his classmates. They were themselves often at sea, frazzled and in debt, and some, who lived in married student housing, had uprooted spouses and small children to worry about on top of schoolwork. Nevertheless, they shouldered a share of his workload along with their own.

That Michael's hints were enough to elicit so much spontaneous generosity says a great deal about the largeheartedness of a much-maligned population. It also says something about Michael's ability to inspire compassionate devotion. This was all the more remarkable because he didn't ask for help so much as he expressed loss in a way that communicated need. His eyesight no longer allowed him to read a page at a glance. His photographic memory was itself just a memory; the literary passages he recited were placeholders for a vast forgotten library, reminding him of all that would not come when he called. When he played his guitar at small gatherings, he looked at his large hands as if they were frozen in blocks of ice, cursing the stiffness that kept his fingers from jamming with jazzman speed and made it impossible at times to use a computer.

Michael shook his head with marveling gratitude as he talked about all his classmates did for him. He hated the thought of receiving charity, but the help he received, which he was quick to say he hadn't requested, was more like a collection taken up for someone who'd been robbed than a donation given to a beggar. In the same way his expressions of loss informed his listeners of the high place he'd fallen from, his account of his classmates reading aloud, typing, and researching for him, mingled humble tribute with guileless grandiosity. There was a sort of competition among his classmates to do things for him, he said, as if he were the one giving *them* a gift.

That Michael couldn't do the work added to his pathos without detracting from the widely held belief that he was a genius, a quality that lived separate from any external measure of achievement. He seemed both wounded and powerful, like Samson waiting for his hair to grow back.

People who knew nothing of Michael's illness accounted for his aura of otherness in symbolic ways, ascribing it to some danger he had passed, a mystical temperament or intelligence itself settling palpably around him, like genius visible. The first time his classmate James Forman Jr. talked to Michael, at a mixer for members of their small-group seminar, he felt instantly intimidated by the stiffly tall, laconic presence who seemed preternaturally at home in the rarefied intellectual atmosphere that had been making James wonder if he belonged there at all.

Michael had managed to bring up, in his offhand disregarding way, that he'd graduated from Yale in just three years summa cum laude and Phi Beta Kappa, tossing in for good measure the exceptionally high scores he'd gotten on the LSATs, for which he had not bothered to study. He said all this with a disavowing shrug, waving away the triumphs he himself brought up to demonstrate the irrelevance of academic achievement.

It is remarkable that Michael, staggered by schizophrenia, veiled by medication, and barely out of a halfway house, had managed to intimidate James, a newly minted graduate of Brown who would wind up teaching at Yale Law School and winning a Pulitzer Prize for a book on mass incarceration.

I *knew* that Michael had spent months in the hospital, and had seen him looking like he'd had the lobotomy he was terrified they were going to give him, but when he phoned and told me that he never really prepared for class but pulled comments out of the ether that stunned his professors, I heard the boast more than the fear. Was law school really that easy? Did his professors really want him to clerk for a Supreme Court justice?

Though James had considered Michael a little "braggy" when they first met, his initial impression gave way to a countervailing, almost mystical image of Michael: "Half professor, half rabbi." It wasn't just the beard or the black kippah perched at times atop his head, but a quality of deep reflection. Michael didn't say much in class, but his deliberate speech suggested careful thought rather than grappling confusion, and his unhurried observations seemed to put a finishing gloss on heated discussions.

Nothing Michael did seemed hurried. He moved through the hall the way he spoke, disregarding the impatient world. This, too, was a sort of confidence, as if he was attuned to some invisible rhythm of his own. James found it impossible to picture Michael running.

Michael didn't run even on the first day of his torts class when he discovered that the room was on fire. Nobody else was paying the slightest attention to the flames that wreathed the walls and lapped at the ceiling like a living thing. Michael didn't shout, "Fire," but he was unable to persuade his body to keep its seat. He rose, gripped by terror, and walked out of the burning room shaking but unmarked.

Michael's classmates were doing for him what Jane Ferber's friend Bonnie knew he would need. A psychologist, Bonnie was the lone member of the Network who disagreed with the prevailing view that nothing would be better for Michael than a return to Yale. Bonnie had been meeting Michael at Jane's house for years. She'd seen him before his psychotic break and after it, and in the interval between his departure from Futura House and the start of law school. What Bonnie saw only reinforced her conviction that brilliant as he was, Michael wasn't ready for the pressures of law school.

This put her at odds with Jane and the rest of the Network, including Michael's psychiatrist. Murray was more important than ever now that Michael was done with the halfway house and the day hospital whose doctors had so outraged Michael and his father by recommending a cashier's job.

When talking to Jane's daughter, Elizabeth, Murray referred to his fascinating patient as "my Michael." His office was on the Upper West Side of Manhattan, just a train ride away from New Haven. As far as the Network was concerned, Yale Law School had already saved Michael and would go on saving him.

Bonnie shared the Network's view of state hospitals as horrible places that would destroy Michael, but she had a different sense of what went into successful community care. For one thing, there had to be a community. There had to be people on the ground applying real clinical judgment. Even a sense of smell, crude as that sounded, had a role because that was what told you when people were not in fact taking medication or caring for themselves, whatever they might say they were doing. She had already seen such fluctuations in Michael.

Like the other members of the network, Bonnie had been an eager idealist in the early days of community care, when it was practically a guerilla movement. In Philadelphia she'd been part of a makeshift mental health center that had set up shop in a former car dealership, an exhilarating, exhausting, and short-lived adventure. As a psychologist, she remained committed to humane care in the community and had been working with people with schizophrenia and their families, often combining several families into a large multifamily support group. She had an intimate awareness of how hard it was: the complexities of compliance, the importance of stability, and the way that change, even positive change, could produce a negative impact.

Nothing Bonnie said persuaded anyone. The day hospital may have been wrong to recommend Macy's, but the real question was how long it took to rebuild a stable self after a shattering blow. There had been other suggestions made, but they'd all been blurred into the vocational equivalent of checkout boy. Somehow Michael's version,

Macy's versus Yale, had become the paradigm that everyone talked about as if it were the only choice. And what did she have to offer in place of Yale?

After much soul-searching, Bonnie did the only thing she could think of. She called up a Yale law professor she had known for years, who was married to an old friend of hers. His name was Robert Burt, but everyone called him Bo. He was thoughtful, compassionate, psychoanalytically inclined, and very smart, and she had no doubt that Michael would find him. She told Bo that he was going to be meeting a young man named Michael Laudor. He's charming and brilliant, she said, and you're going to love him, but he's also very sick. Much sicker than he will seem.

Bonnie told Bo that Michael would need watching. In fact, he would need more than that. Bo would have to create a day hospital for Michael at Yale.

Bo was hardly in a position to create a day hospital. But by the time he met him, Michael appeared to have created one for himself. He had, at least, surrounded himself with people who cared about him and knew he needed help, even if they were unclear about the reasons.

For Guido Calabresi, the support Michael received from his classmates was the sort of thing that made Yale Law School unique. So was Guido. A beloved professor for more than thirty years, dean for the past five, Guido was famous not only for pioneering the field of law and economics but for dressing up like an elf at Christmastime, down to the green tights and curly shoes. His antic energy and moral seriousness were woven through the school.

Everyone told Guido stories, even if they hadn't personally seen him deliver a lecture reclining on his desk like a torch singer on a piano, entertaining the troops while educating them. He hugged everybody high and low, tamed titanic faculty egos by treating them all like beloved bambini, and phoned them up on their birthdays to sing "Happy Birthday" in English *and* Italian.

More than mere exuberance, Guido cultivated what he called "the myths of deanship"—true legends that added to his mystique and made it easier to get things done. One of Guido's triumphs as dean had been negotiating the law school's financial independence from the rest of the university, then shaking the great law alumni tree and raising unprecedented sums from liberals and conservatives alike.

Every fall, Guido delivered his celebrated "treadmill speech" to the incoming class, informing the newbie 1Ls that their time running in the gerbil wheel of academic expectation was over. They might think they were at the foot of one more mountain, but Guido was there to tell them that having been chosen by the best law school in the country, and having had the sense to accept, they were already on top. Instead of knocking themselves out with an assault on their already-assured future, incoming students were invited to "step off the treadmill" and treat the next three years like a second crack at the liberal arts education they'd probably been too anxious to appreciate the first time around. Yale Law School wasn't a conveyer belt for delivering mass-produced legal minds to market; that was Harvard.

The treadmill speech made a big impression on Michael. For one thing, it echoed the educational philosophy of his father, who had taught him never to let school interfere with his education. It also reminded him at a low moment that he was an elite among elites, and that being chosen *was* the achievement rather than a means to some specific end.

Michael said Yale Law School was the only place he knew of besides Telluride and the Institute for Advanced Study in Princeton, where Einstein had sailed in circles, that encouraged you to do nothing but think. And the fact that he'd already spent three triumphant years in New Haven getting a liberal arts education made the prospect of the next three less daunting.

So did the presence of the school's urbane dean. His door was always open to Michael, who walked through it on a regular basis, often in an anxious or insecure state. Even if Guido was on the phone with a Supreme Court justice, Michael said, the justice would get the boot and "Linda" would usher him into the vast wood-paneled office with its paper-heaped desk and high Gothic windows.

Guido had the kind of generous egotism that enlarged rather than diminished the circle of his high regard. He sprinkled his gold dust on everyone, but he had a genuine belief in Michael's brilliance, and therefore in Michael himself. Sympathizing with Michael's frustrated sense that he was no longer "top dog," and that what had once been easy was now hard, Guido lifted Michael's spirits and boosted his confidence. He listened, encouraged, exhorted, and reminded him not to give up. Brains carried a price, and Michael was paying it, but the future would be bright.

Guido was not the only one of Michael's supporters to catch a glint of something familiar at the root of his marginality. "Brains" might be the source of Michael's trouble, but his aura of genius harked back to an older time when brains were the qualifier, the equalizer, the passport, and the country. Like his literary allusions, snatches of vaudeville, and shrugging fatalistic humor, deployed since grade school, Michael's spark of brilliance grandfathered him into the postwar meritocracy that had been the salvation of the brilliant Jewish boys who had grown up to become his mentors.

Cold War pragmatism made it irresponsible as well as immoral to favor "good breeding" over brains, especially after Sputnik was orbiting overhead. If the US government could recruit a Nazi like Wernher Von Braun to put a man on the moon, surely Ivy League universities could let in a few more smart Jews, especially after so many had helped make the atom bomb and only one or two had told the Russians about it.

The WASP guardians who had excluded the pointy-headed and the hook-nosed to preserve Western values began letting them in for the same reason. The belief that Michael and I were raised with, that brains were your ticket up and out, wasn't just a family quirk or an immigrant obsession. It was a national policy, and had launched his professors like satellites into the new liberal order. Law school wasn't exactly the Manhattan Project, but hammering the justice system into a sword to fight for freedom abroad and a shield to protect the rights of individuals at home had been a patriotic act.

A wunderkind among wunderkinds, Guido had arrived in New Haven as a six-year-old refugee from fascism knowing three words of English—"yes," "no," and "briefcase." His success had been meteoric; even now, in his late fifties, the precocious child still beamed from the pater-familial face with its puckish gray goatee. But Guido never forgot what it was to be at the mercy of crushing forces beyond his control; even in his beloved New Haven he'd been taunted for his Italian and Jewish origins.

Sessions with Guido were enormously important to Michael. He sat in a sturdy leather armchair as rainbow light filtered through stained glass medallions set into arched windows bearing the names of former deans like synagogue donors. Sometimes he shared his hallucinations, like the flaming bed he confronted each morning, speaking cautiously and in the past tense to reassure them both. Guido listened with respectful fascination.

A powerful bond had been established the day Michael arrived on campus to begin his new life. He'd been invited to come up early so he could settle into his dorm room before the crush of new arrivals. Chuck had driven up with him. New Haven was less than two hours from New Rochelle—a lot less if Chuck was behind the wheel—and light-years from the halfway house. But even with the blessing of his

family, Jane, Murray, and the rest of the Network, it was a terrifying leap.

The neo-Gothic Sterling Law Building was modeled on the Inns
of Court in London and took up a square city block, with a grassy
courtyard in the middle. It was around the corner from Silliman, and
like his old residential college was a self-contained world: dorms,
classrooms, cafeteria, offices, auditorium, and library were all housed
in one sprawling gargoyled complex.

Everyone agreed that sleeping in the law school rather than off
campus would reduce Michael's stress, but when the helpful factotum
dispatched by the dean's office escorted Michael and his father to his
room, he saw to his horror that there was no bed.

All the doubts and terrors Michael had been holding inside burst
out at the sight of the empty room. Housekeeping screwups were not
uncommon, especially before the start of the semester. The apologetic official tried to explain that a missing bed was a small matter,
easily remedied. Michael wasn't listening; he was shouting and weeping.

When Michael got upset, high spots of crimson appeared on his
cheeks above the beard line just below the eyes. His beard itself seemed
to grow redder. Face aflame, eyes narrowed, he wept and cursed while
Chuck, in his admonishing way, tried to calm him down. But Michael would not calm down. There was no place for him in the dorm,
the law school, New Haven, his life.

There was an echo in the small empty room. Michael's voice rose
and reverberated, and Chuck matched him decibel for decibel. Both
men, when agitated, rocked upward on the balls of their feet, and
Michael was six foot three to begin with. The alarmed official dashed
off to find Guido.

As soon as Guido heard what was going on, he grabbed Stephen
Yandle, his assistant dean for financial affairs, and rushed over. Guido
may have joked that someone with mental illness would fit right in,

but he took the well-being of his students as seriously as he took the cultivation of brilliance. If the law school had failed to provide a fragile student with the most basic piece of furniture, and if that student was coming apart, then Guido and Steve would have to take matters into their own hands, which they literally did. Wasting no time, they found a bed and carried it across the courtyard themselves.

Michael was still raging and weeping as Guido and Steve wrestled the bed into the room and pushed it against the wall. It took longer for Michael to return to himself and the world, but Chuck was persistent and Guido was patient. Perhaps knowing that his bed had been delivered by the head of the law school and his trusted associate would make a difference, if not now, then on reflection. It had in any event been a sincere gesture.

At last, when Guido thought Michael would be able to hear what he had to say, he addressed his troubled student. "Look," he told Michael, "there are any number of people who have a handicap or something of that sort. We've made ramps. We've made elevators. Steve and I will be your ramp."

Guido's words were for Michael, but they were meant for Chuck as well. They were a promise made by the dean of the law school to a student who needed help; they were also a pledge made by one father to another. The law school might be a challenge for Michael, but the real test was the one Michael was giving the law school, and the dean was determined to pass it.

Though Guido taught a class called Tragic Choices, exploring impossible medicolegal dilemmas, he was by nature an optimist. His father had been beaten and jailed by fascist goons, his mother had lost her fortune, but they had escaped Mussolini's Italy with six-year-old Guido and his eight-year-old brother all because Guido's physician father had gotten a one-year fellowship offer from the Yale School of Medicine. That slender promise had been sufficient to get the family from Milan to New Haven. The fellowship had expired by the time they got there, but Yale had saved them.

Over time, Guido's father added a Yale PhD in public health to his medical degree and became a faculty member of the Yale medical school and chief of cardiology at a local hospital. His mother earned a PhD from the Yale French department and became a professor of humanities at a local college. Guido and his brother both got Yale BAs. His brother went to Yale medical school and became a renowned oncologist; Guido went to Yale Law School. The boy who could say only "yes," "no," and "briefcase" got tenure while still in his twenties; twenty-five years later he was the dean.

Small wonder Guido loved the school he presided over and saw it as a sanctuary. A one-year medical school fellowship had saved the outcast Calabresis, who had arrived with nothing but genius and courage. Surely the law school could save Michael.

CHAPTER TWENTY-ONE

MENTORS

The Yale Law ethos is instilled by professors
like Owen Fiss, who inspires his students
by picking up the Federal Rules of Civil
Procedure and literally throwing them
out the window.

—BOB COHN, *Newsweek*, March 28, 1993

Michael found an adoptive Jewish father behind every classroom
door. These brilliant, egotistical, softhearted men, as impossible to please as they were idealistic, terrorized students without even
knowing it. Michael had always been impervious to that sort of intimidation. Besides, he had other things to worry about, like whether
or not the classroom was on fire.

He was as quick to tell his professors about his schizophrenia as
he was determined to keep it from his classmates. His disclosure was
typically prefaced with a beguiling, almost conspiratorial admission.
"They say I shouldn't tell this to anyone, but—" he began, as if he
had singled out each one for his confidence.

It was a feature of Michael's confessional style that his account
of disabling mental illness communicated extraordinary mental ability. He made it clear that he didn't want sympathy or special consideration, and his professors, who understood that he was asking for
both, were deeply affected by his intelligence and vulnerability. They
were also dazzled by his powers of articulation. He talked about the

psychiatric hospital, the halfway house, the doctors who had written him off, and the remarkable father whose fierce faith in him, like Yale Law School itself, had saved him from a Macy's cash register.

There was something incongruous in the almost incidental way Michael disclosed the fiery hallucinations that had followed him to New Haven, like pulling the head of Medusa out of your backpack for show-and-tell. But the very matter-of-factness of his manner suggested that his major battles were behind him.

He was just letting them know that he had won his race with leg irons on so they could disregard the clanking sound he made when he moved. Though medication made him sluggish, and he might take longer on assignments, what mattered most of all, he told them with somber intensity, was that he not be defined by his illness but seen as he truly was.

It was more than compassion that drew Michael's professors to him. They recognized in him that animating spark of brilliance that had made brains the gold-backed currency of the laissez-faire meritocracy. The laissez hadn't been quite so fair when his professors were making their intellectual fortunes and the tariff on smart Jews had been strictly enforced. Anyone who passed through the eye of the Ivy League needle in that quota-filled time had to be brilliant, the way kids who made it out of childhood before antibiotics, germ theory, and vaccines had to have strong immune systems and a lot of luck.

They still bore the scars of their victories. These were invisible to the untrained eye but as obvious as dueling scars to anyone familiar with the outbursts of bullying insecurity and aggressive altruism of a generation abused by the system they had since come to dominate.

Classes were credit-fail for the first semester. After that, in addition to "pass" and "fail" there was "low pass" and "pass with honors." Almost nobody failed, but a pass could feel like a fail, and a low pass could feel even worse. The goal might have been anxiety reduction and, to the students who had lobbied for the change in the 1960s, a step toward greater egalitarianism, but without letter grades your relationship with professors became even more important, because it was their recommendations to the partners who ran the firms and the judges who hired the clerks that determined a lot of what a student would do for the summer and beyond.

The classroom-to-courthouse pipeline was well established at Yale, adding to the luster and stress of the place. Law professors were links in a long judicial chain letter, forwarding favored students to judges whose legal reasoning had influenced them when they were clerks, or to their erstwhile pupils, whose judicial philosophies they'd had a hand in shaping before they ascended to the bench. It was hardly a rule but certainly a custom that Yale-trained judges hired clerks sent to them by their former professors, or by their former clerks who had become Yale professors.

There were no cavernous lecture halls like the one in *The Paper Chase*, where randomly selected victims rose from an anonymous sea to spout case law and spar with a bullying inquisitor before sinking back into oblivion. But no matter how intimate Yale Law School was, no matter how well-intentioned the professor or free-ranging the course, the adversarial spirit of the courthouse prevailed. Even a small seminar was a harrowing proving ground for students unaccustomed to close-quarter intellectual combat.

When Sonia Sotomayor looked back at Yale Law School from the sanctuary of the Supreme Court, she remembered "the threat of being humiliated at any time" no matter how carefully she prepared for class: "Even a correct answer could lead to further probing that might leave you looking for a hole to crawl into." Clarence Thomas recalled the confusion and fear he felt as "new classmates jumped self-confidently into the fray, talking back to the professors as if the tangled complexities of legal doctrine were second nature to them."

Though Michael started law school in what President George H. W. Bush was calling a "kinder, gentler America," professors from Sotomayor and Thomas's time were still teaching, along with a younger generation that had grown up jockeying for sunlight and attention in the long Socratic shadow of their masters. You didn't have to come from a Bronx housing project, like Justice Sotomayor, or a dirt-poor childhood in the segregated South, like Justice Thomas, to wonder, as he did: "Where had they learned so much?"

In Michael's case the answer was 28 Mereland Road, where the cat couldn't lick its own ass without getting an argument, and someone was always shouting about the First Amendment and the ACLU. Michael liked to say that friends who came to dinner stayed for the show. Mike Curtis had wanted to flee the gladiatorial atmosphere of the Laudor family Seder, but it had trained Michael well.

One reason Michael tended to wait until the end of a class discussion before speaking was that listening gave him a chance to reverse engineer the reading he'd failed to finish or had forgotten, even if it had been read aloud to him. His parsing, rational manner had always been persuasive, even when he became psychotic and applied it to irrational things.

Intellectual matters are easier to fudge than practical ones, as I knew from my own educational career. Michael had always been exceptionally good at spackling over cracks in preparation with artful applications of language and an authoritative air, something he'd managed even when he was devolving into psychosis at Bain.

Michael was lucky in the philosophical orientation of the law school in general and his first-year teachers in particular. They prized deep diving over broad mastery, and talking over almost anything.

Whether it was the invisible hand of Dean Calabresi or simple chance, Michael wound up in the small-group seminar run by Joseph Goldstein, whose hatred of prejudice, fondness for Yiddish expressions, and dedication to students—especially if they showed signs of the brilliance he valued above all—made him a natural match for Michael. He had not only spent more than three decades writing about psychiatry and the law, he had been the first law professor in the country to complete training as a lay psychoanalyst back in the 1960s. He had a couch in his office where he still saw occasional patients, as if office hours, psychotherapy, and criminal law were all one.

By the time Michael met him, Goldstein was an eccentric eminence with disobedient white hair, a rumpled suit, and a large bow tie. Famous for Freudian silences and blunt interruptions, he spoke in a soft, amphibious voice that students strained to hear, inviting bold speculation while dispatching shoddy reasoning with a croak of pitiless candor that was like being dissected by a Socratic frog.

Goldstein believed in Michael, who had the special quality of mind he valued, and a purity of purpose that made him seem as far removed as possible from the narrow preprofessional technocrats his class was designed to discourage. He became one of the earliest and staunchest of Michael's supporters—Guido called them Michael's "boosters"—and saw no reason why he should not clerk for a Supreme Court justice when the time came.

"Joe" invited Michael to his house in Woodbridge, where he had entertained Anna Freud—daughter of Sigmund and flame keeper of his legacy—who had taught him that the needs and perceptions of children, so different from adults, could be mapped with the instruments of psychoanalysis and applied to custody cases. He had raised three sons and a daughter with his wife, Sonja, a Yale-educated lawyer who had fled Hitler's Europe as a girl and who helped him research and write his books. Michael had always loved other people's houses, and had an uncanny habit of winding up inside of them. There was a large sunny living room, popovers baked by the professor himself, and mysterious Japanese prints on the walls, a reminder that Goldstein had cracked Japanese codes during the Second World War.

Michael felt at home with the generation formed in the crucible of World War II, who had slain the dragons of tyranny and prejudice abroad and returned to fight the dragons of oppression at home. For them, the Holocaust was endless warning and *Brown v. Board of Education* a beacon of perpetual promise.

Goldstein had run seminars with Anna Freud for two decades, and written enormously influential books like *Beyond the Best Interests of the Child* with Freud and Albert Solnit, the director of the Yale Child Study Center, that emphasized the importance of the "psychological parent" over the merely biological one. The authors went so far as to suggest that in a custody fight between two equally devoted parents, it would be better to draw lots, granting the winner sole custody and banishing the loser to eliminate the conflicted loyalties so detrimental to the development of a child.

Such was Professor Goldstein's authority that whenever he taught the small-group seminar in criminal law, where nobody learned the criminal code, his students were assigned to the civil procedure class taught by Owen Fiss, where nobody learned how to file a motion or take a deposition.

Professor Fiss devoted the better part of the semester to a single Supreme Court case called *Goldberg v. Kelly*, an obscure landmark from 1970 that had done something extraordinary: instead of viewing welfare payments as a stopgap charity bestowed on the poor by the government, it treated them as a form of private property that the government could no more terminate without an evidentiary hearing than it could tow away your car without violating your due process rights.

Turning a single case over and over would always have been up Michael's alley, but in his present condition, a "meta-procedures" course was a godsend. So was the professor, an internationally renowned constitutional scholar and world-class mensch who took an immediate interest in Michael once he learned about his schizophrenia.

There was nothing "meta" about *Goldberg v. Kelly* for Michael,

who knew what it was to stand on a welfare line fearing some clerical error or government caprice could abruptly terminate his benefits.
According to William Brennan, the Supreme Court justice who had
written the majority opinion, the support Michael received wasn't a
"gratuity" but part of the "life, liberty and property" protected by the
Fourteenth Amendment, ratified to safeguard the citizenship rights
of formerly enslaved people and anyone else born in the United States.
Those were *his* property rights, and *his* right to due process that the
case upheld and the class discussed day after day. His secret self wasn't
marginal but emblematic, and in some sense the very substance of
the course.

There was also nothing "meta" about *Goldberg v. Kelly* for Owen
Fiss, who had clerked for Justice Brennan and saw the case as a last
gasp of the golden age of judicial activism—though he did not consider it activism any more than Darwin considered opposable thumbs
a lifestyle choice. Professor Fiss was a tall man in a gray suit, aloof
but attentive as he loomed before his students with monochromatic
brightness, trying to coax from them a recognition that it wasn't the
right answer but the answer that was *right* that made justice possible.

He had grown up modestly in the Bronx, and gotten his first inkling
of what the law could be in 1955 when he took a trip to Washington,
DC, with some high school friends. It was his first time venturing
outside New York City. Eager, like all teenage boys, to experience
freedom, he wandered with his friends into the visitors' gallery of the
Supreme Court, where he saw a tall, distinguished Black man rising
above a sea of white faces and arguing what turned out to be the remedial phase of *Brown v. Board of Education*, known as *Brown II*. The
eloquent lawyer, who was none other than Thurgood Marshall, was
making a case for the immediate implementation of *Brown I*, declaring "separate but equal" schools unconstitutional, which he had successfully argued the year before.

That glimpse of Marshall changed everything for Fiss. Nine years later, he was hired by Marshall to be his clerk on the US Court of Appeals for the Second Circuit. The following year he clerked for associate justice William Brennan, liberal soul of the Warren Court. He worked in the Civil Rights Division of the Justice Department for John Doar, fearless pursuer of the murderers of Schwerner, Goodman, and Chaney, and worked for Doar again in the 1970s as an adviser to the House of Representatives' impeachment inquiry. Shuttling between New Haven and Washington, DC, Fiss translated the Watergate break-in, the illegal bombing of Cambodia, and President Nixon's secret tapes into the articles of impeachment that closed the door on an era.

Teaching *Goldberg v. Kelly* over and over, Professor Fiss was mourning the demise of the Warren Court and the departure of Justice Brennan, his judicial hero and friend. The Supreme Court that had decided the Brown case when he was a teenager had never embraced Marshall's demand for immediate desegregation, substituting instead the vague standard of "all deliberate speed," a phrase that seemed to grow more Orwellian year by year.

For Michael, Professor Fiss belonged to a noble order of legal knights who made Yale Law School a sort of Camelot in exile. To visit his office was to spend time with a man who had not only worked for Thurgood Marshall but also eaten the great jurist's crab gumbo, which he'd learned to make because his grandma had told him that he ought to have a skill to fall back on growing up in segregated Baltimore.

Professor Fiss fit the profile of Michael's mentors: Jewish men born into a land of opportunity and inequality who had managed, with nothing but powerful minds and a parental push, to ascend to the pinnacle of Ivy League eminence. Instead of looking down on those left behind and seeing the dots Orson Welles points to from the top of the Ferris wheel in *The Third Man*, they saw suffering people who needed help. For them, the law was a way of throwing a lifeline to the dots down below. What made Michael unusual was that he was up in the swaying gondola with Orson Welles and Joseph Cotten, and down with the dots waiting for a rope.

If Professor Fiss had walked out of a mythic world, so had Michael, who was in his own way a reminder of the passionate era of the Warren Court and the heroism it had called forth. Fiss was moved by Michael's journey, and was quick to offer whatever help he could. He arranged for paying gigs, including a job as his own research assistant, even after he discovered Michael's skills did not lend themselves to a job typically performed by fast and efficient readers with superior organizational skills and stevedore stamina.

As Bonnie predicted, Michael made his way to Bo Burt's office, arriving in great agitation after hearing that only one other student, a middle-aged woman returning to law school after many years, had signed up for Bo's seminar on law and medical ethics. He was unsettled by the tiny enrollment, but much more upset to learn about the film Bo was planning to show on the first day called *Please Let Me Die*. The documentary, central to the curriculum, had been made by a psychiatrist investigating the sanity of a suffering young man, horribly burned in an explosion, who wanted to end his life.

Michael told Bo that there was no way he was going to watch a film set in a burn unit because every morning he opened his eyes and found his room on fire. That was when he explained about his schizophrenia. Every morning, he told Bo, he lay in bed paralyzed with fear until his father called and told him the flames weren't real. His father didn't just tell him; he proved it. Ordering Michael to put out a hand and touch the fire, he asked him what he felt.

"Does it burn?" his father asked. "Does it *burn*? No? *Good!*"

Then he ordered Michael to do the same with his other hand. Again, the call-and-response: "Is it hot? Does it burn? Does it *burn*?"

When Michael admitted it did not, his father told him, "That's be-cause it isn't real." He got him to sit up and put one foot on the floor. *Never mind the flame.* Even if he had to lift his leg with both hands and force it down, he had to put his foot on the floor, then tell Chuck if the floor was hot. "Is it *hot?* That's right. Now the other foot!"

Michael slipped into his father's voice to tell the story, putting on the bullying Brooklyn accent like a bomber jacket, adding dra-matic urgency and with it that suggestion of mastery that comes with a performance, even if he was performing a terrible reality that tyran-nized him.

As Bonnie had also predicted, Bo was captivated by Michael. Part of what made him so impressive was the way he wore his intelligence and his illness on his sleeve together, though over time Bo worried that Michael, so careful with his peers, was almost profligate in the way he spoke about psychosis to his professors. Despite his canny air, he seemed not quite aware of the stigma that attached to schizophre-nia even in an enlightened environment.

All Michael's professors heard about Chuck and the burning room. They heard the story from Michael and from each other, and they repeated it to each other as the perfect encapsulation of his struggle and strength. He overcame horrible things every day, only to have them happen all over again. He was like Prometheus having his liver eaten by an eagle every morning, growing it back every night in time to be tortured again at dawn.

Bo told Michael he would not have to watch the film and arranged to meet with him to discuss alternative ways of covering the material. Their planning session led to others, and for a time it seemed to Bo that despite having only two students, he was actually teaching two seminars, each with one student. The discussions with Michael to figure out makeup material became the makeup materials. Michael was not simply taking the class with Bo, he *was* the class.

Bo's first book, *Taking Care of Strangers*, looked at the psychological, moral, and legal entanglements of doctors and patients through a psychoanalytic lens. Bo wasn't a psychoanalyst, like his mentors Joe Goldstein and Jay Katz, but he saw the psychoanalytic relationship as a model not only for people in therapy, and for doctors and patients of any kind, but for judges and litigants and perhaps most of all for teachers and students. He was one of those rare listeners whose warmth and shaping intelligence made the arrival of food in a restaurant seem like a crude interruption of the talk that was any gathering's true purpose.

But for all Bo believed in conversation, it wasn't the only thing he asked of his students, and he soon discovered that Michael's brilliance wasn't the same as an ability to produce the sort of sustained thought or disciplined work he expected from his students. Bo didn't find this especially troubling; as far as he was concerned, the most interesting students, and the law school's real success stories, often didn't become lawyers at all. He thought Michael could become an eloquent advocate for people with schizophrenia, someone who had been to Yale Law School rather than someone who was a Yale lawyer.

It was an irony, perhaps, that "Yale lawyer" was a phrase Michael already applied to himself. Recalling his struggle with the day hospital doctors who had dealt him such a bitter blow, he would say: "Why would I bag groceries when I could be a Yale lawyer?" Becoming a Yale lawyer was the whole point.

CHAPTER TWENTY-TWO

PRECEDENT

So I went back out into the world, shoved the
violence and the delusions into a closet, and
leaned against that closet door just as hard
as I could.

—Elyn Saks, *The Center Cannot Hold*

Michael was not the first law student with schizophrenia Joe Goldstein had taught. Elyn Saks had graduated three years before Michael arrived. She, too, found Goldstein a generous mentor, as well as a role model for her own decision to pursue psychoanalytic training after she got her law degree.

Saks had recently been hired as a law professor herself at the University of Southern California; this was impressive not only because of her diagnosis, but also because she had received it during her first semester of law school after she danced out the window of a professor's office and onto the roof of the law building.

The professor had coaxed her back inside and brought her home to dinner with his family, which, as she put it in her extraordinary memoir *The Center Cannot Hold*, "didn't go so well." After hanging up on a psychiatrist from Student Health Services that her professor had telephoned for help, she called her friend Richard, a British neurologist she'd met while studying at Oxford. She knew something dreadful was happening to her and that she needed help, but she told her friend: "I give life and I take it away. Don't try to fuck with me, Richard, I've killed better men than you. Children. Lemon juice."

After hearing a little more, Richard explained to Elyn's professor that she was having a psychotic break, that she needed to get to a hospital right away, and that in her present state she might be a danger to his young daughter. The alarmed professor drove her to Yale-New Haven Hospital, where, after refusing to relinquish the long roofing nail she'd pocketed while dancing on the roof, Elyn was body-slammed onto a gurney and put in restraints.

Three weeks later she was given a diagnosis of chronic paranoid schizophrenia and the news that she was no longer a law student. The hospital had informed the law school's dean of students about her illness and explained that she would not be returning.

In addition to the same diagnosis as Michael, Saks's doctors had offered her the same discouraging prognosis. "I wasn't expected to have a career, or even a job that might bring in a paycheck," she wrote. But after she spent several months in private hospitals, her family brought her home to Florida, where her father, much like Michael's father, gave her a "get tough" speech, insisting that her destiny was in her own hands: "Intelligence, combined with discipline, could overcome any challenge."

Four months after visiting a Florida beach with her family, where she lay in the sand wishing for a gun because strangers and space aliens were plotting to kill her, Elyn was back in New Haven to start over with a new entering class.

Michael had applied to law school before his psychotic break. When the admissions office consulted Guido about the strange case of the brilliant student whose mental health had been one thing when he applied and would be another when he arrived, Guido told his officers that if the testimony of the doctors vouching for Michael, claiming that the worst was behind him, was good enough for them, then it was good enough for him.

Elyn Saks, on the other hand, had been a student when she climbed out the window, twirling and talking about giving life and taking it away. Her studies had been dramatically interrupted only a few weeks into her first semester, so she had to be interviewed by the head of the University Health Psychiatry Department before being cleared to begin again in the fall. Studious as ever, she found an article her interviewer had published explaining how to conduct just such an interview, complete with model questions and preferred answers that she memorized. The psychiatrist stuck to the script and so did Elyn, who was readmitted without a hitch. That was in 1983, when Michael and I were undergraduates.

Elyn repeatedly rejected the help she needed, throwing away her medication and confusing intelligence with sanity. When a professor returned her paper about "The Psychotic Dr. Schreber"—Freud's famous study of a German judge who lost his mind—with a comment calling her work "publishable," she immediately stopped taking her medication. In her memoir she recalled thinking, "I'm publishable, I'm not mentally ill at all—which means I don't need to take medication for the mentally ill. I'm done with this."

This made perfect sense. Artists and intellectuals were the aristocrats in the world Michael and I grew up in, and intelligence bestowed a kind of blessing. Everyone knew dolphins had to be saved from tuna nets because their brains were as big as ours; bigger, actually, which meant they were even smarter than we were and would have much to teach us once they got past that high-pitched baby talk they used in *The Day of the Dolphin*.

What we didn't know was the flipside of this equation: the fate of people considered insufficiently intelligent to be worth saving, like Carrie Buck, a young woman whose forced sterilization was upheld by the Supreme Court in *Buck v. Bell*. She was, in the words of Oliver Wendell Holmes Jr., an "imbecile," and "the principle that sustains

compulsory vaccination is broad enough to cover cutting the Fallo-
pian tubes."

Nobody had taught us that Woodrow Wilson—our only president with a PhD, and a former president of Princeton—signed
a forced sterilization order as governor of New Jersey targeting the
"hopelessly defective" and "criminal classes." President Wilson was
lucky his predecessors hadn't discovered eugenics and his belief that
academic expertise allied with government authority was the path to
progress; otherwise, they might have sterilized his wife's father, who
killed himself in the Milledgeville Central State Hospital the year
before Wilson was married, in which case neither his wife nor his
daughters would have been born.

We hadn't learned that the textbook John Scopes used to teach
evolution listed five "races," with the white "race" on top and the Black
"race" on the bottom. Otherwise, we would have been forced to acknowledge that the creationist rubes singing about "old-time religion"
in the movie version of *Inherit the Wind*, which Michael and I watched
in biology class, were more in tune with the spirit of American equality than Clarence Darrow and the Ivy League eugenicists he planned
to call as witnesses, who had no regard for equality at all.

We also didn't know that the only Supreme Court justice who
voted against the forced sterilization of Carrie Buck in 1927—though
by then Carrie, her mother, and her nine-year-old daughter had all
been sterilized—was a conservative Catholic and future New Deal
obstructionist who took a far more liberal position than progressive
justices like Oliver Wendell Holmes Jr. and Louis Brandeis (a hero
in our homes) who had failed to recognize that the testimony they
heard from eugenics experts was crap, though it wasn't only the quality of the science that made the ruling egregious.

Justice Holmes defended the sterilization of Carrie Buck because he was afraid of the country being "swamped by incompetence." Nothing was more terrifying than mental incompetence at a time when the quantifiable mind was replacing the immortal soul as the unit of individual worth. Eugenics made every disability seem like a contagion requiring public health measures.

Progressive Era reformers saw themselves as the ones needing protection, like the native plants and animals they did so much to save from invasive species. Accordingly, they granted themselves asylum, turning universities, neighborhoods, and as much of the country as possible into a walled garden. They also created hospitals, graduate schools, and public institutions, but blurred science and social science, illness, intelligence, and inferiority, and kept for themselves the power to define which was which.

At the Nuremberg doctors' trial, *Buck v. Bell* was used to defend the physician who oversaw the mass extermination of psychiatric patients; he was hanged anyway. No wonder postwar intellectuals of goodwill were eager to throw out the biological bathwater along with the eugenic baby. It must have felt like making amends, or a way to rescue the tarnished image of expertise.

The rejection of biology played a role in the embrace of psychoanalytic psychiatry and the new world it created. Though it was a psychologist who had administered the IQ test to Carrie Buck that labeled her a "moron"—a different scientific category from "imbecile," the term Holmes chose for reasons of his own.

Psychology was a science of the mind, but the word "psyche" meant "soul" before it meant "mind." Zeus had granted the princess Psyche immortality so she could marry the immortal Cupid; modern psychology reversed the process, turning the soul into the measurable mind. A high score could get you into Yale; a low one could land you in a segregating asylum or get you sterilized.

Reformers eliminated the asylum but forgot to restore the soul as the measure of worth. It was a more reliable indicator of equality than the Stanford-Binet test. The choice between Yale and Macy's had seemed like a no-brainer, but it relied on Michael's greatest strength, which also happened to be his greatest vulnerability.

The flip side of being publishable, for Elyn Saks, was feeling worthless. At Oxford, when her tutor told her that what she'd written made no sense, she had fantasies of setting herself on fire. "I'm not sick," she told her friends when they asked about her growing incoherence, and the burn mark on her arm. "I'm just not smart enough."

If her memoir makes anything clear, it is what a long, slow, lonely journey of error and discovery Saks had to make before accepting the most basic elements of her illness, and before making peace with her need for medication. Five unmedicated days after learning her paper was publishable, she was "convinced that evil beings were about to destroy me." Her doctor got her back on medication before something worse could happen, one of many fitful steps toward recovery.

Elyn was lucky her parents could afford daily psychoanalysis, and lucky they had been able to pay for private hospitals like the Yale Psychiatric Institute, where she'd spent several months after her law school breakdown. Just how lucky she was she realized on her first day at Yale Psychiatric Institute, talking to Eric, a young graduate of an Ivy League school. Like her, he'd also spent time in Yale-New Haven Hospital, the vast teaching hospital whose psych unit she'd found "inhumane and inhospitable." All she'd wanted from any hospital was to be released, but Eric had a different regret.

"I wish they'd made me stay," he told her, "and then maybe moved me here, like they did with you. I fooled them into thinking I was OK. And I went home. And then I killed my father."

Elyn thought she must have misheard.

"I'm sorry," she said. "You did what?"

The young man nodded. "I strangled him."

CHAPTER TWENTY-THREE

SECRETS

> That intuition—that there was a secret I had
> to keep—as well as the other masking skills
> that I had learned to use to manage my
> disease, came to be central components of
> my experience of schizophrenia.
>
> —ELYN SAKS, *The Center Cannot Hold*

Over time, Michael did share his secret with an inner circle of classmates he felt closest to and trusted most, swearing them in advance to solemn secrecy. He told them individually, first administering a hypothetical test, much the way his professors would place a legal dilemma before their students, embellishing it with increasingly complex moral turns of the screw: *What if the mother were a Christian Scientist? What if the killer were sleepwalking?*

Michael asked what they would do if something they knew about him, that they had sworn to keep secret, could be used to prevent something important from happening that they didn't want to happen. Would they resist the temptation?

To illustrate this abstraction, Michael gave them a what-if scenario. What if he changed over time, and turned into their worst political nightmare, someone like Jesse Helms, the senator from North Carolina who'd denounced the 1964 Civil Rights Act as "the most dangerous piece of legislation ever introduced into the United States

Congress" and who was still in office bringing up Sodom and Gomorrah whenever anyone brought up AIDS?

What would they do, Michael asked, if he had morphed into "Jesse Helms and a half," and the president of the United States nominated him for a seat on the Supreme Court? Would they honor their vow of friendship and silence, or would they tell the world his secret and destroy him?

Nobody ever guessed what they were being asked so cryptically to guard. Michael's intense, oblique allusions didn't clarify things. Even for an ambitious Yalie, there was something excessive about preemptively trying to neutralize the possible disclosure of an unspecified indiscretion in anticipation of a future appointment to the nation's highest court.

On one occasion, Michael insisted on sitting with a classmate in her parked car, like a Soviet dissident afraid his room was bugged. She was a generous, public service–oriented law student, one of those who had immediately offered Michael help with his work without needing to know any details. But she was reluctant to swear a lifetime oath to guard a secret knowing only that it would undo him if he turned into Jesse Helms, and Michael was reluctant to reveal his secret until she swore.

They went back and forth until she blurted out hopefully, "Are you gay?"

"Worse," Michael said. "I'm crazy."

He preferred the word "crazy"—as in "I may be crazy but I'm not stupid"—and humor softened the impact of his disclosure. Nobody laughed when he said "schizophrenia." But once the burden of secrecy was lifted, he settled into his telling with a lucidity that erased its dire associations.

One reason people tended to repeat the same stories about Michael's illness was that those were the stories he repeated about himself. Even as an improviser, he'd been someone with a repertoire, a set list sparked by familiar phrases like the segues comedians used to get from one bit to the next in a routine. *Speaking of the devil, anyone here see* The Exorcist?

This could make incidental disclosures a real surprise even to close friends. Once, driving around New Haven with an undergraduate he'd met at the Kosher Kitchen who mentioned that he was going unusually fast even for him, Michael explained that the road was full of bodies; he knew they were hallucinations so long as he could drive through them, and the faster he did this the better. When he'd told this friend about his illness, she'd been completely accepting, but she was upset about the bodies. No wonder he felt safer telling stories he'd told before, which he could turn to when he wasn't sure he could rely on himself.

What must it have felt like for Michael to tell people he had schizophrenia? He called it coming out, but the fear of being discovered by people he did not tell, or disclosing too much to those he did, made it more like inviting a select few to peek inside his closet. His air of gravitas and humor, which gave even his classroom reformulations an intellectual authority, made it all the harder for people to take in what he was saying, since his delivery was so at odds with what people seemed to expect.

None of the friends Michael told thought he was being paranoid. Everyone swore to protect his secret once they knew what it was, and to help him in any way they could.

These classmates did more than simply read to Michael or help him research and type his papers. If he wasn't in class, they went to his room to check on him. They accompanied him to meals, or brought food to him. They calmed him when he was overwhelmed, stayed with him when he could not function. The woman he'd alarmed with his driving came when he called in the middle of the night, and held him as he shivered uncontrollably, gripped by unseen terrors.

It was hard to lose this support when summer came. His routine of classes, dining hall, and pizza study sessions was broken, and his network of teachers and classmates scattered. Even before the bright beds of flowers planted for spring alumni weekend turned brown, the dorms emptied out like transient hotels, and the actual inhabitants of New Haven shimmered into view as if they'd been there all along.

Michael needed a place to stay and a person to stay with. He didn't want to tell a roommate he had schizophrenia, but it was hard to hide hallucinations and hard to conceal the concealments, the medication, side effects, strange sleep, and constant winnowing of reality and delusion that might pass for introspection in a university but was still a lot of work.

Luckily, Linus Yamane was in town. Linus had been a graduate affiliate of Silliman working on an economics PhD when Michael was a freshman who could talk about Keynes, Schumpeter, and the Austrian School with uncanny familiarity. Nine years later, Linus was still working on his PhD, though he was already a professor of economics at Pitzer College in California and was just back for the summer to put the final nail in his dissertation. The kind, melancholy economist agreed to move in with Michael.

They sublet a four-bedroom apartment from some law students who were off doing what most law students did in the summer. The rooms were half-filled with other people's junk but it was a big place, and Linus was an ideal roommate who had known Michael in his precocious glory and had visited him in the hospital at the lowest point of his life. He knew Michael had schizophrenia and accepted him as he was.

Medication made Michael intensely sensitive to heat, as if an increased ability to regulate his mind came at the expense of regulating his body. He and Linus bought an air conditioner, though Michael still sweated with little provocation. His body was like a house with a broken thermostat, but his thoughts also required a sort of manual adjustment. When Linus asked Michael to join him for dinner, Michael became terrified that Linus was planning to eat him.

But Michael was able, at least some of the time, to speak his fears aloud, watching suspiciously for a reaction that might confirm his secret conviction. Sometimes he spoke from behind the closed door. Nevertheless, he shared his thoughts. Linus listened patiently. Some days Michael did not come out of his room or speak, and Linus wondered if it was depression or fear driving him into seclusion.

All four of Linus's grandparents had been born in Japan. Linus had grown up a lone Asian American surrounded by Jews in a left-leaning New Jersey town whose semi-utopian roots still showed in private houses built on communal land. Linus had attended Passover Seders and played his violin in the Reform temple. He was familiar with Michael's whirling intellectual energies and melting-pot pride, but he was respectful of the mystic seeker Michael had morphed into after becoming ill.

As a graduate student fresh out of MIT, Linus had gone to the Yale Christian Fellowship and the Asian Bible study group. He'd signed up for a class in tae kwon do, a physical discipline that is also a state of mind; it became part of a journey toward his Asian American identity. He'd since become a black belt and tried to live by its principles of balance: mastering the mind to cultivate the body; studying violence in order to turn from it; exercising self-control in order to find freedom; and discovering humility, grace, and kindness on the road to strength.

Showing off in Silliman years before, Michael had demonstrated his ability to kick his foot higher than Linus's head, an achievement of height more than flexibility that Michael could no longer accomplish. It was from Linus that Michael had learned the tae kwon do stance he'd taken up whenever the malevolent imposters disguised as his parents appeared in the Neuro Ten unit to kill him.

That summer, in addition to finishing up his dissertation, Linus was reading everything he could find about Asian American studies. The year before Pitzer had hired Linus to teach economics, a young Asian American woman had died by suicide, and the undergraduate's tragic death had not only shaken the college but become a catalyst for thinking about why Pitzer offered no Asian American studies classes, something students had been demanding. Nobody commits suicide because of the curriculum, but the death had gotten Linus thinking about the myth of the model minority, and how easily assumptions of success can mask breakdown or despair.

Most law schools had remained silent during the mass imprisonment of American citizens of Japanese descent, though Eugene Rostow, a Yale law professor at the time, blasted President Roosevelt for bowing to the racist justifications of General DeWitt—"the Japanese race is an enemy race"—and incarcerating more than one hundred thousand men, women, and children in what he correctly called concentration camps. The executive order was defended by California's attorney general, Earl Warren—who would do penance a decade later as a chief justice dedicated to civil liberties—but Rostow was hardest on the Supreme Court for ratifying a belief in group guilt, betraying individual liberty, and echoing the ideology of the enemies America was fighting abroad.

Rostow's article in the *Yale Law Review* was the reason Guido had wanted to teach at Yale Law School, where Rostow, famous for hiring Yale's most brilliant generation, became dean. His essay had been a noble exception, but after the war, Americans who'd been silent began to discover concentration camps all over the place, beginning with state mental hospitals, where conscientious objectors had done alternate service and smuggled out horrific photographs run by *Life* magazine in 1946. The pictures drew inevitable comparisons to the shocking images of liberated concentration camps, though the Nazis had begun emptying their own psychiatric hospitals before the war, building their first gas chambers, disguised as showers, and murdering seventy thousand patients in a dry run for the elimination of Jews, who were also treated as a public health crisis.

The neurologist Walter Freeman was so disgusted by what he saw in *Life*, and the unscientific treatments used by psychiatrists, that he promoted a streamlined surgical solution for both the patients and institutions with the slogan "Lobotomy gets them home." In the 1960s, the sociologist Erving Goffman grouped psychiatric hospitals with concentration camps and classified them as "total institutions"; Betty Friedan labeled suburban homes "comfortable concentration camps"; and Yale psychology professor Stanley Milgram, shaken by the Eichmann trial, ran obedience to authority experiments in the basement of Linsly-Chittenden Hall on Yale's Old Campus, conducting a trial for *potential* Eichmanns.

Dr. Milgram wanted to see if ordinary Americans would give lethal shocks to strangers when told to do so by white-coated authorities, demonstrating that a well-meaning psychologist, haunted by the Holocaust, could manipulate human subjects without their informed consent into thinking they'd killed an actor screaming behind a partition. As one of the participants put it, "We couldn't possibly conceive that anybody would allow any torture to go through Yale University."

Michael was working for Owen Fiss that summer, researching his old friend *Goldberg v. Kelly* for an article Fiss was writing to defend the case not from its detractors but from supporters who admired it for the wrong reasons. These included none other than

Justice Brennan, who had recently given a speech about the importance of passion in judicial decision-making, pointing as exhibit A to the welfare recipients whose benefits the government wanted to take away without a hearing, and whose heart-wrenching testimony had influenced his ruling in *Goldberg v. Kelly*.

This was heresy for Fiss, a philosophical idealist who believed that passion opened the law to ungovernable subjectivities and made justice seem like a lucky bleeding-heart break instead of a force bent to earth by jurists in tune with universal truths. Fiss was calling his article "Reason in All Its Splendor." Despite his reverence for Justice Brennan, he wasn't going to stand by as his former boss spoke of using the heart as well as the head to justify a ruling Fiss considered the product of reason acting through law to fulfill the Constitution's ultimate promise.

Fiss began referring to two cases called *Goldberg v. Kelly*. He called the true version *Goldberg I*, and the fanciful version *Goldberg II*. Paradoxically, *Goldberg II* was upheld by the author of *Goldberg I*, who considered that ruling his finest judicial achievement. Michael understood such distinctions.

His confidence got a much-needed boost from the trust placed in him by Professor Fiss, who treated the Gothic law school like a secular seminary where the pure of mind divined the spirit of the Constitution, inscribed it in law journals, and transmitted it to initiates who carried it into the chambers of appellate and Supreme Court judges. *Goldberg v. Kelly* had itself been inspired by a law journal article called "The New Property." Law professors, it turned out, were the unacknowledged legislators of the world.

Serving as the research assistant for a renowned constitutional scholar was a sort of clerkship for Michael. He was dispatched to discuss the case with Stephen Wizner, who had argued *Goldberg v. Kelly* before the Supreme Court as a young public interest lawyer before becoming a professor at Yale, where he ran the law clinic. He was almost as tall and just as disputatious as Michael. The two hit it off immediately, and stood talking in the street, so engrossed in discussion that neither felt the need to step up onto the sidewalk.

Wizner had run a law office out of a storefront in the Bowery, and recruited the welfare recipients whose powerful stories of poverty and vulnerability had stirred the court's compassion twenty years before. Fiss could insist all he wanted that the Warren Court's "rights revolution" was a rational extension of fundamental principles; Wizner knew there wouldn't have been a rights revolution without emotional stories getting their day in court. *His* essay on *Goldberg v. Kelly* was called "Passion in Legal Argument and Judicial Decisionmaking."

As for Michael, he was happy to be standing in a street in New Haven talking to a law professor about a Supreme Court ruling from 1970.

People are always telling young athletes to get an education so they will have something to fall back on in case of injury; nobody tells the academically gifted what to fall back on if something goes wrong. Michael had fallen back on Yale Law School, where he had stepped off the treadmill and the welfare line both, and was helping a renowned scholar who believed in his abilities. Already he was thinking that academic law was the way for him to go.

Michael wasn't the only undergraduate Linus had become friends with back in Silliman. The first time he went to Payne Whitney Gym for his martial arts class, he'd noticed an attractive undergraduate putting her small, graceful body through a tae kwon do form. She turned out to be a Silliman transfer student. Her name was Caroline Costello, though everyone called her Carrie.

Linus and Carrie had gone to meals, movies, and plays together and had once biked all the way to the Costellos' house in Newton,

Massachusetts, stopping twice along the way to stay with friends. They were so close that some people thought they were dating, and even they had wondered if it might be so, but Linus was mindful of his obligations as a graduate affiliate. Their friendship became one of those pearls that form around affection, confusion, and bad timing.

They stayed connected after graduation, which was easy to do because Carrie had moved to New Haven and Linus always came back to work on his dissertation, even after a stint at the World Bank in DC or teaching in California. That summer, though, was the last time Linus and Carrie would both be in New Haven for the foreseeable future. Carrie came over to hang out with Linus, and wound up spending time with Michael too. He was a good listener as he sat attentively, holding himself very still while the air conditioner hummed.

Technically, Michael and Carrie were reconnecting, though it hadn't been much of a connection the first time around. Michael had been having his brief, intense affair with Carrie's roommate, Robin. He hadn't quite noticed Carrie then, but he did notice her now.

She was blond, pretty, petite, a shade below five feet tall. Michael, at six foot three, towered over her. Superficially she resembled his waiflike girlfriend from the halfway house, but there was a hint of undaunted resolution inside her shy demeanor. She was also athletic. Carrie and Linus had both played wing for Silliman's intramural soccer team and studied martial arts together in Payne Whitney, where Carrie had learned to press her delicate fingers together and break a board with a knife-hand strike and a shout.

Carrie was working for the New Haven regional office of IBM as a systems engineer, which was impressive because she'd been a literature major. A lot of her job was spent in the Connecticut public schools setting up computer networks and telling teachers and administrators how to use them. She had a good head for computers, but IBM especially appreciated her ability to explain technical material in plain English, which is why they bothered training liberal arts students. She spent most of her time on location and liked being in schools explaining things more than she cared about the engineering. The city had some desperately poor neighborhoods where the children needed all the help they could get.

Carrie had talked about going to graduate school in education but had still not applied. Friends like Linus had always recognized the warmth and energy behind her surface self-effacement, but a hairline fracture of self-doubt seemed to run through her life. In Silliman she'd been one of those transfer students who *seemed* like a transfer student, as if she'd missed the moment when everyone else was making friends.

The eager air of the shy arrival looking for a second chance was something she and Linus had in common as they explored New Haven together when Carrie was an undergrad. Six years after graduation, she still seemed a little displaced, as if being a transfer student turned out to be a spiritual condition. There was something a little stalled or provisional about her life, her job, her boyfriends. Linus once asked Carrie what she loved about someone she was dating and was told, "He helps me clean the kitchen."

Michael was a completely different order of person. Carrie loved his expansive way of talking, his intimacy with an intellectual world she admired and had missed after college, and his ability to pull down references from the high branches of culture and present them to her like a bouquet.

Linus did not think it was an especially good idea for Carrie to go out with Michael, much as he cared about them both. Her parents were churchgoing Irish Catholics; her father sang in the choir and her mother went to daily mass. Though Carrie had fallen away from much of the faith, she loved Christmas and all that went with it.

Michael was not just Jewish, he was religious. He had propped himself up in the hospital with God and tradition, and the threads of
that experience were woven through his reconstituted life, adding
to his irony and skepticism a somber, seeking, ecclesiastical aspect.
He often talked about marrying a Jewish woman and having Jewish
children.

Mainly Linus was concerned about Michael's schizophrenia. He
had seen at close range the terrible toll the disease took on his friend,
who seemed perhaps 70 percent of the person he'd been when they
first met. Even with medication, Michael—by his own reckoning—
spent the bulk of his brainpower fending off figments of the unreal
world. But still he was smart, funny, charming, kind, handsome, spiritual. If he sometimes thought Linus wanted to eat him for dinner,
he had always reasoned his way out of it eventually.

By the time Michael and Carrie started going out, Linus had returned to California and Michael was back in the law school dorms.
He waited months before telling Carrie he had schizophrenia, but
if she suspected something, she didn't say. She would not have been
the first person who didn't notice, or who ascribed everything from
surface tremors to elliptical apocalyptic utterances to the hidden depths
of a complex soul.

Carrie wept when Michael told her. She did not reproach him for
having kept his illness a secret. She showed no anger or fear or regret,
only pain for his pain. She wept at the unfairness of what he had
suffered in the past and was still suffering. She knew it was a terrible
illness, but she loved him and that was that.

Michael was deeply moved by Carrie's reaction. In his account,
he told her that he was sorry he wasn't the one on the floor weeping
for himself like that, but he wasn't able to do it and was grateful she
could do it for him.

Linus was not surprised by Carrie's total acceptance. He knew her loving nature, the depths of her compassion, her caretaker kindness. He had gone with Carrie to the Long Wharf Theatre in 1986 to see *The Normal Heart*, Larry Kramer's play about AIDS. Soon after that, Carrie had begun delivering meals to homebound people with AIDS. That was how she was. Once she was committed to a cause or a person, there was no turning back.

CHAPTER TWENTY-FOUR

THE SYMPATHETIC LIGHT
OF SICKNESS

The time will come when stealing or murder
will be thought of as a symptom, indicating
the presence of a disease.

—KARL A. MENNINGER, MD, "Medicolegal Proposals
of the American Psychiatric Association," 1928

The only lowest common denominator of all
civilizations and the only psychological force
capable of producing these perversions is
morality, the concept of right and wrong, the
poison long ago described and warned against
as "the fruit of the tree of the knowledge of
good and evil."

—GENERAL G. BROCK CHISHOLM, MD,
The Psychiatry of Enduring Peace and Social Progress,
with a foreword by Abe Fortas, 1946

The broken world of mental healthcare that Michael had narrowly
escaped by coming to Yale Law School did not disappear from
view but turned up continually in kaleidoscopic form. Legal culture,
itself shaped by psychiatry and social science, had helped create a world
whose policies, paradoxes, and unintended consequences continued
to haunt it in newspaper articles, courthouses, classrooms, and the
streets.

Two of Michael's mentors had been deeply influenced by Judge

David L. Bazelon, a transformative giant who had risen from abject poverty to the US Court of Appeals for the DC Circuit, where he had done more to change the legal landscape for people with severe mental illness than any judge in the country. Joe Goldstein had clerked for Judge Bazelon in the 1950s, and as a law professor sent him his best student every year like a votive offering, including Bo Burt, who clerked for Judge Bazelon in the 1960s. Both professors had contributed to landmark Bazelon rulings that helped shape what would later be known as deinstitutionalization.

The DC Circuit was second in authority only to the Supreme Court, not only because of its proximity to power but because the absence of state courts in Washington, DC, allowed federal judges to deal with everything from petty crime to government agencies whose unassuming acronyms belied vast regulatory bureaucracies with growing budgets and national reach. From his high judicial pulpit, Judge Bazelon handed down rulings that echoed through our childhood—banning DDT, ordering Nixon to hand over his tapes—while presiding over the marriage of law and psychiatry for more than three decades.

His faith in psychiatry was personal; after one of the eruptive outbursts of rage for which he was well known, he told Bo that psychoanalysis had saved his life. If psychiatry could do that for him, why couldn't it play a humanizing role in the criminal justice system that treated the poor, the disenfranchised, and the mentally ill with such indifference?

As it happens, President Truman, who had appointed Judge Bazelon, agreed. One million seven hundred and fifty thousand soldiers had been rejected by the military for neuropsychiatric reasons during the Second World War, suggesting a mental health crisis of epic proportions, and a national role for psychiatry in the postwar world. "Never have we had a more pressing need for experts in human engineering," the president told American psychiatrists in 1948. That year, Brigadier General William C. Menninger, the army's highest-ranking psychiatrist, appeared on the cover of *Time* magazine to explain that "people are beginning to see that damage of the same kind can be done by a bullet, bacteria, or a mother-in-law."

Freud had transformed severe mental illness, which he did not treat, into the psychopathology of everyday life, a universal disorder that turned alienists into psychiatrists and freed them from their rustic asylums. They opened offices with regular hours, like dentists or chiropractors, treating a new class of patient, formerly considered well, and making claims like William Menninger's brother, Karl, who declared in his 1963 bestseller, *The Vital Balance*, that psychoanalysis could make you "weller than well."

After going from the asylum to the couch, and from the couch to the battlefield, psychiatry was ready for the courthouse, where legal experts, too, might become human engineers. As Alan Dershowitz recalled in his memoir *Taking the Stand: My Life in the Law*, Judge Bazelon "knew he could never win his battles by relying on public opinion, which showed little compassion for accused criminals. His weapons were education and elite academic opinion." Dershowitz had been a star pupil of Joe Goldstein's at Yale, and was helping him and Jay Katz edit an eight-hundred-page casebook, *Psychoanalysis, Psychiatry, and Law*, which he drew on when he clerked for Judge Bazelon in 1962.

The ruling Joe Goldstein drafted, *Durham v. United States*, used a broad new faith in psychiatry to liberalize the insanity defense and by extension the entire criminal justice system. *Durham* was a grand social experiment with its roots in psychoanalytic ideas that had been radical before the Second World War, when Freudian concepts breathed life into "legal realism," an obscurely named but enormously influential reform movement incubated at Yale and Columbia. Legal realists gained a radical reputation, in the first place by denying the possibility of blind justice, and in the second place by suggesting that there was something better than blind justice, if only jurists would take off their blindfolds and look beyond the law.

The law was tired of being blind, or at least law professors had lost patience with the legal system's slow groping progress, its pretense of objectivity, and the case method used to teach it. Once you put on Freud's night vision goggles and saw that unconscious forces acted on the mind like a magnet from below, you realized that oral argument, case law—even the Constitution of the United States—were just the tip of an irrational iceberg whose invisible bulk vanished beneath the outermost reaches of the conscious mind. At such irrational depths, the line between a judge *discovering* the law, as tradition maintained, and *inventing* the law, as legal realists argued, melted away.

How could a judge determine mens rea, the "guilty mind" so central to criminal justice, if the judicial mind didn't know what it was thinking half the time, or what half of it was thinking all the time? In the face of such knowledge, the presumption of innocence would have to change—not for the accused but for the judge. So would the presumption of sanity.

The subversive beauty of psychoanalysis was that it could undermine the authority of courts, laws, facts, and judges, by exposing the irrational nature of the human mind, while holding out the promise of a deeper set of laws, like the deeper magic in Narnia known only to Aslan the lion. Having studied the ancient code, Aslan knows he can sacrifice himself to the White Witch and come back from the dead stronger than before. Legal realists liked to claim that "justice is whatever the judge ate for breakfast," but a deficient judicial breakfast, supplemented by self-knowledge and social science, could create enlightened champions of social change, turning law professors into the unacknowledged legislators of mankind.

The traditional insanity defense that *Durham* upended was based on a British law named for a man who had tried to shoot the prime minister, killed his secretary instead, and was sent to an asylum rather than the gallows because a judge considered him too paranoid and delusional to know right from wrong. The M'Naghten rule was more than a hundred years old, though the idea that extreme mental states were exculpatory belonged to a much older common law tradition. The paradox of the traditional insanity defense is that the perpetrator is known but declared not guilty because the court, recognizing states of mind so extreme that a good person can do terrible things and still believe them moral, replaces criminal guilt with insanity, and prison with the asylum.

The *Durham* decision replaced the right-wrong test of M'Naghten—with its stark division between madness and sanity—with the "product test," which held that the accused wasn't criminally responsible "if his unlawful act was the product of mental disease or mental defect." The "product test" rested on the presumption that psychiatrists understood the many factors that produced mental illness, the many mental illnesses that produced crime, and the web of forces tangling them together that could make the accused more like the fly than the spider.

Older versions of the common law spoke of "good and evil" rather than "right and wrong," as if people who lost their reason went back to the Garden of Eden before the fruit of knowledge had been tasted, where they kept their innocence but lost their freedom. The cost was high even without confinement, because someone without the knowledge of good or evil could hardly live in the world.

The M'Naghten rule secularized good and evil into right and wrong, but the Durham rule went farther. It asked the court to see crime the way doctors saw disease, as the neutral "product" of an impersonal system beyond good or evil, and to apply the insanity defense not merely in rare cases of extravagant delusion but to people like Monte Durham, the poor white man who robbed a house and gave his name to the case.

The psychiatrists lobbying for the *Durham* decision had broadened their own mandate from illness to mental health, and from the individual to society, and were arguing for a system that would treat crime the same way. If crime was a symptom of illness, then perpetrators were also victims, or at least bystanders of their own behavior. Doctors would act like lawyers, offering exonerating explanations of illness, while lawyers would become like doctors, demanding treatment in place of prison for those who could be healed instead of punished.

As expert witnesses, psychiatrists would explain to the jury how a particular disorder, in combination with specific environmental factors, had produced behavior for which a defendant could hardly be held responsible. They would also provide the remedy, which would allow the perpetrator turned patient to return quickly to society as a productive member.

That at least was the theory, argued with great care by Durham's pro bono lawyer, Abe Fortas, a former Yale legal realist and future Supreme Court justice who lived in overlapping legal and psychoanalytic circles with Judge Bazelon. As President Truman's undersecretary of the interior in 1946, Fortas had warned that "drastic readjustment of human personality and conduct" was necessary if the species was to survive, arguing that "the role of the psychiatrist in this venture is not merely that of healer; it is the greater task of him who seeks the causes of fear, anxiety, prejudice, and vicious passion, and works to eradicate those causes." No wonder he referred to the *Durham* decision he helped craft as "the Magna Carta of psychiatry." When Fortas became a Supreme Court justice, Joe Goldstein, who already had the Bazelon concession, supplied his clerks too.

Judge Bazelon intended his ruling to give poor people and oppressed minorities a chance to be considered mentally incompetent rather than criminally culpable, likening *Durham v. United States* to the century's greatest piece of civil rights legislation. "It was not mere chance that *Durham* was decided during the same month as *Brown v. Board of Education*," he wrote years later. "In some ways we were responding to the same general awakening of social concern. The insanity defense had been seen as a 'whites only' defense, available exclusively to one seen as suffering from a certifiable illness."

The goal wasn't to make the traditional insanity defense more accessible, but to create a new standard that would serve a different population: "By expanding it to examine human behavior more broadly, we were in practice opening it to minorities and the poor, whose aberrations had seldom been regarded in the sympathetic light of sickness." Judge Bazelon believed that once the insights of psychology, psychiatry, sociology, and economics were used to illuminate the roots of crime, responsibility would be distributed among its constituent causes, and crime itself would lose its sting. Lowering the threshold of insanity would raise the bar for a guilty verdict, which, like raising or lowering interest rates, would affect the economy of crime and punishment. Laws transforming the environment, which psychiatrists identified as a cause of the mental illness that produced crime, would give urban renewal a public health urgency.

Neither Joe Goldstein nor Judge Bazelon had foreseen that the poor and minority defendants they wanted to spare jail time would wind up spending years in state hospitals rather than serving the comparatively short—and more importantly *finite*—prison terms they would have received had they been convicted and sentenced. Hoping to destigmatize criminal activity by curing perpetrators, the Durham rule blurred the line between prisoners and psychiatric patients, which wound up criminalizing illness and further associating state hospitals with prisons.

Monte Durham wrote an irritated letter to Judge Bazelon complaining that he was now branded "Durham the nut." Instead of being healed or exonerated, he had merely been stigmatized. It took real courage for Judge Bazelon to reverse his own ruling eighteen years later, acknowledging that his opinion had produced the opposite of his high hopes, and blaming psychiatry, which he now called "the new wizardry," for overselling its expertise.

By then, Judge Bazelon had served on President Kennedy's Panel on Mental Retardation, whose findings, merged with those of the mental health task force, helped create the hopeful Community Mental Health Act. The combination of psychiatric and sociological ideas, federal authority, and public health aspirations—catchment areas, cures, prevention—like *Durham*, did not turn out as planned. The roots of madness, like the roots of crime, remained obscure.

Eventually, Joe Goldstein lost faith in the insanity defense altogether and called for its abolition, which *The New York Times* reported in a 1970 article: "Modern Legal Test on Insanity Attacked by One of Its Drafters." He called it "a device for automatic commitment to mental institutions, which may be worse than most prisons," and teamed up with Thomas Szasz, author of *The Myth of Mental Illness*, to argue for its abolition in a public television debate. Szasz rejected both legal and biological insanity; Goldstein, when asked about mental illness, snapped, "I have no idea what that is."

Declaring forced treatment of any sort "an offense to the dignity of human beings," he excluded from consideration the most difficult questions raised by the most afflicted portion of the population: people who at their sickest might be no more capable of making realistic decisions about their future treatment and care than someone in cardiac arrest was of calling 911.

A decade after Joe Goldstein drafted the *Durham* ruling, Bo Burt drafted a memo that made its way into another seminal Bazelon ruling, *Lake v. Cameron*, that helped enshrine a right to treatment for psychiatric patients in the "least restrictive environment." The case had become a model for national and state laws, and Bo was proud of the role he'd played in it, but he lacked his mentor's fiery certitudes and utopian optimism.

Bo had once brought up with the judge the unintended consequences of *Lake v. Cameron* and many rulings like it. Courts and hospitals were releasing people onto the street, and not because a less restrictive environment had been found, as that humane directive required. Did he ever worry they were making a mistake?

Judge Bazelon had seen the matter very differently. He understood Bo's concern, but he also believed that releasing so many mentally ill people onto the streets would produce its own positive results. He had faith in the goodness of America, he told Bo. The reason they didn't see these mentally ill people as human beings was that they were swept off the street. Leave them there, the judge said, and the people's empathy would be provoked. Once the American people saw the suffering that had been hidden, and realized the damage caused by their indifference, they would be moved to compassion and finally do the right thing.

When Michael and I were undergraduates, a woman with schizophrenia had frozen to death sleeping in a cardboard box in downtown Manhattan. Her name was Rebecca Smith but the papers called her "the lady in the box" until her daughter identified her from news reports and told her story: a college valedictorian from Virginia who had spent ten years in a state hospital, hid her beautiful face behind makeup and veils—imagining visible scars from the electroconvulsive therapy she received—before fleeing her home and family for New York City.

The death of Rebecca Smith at the beginning of the 1980s was a watershed moment in the backlash against deinstitutionalization, which had become a term of recrimination and regret, like "institution" in the days of dismantling outrage. But deinstitutionalization was an after-the-fact name for a confluence of policies, attitudes, and outcomes, some intended, many unforeseen, that became bureaucratically enshrined and took on a life of their own.

Though a *Times* editorial about the lady in the box asked bitterly, "What should be said about all those who could have helped?" many had tried. New York City's director of protective services for adults told the *Times* that a court order to hospitalize Rebecca Smith, which arrived hours after she had frozen to death, had taken ten days to obtain because Ms. Smith liked sleeping in a box, and it was necessary to show the court that every effort had been made. "We're concerned about people's civil rights," he said.

Meanwhile, the libertarian psychiatrist Thomas Szasz wrote in the *Times* that it would have been a terrible infringement of Rebecca Smith's rights to hospitalize her against her will because she was suffering only from what he called "problems in living." Her failure to take care of herself was "pathetic," he wrote, but became "tragic" when society blamed such troubles on a "nonexistent disease."

It was hard to believe that someone who seemed so indifferent to the plight of people with severe mental illness had helped shape laws governing the treatment of the most vulnerable members of society. But Dr. Szasz's indifference was part of the argument he'd made twenty years before in *The Myth of Mental Illness*. He did not simply deny the existence of Rebecca Smith's illness, or the legitimacy of the state stepping in to help her if her family could not, but insisted on turning the most impaired subset of people suffering from untreated psychotic disorders into a test case of individual liberty. Denying the exceptional nature of Rebecca Smith's illness, he made her autonomy essential to his own, even if she died on the sidewalk to preserve it.

The symbolic role people with mental illness played in legal thinking, and the paradoxes that went with it, did not go away. The legal services program Steven Wizner ran was named for Jerome Frank, an architect of legal realism and early proponent of clinical law programs, who had imagined participants less like medical students honing practical skills in the field and more like "scientists" carrying ivory-tower theories out into the community. When Wizner arrived in 1970, a law student had already organized a class action suit designed to abolish all civil commitment in Connecticut.

As a Yale undergraduate, the law student had helped drive ROTC off campus, and agitated for coeducation by busing in 750 women; but making love not war was easier than casting all psychiatric patients in Connecticut as enslaved Israelites and freeing them in one fell swoop, even if it felt like the next logical step in his activism. The suit had failed in federal court, and Wizner, who knew and loved people who needed involuntary hospitalization, worked hard to rein in such Quixotic overreach, while the law student went on to become the dean of a law school.

Michael didn't volunteer at the mental health law clinic, which was too close to the world he hoped to avoid at all costs. But he'd loved talking to Wizner, who, despite his endowed chair—named for another Yale realist, Justice William O. Douglas—seemed happiest operating at street level, where members of New Haven's invisible majority wandered over to thank him for some unnamed service or friendly counsel.

Elyn Saks had participated in the mental health law clinic in the 1980s for the same reason Michael avoided it, to confront a terrifying area of her own experience and help people "who often looked and sounded like me at my most vulnerable." She celebrated when a classmate won release for a young man over the objections of his parents, who had argued that their son wasn't ready to come home. The student advocate had prevailed and the boy moved into his parents' trailer home, burning it to the ground a few months later and killing his parents and seven-year-old brother while they slept.

Recalling the calamity in her memoir, Saks wrote, "For a bunch of idealistic law students, some lessons were harder to learn than others, and this one—that 'helping people' isn't always a good thing (or, maybe, that 'helping' translates differently from case to case, and must be cautiously scrutinized)—was tragic for all parties."

It was tragic for the young man's parents and their seven-year-old son. It was tragic for the young man, who in addition to the burden of his illness would have to live with the unfathomable burden of killing his parents and little brother. It was tragic for Elyn's friend, Dan, the student advocate, who learned what happened only when his former client called him from police custody to say he'd been arrested on murder charges.

"Dan was devastated," Elyn wrote, "indeed, the entire mental health law class was."

She added that there was "no way of knowing whether Dan's intervention made any significant difference" because the young man's diagnosis, bizarrely, was given only as attention deficit disorder and the hospital might have released him in any case. Still, the story hangs over her memoir, and over the history of law and psychiatry, whose marriage, divorce, and rapprochement are still wending their slow, uncertain way through the courts. The young man had needed psychiatric help but had received legal help. Now he needed legal help. Perhaps in jail he would receive psychiatric help.

CHAPTER TWENTY-FIVE

HAPPY IDIOT

I'm gonna be a happy idiot

And struggle for the legal tender

—Jackson Browne, "The Pretender"

I finally let go of graduate school. I'd taken a full-time job and gotten engaged and, though I still wrote at night, laid aside the dream of literary transfiguration along with academic life. I was working at a start-up newspaper called *The Forward* that had been a socialist Yiddish newspaper for almost a hundred years before Seth Lipsky, an editor from *The Wall Street Journal*, decided there should be an English-language *Forward* too. I was creating its culture section.

"Reason is but choosing," I often told myself, quoting John Milton, who explored the idea so infinitely well in *Paradise Lost*, which I wasn't going to write a dissertation about because I wasn't going to get a PhD. I hated choosing, but feared even more becoming what Milton called "a mere artificial Adam."

Michael and I were in our late twenties. The old friendship that had ended when Michael quit the high school paper had healed but not at the break. It had reconstituted itself around a different break, and was something else. We remained deeply connected, bound by more than memory, habit, guilt, obligation, or even affection, though all those were there too. It was something less than friendship, as I'd come to know it, and also more, and it filled me with a sense of mild dread whenever I encountered it.

Sometimes Michael called, and after greeting me in his slow, deliberate way, fell silent as if I had called *him*. He waited patiently, almost ominously, for me to speak.

His calls were often driven by a mood or a need that would slowly disclose itself in the course of the conversation. The summer after Michael's second year, Owen Fiss helped arrange one of those coveted corporate associateships. He was living in the city, sharing an apartment "out of a Henry James novel" with a friend from law school. The firm was paying him a headshaking amount of money, he told me, and he'd already given his father $8,000 that he owed him.

The welfare office in White Plains had vanished like a dream, and the world of Bain was back: "I don't need to be taken out for eighty-dollar lunches every day," he told me. "It's ridiculous. I wish they'd take me for thirty-dollar lunches and give fifty to charity."

But when I asked, after a particularly long silence, how he'd been spending his time, he said, "Oh, thinking of ways to kill myself. Taking larger doses of medication. Lying on my bed in a fetal position."

What kept me from rushing over on the spot? Was it the unexpectedness of the announcement after so much opulent information about his success? Was it the fact that his words sounded rehearsed, though it was a peculiarity of his speech that they often did? Or was it the feeling—for which I reproached myself even as I was having it—that he was showing off? He was being the best at despair, if nothing else, or trying to show up my naive pretense that we were having a normal conversation, as if I really thought the answer to "How are you?" and "What are you up to?" might be "Fine" or "Nothing much" when his life was a daily scrimmage with demons no matter how much he got paid.

At the same time, he had a way of disregarding my expressions of concern and questions about his illness as if they were either inadequate or demeaning. Besides, the friend who shared the Henry James apartment, an Orthodox Jew with the same name as me, was looking after him. "He carries me on his back the way Aeneas carried Anchises," Michael said.

That was the pattern; Michael phoned in a low state and talked his way into a higher one. When I leaned over in concern, setting me straight about his suffering seemed to be the very thing that brought him a measure of relief, so that he managed the extraordinary feat of turning an argument for why he was worse than I imagined into a case for why he was doing better than I gave him credit for.

Oddly, the mark of his feeling better at these moments was the echo of a familiar contempt creeping into his voice, and with it a certain relief that I may have felt as well because the old competitive equilibrium was restored; striving competitively against each other had been as integral to our friendship as anything.

But often I would find that I had read everything wrong, relying on old instincts that misled me. He would often report on my father's health as if he had a better notion of it than I did, marveling at how old and bent he'd appeared on Michael's last visit to Mereland Road.

"He's my father's age. But he looks so much older."

I'd take this as the old competitiveness, then catch the note of real distress and realize it stirred an entirely different set of feelings in him. My father had always looked older than Chuck, but as his illness advanced, he'd let his white beard grow in part because shaving was difficult, which enhanced his old-world grandfatherly air. But I knew from my mother that Chuck, too, was walking with difficulty, which was connected to cancer treatments that Michael did not bring up.

I didn't ask. I often withheld things, though I was never wholly sure which one of us I was protecting. Mychal and I were planning to get married in the fall, but I decided to save that news, which wasn't hard because Michael tended not to ask what I was up to, though he was interested in my newspaper job. Once, when I blurted out that

I'd finished a novel and was looking for an agent, he said ominously, "Try not to burn it."

I hadn't thought of burning my manuscript, but I did think, in the back of my mind, about Michael cracking up in the Gatsby attic, and telling me with a sort of grim pride as we sat on his bed in the locked ward that his doctors had warned him not to write because he couldn't control his imagination. My mother had told me more than once about James Joyce bringing his daughter Lucia to see Carl Jung after she was diagnosed with schizophrenia. The writer protested that Lucia was simply doing what he did, playing with language, but Jung told Joyce that he was diving to the bottom of a river; his daughter was sinking.

It was only after I was off the phone with Michael, replaying the conversation in my head, or writing it down graphomaniacally in my journal, that I understood Michael had "buried the lede" as we said at the newspaper, or I'd buried it myself in the listening. He hadn't called to tell me about his fancy salary, luxury apartment, or expensive lunches, but to tell me that he hadn't been invited back to work at the law firm after graduation.

This information had followed a story about a woman in the office who found him so brilliant she wanted to see what he could do "just with a phonebook," and concerned a partner at the firm who had turned down his request for a private office. Unable to concentrate in the office he shared with another summer associate who Michael felt was rudely unsympathetic to his needs, he'd told the partner in charge that he needed his own room.

The firm wasn't in the habit of giving summer associates private offices, so Michael told her that he'd been hospitalized for schizophrenia. Whether, as Michael claimed, the partner was appalled, or merely surprised, he wound up shouting, in what he represented as a culminating moment of heroic defiance: "Men like Guido Calabresi don't remember people like you!"

The mystery to me was that he was still there at all.

I recognized how great his frustration must have been. Once, he'd done his homework walking to class in the shoving corridor of a public high school with three thousand students. Now the presence of another associate made it impossible to get any work done at all. But did Michael know that was a terrible thing to say? Or did he really believe he'd spoken harsh truth to abusive power?

The ambiguity unsettled me, but so did the ease with which I'd risen to the bait about Henry James apartments, surrendering to envy and resentment with the speed of a tourist dropping a twenty on a three-card monte table. Only afterward did I see how fully I'd failed to recognize that his job was a disaster from the start; just as I'd failed to take his account of himself curled up on his bed with thoughts of suicide seriously, seeing it as the extravagant return of a hyperbolic habit.

Michael did not pretend his past away, but spoke of Yale Law School as a halfway house with the sort of sly humor that erased the real halfway house, the reasons he'd been sent there, and the advice he'd disregarded about small steps and modest goals. Or maybe he was acknowledging those things, but by joining them to the lives of the best and the brightest, who had stepped off the treadmill with him and lived by a different set of rules, he was making them into a universal condition.

Before demanding a private office at his summer law firm, Michael had gone to New Haven to consult with Bo Burt and other mentors. Bo listened sympathetically to Michael, who wanted to know if he had a case under the Americans with Disabilities Act that had been signed into law by President Bush the year Michael entered law school and that included schizophrenia among enumerated disabilities.

Bo agreed that the situation at the law firm was bad, and that a private workspace was a reasonable accommodation as called for by the act, not to mention by common decency. Nevertheless, he did not recommend any sort of legal action. And he knew about such things, not only because he had worked on what became the Fair Housing Act of 1968 but because he was on the board of the Mental Health Law Project, devoted to legal advocacy for people with mental illness, which would soon change its name to the Bazelon Center.

Believing Michael brilliant wasn't the same as believing he could do the work that a law firm wanted done, or thinking a private office would make a difference. Bo was surprised that Owen, who knew Michael's limitations, had set it up. Law school was one thing, especially at an accommodating place whose teachers prided themselves on stimulating thought rather than imparting information and demanding it back. Bo had already concluded that Michael wasn't going to become a lawyer. So what?

Bo was troubled by Michael's expectation that a law firm would behave like Yale Law School, and a law partner would be as eager to accommodate him as Bo and his colleagues were. He knew that they would not, and he did not think the Americans with Disabilities Act would resolve the matter the way Michael needed. The law had not yet been invented that could create psychological satisfaction.

What Bo feared had in fact happened. The firm, which after all was run by lawyers, found its own way of complying. Michael wasn't given his own office, but he wasn't given any work to do either. If he could not concentrate with someone else in the room, then he would not have to. He got paid, and he could tell other people, as he told me, that he was spending the summer at a fancy law firm. But no work was given to him and nothing was expected of him. He was simply left alone.

CHAPTER TWENTY-SIX

POSTDOC

Intellect annuls Fate.

—Ralph Waldo Emerson, *The Conduct of Life*

The Cold War ended and the walls came down, though not the way we'd feared crouching in the hallway of Roosevelt Elementary. Nothing turned out quite as predicted, but if it had, history would have run on iron tracks and the West wouldn't have won. I still had Michael's well-thumbed paperback of *The Gulag Archipelago* on my shelf; perhaps now I wouldn't have to read it. The protesters who had tried to levitate the Pentagon in 1967, with the aid of Allen Ginsberg's chanting, had somehow lifted up the Kremlin and tipped it over instead. It wasn't their politics; it was their blue jeans. And the music, which hadn't died after all.

It was an exciting time to be at Yale Law School. The school's stock had never been higher. Three dominant candidates in the Democratic primary for president were graduates of Yale Law School, a fact the *Times* covered like a policy position. Guido turned up more than a Page Six celebrity in the *New York Post*, and if he wasn't giving an interview, he was the subject of one.

One third-year law student was quoted saying that Guido told all first years they were brilliant, but the three front-runners had believed him. This did nothing to devalue the Calabresian currency. On the contrary, if taking Guido seriously got you that far, there was clearly something to it. Especially when the front-runner was a saxophone-playing baby boomer who had inhaled everything at Yale Law School but pot and classes. Bill Clinton had spent most of his time working for political campaigns, and even now seemed to be governor of Arkansas in his spare time. He skated over everything with charm, charisma, and chutzpah, which was Michael's kind of story.

The faculty remembered Bill's wife, Hillary Rodham, better than the candidate. A formidable figure in her own right, she'd worked with Owen Fiss on Nixon's impeachment fresh out of law school. She'd also been a research assistant for two of Michael's mentors, Joe Goldstein and Jay Katz, was thanked in *Beyond the Best Interests of the Child*, and credited the Yale Child Study Center with teaching her that it "takes a village to raise a child."

It took a village to raise a lawyer too. Guido was quoted in the *Times* calling the alumni community "this village of 7,000 people," an affirmation of Michael's communitarian values. He might not remember Bill from class, but Guido was so excited waiting for his motorcade that he was literally jumping up and down, according to the *Times* reporter who was waiting with him. The candidate had planned only a quick drive-through, but after being hugged and kissed by Guido, he could not say no to the alumni picnic.

Guido, who had so much faith in Michael's brilliance, knew a winner when he saw one, and GPA had nothing to do with it. As the *Times* explained, "lackluster records matter little at an elite institution where grades have always been considered unnecessary and even redundant." The Yale Law School, Guido declared, was "the closest thing that the United States has to an École Normale Supérieure—the training place for leaders of a society."

When Bill Clinton won the election, Yale Law School declared victory. Guido unveiled a portrait of the new president before he'd even been sworn in. *Time* magazine, which put the president-elect on the cover as Man of the Year, reported that Bill and Hillary had fallen in love with each other and the law in the Yale Law School library. As one law student told the alumni magazine, students were "going around wondering when they'll meet their Hillary or when they'll meet their Bill."

Professors were also in a state of high anticipation, as an unnamed "observer" told the magazine: "We're looking at the prospect of the Law School becoming a sort of shadow government." There was open speculation that Bill and Hillary would do for Yale what JFK had done for Harvard, and FDR, with his "brains trust," had done for Yale, Harvard, and Columbia.

It was also a victory for the sixties generation, whose time had come. George H. W. Bush, emblem of the old Yale, was out; William Jefferson Clinton, avatar of the new, was in. Bush had announced that the nineties would be "the Decade of the Brain," promising cures for schizophrenia and Alzheimer's disease. That work would certainly continue, but a different decade of the brain had also begun.

Nearly 250 university presidents and deans had taken the unprecedented step during the campaign of signing an open letter endorsing Clinton. Giving up their customary neutrality, they'd risked federal funds to back the Rhodes Scholar and Yale Law grad whose "boldness of mind" they believed could restore education to its high place in the culture. Even Guido—who had managed to believe both Clarence Thomas (YLS class of '74) and Anita Hill (YLS class of '80)— had signed the letter.

Intelligence had won. The candidate who had denounced "the brain-dead policies of both parties" was going to put brains back into the White House. The last frayed synapses of Reagan's brain would be swept out, along with the Skull and Bonesman who had all but inherited the job.

When Gennifer Flowers claimed during the campaign that she'd had an affair with Bill Clinton, Hillary denounced her as "some failed cabaret singer who doesn't have much of a résumé to fall back on." The meritocracy had spoken; you might sleep with my husband, but your résumé sucks.

Though Richard Nixon, who turned out still to be alive, told the *Times* that "if the wife comes through as being too strong and too intelligent, it makes the husband look like a wimp," being smart and denigrating other people's intelligence was back. "It's the economy, stupid" was a winning campaign slogan. As for being a wimp, which had worked four years earlier on the hapless governor of Massachusetts, Michael Dukakis—whose wife had been Mychal's preschool dance teacher—Bill flew home to Arkansas to oversee the execution of a mentally disabled Black man. After that, nobody called him a wimp or accused him of seeing a psychiatrist, a charge against Dukakis repeated by all the major papers.

You don't get endorsed by 250 university educators if you can't learn from the past. If dispatching someone with an IQ of 60 inoculated you against accusations of psychiatric, moral, military, or juridical weakness, it was a small price to pay for a chance to effect real change once in office. Even if the impaired prisoner had set aside the pecan pie from his last meal "for later" before being killed by lethal injection.

The biggest consequence of the election for Michael was that the new president nominated Guido to the US Court of Appeals for the Second Circuit. His appointment was a great source of pride for Michael, closer by association to the corridors of judicial authority. It was also a blow. From the day Michael had arrived, and even before that day, Guido had been his guardian angel.

It was a loss for Guido, too, a master educator and institution builder who had transformed Yale into the top-ranked law school in the country. He'd been hoping for solicitor general, but the post had gone to a member of his faculty instead. Still, it wasn't bad for a refugee from fascist Italy.

In addition to chambers in Lower Manhattan, Guido would have a court office in New Haven with a grand view of the New Haven Green and a door that would remain open to Michael, who meanwhile continued his visits. Once Michael told Guido, "You know, when I woke up this morning, I thought you were the devil."

Michael had a way of giving such statements a musing remoteness that made them seem more like curiosities than confessions. Such matter-of-fact declarations fascinated Guido, especially because Michael added that he had come to the conclusion, after thinking it over, that he was probably wrong and Guido wasn't the devil.

That Michael could wake up believing something so irrational was troubling, certainly, but his ability to persuade himself that it was false was a genuine triumph of reason. Just as his ability to articulate his inner conflict so well seemed a victory of order over chaos.

Sometimes Guido phoned up his daughter Nina, who had become a doctor, so he could share amusing stories about the extravagant things Michael told him. "We're all fairly neurotic," Guido liked to say, but still he was amazed by just how neurotic someone with schizophrenia could be.

Nina hadn't seen Michael for some time, though she vividly remembered his intelligence and charm and knew what an entertaining talker he could be. She was also training to become a psychiatrist, and understood that there was nothing "neurotic" about someone who thought his room was on fire, or who believed her mild-mannered father was the devil.

She did her best to disabuse her father of his misconceptions, but Guido, a stubborn optimist, was the product of a legal revolution that had merged law and the social sciences. Though his own area was economics, he'd been shaped by psychoanalytic thinking at a time when psychology had played a heroic role in nothing less than the battle against segregation. He also had the benefit of conversations with Michael, whose ability to put his inner world into words gave their meetings a psychoanalytic authority all its own.

Guido loved and respected his daughter, but he was a lawyer and presided over the greatest law school in the world; he wasn't easily persuaded of anything. And so, father and daughter argued back and forth, the distinguished dean and the young psychiatrist in training who was working with mentally ill homeless people in Boston. The people she cared for, or tried to care for, frequently slept in parks and under bridges, and often refused assistance of any kind.

They had already taught her a great deal.

"Dad," she told him, "you have no idea what you're talking about."

The first time Steve Yandle saw Michael, he'd thought, "He's never going to make it." That was the day he helped Guido carry a bed across the courtyard and into the little room where the towering bespectacled law student was raging and weeping inconsolably. Since that time, Yandle had become one of Michael's biggest boosters and a great believer in his genius.

Michael could not have done better than the custodial duo who had carried a bed into his room that first day. As associate dean for financial affairs, Yandle had been an indispensable ally in Guido's campaign to separate the law school financially from the rest of the university, and in reaping the fundraising bonanza that followed. Yandle ran interference for Michael with the administration and its bureaucracy with such zealous force that Michael called him his "blocking back."

Yandle supported his dream of entering legal academia, the hardest and most competitive path of all. He offered guidance, encouragement, and editorial support as Michael struggled to produce work that could be published in law journals, a necessary step for any sort of scholarly career. Furthering that end, the law school made Michael a postdoctoral associate when his three years came to an end.

This was unprecedented. Michael said the position had been created just for him in recognition of his talents and in anticipation of the work he was going to do. He still had the old witnessing way of sharing good news as if we were both appreciative members of his audience, but it felt freighted with a deep wounded need for affirmation that gave even his grandiosity a poignant desperation. Freed from teaching or attending classes, he would continue to assist scholars with their research while conducting his own. He would also visit classes to discuss disability law, sharing his own experience as he saw fit.

If Michael saw his postdoctoral appointment as a special accommodation from the administration, he did not say so. On the contrary, it was a vindication of the faith Guido had shown in him from the beginning. It was also a rebuke to the doctors who, in Michael's memorable phrase, had regarded him as a high-functioning schizophrenic but a low-functioning person. The prophecy he'd shouted at the law partner who had refused his request for an office, flouted the Americans with Disabilities Act, and shamed him with payment for no work, had come to pass. People like Guido Calabresi didn't remember people like her; they remembered people like him.

Best of all, becoming the law school's one and only postdoctoral associate solved, at least in the short term, the problem hanging over him: What would he do after law school? He had received no job offers and, despite Joe Goldstein's faith, connections, and strenuous efforts, no clerkship, not even the part-time gig for the semiretired justice Lewis Powell that Goldstein had tried to create.

Not only did the providential postdoc defer the question of Michael's next step, it made Yale Law School itself the next step. Perhaps it could also be the step after that, holding out the promise—why not?—of a permanent home.

In the meantime, it allowed Goldstein's academic ambitions for Michael, and Bo's idea of his future as an advocate, to live together peacefully awhile longer. Turning to disability law, Michael, perhaps without knowing it, was working toward a union of his mentors' dreams when he talked about combining scholarship, advocacy, and legal reform to create a society based on what he called communitarian values.

The word "communitarian" had gained academic currency but remained vague enough for Michael to fill it up with his own emphasis on interdependence and what he called "nurturing inclusiveness." He spoke earnestly about the failure of capitalist culture to foster mutual commitments outside of competition, and the pitfalls of an exaggerated focus on the individual who could no longer withstand the pitiless forces of industrial society.

Paradoxically, it was Yale Law School, one of the country's most competitive and elite institutions, that had given Michael a glimpse of the sort of communitarian life he hoped to see replicated in the larger world, and wanted to promote with the work his fellowship would allow him to pursue. For Michael, the law school was itself an emblem of "nurturing inclusiveness."

When Michael told the parable of the bed, he tended to replace Associate Dean Yandle with Chuck Laudor, unable to resist the symmetry of his father and Guido hauling the heavy rudiments of a steel frame and mattress out of a storage basement and up a narrow staircase. And because one embellishment led to another, Michael had the two men getting down on their hands and knees to knock it together with a brick that they passed back and forth, his New Rochelle father and his New Haven father literally making his bed.

The law school really did combine the familial and the professional, especially now that he had been freed from classes and coursework. It had also become a lonelier place. Most of Michael's classmates had left after three years, and those who remained in New Haven no longer lived in the dorms.

The day was long. Michael spent a lot of time outside the cafeteria, chatting with students as they came and went, waving to passersby or sitting meditatively with a closed law book beside him, like one of those men in Harvard Yard or Washington Square Park waiting with a chess board and a game clock for someone to challenge them to a five-dollar round of speed chess. Owen Fiss would see him there as he walked to his office, and found him in the same spot on his way out.

Michael also had Carrie. They didn't live together; Carrie had to get up early for her job at IBM and Michael had no bedtime to speak of. Still, their relationship had deepened, and he spoke with grateful admiration of her beauty, devotion, and self-effacing kindness. There was an earnest innocence in the way he talked, like a kid putting all his coins on the counter and asking what he could buy.

At the same time, I was aware of something a little rueful in the way he made a point of telling me about her Catholic upbringing as if he hadn't told me before. This was different from the melting-pot pride with which he'd celebrated friends and girlfriends in the past, turning them into cartoonish patches on his big multicultural quilt: the intense Asian, the Hollywood Jew, the girl with coffee-and-cream skin, the all-American boy with the Nazi grandma whose cousin—several times removed but still—was hanged at Nuremberg.

Michael brought up Carrie the Catholic—who didn't see herself that way—with a complex confessional air, as if he needed me to know something and was daring me to denounce him while secretly appealing for absolution. I had a feeling this had to do with me personally, or perhaps my father, who had been among the hovering Holocaust survivors keeping watch outside his window during his psychotic break, ringing bells to let him know that all was well.

Next to Michael, whose needs and personality dominated every room, Carrie seemed to recede into protective watchfulness. Still, it was clear that Michael and Carrie were in love with each other. Michael had begun to talk about wanting to get married and have a family. He spoke with passion about his longing to be a father, while agonizing over the fear that he would "give" schizophrenia to his children, or that he wouldn't be able to find a job to support them.

CHAPTER TWENTY-SEVEN

THOUGHTFUL ENABLING

Perhaps outrageous arrogance is needed in
certain circumstances.

—MICHAEL LAUDOR, "Disability and Community:
Modes of Exclusion, Norms of Inclusion, and the
Americans with Disabilities Act of 1990,"
Syracuse Law Review, 1992

Michael liked to refer to Yale Law School as America's most
supportive mental healthcare facility, a wry statement of gratitude that had the added benefit of suggesting that everyone around
him was also in need of supportive services. Both meanings fit easily
into his vision of the good society that lay at the heart of his first
scholarly essay, which, despite a chewy academic title, proposed changes
not merely in law but "basic social attitudes," along with "a redefinition
of standard ways of thinking."

Challenging the narrow application of the Americans with Disabilities Act, which had failed to help him during his summer employment, Michael offered a vision of society where everyone was
a patient as well as a healer, and where the distinction between them
ultimately ceased to matter. Emphasizing what he called "communal wounding and communal healing," Michael sounded like Paul
preaching to the Corinthians—"if one member suffers, all the members suffer"—as he called for a society that knit the able and disabled
into a single interdependent fabric.

In addition to blaming Henry Kissinger and the gunslinger Shane, the outlaw hero of one of the paperback westerns he used to carry around—for reinforcing the myth of "the successful, powerful loner"—Michael blamed Justice Powell for a Supreme Court opinion he'd written in the 1970s that had influenced the Americans with Disabilities Act of 1990. Justice Powell's opinion had upheld the right of a nursing school to reject a deaf applicant because she couldn't read lips when people wore surgical masks, required in many areas of the hospital, or hear the call buzzer pushed by patients in distress, or understand directions shouted in an emergency, despite the school's sending her to an audiologist and paying for hearing aids.

The court decided that because the deaf woman was incapable of fulfilling the core requirements of the program, even after a good-faith effort at reasonable accommodation of her disability was made, the nursing school was justified in turning her away to avoid placing "undue financial and administrative burdens" on the state funding the program. Michael wanted to give "teeth" to the Americans with Disabilities Act by eliminating the ADA's exemptions based on financial considerations. Phrases like "business necessity" and "undue hardship" were "weasel words," he wrote, allowing companies to make economic calculations the basis of the "reasonable compliance" that the law mandated. "Reasonable" was itself a weasel word. Either you welcomed people with disabilities to the table or you cast them out like "lepers shunned in earlier times."

What had sent the case to the Supreme Court, and what interested Michael, was confusion over the phrase "otherwise qualified handicapped individual." Was the law intended to protect someone who was qualified *in spite of* a disability, or was an "otherwise qualified" individual someone who could not do the same work as everyone else even with a reasonable accommodation? In its unanimous ruling, the court, which included Justices William Brennan and Thurgood Marshall, concluded that an "otherwise qualified" person could only mean someone with a disability who could do the same job as everyone else "in spite of his handicap," so long as a reasonable accommodation, like hearing aids, was provided.

To make its point, the court used the example of a blind bus driver, someone who might be considered "otherwise qualified" because the blind driver could do everything except see. But because you cannot drive if you cannot see, and driving was the core requirement of the job, the commonsense reading of "otherwise qualified" had to mean qualified *in spite of a disability*.

Justice Powell expressed the hope that new technologies might change the deaf woman's situation, and the situation of others with disabilities. He called for careful oversight of the law and acknowledged that it wasn't always possible to identify "the line between a lawful refusal to extend affirmative action," on the one hand, and "illegal discrimination against handicapped persons" on the other. Michael rejected the court's finding even with its caveats.

Instead of a blind bus driver, Michael wrote, Justice Powell should have used the example of "a fully qualified software engineer who cannot get up the steps to a place of employment because he is in a wheelchair." But a fully qualified software engineer, who needed only a ramp, was precisely the sort of person the court considered qualified. Climbing stairs wasn't part of being a software engineer but a reasonably surmounted impediment unconnected to the job.

Despite the proud words "Post-doctoral Associate, Yale Law School" glossing his name at the bottom of the first page, and the two-year reprieve it had given him, Michael was racing against a loudly ticking clock. He might find a way to make his own struggle an aspect of his academic work, but he still had to publish more articles and find a job. He was fearful about the future.

Managing a full-time illness wasn't the same as writing about disability law, even if it gave his work a shape and purpose. Though he increasingly drew on his own experience when professors invited him to speak to their students about law and disability, officially he was still in the closet about his schizophrenia.

No wonder he wanted to change minds as well as laws, fix the culture that shaped the Americans with Disabilities Act and the laws that shaped the culture. He wanted to inspire "nurturing inclusiveness" while mandating an "inclusiveness obligation" to make sure it got done, widening the world to receive him through what he called "thoughtful enabling."

Michael was late for the "rights revolution" that had animated his teachers, but he wanted to establish "a right to have the community enfold and nurture a person, even against his will." This wasn't a right to treatment, or a right to refuse treatment; it was a right to be loved and cared for by society. How this right to be nurtured would be established or enforced he did not say, only that "like many a civil rights activist, I remain confident in the ultimate ability of our American community to grow and change and accept."

He wanted a version of the "open warmth of community" that President Kennedy had signed into law before he died, which had never been delivered. Even the "cold mercy" it was supposed to replace was in short supply. Michael was standing with his promissory note demanding his due.

Joe Goldstein and David Bazelon, trying to alleviate the undue burdens of responsibility laid on people of color and the poor arrested for breaking the law, had borrowed from people with severe mental illness the exculpatory nature of their disability, hoping to mitigate punishment in those they assigned it to by temporarily diminishing expectations of autonomy. Michael did the reverse, borrowing from the fight for racial and economic equality and applying it to people with disabilities of every type, gathered into an interchangeable assembly.

Michael knew by heart the opening of the Kerner Commission report, with its ominous warning that America was becoming "two societies, one black, one white—separate and unequal," the way he knew the opening of FDR's "Infamy" speech. President Johnson had assembled the Kerner Commission during the race riots of 1967. This was Michael's version: "The disabled have been systematically excluded from our American community," he wrote. "They have lived in a shadow world, a world of separate but unequal treatment."

But Michael's argument transcended racial and even human distinctions. We all depended on "the blind burrowing of worms aerating the soil," he wrote, and "the microscopic but quietly heroic efforts of nitrogen-fixing bacteria, allowing our food to grow," rendering autonomy not only impossible but a selfish and destructive fantasy. We are "all mutually interdependent," Michael wrote, and all in need of a "nurturing community," an echo of Martin Luther King Jr.'s "beloved community."

It was natural for Michael to speak in the language of the civil rights movement, whose rhythms we had grown up with and whose jurisprudence was built into the classes he took. Just as it was natural for him to reach back to our childhood, when we had sung "We Shall Overcome" at Farm Camp Lowy. There was a haunting symmetry in Michael ending his first scholarly publication with the words "deep in my heart, I do believe."

Michael had been in his last year of law school when I got married to Mychal, who was in her last year of rabbinical school. Our wedding was in my parents' house on Mereland Road, in a ceremony small enough for everyone to fit on the patio if the weather was good, and in the dining room if it was bad. The wedding wasn't small because of the house; we had chosen the house because the wedding was small.

I'd come a long way since my bar mitzvah, more than half my life ago, but I had no intention of beginning married life like one of those fainting goats that keel over every time a tractor backfires. Our small gathering had gone beautifully, even when my father grew confused reciting the refrain of a Yiddish poem—"they burnt us and burnt us"—and simply ended his toast there and wandered off.

Michael loved the fact that I was married to a rabbi. Whenever he saw us together on Mereland Road, he gave his great arcing wave and loped up the hill to greet us. Mychal's presence seemed to vouch for me or restore something our childhood friendship had once supplied. I had been married for over a year and still hadn't mentioned my wedding, embarrassed I hadn't invited him. He'd known immediately anyway, the same way I knew his father had cancer, which he never brought up. We were kept informed about each other by our mothers, who had resumed diplomatic relations and filled in whatever gaps were left with gossip from mutual friends.

Michael knew my parents had sold their house and were moving to Manhattan, which was the main reason I was spending more time on Mereland. He didn't need to be told about my father's illness, which was neurological but worn conspicuously on the outside.

He always addressed Mychal with the courtly formality that had reminded Jo-Ann of her Austro-Hungarian grandfather. The wry spin he put on "Rabbi" wasn't a challenge to her authority but a tribute to the youth and beauty that went incongruously with it.

Michael paid due deference to the guttural sound in the middle of Mychal's Hebrew name. He knew Mychal was the daughter of King Saul, who had accepted two hundred foreskins for her from the future King David, which brought us back to a Jewish joke about a wallet that turned into a suitcase. Her middle name, Batsheva, belonged to the woman King David saw bathing on the roof and claimed for his own, for which he was chastised by Nathan the prophet: *Thou art the man.*

There was something more than flirtation in the single-minded attention Michael gave Mychal as he worked biblical phrases and quo-

tations from Martin Buber into the conversation. The show-off curiosity that had once displayed superior knowledge in the guise of a
question had been replaced by a seeker's sincerity. There were things
he needed to know, even if he could not put them entirely into words.

Mychal took seriously the yearning intensity with which Michael
voiced religious concerns and listened for answers. When he talked
about Carrie, he studied Mychal's face with a stiff scrutinizing expression, relaxing under her approving smile that granted absolution
without even knowing it, just by being happy he'd found someone
he loved.

Neither of us had met Carrie, but Mychal had grown up in Brookline, the Boston suburb next to Newton where Carrie had spent her
high school years. They'd also been neighbors of a sort, having lived
in adjacent suburbs connected by a trolley line. They were both Yale-
educated, literature-loving Red Sox fans, intelligent and empathetic
women who wanted to devote their lives to helping people. Carrie
delivered meals to homebound AIDS patients and dreamed of bringing computers to kids in low-income neighborhoods; Mychal was training to become a hospital chaplain and spent her day visiting patients
in a cancer hospital.

Friends of Michael, and Michael himself, tended to describe Carrie as someone who preferred to remain in his shadow, peering out
shyly while keeping a protective eye on him. Nobody talked about
ideas at her dinner table, Michael said sorrowfully, as if describing
a childhood of extreme poverty. The verbal sparring he'd taken for
granted at home, where ideas were a blood sport, daunted Carrie.
She sat out the battles of wit and one-upmanship at Ferber gatherings,
where Michael held court and was treated like a minor celebrity even
by his psychiatrist, who was a frequent guest.

Michael described their families with an eye for comic difference.
Carrie's mother was a pious Catholic who went to mass every day
and had raised her three daughters to think of others before themselves.

Michael's mother had raised three titanic sons who fought like the Stooges over food and politics while she tried to stay sane with singing and outbursts of abrupt laughter. Still, they shared a devotion to people in need; Carrie's mother was a nurse specializing in the care of people with colostomy bags, while Michael's mother worked at an agency that administered group homes for people with intellectual disabilities.

Frankly, the families did not sound so different to me, though Carrie's father had served on submarines, which Michael considered the quintessence of goyish activity and was why Carrie had been born near a giant naval base in Norfolk, Virginia. Her father was a taciturn mercurial man who sang in the church choir, got a PhD in biostatistics, and moved the family north. Michael's father, who had a PhD in economics and had learned to swim off the coast of Brooklyn, was a voluble mercurial man who did not run silent but could be heard at the top of Mereland talking at the bottom. He was known to curse at the television set because, as Michael explained to Carrie, shouting at the news was something Jews did, a perfectly normal response to a crazy world, like throwing furniture.

Carrie's practical skills had served her well in her work for IBM, but Michael had encouraged her to get a one-year master's degree in education at Harvard so she could follow her dream of using computers to boost the quality of education for poor kids in neighborhoods with lousy schools. This was a generous act on Michael's part because New Haven was a lonely place for him without classes, grateful as he was to have his postgraduate fellowship, which may have been why we saw him more on Mereland.

According to Michael, Carrie's parents weren't happy that their daughter was in love with a Jewish man who had schizophrenia, or as he put it, "a crazy Jew." He said it with humor, but it was bitter humor and clearly a source of pain. It wasn't hard to imagine that practicing Catholics wanted their daughter to be with a Catholic man.

Michael talked about wanting a Jewish family, and could hardly be surprised that practicing Catholics wanted their daughter to marry inside the church. But it was hard for him to keep that expectation separate from an ancient antipathy to his religion, just as it was hard for him to distinguish between a parental preference for someone who *hadn't* set his own novel on fire, and Oliver Wendell Holmes Jr.'s 1927 support of forced sterilization to prevent being "swamped by incompetence" in *Buck v. Bell*.

Such distinctions were especially hard for someone who couldn't be sure a room *wasn't* on fire just because nobody else saw the flames. Plenty of serious people in the not-so-distant past had considered his religion a genetic disease, and his illness the work of the devil, or vice versa. Even Louis Brandeis joined the 8–1 majority opinion that justified the sterilization of Carrie Buck, her mother, and her young daughter because, in Holmes's fateful phrase, "three generations of imbeciles are enough."

Everyone learned about the 1967 Supreme Court case *Loving v. Virginia*, which had struck down the portion of Virginia's hateful "racial integrity" act preventing Black people and white people from marrying. But how many people knew that the 1924 law—which had been used against Carrie Buck, who was white—contained other marriage restrictions besides race, requiring husbands to swear that "neither is she nor am I a habitual criminal, idiot, imbecile, hereditary epileptic, or insane person." Even the Warren Court had left those provisions on the books, where they remained until 1976.

Michael himself wrestled with what he considered a religious obligation to have children, and a conjoined fear of passing on schizophrenia like a curse. The essay he'd been working on since "Disability and Community" argued that certain miserable children had the right to sue their parents for violating a "right not to be born in such a state that we would have been better off never to have existed." The essay, which he wound up calling "In Defense of a Wrongful

Life," was a declaration of rights for those not yet alive: "All we need is a right to be born not tortured, not miserable, not utterly wretched." He wanted to protect, as well, "those harmed by the birth of a person whom we cause to be born." All this made having children an even more daunting responsibility. As Michael explained, "in the timelessness of God, future people are as important as we are."

CHAPTER TWENTY-EIGHT

CAREER KILLER

The worst part about having schizophrenia in
my life, without a doubt: no jobs. Nobody will
hire me. A hundred different interviews, and
every one of them will say, "Oh, mentally
ill—we don't hire you people." That's tough.

—Dr. Frederick J. Frese III, director of psychology
at Western Reserve Psychiatric Hospital

Michael applied for academic law jobs when his two years as a
postgraduate associate were up. His dream was to be a professor at Yale Law School. His short-term plan was to find something
in the New York area so he could stay near friends, family, doctors,
and mentors.

Advised to avoid any mention of schizophrenia—a "career killer"—
Michael was unable to explain in interviews why he had never clerked
for a judge or worked at a law firm beyond a single summer. Michael's answer—that such work lacked the intellectual stimulation he
required—didn't help his case. He got no offers at all, a bitter blow.

His mentors remained supportive and kept their eyes out for research opportunities. They continued to invite Michael to speak to
their classes, but Yale Law School was no longer his home. He lived in
a tiny apartment in the Riverdale section of the Bronx, which he shared
with Carrie until she got her own place in Tuckahoe, a Westchester

town fourteen miles north of New York City. They were still to-gether, but the Bronx apartment was too small for two people with such different habits and routines.

Carrie was working in Manhattan, where she'd been hired by an ambitious start-up called the Edison Project, launched with great fanfare by Chris Whittle, a charismatic media entrepreneur. The Ed-ison Project's goal was nothing less than the transformation of pub-lic school education, which Whittle hoped to replace with a for-profit system that would allow the poor to attend for free.

Carrie's expertise in computers, and the education degree Michael had encouraged her to get, made her a good fit for the project, which put technology at its center and promised to give every family a free home computer, a novel idea at the time. It was an exciting job, and Whittle had hired away the president of Yale University, Benno Schmidt, to be Edison's CEO. Schmidt, who had raised a billion dollars for Yale in his relatively brief tenure, had likened the project's scale and ambition to the D-Day landing.

While Michael wondered if his academic dreams were over, Car-rie was commuting to the Edison Project's fancy Fifth Avenue digs and working, though not directly, for Schmidt, a noted First Amend-ment scholar who had clerked for Earl Warren and served as dean of Columbia Law School before running Yale.

Michael and I no longer had chance meetings on Mereland. When we spoke on the phone, which wasn't often, he sounded sunk in gloom. He'd lost the world that had sheltered him for five years and hadn't found a job or community to replace it.

Meanwhile, Carrie was swept up in a demanding new enterprise. She was incredibly busy, traveling to pilot schools, connecting home computers to a larger network that she was helping to create. The schools were frequently in the poorest part of town, in districts most amenable to outside intervention because they were failing. Carrie was devoted to the job; the goals were noble and the work engaging.

But the hours were long even when she wasn't on the road. Her absences made a hard year for Michael even harder.

Michael was volunteering at the Westchester Independent Living Center in White Plains, which offered peer support, referral services, and advocacy for people with physical and psychiatric disabilities. He admired the center's energetic director, Joe Bravo, a scrappy disabilities advocate in his late thirties who had been in a wheelchair since the age of twelve, when he was shot in the chest while riding his bicycle in his Bronx neighborhood.

The first independent living center, like the disability rights movement itself, had been created at Berkeley. Without the struggle for disability rights—born even before the free speech movement took flight—Guido could not have told Michael that he and Steve Yandle would be his ramp. There had been no ramps, and no people in wheelchairs in either the back or front of the bus when Ed Roberts, an unfathomably courageous man with post-polio quadriplegia, sued Berkeley and won admission to the college in 1962. He turned the empty wing of the university hospital, where he slept in an eight-hundred-pound iron lung, into a dorm, a clamorous hangout space, and a political movement.

When Roberts and 150 other disabled activists occupied a federal building in San Francisco in the 1970s, the Black Panthers brought them food. The Westchester center Joe Bravo ran was an offshoot of the independent living movement that had been born as a renegade act of communal self-help at Berkeley and grown into federally mandated associations operating in every state.

No wonder Michael was drawn to metaphors of physical disability, which conveyed so much more concretely the social condition of people with disregarded potential and the changes needed to accommodate them. Setting the imprisoned self free had a different valence when told about someone who couldn't walk.

Joe Bravo was impressed with Michael, a Yale Law School graduate who dressed like a Wall Street banker and talked about himself with startling candor and eloquence. Michael had been a peer counselor as an undergraduate, and he worked with Bravo to create the Westchester Consumer Empowerment Center, which offered counseling to people with mental and physical disabilities. Michael's willingness to share his story, and the story he had to tell about finishing Yale Law School despite schizophrenia, made him an inspiring figure.

Michael was dividing his time between Riverdale and his parents' house. Chuck's prostate cancer was no longer responding to treatment, and Michael wanted to spend more time with him. His fear of losing his father loomed over everything. Chuck was the booster of all boosters, who had not only propelled Michael into law school but also talked him through fire each morning. There were days now when Chuck could not get out of bed himself.

The struggles and triumphs Michael shared so inspiringly at the independent living center, and in the seminars his former professors asked him to address, were precisely what he had left outside the door the year before when he'd applied for professorships. What if people had to see the shadow in order to appreciate the light? What if concealment was as dangerous as confession?

And there had been no victories. He'd betrayed his experience without accomplishing the desired end. The upside was that the person who'd been rejected the year before wasn't really him.

If Michael had agreed with those advising him that his only hope of success was in disguising his illness, he might have been doubly despondent. But he'd always believed in the power of his own story.

He applied for academic jobs the following year, and this time he did not deny his illness. It no longer seemed possible to conceal so much of himself.

Unfortunately, telling prospective employers in 1995 that schizophrenia was the reason he hadn't worked at a law firm was no more persuasive than telling them the year before that such work was intellectually beneath him. Hearing how delusions, imperfectly extinguished by enervating medication, made the stress of such places intolerable left them wondering what else he would find intolerable.

His honesty and eloquence asked them to find in what he could still do—and in the quality and clarity of his explanation of what he could not—a compensatory reason for hiring him. That did not happen. It was still early in the process when Chuck died.

Michael spoke at his father's funeral. Someone told me it was a "tour de force" without remembering what he'd said. Someone else described it as an elegiac outpouring delivered in the rollicking manner of a spellbinding Black preacher. I'd seen Michael deploy that mode, with its kinetic gestures and rhetorical flights, but only for comic effect. This was different, a sincere channeling of religious charisma fueled by grief, love, mania, and psychic turmoil.

During shiva, the traditional week of mourning, Myrna Rubin visited the Laudors with her son Eric. The families had been neighbors before the Laudors moved to Mereland, and Myrna had known Michael since he was a little boy in a superman costume.

Myrna was also a psychiatric social worker, Jane Ferber's best friend, and part of the Network. Jane was the reason Myrna had become a social worker; she'd encouraged her to go back to school, found her a job, first with Andy Ferber in the Bronx, and then with her at the Huguenot Center. It was Myrna, to her great regret, who had told Andy about her yoga teacher, just back from India, where she'd learned a new leaping technique, which had launched Andy's flight to Bhagwan.

Like Bo's friend Bonnie, who was Jane's other best friend, Myrna was one of the small group of women who gathered in Jane's kitchen and kept a watchful eye on Michael over the years. Seeing him in the Laudors' living room, Myrna found Michael in an alarming state. His eyes were wild, his words and emotions out of tune, not only with the occasion but somehow with himself. He spoke like someone in a badly dubbed movie, or a film with the sound out of sync so that what he said and how he looked when he said it were misaligned, as if the words and the feelings behind the words couldn't catch up with each other.

Michael spoke rhapsodically about his parents' marriage, praising their sex life, which he abruptly began describing in minute and graphic detail. This shocked Myrna, who worked at Creedmoor Psychiatric Center and wasn't easily shocked. The room froze. Michael's mother looked at him with weary reproof.

"Those are private things," Ruth told him in a low, careful voice. She spoke almost ritualistically, like someone used to repeating phrases. "We don't talk about things like that in public. They're private."

Part IV

✻

The House of Dreams

A hero ventures forth from the world of common
day into a region of supernatural wonder:
fabulous forces are there encountered and a
decisive victory is won: the hero comes back from
this mysterious adventure with the power to
bestow boons on his fellow man.

—Joseph Campbell,
The Hero with a Thousand Faces

If I am not what I've been told I am, then
it means that you're not what you thought
you were either.

—James Baldwin

CHAPTER TWENTY-NINE

ROLE MODEL

People with schizophrenia are negated
constantly, and I can be a role model.

—MICHAEL LAUDOR, quoted in *The New York Times*,
November 9, 1995

Two months after Chuck's death, in the fall of that difficult year, something extraordinary happened that changed Michael's fortunes almost overnight. Destiny was calling in the guise of an article in *The New York Times*.

The article was called "A Voyage to Bedlam and Part Way Back," and it ran on the front page of the Metro section on November 9, 1995. Under its poetic headline, in smaller type, a second headline—we called this "the deck" at my newspaper—modified the first: "Yale Law Graduate, a Schizophrenic, Is Encumbered by an Invisible Wheelchair."

"The most interesting feature of Michael B. Laudor's résumé," the article began, "can only be glimpsed between the lines." The reporter, *Times* staffer Lisa Foderaro, pursued a dual narrative, tracing the lines of Michael's conventional success while fleshing out the clues glimpsed between them. "Sprinkled among the stellar nuggets of his life," the story continued, "from graduating summa cum laude from Yale University in three years to being awarded a coveted postdoctoral associateship at Yale Law School, are references to his work as a mental health advocate and consultant on ethics in psychiatric research."

Foderaro offered a sort of alternate résumé: "Mr. Laudor, 32 and by all accounts a genius, is a schizophrenic who emerged from eight months in a psychiatric unit at Columbia-Presbyterian Medical Center to go to Yale Law School."

At the heart of the story was Michael's determination to find a job as a professor at a law school without denying or disguising his schizophrenia. "Some people at Yale Law School told me not to tell anyone because mental illness is a career killer," Michael explained. "They won't let you work in law firms, they won't let you work as a professor." This was the era of President Clinton's "Don't Ask, Don't Tell" policy regarding gays in the military. People with schizophrenia were practically unheard of in academia.

When Michael came out of the closet, he came out all the way. "Dubbing himself a 'flaming schizophrenic,'" Foderaro wrote, "Mr. Laudor said that his decision to make his illness public and work closely with others with mental disabilities was a political and religious one." The article resolved the tension between an academic career and a life of activism; Michael's quest to become a law professor without denying his mental illness *was* activism, like Ed Robert's quest for admission to Berkeley despite being told there was no place there for a quadriplegic student.

Guido Calabresi was given his due as the dean who "set the tone" for Michael's law school years, telling him "that he was in a sort of invisible wheelchair and that he would place ramps wherever needed." His faith was fully vindicated, and by the time Michael graduated, "Mr. Laudor had so impressed his professors that they asked him to join the school as an associate."

Chuck was the heroic father who had urged Michael to go to Yale Law School in the first place, after making the fateful trip with him to Herald Square, where they watched a Macy's cashier "besieged by snippy customers." Chuck's recent death, and Michael's devotion to his father during the final year of his illness, gave Michael's determination to succeed on his own terms an added poignancy.

I wondered if Chuck's death had been a factor in Michael's decision to go public. I wasn't sure how Chuck would have felt reading that "mental illness runs deep on his father's side of the family." Michael's triumph despite a stacked genetic deck was all the more impressive, but I remembered Chuck's pained, cautious allusions to family history after Michael's hospitalization.

Michael also spoke openly about his faith. "I am a religious person," he told the reporter, explaining that "we are all, as a nation of priests, called upon to do our part to heal the world." He took his part in the project of cosmic correction seriously. "People with schizophrenia are negated constantly," he said, "and I can be a role model." He could "stand up and say I am a person with schizophrenia" while also declaring himself "a reasonable candidate to be a law professor." Discussing his decision with *The New York Times*, along with his mental illness, took an extraordinary amount of personal courage.

Above the article, spanning four fifths of the page, was an enormous photograph of Michael leaning against a column in the Gothic gloom of the Yale Law School entranceway. He looked grimly dapper in a dark suit without a tie, his white shirt open at the throat, his beard and mustache neatly trimmed. The frame of the photograph was deep enough to show Michael at full height, his hands in his pockets, one foot crossed over the other.

The reporter described Michael as "tall, with fine features and big round glasses," though he had removed his glasses for the photograph, the way he did for school pictures. "He is charming and well dressed and makes the right amount of eye contact," she added.

I wondered if Michael would be insulted by those observations, though they were clearly intended as compliments, and perhaps a refutation of the notion that people with schizophrenia wore shabby clothes and looked away.

Describing schizophrenia as "the most common major mental illness—afflicting 1 in 100 people—and the most disabling," the article treated Michael's achievements as both emblematic and anomalous. "Some people do not respond to medication, and many do not have the constancy of support that Mr. Laudor has had from friends, relatives and a talented psychiatrist."

The heroic nature of Michael's recovery, those who helped him, and Michael himself were central to the story: "His success is about many things: the efficacy of new drugs in treating mental illness, the support of family, friends and colleagues and the steely refusal of a young man who became very sick at age 24 to be capsized by his disease."

It was a glowing profile that captured Michael's wry sense of humor—"I went to the most supportive mental health care facility that exists in America: the Yale Law School"—as well as his knack for harrowing formulations: "My reality was that at any moment they would surgically cut me to death without any anesthesia." He recalled the pain of his hospitalization with touching frankness: "I spent my 26th birthday there crying on my bed."

The story featured so many of Michael's telltale phrases and touchstone encapsulations, even when he wasn't being quoted, that he seemed as much the author of the piece as its subject. It wasn't just the stories but the shape and meaning the article gave his experiences that bore his distinctive stamp and style. Foderaro described Michael's childhood as an idyllic before-time: "Growing up in New Rochelle, Mr. Laudor was a standout from an early age. He often cut classes to play jazz guitar but got A's anyway."

"Mr. Laudor breezed through Yale in three years," the reporter wrote, and "had never been happier." Then came Bain and growing paranoia that his phone was tapped and musicians he jammed with were following him home. In New Rochelle, guardian neighbors rang bells of warning to ward off evil, protecting him in accordance with his reading of Psalm 130.

It was remarkable to see Michael lift the lid off stories he'd labored for years to conceal. No more sitting in parked cars swearing friends to secrecy; he poured his private life onto the pages of *The New York Times*, a newspaper with more than a million readers, confiding even his present experience with liberated eloquence: "I feel that I'm pawing through walls of cotton and gauze when I talk to you now," Michael told the reporter. "I'm using 60 or 70 percent of my effort just to maintain the proper reality contact with the world."

The article didn't say if his struggle to maintain "reality contact" was caused by the fog of illness or the fog of risperidone, the antipsychotic medication he took (another revelation). Either way, it was no small thing to tell the world you needed 70 percent of your mental energy just to maintain "reality contact," leaving you just 30 percent to be sane with, while claiming you were "a reasonable candidate to be a law professor."

Michael didn't seem concerned he might compromise his case. On the contrary, he spoke with the relaxed authority of an expert expounding a subject he knew well. Describing his illness from the inside out, he took his place among the pathologists peering down with fascination at the figure on the table mysteriously talking. Whether it was because Michael's 30 percent sounded like another man's hundred, or because people still thought we used less than 10 percent of our brains to begin with, Michael's confessions seemed only to enhance his authority. "As he quotes from Virgil's *Aeneid*," the reporter wrote, "and talks about synapses and dendrites with the ease of a neurologist, the pyrotechnics of his intellect are on full display."

Brilliance was the fulcrum of the story, the point at which Michael was lifted above the stereotypes of schizophrenia, much as intelligence elevated him beyond ordinary expectations before he got sick. "Far from knowing that Mr. Laudor had a severe mental illness," the reporter wrote, "the other students were somewhat in awe."

The timing of the article could not have been better. Michael was still applying for academic appointments, and the profile gave him a chance to take his case public. Guido, now a judge on the US Circuit Court of Appeals, offered a ringing if obliquely worded recommendation. "I think somebody who has the abilities Michael does should have an easier time than many because he is so talented," the former dean told the *Times*.

Despite Guido's optimism, the article described the insensitivity, ignorance, and fear that Michael was often forced to confront. "One interviewer asked if he was a violent," the reporter wrote, "which Mr. Laudor said reflected a common and painful stereotype."

I understood Michael's indignation, but I wished the article had addressed the question even a little instead of leaving it to Michael to dismiss in a way that made you feel as if even to ask were an insult. I could well believe it was a painful stereotype, but I also knew that before he was medicated, Michael had armed himself with a knife in fear of his imposter parents.

I felt even more confused by another painful stereotype Michael described encountering, ironically from the doctors at the day hospital. Foderaro quoted Michael's explanation without comment: "'They saw me as a very high-functioning schizophrenic but not a very high-functioning person, and what high-functioning schizophrenics can do is limited,' he said bitterly. 'I could aspire to working a register at Macy's.'"

I'd heard Michael tell this story before, and the doctors' employment suggestions did seem terrible. I could scarcely imagine the doom

Michael must have felt scouting Macy's with his father. But I also knew that Michael had found the halfway house an infantilizing insult to his abilities and independence, and he'd left before the staff considered him ready to go.

And even the ham-fisted doctors who had recommended Macy's or its equivalent had only been trying to come up with a temporary, low-stress way to help Michael find structure while he consolidated his gains and rebuilt skills it took time to recover. The work suggestions were intended to be slow steps on a long road back, not the final destination, as Michael implied when he said, "I could aspire to working a register at Macy's."

It was almost as if—a strange thought—he didn't want to raise the bar of high functioning to include success at Yale Law School, or an academic teaching job, but to eliminate the idea of schizophrenia itself, ironically at the very moment he was coming out of the closet.

One of the things that haunted me about Michael's breakdown was how frightened his parents had been. He'd been taken to the hospital against his will, and without a father like Chuck—capable of bullying, bluffing, and threatening Michael into signing himself in for his own good, as it certainly was—he might not have gotten those eight months of care he'd so desperately needed. Without that, who could say what might have happened?

Knowing even a portion of what Michael had been through, the death of his father, the inability to find work, the dark moods, stomach ailments, insomnia, and all the other large and lesser symptoms that his schizophrenia seemed to drag behind it the way a glacier gathers up trees and boulders—to say nothing of the medication he had to take, as if delusions and hallucinations weren't enough—I was shocked to discover what a storm of confused feeling the article stirred up in me. Afraid it was nothing but envy, I did my best to push it away, but the feeling persisted, a sense of something missing or out of tune, which hung in the air like an unanswered question I did not know how to ask.

The only doctor quoted in the article was a psychologist who had studied patients released from a state hospital in Vermont in 1950, where they had spent many years on a hopeless back ward. After twenty-five years of therapy and support in their rural communities, two thirds of the released patients, half of whom had schizophrenia, had "improved considerably or had fully recovered." Others had gone back to the hospital; some had died.

The study was a strong argument for the importance of community and home care, a reminder of how much patience and sustained dedication supportive care of any kind requires, and an argument for available beds in psychiatric hospitals for those who still needed to return for long or short periods of time. It didn't really address the efforts of a brilliant young lawyer trying to participate at the highest level of an elite intellectual culture despite prevailing prejudices, which was how the article framed Michael's dilemma.

"If somebody in a white coat tells you you have a terrible disorder and you're never going to get better," the psychologist told Foderaro, "chances are a whole group of people are going to buy off on that and it becomes a self-fulfilling prophecy."

That observation seemed both true and important. Michael, despite the caution of the day hospital doctors, had a network of champions; his father had all but carried him to Yale Law School, where he was welcomed with open arms by the dean, who knew he had schizophrenia. He had just been called a genius in the first paragraph of an article in *The New York Times*.

In the *Times* article, Michael only needed society to widen its gate the way Yale Law School had done. What was the meaning of the deck—"Yale Law Graduate, a Schizophrenic, Is Encumbered by an Invisible Wheelchair"—if not to suggest that it wasn't schizophrenia weighing Michael down but society's refusal to extend the ramps that Guido had metaphorically installed with such success? Refusing to accommodate his accommodations, the way a city bus with a lift accommodates a person in a visible wheelchair, society turned his simple need into a cumbersome burden.

The reporter, hailing Michael's success, summed up his challenge: "But shadowing his progress is always the question of whether to reveal himself as a person with schizophrenia." Stigma was real, and its consequences serious, but having visited Michael in the hospital, I didn't think the only question shadowing his progress was whether to disclose his schizophrenia.

I thought schizophrenia itself was the question, with its paranoid thinking and "negative symptoms" muffling the mind and the body alongside the medication whose side effects might someday outweigh its benefits. I heard other questions when Michael called me in a bottomless mood to say he was curled up in a fetal position thinking of ways to kill himself. Or when he agonized about whether his children would be genetically doomed, or sounded as he had when he shouted at a law partner that Guido Calabresi doesn't remember people like her.

At the end of the article, the reporter returned to Michael's job search, and sounded a hopeful note about the future: "Now, he is once again sending out résumés. Those who know him well are guardedly optimistic."

She gave Guido the last word, which was fitting, because his unguarded optimism had greeted Michael at the start of his hero's journey and given him a sense of belonging and purpose when he most needed it. Like the cupbearer remembering Joseph in the Bible, Guido had indeed remembered Michael. Now a federal judge, he offered up a final benediction: "He is a brilliant young person who has conquered what is always difficult—an illness—but conquered it extraordinarily well."

CHAPTER THIRTY

TWICE BORN

The inward journeys of the mythological hero,
the shaman, the mystic, and the schizophrenic
are in principle the same; and when the return
or remission occurs, it is experienced as a
rebirth: the birth, that is to say, of a
"twice-born" ego, no longer bound in by its
daylight-world horizon.

—Joseph Campbell, *Myths to Live By*

The profile in the *Times* didn't land Michael a job as a law professor, but the torrent of support that flowed from the article's
publication lifted him up after so many blows to his fractured identity. He had spoken up for a disparaged population, offered himself
as a role model, and given people with schizophrenia and their families desperately needed hope.

Laurie Flynn, the director of the National Alliance on Mental
Illness, recognized in Michael's story a tale she had heard over and
over: the golden child who goes off to anticipated glory only to come
home broken by severe mental illness. But Michael reminded the world
that this wasn't the end of the story. The outcome wasn't fixed, and
in the hopeful Decade of the Brain a new story was being written
every day by researchers, doctors, advocacy groups like NAMI, and

above all by people like Michael, who had stepped out of the shadows to tell his own story.

NAMI had been created in the aftermath of deinstitutionalization by parents caring for children with severe mental illness, many already adults with no place to go. A group nearly as maligned as their ailing children—often by the very doctors they turned to for help—these parents sought each other out amid the ruins of the state hospital system and the failed promise of the community mental health movement that had vowed to replace it.

Banding together in 1979, the caregivers and practitioners who created NAMI offered emotional support and practical information while fighting absurd laws, inadequate services, and the stigmatizing ignorance of society. They knew firsthand the danger of the mythologizing impulse of a society that had once elevated untreated victims of a terrible disease to the symbolic status of free spirits, only to turn the untreated victims of utopian intentions into demonic emissaries of a dangerous population.

Flynn had become the director of NAMI in 1984, the year her seventeen-year-old daughter was hospitalized after a suicide attempt. "When a loved one has been in the mental hospital," Flynn said, "nobody brings you a casserole." But times were changing, and Michael, telling his story to the widest imaginable audience, was living proof. To Flynn's daughter, bravely battling her up-and-down illness, Michael was a hero whose story offered real hope.

Everyone needs hopeful stories. The *Times* article reverberated in unexpected places, inspiring other portions of the population as well. Hollywood and the publishing world came calling.

Michael sounded exhilarated and slightly manic when we talked on the phone that winter. The money was astronomical, the names famous and symbolic. Disney wanted to make a movie about his life and was offering him a million dollars and the interest of director

Michael Mann, whose latest feature was a successful crime thriller called *Heat*. Twentieth Century Fox saw Disney's million and raised it Robert Redford, who had won an Academy Award for directing *Ordinary People*, released when we were in high school.

Groundbreaking for its time, *Ordinary People* was a landmark in the cinematic treatment of mental illness, featuring a traumatized teenage boy who attempts suicide and spends four months in a psychiatric hospital because he feels responsible for his brother's accidental death. Back home, the boy gradually learns to forgive himself and blame his mother with the help of a psychoanalyst in a shawl-collar cardigan, played by Judd Hirsch, who also played the wise cabbie on Michael's favorite sitcom, *Taxi*.

Instead of four months in a psychiatric hospital with PTSD, Michael spent eight months in a psychiatric hospital with schizophrenia. Instead of going home to confront family demons, Michael went to Yale Law School, defeating madness with the power of his own mind. This was more like *Extraordinary People*, but Michael was also an underdog everyman who overcame obstacles with the support of a father devoted to his success.

That was the view taken by Ron Howard, who played the all-American high school student Richie Cunningham on *Happy Days*—the show I was watching in reruns when Ronald Reagan got shot. Howard also wanted to turn Michael's story into a movie. He'd been interested in mental illness ever since he was an eight-year-old star on *The Andy Griffith Show*, watching in fascinated terror as a guest actor suffered a breakdown on the set. While the cameras rolled, the actor began babbling incoherently before collapsing in a flood of tears and contracting into a fetal ball.

Howard had graduated from television and turned into an A-list movie director with a production company, Imagine Entertainment, that he owned with the producer Brian Grazer. Their most recent movie was *Apollo 13*, a critical success and box office smash that turned "Houston, we have a problem" into a household phrase. Imagine had a deal with Universal Studios, which offered Michael a million and a half dollars for his story. They wanted to "fast-track" the project for Howard.

Meanwhile, in a parallel universe, book editors were in a bidding war for a memoir Michael was going to write called *The Laws of Madness*. The memoir was going to be the basis of the movie that Ron Howard was going to direct, which was also going to be called *The Laws of Madness*.

The book offers, though considerable, were for a lot less than he was getting for the movie rights, but the meaning of a publishing contract loomed larger for Michael. In the hospital, he'd been told to stop writing while he strengthened the slender filaments anchoring him to the world. Doctors fitted him with antipsychotic medication, a neuroleptic dream catcher for ensnaring hallucinations. Instead of a universal balm, imagination had been declared the enemy, or at least an unreliable friend.

But his literary aspirations, like his way with words, hadn't disappeared. He'd spun the straw of suffering into the gold of literary achievement. This was the magic of writing as we'd always understood it.

Michael had once talked about spending ten years working at Bain to earn enough money so he could retire and write. Illness had interrupted that dream, but the interruption had become the paradoxical source of its fulfillment. Instead of following the steps of his ten-year plan, whose first phase would only now be coming to completion, Michael became a writer, famous and rich all in one go.

The events of the winter sounded so fantastic they might have been the symptom of a relapse, but they were all real. It was also the case that Michael, who spoke with precision even when describing delusions, initially left out certain details in the rush of excitement. These omissions contributed to the feeling everything had happened with the abruptness of a dream.

In his early exuberant accounts, Michael left out the months he'd spent writing a proposal with a literary agent who had orchestrated the frenzy, though knowing this actually made the story more impressive, a tribute to his talent and determination. He'd met his agent, Tina Bennett, when he was at Yale Law School and she was at the graduate school getting a PhD in English literature. Abandoning her degree, Tina went to work for Janklow & Nesbit, one of those powerhouse agencies that a decade before had brought Hollywood luster and big money to book publishing. Tina brought her love of literature and her memory of Michael's brilliance with her.

The day the profile ran in the *Times*, Tina was calling up book editors to make sure they'd seen the story, and to let them know that Michael was as dazzling in real life as he seemed in the article. She told them he was working on a book proposal, and promised to keep them updated.

I got *Publishers Weekly* and *Variety* at my office, and Janklow & Nesbit seemed to pop up whenever a novelist "inked" a deal for "seven figures," or a journalist got a payout like a Yankees shortstop for a magazine story and a book to be named later. Tina was earnest, intense, and righteously committed to authors and ideas. She already displayed the qualities that would make her a big-time agent when she cold-called editors and introduced herself.

Michael worked with Tina into the early months of 1996 to produce an eighty-page proposal for *The Laws of Madness*. The story followed the general outline of the *Times* article, which had followed the general outline of Michael's life as he'd described it: a brilliant young man growing up in an idyllic suburb, who found everything easy until he was stricken by a terrible disease that threatened to sideline him permanently. Defying convention, the pessimism of mental health professionals, and the prejudice of society, he rose to the pinnacle of intellectual attainment, helped by classmates, professors, and above all the love and support of an extraordinary father who refused to let him quit.

Tina sent the proposal to editors whose appetites had been whetted months before. The eighty-page document caused an electric stir. How often, in those days especially, did anyone narrate schizophrenia from the inside out?

Michael described his hallucinations with such vivid intimacy that the terror he felt chatting with the secretary at Bain became the reader's own: "One minute we were standing in a well-lit room, and in another second, like a candle flickering, we were in darkness flashing on and off and there was blood dripping from her teeth as her clawed hands reached for me."

His precise, cerebral prose, lit by pulp-fiction flashes of horror, seemed uncannily suited to the subject matter. All the competing genres that had unsettled me when I read Michael's short stories had found their proper outlet. The spy thriller outlived the manuscript he'd burned in his parents' driveway, even as he explained why he had to burn it: "I would be walking through Wykagyl in New Rochelle when suddenly I would see Nazis in trench coats with their hands dipping into their pockets, reaching for guns as I would dive for cover. I was terrified."

The proposal read in places like the science fiction stories he'd narrated in the schoolyard, where I heard about mind-reading "precogs" and the scalpel-wielding doctor who has to take down the parricidal baby he brought into the world. Michael described what it had felt like to discover that his parents were evil imitations of themselves: "I soon burst in at 3 in the morning, to accuse my parents of being impostors, of having killed my real parents while they themselves were neo-Nazi agents altered by special surgery and trained to mimic my parents."

The technical name for the condition Michael was describing is Capgras syndrome, but even the clinical literature refers to *Invasion of the Body Snatchers*, according to Elyn Saks, who experienced its horror for herself while a law professor at USC. The thrill of fear that ran through readers of the proposal for *The Laws of Madness* heightened the sensation of bearing witness to something authentically new. So *this* is what it's like when someone you love becomes a sinister double sent to assassinate you. No wonder Michael screamed at the imposter pretending to be Chuck—"I don't know why you killed my father or who you are!"—before rushing upstairs to hunt for the corpses of his real parents.

But the proposal, and its protagonist author, rose from the depths of such delusions, tracing the archetypal tale of a young man's triumph and a father's love. Even as it offered vampire glimpses of bloody fangs and Nazi spies, the narrative arc bent toward Yale Law School. This novel combination of elements gave *The Laws of Madness* a paradoxical power encapsulated in its brilliant title, which suggested a rational treatise or rule book ordering a condition famous for irrational mystery.

After sending out the proposal, Tina sent out Michael. She escorted him to publishing houses, where he spoke with undaunted eloquence to editors flanked by the thrones, dominations, powers, and publicists whose approval was needed for big contracts. He put a familiar face on schizophrenia, a name that still sounded like an ancient curse in modern ears, the way polio and typhoid had once vibrated with primeval terror before becoming the names of vaccines, and joining the roster of disasters that afflict other people in faraway places.

Michael talked not only about schizophrenia but about the "the nurturing male," a concept central to his project. He paid tribute to his father and men like Guido Calabresi, whose open-armed affection and support had been as important as their recognition of his brilliance. In the proposal, Guido, Steve Yandle, and Chuck worked together to assemble Michael's bed.

Not everyone responded with enthusiasm. One senior executive shut down the bidding of a junior editor, who had already driven up the price. Married to a physician who spoke darkly about the nature of schizophrenia, the executive declared simply, "We're not doing it; he's crazy."

But the overall excitement, high to begin with, increased as the interested parties sat with the thoughtful, handsome lawyer who talked about difficult things with articulate authority and self-deprecating humor. *I may be crazy but I'm not stupid.*

Interviewing for law school jobs, Michael had disclosed his schizophrenia so that it could be disregarded, a stressful double action. Meeting with publishers, his illness was the centerpiece, the selling point—though just what *it* was remained murky. That, too, was part of the appeal. Everyone wants to hear, and publish, a new story. Michael arrived like a traveler from an undiscovered country, eager to talk.

He had lately begun referring to "the country of illness," a phrase from a recent book by Lauren Slater called *Welcome to My Country.* Slater was a writer-therapist who dove headfirst into her patients' lives and stories. One of her patients, a former Ivy League student with schizophrenia who scribbled incessantly into notebooks, spoke of being "inside the dragon." Slater helped him get into a writing program, but she remained the transcriber and framer of his and other patients' lives. Michael spoke from inside the dragon, but he spoke in his own voice and gave his listeners a glimpse of authentic fire.

When the president of Scribner asked Michael if he still hallucinated, Michael told her, "I'm hallucinating right now." She asked what he saw, and the room grew quiet as Michael described a burning waterfall emptying into a lake of fire. He also saw a peaceful house with shutters and vines. Michael explained that he managed these and other competing images by ordering them on a great screen, arranged in a hierarchy of terror from greatest to least. The burning waterfall was at one end of the spectrum; the house with vines at the other.

Bidding began at $200,000 dollars and rose quickly.

Michael discussed his technique for controlling hallucinations with Ron Howard when he met with the director and members of his production team. The former television star was fascinated by Michael's ability to treat his mind like a giant television set, assigning images to different channels, or doling them out to various quadrants of a single screen. Michael left a central portion of the screen free to serve as an unclouded window on reality.

The screenplay was being written by Chris Gerolmo, who had written the screenplay for *Mississippi Burning*, a fictionalized account of the FBI's hunt for the killers of Goodman, Schwerner, and Chaney, the civil rights workers murdered in Mississippi in 1964 whose martyrdom haunted our childhood. The three men appeared at the beginning of the movie, unnamed but unmistakable, their killing performed almost like a pantomime or shadow play to set the grizzly stage for the drama to come.

Michael accepted an offer of $600,000 from Scribner, not quite the highest bidder but close enough. Scribner was the house of F. Scott Fitzgerald and Ernest Hemingway; such things mattered. So did the connection he felt with his smart, literary editor, Hamilton Cain, who had written his college thesis on Sylvia Plath, was our age, and was very enthusiastic about *The Laws of Madness*.

Despite coming from a different world, Hamilton had an intuitive understanding of what Michael was trying to accomplish. That different world was in itself part of his appeal. Hamilton had grown up in a southern evangelical home where Jesus, sin, and hell were real presences, before fleeing to New York City. This was the sort of thing Michael loved. They were both trying to escape from hellfire.

Hamilton heard in Michael's apocalyptic hallucinations an eerie echo of the soul terror he'd felt at the age of seven watching *A Thief in the Night*, the 1972 film about the harrowing struggles of sinners abandoned to a doomed earth in the aftermath of the Rapture. He still knew the words to the Christian pop song "I Wish We'd All Been Ready," famous from the soundtrack.

Hamilton, who wore his wedding suit to the meeting with Michael and Tina, had recently married a secular Jewish woman from LA. Michael was planning to marry his secular Catholic girlfriend, despite her religious parents' objections. In the course of the meeting, Hamilton mentioned his new father-in-law, Mike Goldstein, who was famous for studying the families of people with schizophrenia.

Michael was fascinated by Goldstein, an eminent psychologist at UCLA who had grown up in the shadow of mental illness; his own father had been diagnosed with schizophrenia when the psychologist was young. Goldstein didn't study families in the blaming manner of an earlier era, which discounted biology, but in an effort to balance medical understanding and genetic awareness with a psychoanalytic perspective. He explored the role families could play in triggering as well as healing mental illness. The meeting was full of magical connections.

CHAPTER THIRTY-ONE

CREATIVITY, INC.

riverrun, past Eve and Adam's . . .

—JAMES JOYCE, *Finnegans Wake*

The money from the book and movie deals allowed Michael to get out of the tiny Bronx apartment. He moved with Carrie into a two-bedroom apartment in Hastings-on-Hudson with a balcony and a sweeping view of the river.

Hastings was a quaint, hilly river town twenty minutes by car from New Rochelle on the Saw Mill and the Cross County. It was also where Michael had gone to play music at Riverrun Books after quitting Bain in the year of deepening confusion and paranoia.

Riverrun was a short walk from Michael's apartment, but whatever worries he might have had about its haunting proximity were outweighed by the triumphal nature of his return. A great deal had changed in ten years, including the fact that he was living there with Carrie. He had money in the bank and a book and movie deal worth $2.1 million.

He'd even incorporated himself; inspired by Imagine Entertainment, he called his one-man company Creativity, Inc. Nevertheless, Carrie felt it was important to treat Michael's earnings as a onetime windfall that might have to last for a very long time. They were talking about starting a family and would need all they could save.

Their garden apartment was in the River Edge, a modestly prosperous complex of low redbrick buildings with white railings built on the eastern bank of the Hudson opposite the Palisades, whose plunging red cliffs were tamer here, sloping rather than falling into the river. Their balcony felt higher than the second floor and overlooked a wide arcing expanse of the Hudson that swept northward in its broad, deep channel all the way to the Tappan Zee Bridge.

Michael was a writer now. Whether or not Riverrun was next door, *The Laws of Madness* required him to revisit old wounds. He would have to retread the downward spiral circling him back to the brink of an abyss that had yawned under him a decade before, and that still divided his life into a jagged before and after. Even monuments of past success could be painful reminders of loss.

But Hastings-on-Hudson was a peaceful place, and the genteel pretension of its name had literary appeal, like Stratford-upon-Avon. Even the local pizza place was called Villaggio Sereno. Hastings was serene, and technically a village, with fewer than eight thousand people taking up less than three square miles. The streets were safe—the police station was a stone's throw from Michael's front door—and there were cafés, antique stores, and the river itself in walking distance.

The train station was also in walking distance. Manhattan was a short train ride away, a convenience for Carrie, who had been tasked with designing a new email system linking all of the Edison Project's schools. New schools were opening around the country—there were forty-two and counting—and in addition to commuting to the city, Carrie was traveling to Michigan, Kansas, and Texas.

Michael was busy too. He had the book to write, of course, but in the first flush of success, his excitement seemed in itself like a form of activity. Visits to New Haven were a combination victory lap and thank-you tour. He told professors they were going to be in his movie like a man paying off debts with double interest. They'd helped him achieve a dream of success that the movie itself had mysteriously come to represent. When he spoke to their seminars, it was with the added luster of *The New York Times*, Scribner, and Universal Pictures, advanced degrees conferred by the culture itself.

He took the train to Manhattan to meet with Ron Howard and assorted members of the Imagine team including Chris Gerolmo—a group Michael referred to collectively as "the suits." The suits were retracing in person the stations of his illness, the hospitals and the halfway house that Michael would have to return to in his mind as he wrote his memoir. They had a fat file of articles and information about him but seemed eager as well to soak up his essence, what he wore and how he talked.

For people who took large liberties, they were sticklers for accuracy. Ron Howard had even brought the team to meet Michael's old nemesis, the social worker who had run Futura House. To Michael's disappointment, the suits had found Sylvia charming and professional and failed to see the petty martinet he still referred to as Nurse Ratched, just as he spoke of himself as the McMurphy type.

Admiring of Michael as they were, the suits could hardly share his idea of himself as the McMurphy type; they wanted to showcase his heroic recovery, which was only possible if they showed his battle with schizophrenia. McMurphy wasn't fighting an illness but a system, which is what the director Miloš Forman, an exile from Soviet-crushed Czechoslovakia, had found so resonant about Ken Kesey's novel. *One Flew Over the Cuckoo's Nest* was a parable about the terrors of state control; mental illness had nothing to do with it.

Michael's story was different, and Imagine's enthusiasm was very high. Brian Grazer told a Hollywood reporter that *The Laws of Madness* "is the perfect thing for us to do after *Apollo 13*." The producer was especially excited about the powerful father-son relationship at the heart of the story: "It will get great casting because the two key roles are emotionally complicated, challenging and also very castable."

The "castability" of the movie became a sort of parlor game Michael loved playing. What did Bo think of Danny DeVito for the part of Guido? Who did Bo want playing himself?

"If you say Danny DeVito," Bo told him, "I'll kill you both."

DeVito was a running joke, and Michael always laughed. It's possible, though, that he really did think the actor who had played the irascible dispatcher on *Taxi*—and a patient in *One Flew Over the Cuckoo's Nest*—would be good for the part of Dean Alfieri, which is what they were calling Guido. You could do a lot with a goatee and glasses.

As for Michael, *Variety* was reporting that Leonardo DiCaprio was interested in playing him. Just twenty-one years old, DiCaprio had been famous since playing a teenager with intellectual disabilities in *What's Eating Gilbert Grape*. The young actor was clearly on the brink of breakout superstardom.

Even Guido's successor as dean, Tony Kronman, was in on the law school's movie excitement. He'd never had Michael as a student, but Owen Fiss was a close friend, and the actor Ron Silver, who had played Alan Dershowitz in *Reversal of Fortune*, had sat in on his contracts class. Between the two of them, or so Kronman imagined, he'd gotten a phone call from Ron Howard, asking if he and the Imagine team could tour the campus.

Yale was halfway to a movie set already, with its ersatz Oxford architecture and intentionally broken windows repaired with seams of lead that reminded my father of the wrinkles Mrs. Peachum irons *into* the rags worn by the army of beggars in *The Threepenny Opera*. When Sean Connery played Indiana Jones's college professor father, Steven Spielberg turned Yale's law faculty dining hall into Professor Jones's office, and the tickled law professors kept one of the faux oriental-style paintings on the wall as a memento.

Michael got along well with Kronman, who had a PhD in philosophy from Yale and a law degree he'd added on because he'd finished his dissertation before his psychoanalysis and wanted to stay in

New Haven to complete his inner journey. It took time for him to work up the nerve to ask Michael if the break from reality he talked about had been total, and if any of its symptoms ever came back. Michael answered yes to both questions, and explained that angels were waving fronds of fire just outside his field of vision at that very moment. The wrought quality of the images suggested borrowings from Dante's *Inferno* or from *Paradise Lost*, and it occurred to Kronman to wonder if he was being bullshitted, but he'd taken Michael at his word, the conversations continued, and the two became friends.

Kronman considered Michael remarkable not only in his own right but also as a source of institutional pride. He shared Guido's belief that no other law school in the country would have taken a chance on someone who could so easily have been written out of the picture. The law school prided itself, Kronman later explained, "on looking beyond or through disabilities of all sorts and disadvantages to spy brilliance in whatever form it appears." Michael was an affirmation of Yale's best self, and the movie would be a feather in the law school's cap as well as Michael's.

The dean was happy to grant Ron Howard permission to tour the law school and offered to act as tour guide.

The first time Chris Gerolmo met Michael in a Midtown coffee shop, the screenwriter had the impression of being with someone restrained by a five-point harness of the sort worn by race car drivers or fighter pilots. Michael sat with his back pressed against the chairback, feet flat on the floor, ass flat on the chair, hands flat on the table. He was hanging on, Gerolmo thought, for dear life.

But it was Michael's determination to resist the pressure, as much as the pressure itself, that so impressed the screenwriter. Despite the g-forces bearing down on him, Michael wasn't about to eject. On the contrary, he was going to use all of his considerable powers to persuade you that everything was all right. For Gerolmo, this was the key to his character.

He was excited about creating a character like Michael, who thought in long paragraphs, wanted to talk for a living, and used his obvious intelligence and eloquence to hide his illness as soon as he started discovering he was sick. Gerolmo had taught screenwriting at Harvard, where he'd gone to college, and couldn't help thinking that if things had been a little different, he might have written about the world of academics and intellectuals more often.

Mississippi Burning had been a prestige picture, and he was sometimes brought in to give other projects an Oscar-worthy gloss, but he'd spent plenty of time polishing gory crap. He had once named a doomed character in a Steven Seagal picture Lapoleon for the private pleasure of killing him off a minute later with the stage direction "Lapoleon blown apart."

Gerolmo was impressed by Michael's explanation that it took 90 percent of his mental force just to pierce the fog enveloping his brain. He admired the formulation as much as the fact; even if it was a "canned rap," and the percentages changed with every telling, Michael had found effective ways of sharing his battles with civilians.

The Laws of Madness was more than an A-list writing assignment for Gerolmo; he'd been promised a chance to direct the picture if Ron Howard was waylaid by one of the many projects coming his way. The year before, Gerolmo had won great praise for a thriller he'd written and directed for HBO, about a real-life Soviet serial killer who murdered fifty-three women and children, evading capture throughout the 1980s in part because of apparatchiks fearful of crossing the official Soviet line that serial killers were found only in the decadent West. The murderer, a member of the party in good standing, was caught only after the fall of Communism when his longtime pursuers, played by Stephen Rea and Donald Sutherland, enlisted an eccentric psychiatrist played by Max von Sydow, the knight who played chess with Death in *The Seventh Seal* on my dorm room wall in college.

When Leonardo DiCaprio met with the Imagine team to discuss *The Laws of Madness*, the screenwriter handed him a Sony Walkman, and asked him to put it on and hit "play" as the meeting got underway. Instantly, DiCaprio was assaulted by strange sounds—crunching metal, whispered words, a horrific car crash, gunshots, screams, and spliced voices unspooling in an interrupting jumble without rhyme or reason while he tried to follow what was going on around him.

Gerolmo had asked his friend, the film editor Billy Goldenberg, who'd edited *Citizen X*, to create the tape as a way of giving the young actor a taste of what it was like to contend with a competing reality renting space in his head and banging on the walls while he tried to act like nothing was wrong. What ambitious young actor could resist the challenge of an interior world utterly at odds with what was really going on?

DiCaprio loved it.

What many people saw when they looked at Michael, and what I sometimes saw myself, was someone catapulted by success to the top of Abraham Maslow's famous "hierarchy of needs," where those who achieved "self-actualization" stood at the pinnacle of human fulfillment.

One of the fathers of humanistic psychology, Maslow had designed his hierarchy as a sort of government food pyramid for the psyche, with physical necessities down at the broad bottom—where our health teachers had put bread, Frosted Flakes, and other essential carbohydrates that formed the foundation of a healthy diet—followed by narrowing bands with needs like security, love, and self-esteem, until you came at last to self-actualization at the protein-rich peak.

Guided by Aldous Huxley's faith in "human potentialities,"

Maslow believed that "What human beings can be, they must be," and that psychology's purpose was to help people give birth to the ideal version of themselves that environmental constraints and social convention conspired to abort. Some people never advanced beyond the basics, but self-actualization, like artistic expression, was the high ground you graduated to after other aims and needs were answered. Wasn't that why I'd gone to Berkeley? Not to get a PhD in literature but to take what was potential in me and make it actual? That was why I'd thought Michael had left Bain and moved into the attic of the Ferber house, and though I was wrong, I wasn't wholly wrong, because Michael's strange journey had led him to the very place he'd been planning to go. Somehow, he'd scooped up all of Maslow's stages like jacks on a single bounce.

Maslow's theory formalized many of the assumptions Michael and I had grown up with. We were free to be you and me, but our models were artists and intellectuals drawn from the one percent of the population that Maslow identified as having risen above the "pathologically average" as he called the remainder of humanity, and fulfilled their promise. It is ironic that Maslow's self-actualized one percent, capable of "peak experiences," resembled the one percent of the population R. D. Laing identified as the only sane members of a crazy society, who overcame the confines of convention to become outwardly what they were meant to be deep inside.

Maslow had in fact borrowed self-actualization from Kurt Goldstein, a neurologist and psychiatrist who studied schizophrenia. But Goldstein used the term to suggest the ways in which the "total organism" labored at every level, from the cellular to the emotional, to come as close as possible to doing what it had evolved to do. In Goldstein's usage, someone with a severe mental illness or traumatic brain injury might yet be heroically self-actualizing within the borders of an unforgiving biological reality.

Maslow had other ideas. Hoping to save psychology from "the

study of crippled, stunted, immature and unhealthy specimens," he had turned to the lives of the best and brightest, intellectual heroes like Einstein and Huxley whose gifts might also help him understand how he'd managed to escape the malign influence of a mother he considered schizophrenogenic.

And what of those on the lower rungs, who needed the care and support of others just to get by? What was left for them? Reaching into the asylum, Maslow had borrowed a concept devised to help people with severe impairments find wholeness, and adapted it to ward off a condition he called the psychopathology of the average. As my father sometimes said, quoting a Hasidic story about a rich man who lives like a poor man out of sympathy, it was better for the rich to eat cake, because when they ate only bread, the poor ate stones.

For a time, Michael seemed to be everywhere even without leaving Hastings. He turned up in Hollywood trade publications and in *The New York Times*, which sought him out as an authority on matters pertaining to mental illness, not merely as someone who had overcome it.

Contacted by the *Times* about a medical student who was hospitalized by psychiatrists at his own medical school for what they called "dangerous behavior," Michael delivered an angry judgment:

> "He lost five weeks of his life and maybe his medical degree," said Michael Laudor, a legal scholar with a history of schizophrenia. "What happens to someone who can't marshal those resources? Many commitment hearings are an outrage."

In truth, it seemed hard to know precisely what to think, since the medical school and the hospital were constrained by confidentiality, and the woman who had filed an assault complaint against her medical school classmate refused to speak to the reporter, who printed her name anyway. Still, the article, which was called "Medical Student Forced into a Hospital Netherworld," shared Michael's perspective that the student should not have been hospitalized in the first place. "Most commitment proceedings," the reporter explained, "involve serious acts of violence or severely distorted thinking; for instance, trying to throw a child out a window in the belief that he is possessed by the Devil."

The medical student, who had gone off his medication for bipolar disorder, had been hospitalized on six previous occasions, twice involuntarily, though he did not say why. He was thirty-seven, just a few years older than Michael—"a legal expert with a history of schizophrenia"—who may have felt that but for the grace of God he could have been the subject rather than the authority. To be the quoted expert instead of the victim offered a small measure of protection against a netherworld he feared as much as illness itself.

CHAPTER THIRTY-TWO

MICHAEL CALLED KEVIN

And we are magic talking to itself,

noisy and alone. . . .

—ANNE SEXTON, *To Bedlam and Part Way Back*, 1960

Chris Gerolmo's job was to tell a compelling story robed in the details of Michael's life, anchored in the reality of his illness, and infused with Hollywood magic. Accordingly, Michael was now called Kevin. His parents lived in New Rochelle but were no longer Ruth and Chuck; they were Miriam and Edward. Laudor had been turned into Lauton, much as Chuck had turned Lifshutz into Laudor years before.

Factually, Gerolmo could learn what he needed from the book proposal and the fat file Imagine had put together. What he learned from meeting Michael was something else. Only someone who had listened to Michael talk could have his character say, "I find it just as irritating as you would if you weren't narcotized into a completely fake Zen-like acceptance of the vexatious shit of everyday life."

The line was spoken at Dray & Company (the fictionalized Bain), by Kevin (the fictionalized Michael), chastising a member of his management consulting team who's just smoked a joint in celebration of their successful presentation. The young colleague doesn't understand why Kevin is acting so paranoid. The reason, of course, is that he *is* paranoid, and his boss's compliment—"We have our eye on you"—completely unnerves him, but nobody knows that yet, least of all Kevin.

The Laws of Madness was Michael's story, except that it was about somebody called Kevin, mysteriously casting Michael's shadow, unless Michael's shadow was casting Kevin. Either way, Michael called Kevin was the wunderkind youngest of three brothers; his comedian middle brother was now called Terry and promoted to eldest; he got a new middle brother named Jonathan, a classical pianist, and a father called Edward who taught medieval theology at Baruch College, where my father taught.

Professor Lauton was the other great role Brian Grazer had mentioned. I don't know if it was hard for Michael to talk about casting Chuck, given his father's recent death, or if he was haunted by what had happened the last time he thought someone was pretending to be his father.

The article in which Grazer touted the castability of The Laws of Madness quoted another Imagine executive explaining that Michael's father "has become integral in changing the way the system works when an individual is trying to repair." Even before shooting began, the movie was altering the world it drew inspiration from, like a planet bending light with gravity.

Gerolmo was so excited by the cinematic possibilities of Michael's illness that in a rare burst of prophetic optimism he told Ron Howard, as they walked along a quiet country road discussing The Laws of Madness, that he'd hit on an approach that would win the movie seven Academy Awards.

This was his decision to tell the story from the point of view of someone unaware he was developing schizophrenia, and to put the audience in the same unsuspecting boat. If Kevin thinks he is being followed home from a jam session at the Riverrun bookstore, the audience would think so too. For one thing, they made Kevin a consultant for a military supplier, setting up plausible government involvement in an actual plot. For another, the audience would really see the "black Crown Vic sedan" turning slowly onto Mereland Road with the headlights off, trailing Kevin as he lopes toward his house, his guitar case swinging at his side.

Why would the car exist only in Kevin's head when the audience could see it as plainly as they saw Kevin and the street and the guitar case he flings away as the Crown Vic roars suddenly toward him, swerving to hit him as he dives behind a stand of curbside garbage cans just in the nick of time? When the black sedan comes screeching back for a second pass, the audience, watching as the rear window rolls down and "the silenced muzzle of a TEC-9 pokes out," would have no reason to suspect that delusion was calling the shots, and hallucination was the filter screwed over the camera lens. Movies were made for madness.

The most harrowing application of this approach would come in the psychiatric hospital where Kevin, held against his will, accuses his father of being a "replicant with a computer for a heart" sent by Nazis to murder him.

"If I killed you," Kevin tells the replicant, "any court in America would acquit me."

His father, usually able to stand up to anything, glances toward the two-way mirror where a psychiatrist had been watching in an earlier scene before marching in with orderlies when things got heated. On that occasion, Professor Lauton had accused the doctor of spying and told him to stop meddling. This time, nobody opens the heavy door, and the professor turns back to his enraged son, who grabs him by the throat.

"Snap out of it!" Edward tells his son, choking. "I am your father! I'm Edward!"

But Kevin doesn't snap out of it, and doesn't remove his hands; he wraps them tighter around the imposter's throat. Unable to speak,

Edward struggles and attempts to rise, but Kevin is bearing down in fury, shouting, "Die, you son of a bitch!"

The rest was silence, and a stage direction: "(With every ounce of his strength, he strangles his father, until the old man stops coughing, until he gradually sinks to the floor, inert, until he's limp and lifeless.)"

It was the sort of passage Michael might have written in one of the stories I flung under my bed, or in his incinerated thriller. But it was something he would never have written now about himself or someone suffering from mental illness. He was adamant in discussions with the Imagine team that any imputation of violence to people with severe mental illness was a hateful canard.

Technically, the script didn't violate Michael's assertions. Though the scene ended with Kevin on the floor beside his father's lifeless body, gripping his own head in his hands and rocking back and forth, in the next scene Kevin, lying in bed, opens his eyes and sees his father sitting beside him, alive and well and reading the newspaper. Rocked by horror, relief, and confusion, Kevin realizes how sick he really is and tells his father he'll need all the help he can get.

Nevertheless, the image of the killing would remain in the watcher's mind. Gerolmo thought of the scene as a flash of light that couldn't be blinked away all at once. Those lingering spots would cling to the viewer's perception, deepening the audience's understanding of Kevin and the insidious illness he was battling.

Did Michael divine any of this? Even without reading the screenplay, he was aware that he was not entirely the hero of his story. His father was the hero, however heroic Michael's character might appear. His father was going to be the hero of his memoir, too, but the writer is also the hero of his book, just by writing it. This made the literary version of *The Laws of Madness* all the more important.

The suits didn't tell Michael about the patricide, which wasn't patricide but a hallucination, and wasn't about Michael Laudor but about Kevin Lauton, who was himself a sort of hallucination wearing the body of Leonardo DiCaprio—though at a certain point it ceased to be DiCaprio and became Brad Pitt, who had stepped in when DiCaprio, despite his enthusiasm, was unable to commit in time to the project, which was tentatively set to begin shooting in September 1998.

Nothing was fixed, even when *Variety* reported the story: "Already booked to star with Edward Norton and possibly Courtney Love in Fox 2000's 'The Fight Club,' Pitt is hoping to make 'Madness' his fall project, sources said."

Deadlines were an added pressure on Michael, and the publisher understandably wanted to coordinate publication with the movie. Books with actors on the cover tended to be bestsellers.

Michael's book was the basis of the movie, but he hadn't written the book, and the screenplay was already drafted. The cinematic *Laws of Madness* would inevitably deviate from the written version.

I assumed Michael was getting the attention he'd always wanted, but he talked about the suits with increasing irony, shaded by something else. It no longer sounded like amused self-deprecation when he burst out with "I'm talking to someone who made a movie about a mermaid!"

That was a reference to *Splash*, Ron Howard's directorial debut in the 1980s starring Tom Hanks and Daryl Hannah. The movie had been so successful that the joke was lost on contemporary audiences when Hannah's beautiful mermaid, walking naked on new legs in Manhattan, chose the name Madison after seeing it on a street sign. When the movie was released, Madison had been an East Side avenue and a Founding Father; a decade later it was one of the most popular girls' names in the country.

At some point in the development of *The Laws of Madness*, Ron Howard committed himself to a movie called *EDtv*, about a guy whose life is ruined when he's made the subject of a 24-7 television show. The concept spoke to the former child star much as Michael's method of managing his hallucinations had. With Howard committed elsewhere, Imagine honored its pledge to Gerolmo, not a given in Hollywood, and handed him the directorial reins to *The Laws of Madness*.

For the screenwriter, this was a once-in-a-lifetime alignment of the stars. Gerolmo had directed *Citizen X* from his own screenplay using top-notch actors and getting excellent reviews, but a picture set in the former Soviet Union and filmed in Hungary for television, even HBO, was one thing. Stepping in for Ron Howard on a picture with a $50 million budget was of a different order. The time was right for a serious movie about madness and recovery, and Brad Pitt would secure the $50 million.

Gerolmo told Pitt about Michael, rigid with tension in the coffee shop as he talked about flipping from the bloody horror of the Suicide Channel to the soothing Vacation Channel where the Girl from Ipanema went walking. The actor had appreciated at once the challenge of playing someone whose "whole show," as Gerolmo put it, was demonstrating to everyone that he was in total control while his body told a different story.

In addition to thinking that Danny DeVito should not play Guido, or himself, Bo had begun to wonder if the manic exhilaration the movie seemed to stir up in Michael might not be good for him. This view was shared by Bonnie, the psychologist who had called Bo seven years before to tell him about the impressive young law student who was much sicker than he seemed.

Bonnie's experience as a therapist caring for people with schizophrenia in multifamily groups, and studying that type of care, had taught her to evaluate life events not as objectively good or bad, or merely neutral, but as "stressors." Good news could wreak as much havoc as misfortune, and a new job could prove as destabilizing as the failure to find one. The "stimulus levels" of Thanksgiving could require days of psychological preparation, and even then, a casual question like "What've you been up to?" shouted across the table could upend months of painstakingly recalibrated expectations.

Since going to Yale Law School, Michael had grand things to shout back across the table, and even grander things now. He also had deadlines, meetings, and the mind-bending awareness that his life would be projected on a screen for millions to admire. The book and movie deal were fabulous in many ways, but Michael needed a calm, regulated life, and a caring, attentive community.

He was spending hours alone each day trying to write. Alone was not the same as calm. He was still hallucinating, still grappling with delusions. Bonnie thought he was on a runaway train, but could not persuade the rest of the Network to share her fears. Michael had not merely beaten the odds by what he'd accomplished but by what he'd avoided. Since his release from the psychiatric hospital, and his departure from the halfway house, he'd completely avoided "the system."

Bonnie's roots were in community mental health. She was steeped in the values of the Network, and totally devoted to Jane, but she felt like a lone voice of unwelcome warning at the feast. She was dampening a victory that belonged not only to Michael but also to those who had believed in him and still felt they were watching over him. Jane was in touch with Murray and had even found Carrie a therapist, a psychologist from the Network and a long-standing Creedmoor colleague who saw patients privately.

What was Bonnie's talk of stimulus levels, expressed emotion, and models of harm reduction compared to Yale, Hollywood, a book deal, and a voice in *The New York Times* denouncing the "netherworld" they were committed to sparing him?

Michael had gone with his mother to the party Bonnie hosted on the Upper West Side for Elizabeth's new baby, Gideon, who was Jane's first grandchild. Michael was in a celebratory mood and burst into "Joshua Fit the Battle of Jericho" in the elevator, serenading baby Gideon, who was in the elevator with his parents, wrapped up for the return trip to Brooklyn. Ruth joined in, mingling her high melodic voice with Michael's reverberating baritone, adding the "hallelujahs" while Michael stomped and clapped in the little space as if the walls really had come down.

CHAPTER THIRTY-THREE

SHAMANS

Carl Jung thought that we should see each
dream as a message from God. Why not
a hallucination?

—MICHAEL LAUDOR

On Friday nights, Carrie and Michael went to Temple Beth Sha-lom, Hastings's Reform synagogue. They arrived an hour early to study with Rabbi Edward Schecter. Carrie was planning to convert to Judaism.

Rabbi Schecter—but everyone called him Eddie—was a trim, quick, emotional man who liked to say that all he'd ever wanted to do was run a Jewish camp. Even in prosperous, suburban middle age he exuded campfire enthusiasm. He had in fact been the head coun-selor for my sister's teenage cohort at Camp Ramah in the Berkshires, leading sing-alongs in the longhaired, sandaled past.

Eddie remained a soulful, gregarious child of the 1960s, who kept multiple copies of books he loved in his study and in the trunk of his car, handing them out as needed to friends and congregants. Eddie gave out books the way wonder rabbis had once distributed amulets. Hastings was an artsy, intellectual suburb, but the world of people who wanted textual healing was shrinking. Michael was one of those who still did.

The rabbi felt an immediate connection to Michael the first time he met him. He seemed to Eddie a sort of tzaddik or Jewish saint, a suffering soul with an aura of righteousness. He reminded the rabbi of Elie Wiesel. Eddie was so impressed with Michael that he offered him a job teaching in the Hebrew school. Michael declined, for the same reason he declined an offer from Joe Bravo to join the board of the Westchester Independent Living Center. He had a book to write.

It said a lot about Eddie's feelings for Carrie and Michael that he gave them the hour before Friday night services. Though generous with his time, he liked to prepare for Sabbath services alone and had always reserved that time for himself. He was deeply moved by Carrie's shy intensity and Michael's mystical aspect. And he was moved by their devotion to each other.

Carrie liked to keep a hand on Michael's shoulder while they sat together during services. They always sat in the same seats on the aisle, about a third of the way back. Michael wore a suit and tie. Carrie was pretty, petite, almost elfin beside Michael, who pointed out the place in her prayer book from time to time. When they stood for the opening of the ark, Michael towered over her, but they leaned toward each other and Carrie continued to touch his shoulder, maintaining her gentle contact.

Seeing them like that, Eddie thought of the biblical phrase "one flesh" used in Genesis to describe Adam and Eve. *Therefore, a man shall leave his father and mother and be joined to his wife, and they shall become one flesh.*

Eddie had wandered into Temple Beth Shalom twenty-five years before to take his first and only rabbinical job. He knew every shopkeeper and restaurant owner in Hastings, and was friendly with the eccentric supermarket manager who dispensed advice at the checkout counter the way Eddie gave away books. He was also the Hastings police department chaplain and got along well with the cops, who'd asked him at his swearing in if he wanted a hymn and proceeded to chant "Hymn, hymn, fuck him!" while Eddie roared with laughter at the razzing.

The book Michael had sold but not yet written hung over him. Recollecting madness in tranquility was no easy task, and he wasn't tranquil. He was making very little progress, possibly none. The movie, on the other hand, raced along like the Hudson outside his window, whether he willed it or not. Of course, Imagine had a whole team working on the picture. Michael was alone.

Even before the year was out, his publisher had begun getting nervous. Gerolmo had heard reports—the Imagine people kept tabs on such things—that Michael wasn't producing. The screenwriter could have told them after his first meeting that Michael had a phenomenal mind but was never going to finish his book.

It wasn't the first time he'd had to base a movie on a book that didn't exist. The problem wasn't critical, and could even be an advantage. The movie was on track; a big star was attached. Why not let the filmmakers do their thing and then join in the promotion, which would create other opportunities?

For Michael, leaving his story to Hollywood was unthinkable. The closer *The Laws of Madness* got to becoming a movie, the more important the book became. Selling "life rights," a term I'd never heard before, was like selling a kidney to a stranger so he could put a living piece of you into his own body. Writing a book meant something else entirely. It was yours. In some sense it was you.

He needed the movie money, but the book restored a dream of creative achievement that had gone up in smoke even before he'd burned the manuscript of his thriller. It was his chance to redeem the fluttering rejection letters tacked to the rounded wall of his attic room that had signaled to Jane Ferber ten years before that a storm was coming.

Michael had been keenly aware when I'd sold my first novel to

Random House two years before. He was admiring, curious, envious in the frank, inquiring way that was itself a sort of compliment. He always checked on the book's progress warningly or wistfully, the way you ask about someone else's child. Now it was his turn.

If only he could get away from the suits and *Splash* and return to the purity of literature, but those worlds were increasingly connected. Scribner was part of Simon & Schuster, which was owned by Viacom. Publishing was, if not the movies, at least a part of the entertainment industrial complex.

It was a time of mergers and mega-agents collapsing Hollywood and Manhattan, and spawning bookstore chains that operated like multiplex theaters for first-run blockbusters, ordering in bulk from a central office that allowed the chains to offer bestsellers at a discount, putting small bookstores out of business and consolidating not only the distribution but the acquisition of books.

Michael might envy what I had, but he had what everyone wanted. The influx of Hollywood money didn't kill the old dream, just gave it jackpot glitter. It was Michael who had told me the Woody Allen joke about forging the uncreated conscience of his race in the smithy of his soul and having it mass-produced in plastic. He no longer found the joke funny. He'd been paid a lot of money and was expected to produce.

In an effort to shore up Michael's resolve, his editor took the train to Hastings-on-Hudson. Hamilton brought a tape recorder, hoping an interview might jump-start the process, or become in itself a way around his block, supplementing what was already there with spoken words that might be edited into place. It was hard to know what *was* there because Michael had not sent in any pages, but Michael liked the idea of a conversation, and he and Hamilton envisioned a series of sessions.

Michael's apartment in the River Edge had an under-furnished, almost temporary feel. When Hamilton asked for a glass of water, he followed Michael into the spartan kitchen. He drank while they stood in the narrow space.

Carrie was at work, the apartment was quiet, but Michael was animated and reassuringly articulate. He and Hamilton sat facing each other in the living room and moved from easy preliminary talk to recorded conversation.

For Michael, discussing his book and what would be in it often seemed indistinguishable from talking about his childhood. It was the starting point of his story but could seem like its destination, too, as if a return to that good time waited on the far side of all his struggles.

The session began with Michael talking about Mereland Road and me: "There were only six or seven houses in the most immediate part of our neighborhood, our street. I was inseparable from a friend who moved in when I was in fifth grade, Jonathan. Another lover of books, another son of a professor. And, perhaps most of all, the son of a novelist."

What connected us in his mind, as much as the short street, was writing and the dream of writing. I might have said basketball. Or Monty Python. Listening to comedy records. But looking back, he saw us as writers in embryo, and maybe even in fact: "As Jonathan and I wrote stories and poetry and discussed what we were reading, the sheer reality that one of the things an adult did was be a novelist stared us in the face."

Our later lives and hopes were collapsed into his memory of our childhood. We did swap books, though mostly they came from him to me, but we didn't share stories and poems of our own. On the contrary, those may have been my happiest childhood years because I didn't think everything, or even anything, had to be turned into something else.

He thought I might have taken writing for granted, because of my mother, but he also understood that "when it's your own mother

who is the family novelist, it may be something to overcome in finding your way as a writer." Mainly, he was aware that I had published
my book. "But Jonathan has a novel out now," he told Hamilton. "He's
done it; he is a novelist. I was sure that I, too, would be one."

Michael had always been the hare to my tortoise, and to me he
still was, even then. He was living by the river writing a book for
which he'd received more than thirty times the advance I'd gotten
for mine. And that was the least part of Creativity, Inc. But to him,
I'd already crossed the finish line. And though, after telling Hamilton, "Jon's a good writer," he added, "I'm better," he was paying tribute to me for doing something he seemed to doubt he would ever do.
His elegiac tone, almost posthumous, was for himself.

He'd always been able to sprinkle gold dust on the people and
things he valued, and on his childhood in particular, a habit that intensified after he became ill. The good were very good, the smart
were geniuses, and the prominent were at the top of their field. This
may have been a counterpoise to his losses, or perhaps the flip side
of paranoia; a way to keep the dark delusions at bay with assertions
of innocence and harmony. Or perhaps they were a dream of dry land
to someone lost at sea, more a promise that the good world was waiting than a memory of it.

In any event, New Rochelle increasingly became an Edenic place
in his telling; men were nurturing, women were breadwinners cheerfully going to offices, while children of every race and religion played
in harmony, like the children on God's holy mountain in Martin
Luther King Jr.'s Dream speech. He conjured the world as he wanted
it to be; was it his fault people believed it was all real? I half believed
it myself, and I'd grown up there.

He told Hamilton about my mother's friend Cynthia, a great writer
who had encouraged his writing and told him never to give up. Cynthia was always around, he said; she turned up at gatherings at the

optometrist's around the corner, for example, and he saw a lot of her daughter, Harriet, who also went to parties in the neighborhood, though in fact he'd never met Cynthia's daughter, whose name wasn't Harriet, and who didn't go to parties in the neighborhood or possibly anywhere, and neither did Cynthia, who did not visit the optometrist around the corner, though he was a lovely man who fitted me for contact lenses gratis and had driven my father to the train station and Michael and me to school.

Hamilton and Michael broke for lunch. They talked all the way to a local café and all the way back to the apartment, which was filled with late-afternoon light the color of fall leaves. They resumed their places, Hamilton on a low sofa, Michael in the chair opposite. The recorded conversation was freewheeling, associative; Hamilton drew Michael back when he could to the structure of the book and the chapters it might contain.

Michael talked about law school and Telluride, about Guido's faith in him, and the power of prayer, which he illustrated with a story about Carrie. She used to get frightened in the car because whenever anyone tried to cut him off, he got so angry he'd drive after them in hot pursuit, until he added a prayer at night: "Please purify my thoughts O Lord, that I do not act out of vengeance, violence, anger." It wasn't part of the traditional liturgy, Michael explained, but after he'd said it every night for a year or two, he was able to hold back even when his foot was itching to slam on the gas. Even his psychiatrist had to admit that you don't knock something people have done for thousands of years.

Hamilton had sent him a collection of essays he'd edited by Robert Sapolsky, a neuroendocrinologist, Stanford professor, MacArthur "genius grant" winner, and polymathic science writer who spent part of every year in Kenya wrangling baboons with biblical names he'd bestowed in tribute to the Orthodox Jewish childhood he'd broken from. The specter of childhood faith lived on, transmuted, in baboons named Saul, Benjamin, and Bathsheba; an interest in free will and neurobiology; and a beard of Levitical proportions that Sapolsky's ponytail, T-shirt, and jeans prevented from winning the argument.

The essay Hamilton thought would interest Michael was about shamans and schizophrenia and was called "Circling the Blanket for God." Michael, who forgot that Hamilton had sent him the book, told Hamilton all about it. He'd also forgotten that Sapolsky's question, why a disease as terrible as schizophrenia would continue to exist, was answered by exploring the possible benefits conferred on those *related* to people with schizophrenia rather than those suffering from the "full-blown" illness, which Sapolsky called "one of the most catastrophic ways in which the mind can go awry."

Sapolsky's essay was about people he called "schizotypal," relatives of the truly ill who suffered a milder version of the disease, a sort of schizophrenia once or twice removed. Maybe that's what Philip K. Dick meant when he called a character a "part time schizophrenic." Sapolsky speculatively associates the schizotypal with shamans in tribal cultures, people who had visions but were socialized into a world that both allowed them their difference and assigned them a special role as sacred healers living apart from others, powerful and remote.

Sapolsky was quick to acknowledge the speculative aspects of his essay, which drew on the work of an anthropologist from the 1930s, Paul Radin, the Polish-born scion of a rabbinic family who studied Native American cultures in the American West and was possibly the only person capable of producing a Yiddish-Sioux dictionary, as Sapolsky wryly noted, sensing a kindred spirit. But what interested him about Radin was that he was "the first to advance the idea that many shamans, witch doctors, and medicine men (and women) are 'half-crazy.'"

The emphasis was on "half"; tribal societies would have had no more place for someone in the full grip of psychosis than any other society. This was the distinction that Joseph Campbell and Julian

Silverman, speaking at Esalen and elsewhere in the 1960s, tended to ignore when, inspired by Radin, they embraced the idea of schizophrenia as a journey of enlightenment. Michael also skipped the distinction, though Sapolsky did not.

Michael retold the essay the way he recalled his childhood and our neighborhood; it was related to but different from what was actually there. He described Sapolsky as an agnostic, though Sapolsky made a point of calling himself a "fervent atheist," and transformed Sapolsky's speculation that God and religion sprang from mental illness into the suggestion that mental illness came from God. "Carl Jung thought that we should see each dream as a message from God," Michael told Hamilton. "Why not a hallucination?"

Michael agreed with what he considered Sapolsky's lament for our "perverse, wholly Westernized scientific way of looking at behavior." In fact, Sapolsky speculated that both shamanistic religion and major Western religions owed their existence to misunderstood mental illness, transmuted over time into normative values to comfort and soothe anxious masses. Radin thought only "primitive" societies had shamans; Sapolsky extended his theory to the West as well, using Martin Luther's obsessive-compulsive disorder as an example of the process. Cracks in the human mind didn't let divine light in; the divine light *was* the crack, a symptom refined and ritualized over time into a habit of mind.

Michael drew a different set of conclusions. He saw himself among the "tribal visionaries," and while he owned that "science can be a very helpful tool in treating disability, whether the affliction has divinity-endowed causes or meaning or not," he was clear about the limits of such thinking. "Who knows," he asked Hamilton, "when Satan is roaming the world and wandering about, looking for someone whose faith he can bet God he can break?"

The reference was to the book of Job, but it wasn't hard to imag-

ine whose faith Michael was talking about attracting unwelcome
satanic attention.

The apartment glowed and grew dim as the December sun crossed
the river and disappeared behind New Jersey. The recorded conversation was over. Michael had never turned on the lights and made no
move to do so now as the winter dusk crept inside. The river was
faintly audible. Who knew how many hours Michael had spent staring at it? There were days when the tugging current got inside your
blood, and you felt the chill entirety of the river sifting through your
rib cage, depositing cold silt directly into your soul.

Hamilton was scribbling in the interior gloom, eager to capture
a few last thoughts from what he thought had been a very successful
first session. He was only half-aware of the solidifying silence when
Michael spoke suddenly in a voice that seemed to have dropped an
octave. Hamilton looked up startled and saw Michael, still sitting
across from him, rocking back and forth.

"I'm very tired," Michael said in a deep, denatured voice. "I think
you'd better go."

Hamilton didn't argue. He had only a few more things to get
down.

"We'll wrap it up," he said, turning back to his notebook. Every
word captured now might be a piece of the book, which artful collaboration might yet save. He would still have time to make his train.

He was scribbling fast when he suddenly became aware that
Michael had risen and come over to the couch where Hamilton was
sitting. He felt his looming presence, rocking back and forth. As he
looked up, Hamilton felt the hairs on the back of his neck stand
straight. Michael was towering over him, his face utterly transformed.
Without its familiar spark, Michael's face was a mask. He remained
standing over Hamilton, peering down without saying a word, rocking slowly.

"Is everything okay?" Hamilton asked.

"I think you should go now," Michael said, his voice deep and slow. "I'm really, really tired."

Hamilton was all speed, gathering up tape recorder, notebook, backpack, coat, but by the time he was at the door saying goodbye, Michael had recovered his old self and insisted, with customary gallantry, on walking Hamilton to the train station. He talked easily on the short walk, and at the platform gave Hamilton a big, stiff scarecrow hug.

On the whole, it had been a productive day. Neither of them had mentioned the anomalous moment in the gloom. Still, the impression troubled Hamilton, and stayed with him on the train back to the city.

It took several months for the tape-recorded conversation to get turned into a transcript that Michael would approve. His agent had undertaken to get it typed and there had apparently been some objections on Michael's part to the initial effort. Hamilton wasn't sure what they might be, a transcript was a transcript, but it was February 1997 by the time he got it, and by then he had decided to leave Scribner for a job at Dutton.

Like untenured faculty, junior editors often wind up leaving the place where they start out to make a lasting home elsewhere. Hamilton hated the thought of saying goodbye to Michael and *The Laws of Madness*, though he'd also begun to have doubts about the book getting written.

Hamilton had hoped his interview would be the first of several, gradually supplementing the proposal with Michael's own words and turning it into a full-fledged book. Not that the next editor couldn't do the same. The book would be left in good hands, but Hamilton had a strong relationship with Michael, established in what already felt like a different era.

Hamilton's departure was a blow to Michael. Tina told the editor that "some people" were very upset about the news. It wasn't hard to know who "some people" were, but what could he do? Meanwhile, Hamilton's father-in-law, Mike Goldstein, was dying. The psychologist, whose schizophrenia research had fascinated Michael, had received a dread cancer diagnosis that gave him mere months to live. He was receiving home hospice care, sleeping in a hospital bed in the living room of his house in the Hollywood Hills.

Hamilton's wife had gone to stay with her dying father, and Hamilton, who was close to Goldstein, flew to Los Angeles over Presidents' Day weekend to say goodbye. He found his father-in-law weak but alert as he lay hairless, wasted, and practically immobile in his hospital bed. Still lit with the warm light of consciousness Hamilton admired, the psychologist told his son-in-law he was eager for distraction.

Hamilton had brought along the new-minted transcript of his conversation with Michael. "Well, I've got this thing if you want to read it," he said.

When the psychologist had finished reading, he looked intently at his son-in-law.

"I don't believe it," he told him. "He's either faking it, or he's much sicker than he's letting on."

CHAPTER THIRTY-FOUR

EQUAL OPPORTUNITY

We need the dominant culture to recognize
our biologically driven illnesses as disabilities
that can be greatly accommodated, often with
little effort, when the fear of us is removed.

—MICHAEL LAUDOR, *The New York Times*, "Mentally
Ill Don't Need Lessons on 'Real Work'"

Hamilton's colleague, Jane Rosenman, took over the editing of *The Laws of Madness*. There was nothing to edit yet, which was part of the challenge. Michael was like a mountain richly seamed with ore that nobody could figure out how to extract.

Jane had felt the pull of Michael's story ever since she'd opened *The New York Times* on her morning bus ride to the Simon & Schuster Building in Rockefeller Center and discovered him looking out from the shadows of the Metro section. She had a young son at home, a toddler, and was deeply stirred by the story of a brave and brilliant young man refusing to submit to a terrible illness. Here was something no amount of childproofing could guard against.

As soon as her day permitted, Jane had tracked down the reporter at the *Times*, Lisa Foderaro, who laughed when asked if she'd thought about turning her extraordinary article into a book. Jane was the seventh editor to ask that day, and it wasn't even lunchtime. Foderaro explained that she wasn't writing a book about Michael, but Michael was writing a book about himself and was already working with an agent. Jane called Tina that day, too, only to learn that the proposal had already been promised to her Scribner colleague.

When Hamilton left for Dutton, Jane was the right person to take over. Tina brought Michael in to meet her, and they established an immediate and easy rapport. Jane was conscious of Michael's conspicuously slow speech and rigid bearing, which she suspected were the result of medication, but what she felt above all was Michael's overwhelming warmth.

Even in his diminished state—and Jane knew she was getting only a tiny piece of Michael—he reminded her of Jewish men she'd known and loved in her own family, including her husband, whom she'd met at a synagogue on the Upper West Side. Michael loved that story, and when he called his new editor to talk about his book, and a host of other subjects, his conversation often led back to Jane's synagogue, where I also went. Jane valued these conversations, but the deadlines came and went, and the promised pages never arrived. Eventually the calls stopped too.

I knew Michael was struggling with his book, but I'd grown up surrounded by published writers and had never once heard one say, "It's going well." On the contrary, even the most successful talked about their work in progress the way aging relatives talked about angina or diabetes.

It did not occur to me that he could not write the story he had sold, which had already saved him in just the way we'd imagined writing could. Struggling with illness, unable to find a job, he'd told his troubles and suddenly didn't need a job—or rather, telling the story of struggling with illness and not getting a job became his job.

You would have to be very ignorant about schizophrenia, as I certainly was, and deluded about writing, as I continued to be, to think that telling the story of your struggle with psychosis could turn it into a past-tense affliction, like sorrow transmuted into words.

One problem, perhaps, was that Michael was a story before he had become a writer. Even when he appeared to be the narrator, other people were telling his tale. They told it to each other, to readers of *The New York Time*s, to him. The headline above his profile, "A Voyage to Bedlam and Part Way Back," was an allusion to a collection of poems by Anne Sexton—*To Bedlam and Part Way Back*—published in 1960 at the dawn of a confessional age. Like her friend Sylvia Plath, Sexton suffered from severe mental illness; many of her poems were set in psychiatric hospitals, the bedlam of the title, and addressed to her psychoanalyst.

Freud had borrowed freely from literature for his new science, but he gave it back the idea that telling a story was an act of healing. What made "part way back" so much more promising than "halfway house," which Michael hated, was the hopefulness of literary allusion itself, whether or not you knew where it came from. In fact, if you knew too much, it might undercut the article's optimism, because Sexton, like Plath, had killed herself. But even the archaic word "bedlam" shed a poetic rather than a medical light, and made it possible to feel that Michael was being gathered into the arms of literature, which had been the destination all along.

The idea of writing as redemption, a secular pursuit with a religious reward, was another of those unexamined givens Michael and I had grown up with. Even my father, who told me that writing "destroys everything," had imagined himself in retirement overlooking the Hudson and dreaming back on the Danube, writing a book called *Two Rivers* that would harmonize the divergent streams of his life, though the epigraph he'd chosen years before—a passage from a Yiddish poem that ended "I live like a war invalid with sensations of shot-off fingers"—suggested it might not have offered the resolution he intended.

I'd fended off Mychal's eagerness to start a family in the belief that I needed to finish my novel first, only to wonder, as Mychal and I struggled with fertility, where I'd gotten the perverse idea that one form of creativity competed with another.

Michael remained determined to write his book without assistance, to tell his story in his own way and his own words. Whatever Hollywood distorted, he believed, could be made right in his own telling. His dream of literary purity, a solitary pursuit of attic rooms, was at odds with the interdependent world he'd imagined in his law review essay. Writing was a very lonely business.

My mother had recently described the writer's journey as "a single-file trudge through treacherous terrain" in a back-page essay in *The New York Times Magazine*. She added, "Nobody plucks you out of the quicksand."

I'd published my own novel at last, and while every review felt like a public colonoscopy, it had been generally well received. My editor had thrown me a party in his grand apartment in the old beaux arts police building on Centre Street; he lived on the same floor as Toni Morrison, but I woke up back in my own apartment. Publication had not freed me from my full-time job, as I'd irrationally hoped, and had led to conflict with my mother, which I hadn't expected at all. Her dark musing about the loneliness of the long-distance writer had been occasioned by the publication of my novel. Her essay was called "My Son, the Novelist," and its purpose, she'd told me in advance, was to explore "the taboo of ambivalence." She'd gotten the assignment at my book party.

There was love and admiration in her piece, to be sure, but also the wish that I'd "found something else to do." What if my books sold more than hers? Or encroached on material she'd "marked" for herself? She worried that one of us would have to say "what F. Scott

Fitzgerald said to his wife, Zelda, about her own autobiography—You can't use that material, it's mine!"

Why was the choice always Zelda or F. Scott Fitzgerald? Hadn't Fitzgerald himself written that "the test of a first-rate intelligence is the ability to hold two opposed ideas in mind at the same time, and still retain the ability to function"? True, he'd written that in *The Crack-Up*; nobody said it was easy.

The flip side of the idea that writing heals you, perhaps, was the fear that failing to tell your story, and fulfill your dreams, cast you into outer darkness. And I'd always suffered from anxiety. It didn't matter if Harold Bloom turned anxiety into a literary theory, or Kierkegaard called it "the dizziness of freedom." With freedom like that, who needs food poisoning? But I was no longer as dizzy as I used to be, and I had drugs to thank for it.

Writing itself had driven me over the psychopharmacological cliff. I'd suffered a massive panic attack in New Mexico, where I'd gone for *Vanity Fair* to interview Henry Roth, a very old writer who'd published a masterpiece in 1934 followed by sixty years of silence, exile, and depression. Roth was about to publish his second novel, at the age of eighty-seven, when I went to see him. The interview had gone well, and I was driving the writer from the converted funeral parlor, where he symbolically lived, to the hospital where he had an appointment, when I missed an exit. This was nothing new for me, but suddenly I found myself drenched in sweat and overcome with dread, with a very agitated octogenarian beside me like the ghost of Christmas future, who told me with dooming certitude, "You make one wrong turn, the errors tend to compound." I returned home vowing to change.

Earlier that year, I'd found a cast-off copy of *Listening to Prozac* in the lobby of my building. The drug and the book were both bestsellers, two things I'd been raised to be suspicious about. The possibility of instant relief, and the promise—or threat—of a remade self, were seductive and shameful. I smuggled the book upstairs and hid it in my apartment. When I got back from New Mexico, I took it out of hiding.

Prozac was an antidepressant, and I didn't have depression, but curbing anxiety was a sort of side effect. The main effect was also a side effect, which was true for a lot of psychiatric drugs, which tended to be accidental discoveries. Nobody knew how Prozac worked, only what it did, or *maybe* did. This didn't stop drug makers from describing it as a simple fix for a chemical imbalance, a sort of vitamin supplement for serotonin deficiency.

The book was thoughtful and surprisingly ambivalent about the changes the author's patients noted in their personalities. The author, Peter Kramer, was a psychiatrist, analytically trained and biologically knowledgeable. Psychiatry had stopped healing the world and was trying to fit its own broken halves back together. There was nothing wrong with feeling bolder, less ashamed, or more adept, but if those were reasons people sought out the drug, the author suggested it might better be called "cosmetic pharmacology." Dr. Kramer was afraid patients might sidestep therapy.

For me, the appeal of Prozac was that it addressed the brain but required no thinking. There was no talking your way out of neurosis, no deciphering clues or tracing conflict back to unconscious childhood desire. You took a pill.

Freud had insisted that every stray thought was meaningful, and even told you what the meaning was, which made the unconscious more like Levittown than an uncharted deep; you could put up your own posters but the floor plan was poured concrete. In that sense it was, like Marxism, an anti-intellectual magnet for intellectuals. Prozac wasn't about finding meaning in mental discomfort, or thinking at all. That's what I found so exciting.

Some of the author's patients described feeling "better than well," which was just what Karl Menninger had promised psychoanalysis could do back in the 1960s, in his book *The Vital Balance*, though nobody called it cosmetic psychoanalysis. My goal wasn't anything so lofty.

The dose I started with was so low it had to be titrated into cranberry juice by unscrewing the capsule and shaking in the few micrograins of medication. I drank half the dissolved mixture one day and the remaining half the next, increasing the amount in small increments over days and weeks. Even those first mild Jekyll doses produced a palpable change. My fingertips tingled and my skin felt a kind of internal agitated heat, as if the molecules were moving too fast. This at least meant *something* was happening. Even better, something *wasn't* happening.

My nervous system seemed to be acquiring a buffer zone, or a lag of several seconds, like the gap a live TV show uses to edit out swear words before broadcasting to the world. If my neurons blurted out an inappropriate response to some innocuous stimulus, my body got an extra beat before going to DEFCON 2.

I still had anxiety, of course, but over time it ceased to be the constant, consuming companion I'd known all my life. If that was the placebo effect, it was all right with me. I'd always been highly suggestible, but the staircase of my suggestibility typically spiraled down and this was leading someplace else.

Responding to psychiatric medication is as much a diagnosis as a cure, which sounds like a vaudeville joke: if the medicine works, you're sick. Because there are no cures, you remain sick, but you do get relief. Aspirin doesn't cure a headache; you just don't notice it anymore.

And what did I have? "We're giving you generalized anxiety disorder," my psychiatrist said.

Vagueness was built into the diagnosis, and its acronym, GAD, made it sound like a minor irritation, which, compared to schizophrenia or bipolar disorder, it certainly was. But taking Prozac for a disorder in the *DSM* confirmed that I had a mental illness. It was easy to forget that the *DSM* included arachnophobia as well as psychotic depression. If it was in the book, and insurance covered it, I was a conscript in a vast invisible army whose staggering proportions were frequently reported in newspapers informing their readers that half the country suffers from mental illness at one time or another. Michael and I were, in that regard, in the same boat.

I mention this not because we were in the same boat, but because it was so easy to think we were, just as it was easy to imagine that my medication and illness were analogous to his. I didn't want anyone telling me I had to take medication or stop taking it, or even knowing that I took it. Why should I think Michael's situation was any different, or believe that if he decided to stop taking his medication it was any business of mine?

The paradox of binaries is that they don't mean there is no spectrum, just as a spectrum doesn't mean there are no essential differences. A murky border is still a border. The problem was knowing who had the authority to establish it. Public debates about who was ill, who was merely different, when it mattered, and what to do about it remained confusing and contentious.

At the time, a battle was raging over new guidelines issued by the Equal Employment Opportunity Commission to explain how to apply the Americans with Disabilities Act of 1990 to employees with mental illness. Businesses were pushing back against the EEOC's guidelines that told employers to be mindful of the fact "that traits normally regarded as undesirable—chronic lateness, poor judgment, hostility to co-workers or supervisors—'may be linked to mental impairments.'" How could they combat the "myths, fears and stereotypes" of disability if they had to parse the difference between a "substantial" threat of physical violence and a merely "elevated" risk?

And what to make of the reference librarian, given as an example in the blizzard of press coverage, who shouted at patrons and colleagues, and disclosed her disability only when disciplined for a second time but—according to the new guidelines—still had to be given time off to reduce stress?

In many ways, federal regulations were catching up with Michael's inclusive understanding of disability and community. He was cited in a law review article by two members of the EEOC's legal counsel making a case for the guidelines. They referred not to Michael's own article on the subject but to the profile of him in the *Times*. His story was an illustration of the reality of stigma, whose elimination was one of the ADA's goals, but it was also an argument for accommodating psychiatric disabilities as if they were physical ones. His invisible wheelchair was becoming a reality.

But it wasn't only businesses who protested the new guidelines. Michael was incensed by an opinion piece that ran in the *Times* in the spring of 1997 that accused the EEOC of committing "the occupational equivalent of malpractice." The article was by Sally Satel, a psychiatrist and lecturer at the Yale School of Medicine, who argued that bending the rules, whether in "the workplace or the courtroom or the classroom," was a "cruel ploy" that would only make her patients with personality disorders worse.

Though Satel did not mention schizophrenia, Michael took the entire argument personally, and fired off a letter to the *Times* rejecting her premise and presenting himself as its refutation: "We don't need to 'internalize the psychiatrist's "limits,"' as Dr. Satel proudly describes her patient doing." She had failed to see that "those of us with organic brain diseases are in a kind of invisible wheelchair." He wasn't responding to her argument about personality disorders—which he said "borders on irrelevance"—so much as redefining her words, and the people they described, as if a diagnosis, perhaps any diagnosis, could be cured by redefinition.

But sometimes, Michael talked about William Styron's *Darkness Visible*, a short memoir that lifted the lid off major depressive illness when it was still shrouded in shame and secrecy. Sunk so deep in suicidal despair that "the kitchen knives in their drawers had but one purpose for me," Styron asked his psychiatrist about going to the hospital, only to be told he should avoid it "at all costs, owing to the stigma I might suffer." For Styron, mental agony was the Miltonic hell of the title, not the hospital that his psychiatrist, clinging with "stubborn allegiance to pharmaceuticals," was determined to spare him.

An earlier generation of psychiatrists, shaped by psychoanalysis, had looked on medication the way Styron's doctor viewed the hospital. Resorting to psychotropic drugs was considered "a failure of imagination on the part of the doctor," Peter Kramer recalled of his time at Harvard Medical School in the 1970s. Psychiatrists, too, feared stigma.

Sometimes they even reinforced it. The reforming superintendent of the Oregon State Psychiatric Hospital, where *One Flew Over the Cuckoo's Nest* was filmed, had not only invited a film crew into the institution he presided over, but had a cameo playing Randle McMurphy's psychiatrist. He knew that the movie's violent representation of electroconvulsive therapy was more than thirty years out of date, before muscle-relaxants and other safeguards were introduced, and that there hadn't been a lobotomy performed at his facility since the advent of antipsychotic medication in the 1950s, but he hoped that setting the movie in 1963, and adding a disclaimer in the credits, would make it clear the movie was an "allegory" rather than a literal representation of a psychiatric hospital.

Weeks after Styron had been warned away from the hospital, he was rushed by ambulance to Columbia Presbyterian, the same place Michael had been. Even with "its locked and wired doors and desolate green hallways," Styron wrote, and the noise of ambulances drifting up to the tenth floor at all hours, the hospital "was my salvation."

CHAPTER THIRTY-FIVE

THE BACKWARD JOURNEY

And I realize the unbearable anguish of
insanity: how uninformed people can be
thinking insane people are "happy," O God.

—JACK KEROUAC, *Big Sur*

Michael no longer returned calls from the Imagine team, but work on the film was racing ahead. Films are fluid things, and the suits were always mulling changes. One of Imagine's executives, a woman Michael liked, had wondered from the start about a stronger female presence. Michael had been clear that his mother was a minor character in his story, just as his father was the nurturing anchor, but perhaps a love interest beyond the woman at the halfway house could be introduced.

Someone had even contacted Jo-Ann to explore the possibility of including her in the movie's narrative, or so she thought; she was never wholly sure what the conversation was about, though it stirred up uncomfortable memories. The last time Jo-Ann had heard from Michael, he was calling around the clock, until her boyfriend had picked up the phone and told him sternly never to call again.

But that was years ago, when she was at Yale studying musicology and Michael was in New Rochelle heading toward his crack-up. Since then, Jo-Ann had become a professional musician, married the boyfriend who'd answered the phone, and become the mother of a daughter. She felt affection, respect, and sympathy for Michael, whose life had also changed. She wanted to be helpful if she could; if the movie was something positive for Michael, as it seemed, she wouldn't object to being portrayed, though she didn't want to be blamed for his breakdown, if possible.

Imagine had also contacted Laurie Flynn, who was still executive director of the National Alliance on Mental Illness. The movie people set up a meeting with NAMI to talk with the organization about consulting on the movie. It said something about the filmmakers' intentions that they wanted to get things right.

Like her daughter, who had been diagnosed with a severe mental illness, Laurie saw Michael as an inspiring role model. Laurie had been in touch with Michael intermittently since his profile in the *Times*. He'd not only finished law school despite schizophrenia, but had become an advocate for people with disabilities who was outspoken about the role played by teachers, friends, psychiatrists, family, and medication. The film was an opportunity to give the world a positive image of someone with serious mental illness.

Times were changing, but even in the second half of the 1990s a group like Stigma Busters, which had grown out of a NAMI project, had its hands full tamping down misinformed and negative representations of people with severe mental illness. John Deere's ad for the Tricycler, "the world's first schizophrenic lawn mower," not only turned schizophrenia into multiple personality disorder—three lawn mowers in one machine!—but trivialized a debilitating brain disease while stigmatizing those who had it.

It was impossible to imagine another major illness so casually abused to sell products. *Our grass seed grows faster than stage four pancreatic cancer!* For some reason, people felt free to borrow mental illness, and the ones who paid the price for it were the people already suffering from the illness. Nike had a "Just do it" ad featuring a pitcher on a baseball mound who hears voices telling him to throw a fastball. "Crazy people talk to themselves; it doesn't matter."

It might matter if the pitcher were experiencing a psychotic episode. Calling people with mental illness "crazy" while simultaneously discounting their symptoms was the worst of both worlds. The NAMI volunteer who got Nike to pull that ad—though not its ad for the shoe with "multiple personalities"—had a mentally ill son too sick to live with her at home, a constant source of heartbreak. She also got John Deere to kill its ad for the Tricycler. Her letter to the company asked why she would want to buy a machine afflicted with an illness that caused severely impaired brain functioning in people? To bust stigma, you had to be honest about the actual illness; otherwise, someone would harness it to a lawn mower.

But it was one thing to get the president of the Madame Alexander Doll Company to pull its *Psycho* collectible—a Janet Leigh doll wrapped in a towel, standing in a Bates Motel shower with a knife-wielding silhouette on the shower curtain. It was something else entirely to make a positive, realistic, and uplifting movie about someone like Michael living with severe mental illness. *The Laws of Madness* had the potential to influence millions of people.

Michael, however, was trying to outrun the movie version of his life. As the Hollywood juggernaut raced ahead, it threw his lagging book into relief. He was afraid a movie would replace the story he wanted to tell in his own words, which was after all the story of himself. But he was also afraid he wouldn't be able to tell it, which made both the book and the movie twin pressures.

His proposal for *The Laws of Madness* had generated excitement among publishers and producers in part because it promised to follow the pattern Joseph Campbell had distilled into the hero's journey, that thrilling formula absorbed into *Star Wars* that was now the cornerstone of Hollywood character development.

But Michael's life really was part of a modern myth that Campbell himself had helped define about the similarities between schizophrenia and the hero's journey. Campbell had read the same anthropological studies that Robert Sapolsky had examined, but had hurried past the very distinctions Sapolsky had been at pains to explore. He'd been inspired by the work of Julian Silverman, the NIMH psychologist, who invited Campbell to speak at Esalen's "Shamanism, Psychedelics, and the Schizophrenias" conference.

"Let me tell you," Campbell proclaimed ecstatically, "something of what I have recently heard about the wonders of the inward schizophrenic plunge." Drawing examples from the Inuit society Michael and I had learned about with Miss Waldman in fifth grade during Man: A Course of Study, Campbell described how adolescent Eskimos suffering psychotic breakdown were transformed into healers under the mystical tutelage of wise shamans. "Interpreted from this point of view," Campbell wrote, "a schizophrenic breakdown is an inward and backward journey to recover something missed or lost, and to restore, thereby, a vital balance. So let the voyager go."

Those who knew Carrie primarily as Michael's girlfriend tended to think of her as the shy guardian watching from the shadows, listening to the roar of conversation, or fanning Michael with a printed program at Elizabeth Ferber's wedding when the heat conspired with his medication and he couldn't stop sweating. To others Carrie was just a name, or a movie character in need of development. But Carrie was at the center of her own vibrant world and the technological heart of the Edison Project, where she was part of a tight-knit band of dedicated computer geeks who called themselves the five musketeers, worked sixty hours a week, and went for drinks at the Blue Bar in the Algonquin Hotel, around the corner from Edison's offices on Fifth Avenue between Forty-Third and Forty-Fourth.

Carrie was Edison's associate director of technology, admired for her energy, optimism, and uncanny technological prowess, her shy demeanor and booming ha ha laugh that her boss, Tom, could hardly believe had come from so small a body the first time he heard it at the Blue, where the musketeers knew she drank gin and tonic and made sure she had a nice one waiting when the demands of work and the pressures of home allowed her to join. That hadn't happened for some time.

It took Carrie five minutes to walk to the Hastings train station, approximately half an hour on Metro-North to get to Grand Central, and five minutes more to walk to 521 Fifth Avenue. Timed right, Carrie could get from the River Edge to her office on the fifteenth floor in under an hour.

Getting out of the house was another matter.

Her boss, Tom, had learned long ago that Carrie wasn't a morning person and was unlikely to appear in the office before ten. He also knew that whatever work Carrie missed in the morning she would more than make up for by the end of the day, or in some mysterious pocket of the night where she seemed to hoard extra hours.

Her colleague Barb had often come to work expecting to tackle a project she and Carrie had discussed, only to find it had been finished in the night, like the shoes made by the elves in the fairy tale. Carrie would explain in her understated way that Michael was going through a rough patch. She'd wanted to keep him company and had stayed awake working and keeping watch till morning.

Carrie spoke of these things without complaint or apology, and with the implicit optimism that made every impossible task sound manageably under control, like the creation of a full electronic report card to allow gym teachers and math teachers and everyone in between to funnel grades and comments into a centralized portal individually accessible to parents and students. This was novel at the time, and part of a larger intranet known as the Common, which not only connected students, parents, and administrators at an individual school but also linked all Edison schools to each other.

Lately, Carrie had been deeply absorbed in the problem of clones. These were knockoff Macintosh computers that Apple Inc., which made the real Macs, had licensed to run its operating system. The Edison Project was hemorrhaging money and could no longer afford the Apple-made computers it had already spent millions of dollars buying for every child and every school. The clones were cheaper but riskier; Carrie had to fiddle with the OS to make sure the new machines were compatible with the old and would mesh with the system she'd worked so hard to create. The number of Edison schools was more than doubling by the fall of 1998, so a lot was riding on Carrie's ability to make the switch work.

Everyone in the tech department knew that Michael had schizophrenia, a biological illness affected by external stressors, like the deadlines he kept missing. They knew there were times Michael was in "the zone" and Carrie's life became harder. His illness was part of Carrie's mystique; she waxed and waned with its vicissitudes but never wavered.

Barb vividly remembered how stupefied Carrie had been by the book and movie deal. She'd never imagined they would have any money and hadn't expected Michael to make any, and the windfall had allowed her to glimpse a more stable future for the two of them. Barb knew Carrie was committed to Michael, and wanted a family very much, but when she'd asked if it meant they could get married, she'd been aware of a certain particle of hesitation. "He has to be well enough first," was all Carrie had said at the time.

Carrie was as matter-of-fact about Michael's illness as she was about her devotion to him. Her frank, understated style gave her explanations a spare wholeness that rendered whatever might be missing temporarily invisible. But she was private as well as shy, and if you asked too much, or listened too hard, you suddenly realized she wasn't talking about it anymore.

The same thing happened when she talked about her plans to convert to Judaism; her colleagues knew she was doing it, not that she'd grown up in a Catholic family where the religion was still practiced. They knew what she was moving toward, not what she was leaving behind. Barb had gotten to know her best when they traveled to schools together. That was how she'd learned that Carrie talked to her mother every day, and that she'd agonized about going into the field at all, afraid of leaving Michael alone, a concern that never left her. Barb often had a sense that programming was a kind of therapy for Carrie. No matter what was going on in her life, she seemed capable of accomplishing complex technical tasks with extraordinary focus and facility.

In addition to being a decade older, Barb was married and settled comfortably in life. She took a maternal interest in Carrie, and on one early trip had asked her, as delicately as possible, if it was perhaps too much of a burden to be with someone so sick.

"Unfortunately," Carrie had told her simply, "I fell in love with him lock, stock, and barrel."

The old-fashioned phrase was itself quaintly reassuring, like something you sang in a 1950s musical.

"Once you're hooked," Carrie added, "you're hooked."

To the seasoned observers of the Network watching over Michael, his relationship with Carrie was one more example of his exceptional nature. In their experience, it was practically unheard of for people with schizophrenia to sustain long-term relationships, though Fred Frese, one of Michael's heroes, spoke openly about the role his wife played in keeping him out of the hospital. A crusader for the rights and dignity of people with severe mental illness, Frese had a PhD in psychology as well as a diagnosis of paranoid schizophrenia. His wife, Penny, patrolled the borders of his illness like a UN peacekeeping force, except she didn't run off when conflict started. When Penny told him, "Fred, you're going there again," he took the extra pill she handed him even if he saw no logical reason for it.

One reason he relied on Penny, Frese told audiences, was that knowing your diagnosis wasn't the same as believing it. He'd been hospitalized for the first time as a young captain in the Marines, convinced that America was losing the Vietnam War because its adversaries were brainwashing the country. He'd recently seen *The Manchurian Candidate* and, like the CIA, found it deeply persuasive. When he looked at his hospital chart and saw "paranoid schizophrenia," he understood that his doctors were protecting him, because if the enemy knew that he'd figured out their brainwashing plot, they'd kill him.

Frese told this story to emphasize the importance of having someone you trusted. It didn't have to be a wife or a husband, just someone whose opinion you could take on faith, because once you were in the grip of a delusion, that was all you had to go on. As he reminded audiences, a delusion is only a delusion *if you don't think it's a delusion.*

He'd become the head of the psychology department at the state institution where he'd first been hospitalized, but it had taken him five hospitalizations and more than a year of homelessness before he'd even begun to consider the possibility that there might be something really the matter with him. There had been five more hospitalizations after that. When he told audiences, "I believe there should never be forced mental health treatment, ever!" he waited for the applause to die down before adding, "Unless it's absolutely necessary." But Frese had not been hospitalized since his marriage.

The Network might wonder why Carrie stuck with Michael when he was spiraling, but they took her very existence as proof that he was beating the odds. When he was good, they knew, the relationship was incredibly normalizing for him. It made him feel part of the rest of the world, which was important. Even Bonnie considered his relationship an indication that Michael was a special case, though she worried when she saw the telltale signs that he was unmedicated.

For Carrie's colleagues, the equation was reversed; Michael's illness was evidence of *Carrie's* exceptional nature. It was Michael who was the hidden figure, though Carrie gave them glimpses lit by love and concern. They were, however, only glimpses.

She did not like to talk about the times when she came home from work and Michael refused to let her into their apartment because he didn't believe she was who she said she was. No matter how much Carrie insisted, she couldn't persuade him of the truth. There was no telling him, like Penny, "Michael, you're going there," and getting him to take an extra pill, or any pill at all. How could he trust her words when he didn't believe it was her body? At such times, the terror and fury on the other side of the door were enough to send her to a friend's couch. Those were hard nights.

M ichael's editor and agent conferred and agreed that getting him outside help was the obvious next step.

"We really have to start thinking about trying to bring in a writer," Jane told Michael, who wouldn't hear of it. He remained unmoved by Jane's assurances that a hired professional would only tell his story *with* him, not *for* him.

And so, like Hamilton, Jane and Tina took the train to Hastings-on-Hudson to see what they could accomplish in person. A friendly, united front, they would promise to find a truly terrific writer to help him get the book done.

It was a radiant Friday in April, the most beautiful spring day Jane could remember, which made it all the stranger that Michael didn't meet them at the station. They walked the few hilly blocks to the River Edge apartments. Jane was second-guessing her Friday jeans and dress-down shoes. Tina was in her business usual, looking elegant but ascetic in the corporate way, her high heels stepping on their own echo as the river flashed through blossoming trees.

As soon as Michael opened the door, Jane had a sense that something was terribly wrong. Nothing specific had changed in his outward appearance, and yet he was utterly transformed, crushed inwardly by some vast invisible weight for which the word "depression" felt entirely inadequate. It was more than a mood or feeling, charging the atmosphere of the apartment that engulfed them.

Michael wasn't wholly gone beneath his leaden exterior, and when Jane apologized for her "shlumped-down" look, Michael made a wan, mechanically gracious effort.

"No, no," he said. "You look fine, Jane."

They received a perfunctory tour of the apartment when they asked for one, but Michael stopped before a closed door without opening it.

"Carrie asked me that I not show you the bedroom," he said.

It seemed to Jane the sort of respect a certain type of Jewish man would show for his wife's wishes. Carrie was at work, as she had been when Hamilton visited. Edison had a big conference coming up in Chicago in June, and Carrie was even busier than usual preparing for it.

Sitting in the living room, Michael lamented how much Carrie's father hated him. "He has three things against me," he told them. "Chronic unemployment. Judaism. And schizophrenia." He'd said the same thing to Hamilton, but his defiant humor had seemed larger than the pain of the perception. Now, the few flashes of humor only made the underlying darkness deeper.

Michael had led Hamilton to a local bistro for lunch and urged him to get the onion soup. Now he did not want to leave the apartment, and Jane and Tina ate their sandwiches in the living room. Jane asked if she could have a cup of tea, and Michael rose heavily and led her to the kitchen, where he filled the kettle and put it on the stove.

It was a bright galley kitchen, nicely appointed, but all the pleasant externalities of the garden apartment, like the river and the day itself, only added to Jane's feeling of irreparable loss. The sense of something broken made her heartsick.

Michael declined to walk with them to the train station, and they returned as they had come. Jane was reeling. Their efforts to talk practically about *The Laws of Madness*, and persuade Michael to accept an outside writer, had gone nowhere.

"You know, Tina," Jane said when they were on the train, "I've got to tell you I'm just devastated. Just undone."

Tina, on the other hand, spoke hopefully about the book and its future. But Tina did not have children, and Jane was thinking about the four-year-old son she'd brought to day care that morning. It was hard not to extrapolate from that aching awareness of entangled vulnerability, the guardian vigilance that subtly infiltrated everything and came with loving someone you could not always protect. Her sense of Michael's illness as an unbearable load pressing down on him, a force over which she had no power, was visceral. It made her feel crushed inside herself in a way that was hard to communicate.

"I've never seen anyone in that situation," she told Tina.

What she thought was, "This book will never get written."

CHAPTER THIRTY-SIX

THE TWO ADAMS

What is the message that is embedded in
organic and inorganic matter, and what does
the great challenge reaching me from beyond
the fringes of the universe as well as from the
depths of my tormented soul mean?

—JOSEPH B. SOLOVEITCHIK, *The Lonely Man of Faith*

Carrie and Michael hadn't been to Temple Beth Shalom for eight
months when they appeared at Friday night services on the
evening of June 12, 1998. Eddie hadn't seen them since the High
Holidays in the fall of '97. The study sessions had ended then, too,
without explanation.

They hadn't quit the synagogue, because they'd never joined. Michael had worried so much about money that the rabbi had assumed
the couple didn't have any, and he wasn't one to demand dues in any
case. As Eddie saw it, there are very few things that really matter in
life, and if you have a few, it's a lot. Carrie and Michael had mattered
a lot when they were there, but when they'd stopped coming, it turned
out nobody knew them well enough to say where they'd gone. Even
when they'd seemed like regulars, Eddie realized, they'd been strangers
in Beth Shalom's midst.

They'd returned as mysteriously as they'd arrived the first time, sitting in the same seats, five rows back on Eddie's left as he looked out

over the congregation. They hadn't gone anywhere but had been going through some difficult times, as Carrie explained to Eddie when he spoke with the couple briefly before the service began. She had a way of acknowledging hard times that suggested things were all right now, or would be soon.

Carrie was still Michael's rock, small but strong, leaning toward him as he clung to her. *V'dabak l'ishto: And the man cleaved to his wife.* Michael had grown heavier, more neglectfully bearded, sadder perhaps, but his Hasidic aura still intimated that beyond the melancholy world, there was radiance. It was this quality Eddie had felt so connected to the first time they'd met.

Michael, who was visibly moved during the service, had asked the rabbi if they could meet. The request seemed general rather than urgent, so instead of asking Michael to stay after services or come the next day, Eddie suggested they meet Tuesday morning in his study. Michael said Tuesday would be fine.

To Eddie's surprise, his wife, Laurette, told him not to meet with Michael alone. She didn't have a reason beyond intuition, but called out her warning as he was leaving that morning. He couldn't understand where his wife's alarm was coming from. Laurette had participated in the study sessions Eddie had conducted for Carrie and Michael; she'd been the fourth person at the table and knew Michael almost as well as he did.

"I won't be alone," Eddie called back. "Linda will be there."

Linda was the receptionist of the Hebrew school, though it turned out she wasn't there that morning, as Laurette learned when she phoned Eddie in his office.

"Judy's here," he told Laurette. Judy ran the synagogue's nursery school program. His wife told him to leave the door open.

All this seemed entirely unnecessary once Michael was seated across from Eddie. He was down, to be sure, certainly depressed. But he was a gloomy, familiar version of himself. Eddie knew he had psychiatric problems without knowing a great deal about the details. He knew Michael took medication, but so did many in his congregation. There were no burning questions or confessions, just the old sorrows. Michael was burdened by his book, by illness, by the weight of a materialistic society pressing on his soul, and by a hunger for God. His loneliness was palpable.

Eddie was a good listener, actively empathetic but grounded, allowing the pain of others to pass through him without cracking him in half like a tree struck by lightning. After listening to Michael, Eddie asked if he'd ever read *The Lonely Man of Faith* by Rabbi Joseph Soloveitchik, known to his followers as "the Rav." Born in Russia to a line of eminent rabbis in 1903, the Rav had died ninety years later in Boston, his life shaped by Jewish tradition, Western philosophy, and the brute forces of twentieth-century history. *The Lonely Man of Faith* was one of those books Eddie kept in multiple copies on his shelf, though it seemed especially well suited to Michael. Originally published in 1965, it was in its way a countercultural work by a great rabbi standing up in prosperous postwar America and crying out to God.

Michael hadn't read the book, and Eddie retrieved a copy and handed it to him. He asked Michael to read it and come back the following week so they could talk about it. "It says *Lonely Man of Faith*," Eddie told him, "but it's a positive book."

My father kept a copy of the Rav's little book on the shelf near his bed, and I can see why Eddie thought a confession addressed to the suffering soul who "looks upon himself as a stranger in modern society" would speak to Michael. He also loved Bible stories and had begun his "Wrongful Life" essay with Genesis. Eddie had focused on the weekly Torah reading at their Friday-night study sessions, and the *Lonely Man of Faith* used the two different versions of God's creation of Adam in Genesis to talk about two different visions of human nature. The Rav called these "Adam the first" and "Adam the second." We were supposed to embody both Adams, because both represented God's will, but lately, Adam the first had been getting the upper hand.

Adam the first was the one fashioned in God's image at the same time as Eve—how, you aren't told—who marches forth to be like God, dominating and subduing the earth, creating new worlds with strength and ingenuity. This Adam finds his separateness from nature a source of strength because he transforms what's around him, achieving dignity through action. Before he fell ill, Michael was more like Adam the first.

By contrast, Adam the second was made out of dust and never forgets it. Rather than doing and making, he wants to know why things exist in the first place, and what their meaning is. He is alone and lonely, and finds his separation from the rest of creation a source of sadness. Out of loneliness, Adam the second asks for a companion and gives up a rib, a sacrificial gesture, so God can make Eve, as much a clone as a wife.

This Adam wants to be part of creation more than he wants to be in charge of it, and would rather submit to God's will than subdue the material world. He craves contact with eternal things, and his idea of community is based on love and faith, like Michael's accommodating communitarian world.

The paradox for the Rav was that redemption could only come from submitting, like Adam the second, to God's will, but dignity could only come from dominating and transforming the world. Adam the first, who wants to be *like* God more than he wants to *know* God, finishes his projects on time; his social ties are practical and utilitarian, forming factories and offices designed for making and doing, without offering reasonable accommodation.

The forces of the two Adams were supposed to be balanced inside of us, but in a world that favored makers and doers over contemplators, and secular achievement over the journey toward God, Adam the first was growing like a golem. Adam the second meanwhile seemed to get smaller and lonelier. Increasingly, Eddie couldn't help thinking that there ought to be a third Adam, and that something was missing from the equation.

Eddie thought Michael was Adam the first when he was with Carrie and Adam the second when he was by himself. He wanted to help Michael find the courage to be alone with what he had.

Michael left with *The Lonely Man of Faith*. He was still heavy with sorrow but would be back to talk the book over, which would give Eddie another chance.

Eddie did not imagine, as he discussed the two Adams, that Michael had stopped taking his medication and was grappling with delusions, including the belief that there were two Carries, and the one he was living with wasn't human.

That the tough times were getting worse was no secret to the members of the Network who had watched over Michael personally and professionally for years, and who now watched over Carrie as well.

The day Michael met with Eddie, Jane Ferber got together with her old friend Myrna for dinner in Larchmont and poured out her distress about Michael's backward slide. His decline had been apparent for some time but had lately gotten manifestly worse. Myrna knew Michael had stopped taking his medication, but was shocked to hear that he thought Carrie was a space alien.

"You have to call Murray!" she told Jane.

Jane had been talking to Michael's psychiatrist and said she would call Murray again. Not that he didn't know. Myrna had heard that nobody, his psychiatrist included, had been able to get Michael to go back on his medication. But delusions were no more a justification for forced medication than refusing medication was a justification for forced hospitalization. The only question was whether Michael was violent, and Murray didn't see him that way.

Bonnie, the Cassandra among Jane's friends, had been watching the ebb and flow of Michael's illness for years and noted the falling off of his ADL, the activities of daily living—like toothbrushing and showering—that served as outward indicators of inward trouble. Such humble units of measurement often revealed more about mental trouble than eloquent assertions to the contrary.

Bonnie knew how easily brilliance could be mistaken for sanity, and how devastating the misunderstanding would be if Michael were left thrashing on his own. Where was his day hospital now? Michael wasn't her patient, or Jane's for that matter, though in a larger sense the Network had collective custody, much as Michael was an honorary member of the Ferber family.

Being in the family hardly precluded treatment; Josh, who'd shared the attic with Michael during a dark time for both of them, had been treated by his mother for years. At present Josh was in Poona, India, visiting his father at the ashram that was carrying on in the name of Bhagwan, who had "left his body," as his followers said, in 1990. They called him Osho now.

Josh's father, who was still called Bodhicitta, had weathered all the storms, and had literally been struck by lightning in Nepal, where he had a revelation about the irrelevance of his own body. He'd also come full psychiatric circle at an ashram where, in addition to tending the roses, he was tasked with figuring out when an ecstatic spiritual experience was really a psychotic episode. It had taken many years, eight thousand miles, and perhaps a bolt of lightning, but the former Dr. Ferber had arrived at the melancholy conclusion that there were some people who could not be healed even by a spiritual community dedicated to love, but needed to go to the hospital for treatment. Otherwise, they risked destroying the fragile balance everyone had worked so hard to achieve, and themselves along with it.

Elizabeth Ferber had been hearing harrowing reports about Michael from her mother. The stories were disturbing in themselves, but what made them especially frightening was the constrained intensity of her mother's voice. When Jane said, "He isn't doing well," it didn't sound like the neutral assessment of a remediable situation. Her mother's foreboding tone seemed to suggest something awful was imminent. In which case now was surely the time to act.

"What are you and Murray going to do about it?" Elizabeth demanded.

"We can't do anything," her mother told her.

Elizabeth was astonished. Her mother wasn't just a psychiatrist but a thirty-year veteran of community mental health. She didn't just care about Michael; she'd all but adopted him. Jane and her friends had devoted their lives to creating humane options for people with mental illness. It was crazy to think there was no place for Michael.

"How can you do nothing?" Elizabeth asked.

But all her mother could say was, "We can't."

The police *might* take Michael to a psychiatric hospital, but the hospital wouldn't keep him if he wasn't dangerous, and the danger had to be imminent. Thinking your fiancée was a space alien did not necessarily make you dangerous.

Nevertheless someone, possibly Murray, had recently dispatched the mobile unit of a local psychiatric hospital to the River Edge. It's possible someone else had requested it, perhaps even Ruth, who was increasingly alarmed about her son's behavior. She couldn't help thinking that if Chuck were alive, he would get Michael to go back on his medication, or would do *something*, the way he'd been able to talk Michael into signing himself into the hospital. But Chuck had been dead for two and a half years. Michael had turned thirty-five in May and couldn't be made to do anything.

It was Michael who answered the door when the crisis intervention team rang the bell. He chatted with them convincingly and sent them on their way. Before leaving they gave him their card and told him he could call them anytime, day or night. Michael took the card and shut the door.

This surprised nobody. Bonnie knew how easy it was for someone like Michael to avoid the buzzwords that could trip a psychiatric alarm. Everyone in the Network knew; they'd worked at the same places and understood that you didn't have to act sane, just "not act crazy," as Myrna put it, when the need arose. In her crisis intervention handbook, Jane described coaching patients to avoid commitment, but Michael did such things automatically. Even in the grip of a delusion, he seemed capable of bending his behavior around the kernel of other people's expectations of sanity.

The foreboding Elizabeth had heard in her mother's voice wasn't fear of Michael but fear for him. The danger that weighed most heavily on the Network was that Michael would suffer a break from which he might never recover; that he would end up with a hospitalization that would never end, despite the trend of emptying beds and closing hospitals. They doubted the efficacy of the system but feared its capacity for destruction and were determined to save him from it.

For her part, Carrie had lived through many ups and downs with Michael's illness. The night Jane had dinner with Myrna, Carrie was shopping in the A&P when she ran into an old friend who lived nearby and couldn't help commenting on how strained she looked. Carrie explained that she and Michael were in a rough patch but added, "We'll get through this. We always do."

The following morning, Carrie called the Edison Project office to say she had a personal emergency and would not be coming in. It was Wednesday the seventeenth, the day before the team was flying to Chicago. It was unusual for Carrie to miss a day of frenzied preparation, but the tech team had been with her in up times and down too. Tom had no doubt she would be there the next morning with her mountain of materials in order.

But Carrie wasn't there the following morning. It was early yet, but there were thirty people with suitcases from all departments crowded into the open space between offices with that stressed, expectant, festive air of kids before a class trip. If she wasn't in transit, someone would have to get ahold of Carrie and figure out how to get her materials for what Tom called the dog and pony show.

Carlo from development approached Tom. He'd been talking about something he'd heard on the all-news station, asking everyone the same question.

"Did you hear the weird thing on the radio this morning?" he asked Tom.

"No," said Tom, "why?

"What's Caroline's boyfriend's name?"

Strangely, Tom couldn't remember.

"There's this weird news story," Carlo was explaining, "this guy in Hastings stabbed his girlfriend and they're trying to track him down." The woman hadn't been named, but Hastings—

"Oh, Carlo," said Tom, "he wouldn't do something like that. Go away!"

Carlo went away, and Tom went into his office to answer the phone. There was a woman on the line.

"Tom, I'm Carrie's sister," she said. "I'm calling to let you know that Carrie won't be coming to work today." There was a jittery, fraught pause. "And she won't be coming to work anymore."

Tom closed his door.

"I heard something very odd this morning," he said. "I'm putting two and two together. Has something horrible happened?"

"Yes."

Tom shared his grief, offered condolences, hung up the phone, and found himself staring stuporously out the window. Everything that had seemed to matter a moment before, the trip to Chicago, the computers and presentations, had disappeared.

CHAPTER THIRTY-SEVEN

PERSONAL EMERGENCY

They're struggling with thoughts of wanting
to hurt themselves or others, and at the same
time, they desperately need the help of those
they're threatening to harm.

—Elyn Saks, *The Center Cannot Hold*

Eddie had noticed a helicopter hovering overhead when he took his recyclables to the curb late on Wednesday afternoon, the seventeenth of June. Helicopters were unusual for Hastings. Soon after, a patrol car pulled up to his house. That was how he learned that Carrie was dead, and that Michael had killed her and vanished. The newspapers the next day would still say Michael was only wanted for questioning, but the police car was there to take Eddie and Laurette into protective custody.

It was Ruth Laudor who had told the police to find Eddie. She knew Michael had met with the rabbi the day before, which made him the last person her son had seen before killing Carrie. Not the last person Michael had talked to, Eddie was relieved to learn, but the last person he'd seen. Ruth feared for Eddie's safety. The synagogue was being evacuated.

Ruth was also the reason a patrol car had been dispatched to the River Edge. A day that had begun with Carrie calling her office to say she couldn't come in had escalated into a frenzy of desperate telephone exchanges. There were calls with psychiatrists, with Ruth, with members of a crisis intervention team, who arranged for a visit that evening. Michael was intermittently on the line sounding like a hostage negotiator, a hostage, and a kidnapper backed against a wall of rising terror.

Michael had bombarded his mother with turbulent calls of increasing intensity, making wild accusations and irrational threats. After one harrowing call—Michael ranted about suicide and murder—Ruth had called back in a panic. Michael picked up, and Ruth told him to give the phone to Carrie. Michael said he couldn't do that because he'd killed her.

Ruth's call to the police came in at 4:17 p.m. on Wednesday. She urged speed and gave few details. The desk sergeant heard the panic and put out a radio call to check on the welfare of a couple in the River Edge apartments. The man had psychological problems and his mother hadn't heard from him and was worried about him and his fiancée, who lived there too.

Eddie knew the Hastings police department well; he'd been sworn in as police chaplain in the courtroom upstairs. Even before becoming their chaplain, he'd gotten to know many of the officers who had guarded Beth Shalom during the High Holidays after one or another of the bomb threats that were semi-regular occurrences in the 1970s and early '80s. Now they were guarding him and his wife, not from a hate group but a holy soul who had killed his beloved partner. Was it possible?

The investigation was being directed by Vince Schiavone, who'd been the youth officer when Eddie had arrived in Hastings. They'd gotten along immediately, different as they seemed; it was Vince who'd suggested Eddie when the old priest who'd been serving as chaplain died.

Vince was now Lieutenant Schiavone, the department's executive officer and—that week—acting chief of police as well. When the officers ringing Michael's bell got no response, and found the door locked, they radioed their sergeant, who called Vince at home. Officers couldn't go around opening doors, but the desk sergeant had felt the mother's distress, and Vince told them to get the key from the super and check out the place at once.

The officers found a woman's body in the kitchen, fully clothed, lying in a pool of blood. There were multiple stab wounds and her throat was cut. Signs of struggle suggested she'd fought back. Blood was everywhere, soaking the floor of the narrow kitchen and spattering the walls and the refrigerator. No weapon was found, but a chef's knife was missing from its slotted space in the slanted block that housed it. The man was also missing.

Vince soon received a second call: "Lieutenant, come back to work. We've got a homicide."

He told them to seal off the apartment and post a uniformed officer outside; nobody gets in but the two detectives. The department only had two detectives, one of them minted just six months earlier. There hadn't been a murder in Hastings for nineteen years.

Yonkers, on the other hand, just across the border, averaged twenty or thirty murders a year. Its police department had a helicopter and a crime scene unit, and Vince reached out to them. They sent a forensic team and coached him through the investigation. Everything had to be done by the book, even if you thought you knew who did it. Vince didn't want to be the guy on TV explaining that the Hastings PD had screwed up a homicide.

Vince visited the crime scene briefly, a horror show, then drove with an officer to New Rochelle to deliver the news to 28 Mereland Road in person. The moment Ruth Laudor peered through the glass, and opened the door, she asked, "Is she . . . ?"

"Yes," Vince told her. "She is."

Ruth burst into tears. Vince would never forget the look on her face. It seemed to say, "Oh my God, I failed," and, "We didn't move fast enough."

The officers passed through the cramped vestibule with the Indian print of the buxom dancer, and into the living room with the piano and the books. Vince didn't feel it was necessary to give Ruth the details. For one thing, they were shocking. For another, it seemed clear that she knew. No doubt she'd hoped that what Michael had said to her on the phone was a delusion, but Vince had never seen a person who *knew* the way Ruth did.

What can you do in such a situation but listen? Ruth told them about her son, explained that he had schizophrenia. She gave them a lot of background information and told them his story.

"I knew something like this could happen," Ruth said. "But he was getting happy. They were going to be married . . ."

Her anguish was intense, shot through with what Vince's wife called *woulda coulda shoulda*. They'd been trying to find him a psychiatrist or someone who could get him the help he needed, she said. Not that he wasn't getting help already. She wanted Vince to know, he felt, that they'd been working on this and it had gotten away from them somehow.

Vince was a person of enormous empathy, who had created the position of youth officer despite ribbing from fellow officers who called him a "social worker" just because he thought someone ought to reach out to delinquent kids who often lacked only direction or a decent home. It still smarted. Didn't he carry a gun and keep handcuffs in his pocket? Didn't he do police work too? Now all the departments had youth officers, and cops were expected to step into the breach for both young and old.

While Ruth was talking, a radio call came in from the detectives at the River Edge; *his* car was still in the lot but *her* car was gone. Someone had seen Michael driving away in Carrie's black 1989 Honda Civic.

Vince told Ruth he was sorry but had to ask, "Do you know where he is?"

"No," said Ruth. "I don't."

She seemed like a lovely woman, and so distraught. Nobody should have to go through that with their own child. The grief and guilt. The second-guessing. Even the cops at the station felt guilty. The River Edge was perhaps one hundred feet from the station. Michael could see the building from his balcony. As one patrolman put it, "To think that was going on right next to us. If we'd got there maybe fifteen minutes sooner, half an hour sooner . . ."

The police station was so close that Eddie, looking out the window in the June evening, could see the gurney with Carrie's covered body wheeled along the path. It was guided away from the low brick buildings and toward the ambulance that would take it to the morgue. Vince would have to bring the Costellos there once they got to town to identify their daughter's body.

The coroner's report, released quickly, told its stark forensic story. The death was a homicide. The cause was "sharp force injuries of head, neck, back and upper extremity involving lungs, aorta, esophagus and thyroid cartilage."

Carrie had been grabbed from behind and stabbed repeatedly. Her killer had used two knives. Her throat had been cut. But despite her assailant's size and weight, which was put at six foot three and 230 pounds, the victim had fought, trying to hold off her attacker till the end.

The medical examiner's report included an additional piece of information that deepened the tragedy for those who knew the couple, and compounded the crime for the DA's office. Carrie was pregnant.

Jane Ferber called her daughter that evening to tell her what had happened. Elizabeth was in Brooklyn with her son, Gideon, now two years old. Along with the shock and horror, she felt again the sense of a tragedy foretold.

"The police are looking for Michael," Jane said.

"Well, lock the doors and the windows!" Elizabeth shouted at her mother.

My mother called me at my office and told me not to go home. She'd heard an approximate version of the story from a New Rochelle friend who must have heard it from Ruth, or maybe it was once or twice removed already because it was garbled, or maybe just preliminary. When I asked why I shouldn't go home, my mother told me that Michael had hurt Carrie.

"Hurt her how?" My mother wasn't sure but she thought with a knife.

"A knife? My God, is she all right?"

She thought it was serious but didn't know the details. She didn't say Carrie was dead, and perhaps she didn't know, though it's not impossible she wanted to spare me. I'd find out soon enough. But my mother knew they couldn't find Michael, and repeated that I shouldn't go home.

I felt an overwhelming nauseous dread, but not about going home. Why would Michael seek me out? But I felt as if a great calamity had befallen me already in a way I couldn't yet identify.

Jane must have listened to her daughter, because when Josh Ferber got home from India that night and drove straight to his mother's house from JFK, he twisted the knob to push open the door and found it wouldn't budge. He knew at once that something terrible had happened. His mother never locked her doors, at least not when she was awake. And she was wide awake.

Eddie was also awake. Released from protective custody, safe in his own soft bed, he could find no rest. He got up and dressed around midnight and drove to the all-night A&P where, the day before, Carrie had assured a concerned friend that she and Michael would get through their tough time.

Wandering the aisles aimlessly, Eddie was lost in thought when his cart was grabbed at the opposite end. He looked up and saw the store's manager, Wally Urtz, blocking his path.

"Rabbi, I know why you're here," Wally said, like a figure in a Jewish fable. "And I want to tell you a story."

Wally was an older man with a limp, which did not deter him from helping overburdened shoppers carry groceries to their cars. He was so attuned to people's troubles that when Eddie wanted to give to charity, he gave Wally cash to distribute because he always knew which families needed money. Eddie considered him a lamed vavnik, one of "the thirty-six righteous" on whom the fate of the world depends. That he wasn't Jewish made no difference.

"Years ago," Wally began, "it was the middle of the night, just like this. I had a young Black woman working her way through school at the checkout. A white woman was here and she says, "I'm not letting you check me out. I want a white woman checking me out . . .'"

The young woman, Nicole, was only sixteen and crying when Wally got to the register. The white lady kept repeating that she wasn't letting a Black girl check her out. Wally told the customer, "You're letting her check you out or I'm calling the cops."

Then he turned to Nicole, who was still crying and didn't want to do it, and said, "You're not going to let her get the best of you." He told her that life was full of tough challenges and that she'd have to learn to deal with them. He'd be right beside her, they'd go through it together, but she was going to check that woman out. And she did. Years later, Nicole returned and told Wally, "I graduated college, I graduated law school, I became an assistant DA, and it's all because of that night."

In the manner of Jewish fables, Wally's story was only obliquely fitted to the present crisis. But the moral, delivered separately, was a direct hit. "People walk into your synagogue and my A&P," he told Eddie, "and we have no idea what's going to happen. Now go home to your wife."

And the rabbi went home.

CHAPTER THIRTY-EIGHT

GOING BACK

You can't go back and you can't stand still

If the thunder don't get you then the
lightning will

—"The Wheel," 1972, words by Robert Hunter;
music by Jerry Garcia and Bill Kreutzmann

Michael drove Carrie's black Honda west, away from Hastings-
on-Hudson toward Binghamton. He was no longer the lonely
man of faith passing through the dark night of the soul. He was a
thirty-five-year-old man with untreated schizophrenia who had done
something terrible, covered in blood and hounded by horrible thoughts.

Twenty minutes outside of Binghamton on Route 17 he approached
the exit to Farm Camp Lowy, a pocket of lost time even when we
were there in the seventies singing "Happiness runs in a circular
motion." As a counselor in training, Michael had been told to stop
diving into the lake and towing the little kids to the raft whenever
he saw them struggling. "If they take the bus," the swim counselor
said, "why would they want to walk to work?" He'd felt like the
Catcher in the Rye, he told me proudly, but had stopped saving them.

The lake and cabins were operated by Evangelicals now, and Michael didn't get off at Farm Camp Lowy. He drove on to Binghamton, where he'd once sat with counselors from Farm Camp Lowy on
dorm room floors, talking and smoking pot in that easy suspended

way that lasted forever, like holding your breath and breathing at the same time because time, like happiness, ran in a circular motion, carrying you forward and taking you home.

Binghamton wasn't his final destination either. Michael abandoned Carrie's car in a big lot near the university. He bought a ticket on the 10:30 p.m. Shortline bus to Ithaca, which you can do even with blood on your clothes, especially if the light is poor and you ask in the right way. He changed seats several times, filled with restless terror.

Carrie and her family had lived in Ithaca, and in Buffalo, too, on their way from Virginia to Newton, Massachusetts. Michael's Ithaca was Cornell University. It was Telluride House where he'd discovered the poem "Ithaka" by C. P. Cavafy:

> As you set out for Ithaka,
> Hope the journey is a long one.

The journey by bus was an hour and ten minutes, but time wasn't passing in the usual way. Michael's Ithaca was the Stone Arch Bridge he crossed when he walked from Telluride House into Collegetown with friends for a late-night burger and maybe a beer if they could bluff the waitress out of carding them. If anyone could, it was Michael; you just had to ask in the right way. He was sixteen but the drinking age in those days was only eighteen.

> Keep Ithaka always in your mind.
> Arriving there is what you're destined for.

It would be good to go back, if only he could. To Telluride, to being sixteen, to literature and revolution, to his summer girlfriend, Tocqueville's furious sheep, Flaubert's *Sentimental Education*, and dirty limericks composed on the communal blackboard. Back to the Stone

Arch Bridge, also called the College Avenue Bridge, which connected campus to Collegetown. Under the bridge, where trolls live in stories, was the drop they joked about nervously, the flip side of every deep dream. Cascadilla Gorge wasn't as deep as the gorge at the other end of campus, but it was deep enough to swallow people and their dreams in one gulp. It was like in that Grateful Dead song, "If the thunder don't get you . . ."

Michael got off in Collegetown. The bus driver, who had noticed the blood on Michael's clothing but didn't think it was any of his business, watched the tall, agitated man walk onto the Stone Arch Bridge. The man stopped at the midpoint and looked east, leaning out over the rocky drop where rushing water eddied around boulders and trees. The sucking power of the gorge could be felt as well as seen in the illuminated darkness, and made more noise than the roar of traffic.

CHAPTER THIRTY-NINE

THE FATAL FUNNEL

Sergeant Mospan: Did this occur today?

Michael Laudor: Yeah, she was threatening to have me put away, so I might have killed her or her windup doll, I'm not sure, can we check on her?

—Interview with Cornell campus police

After five years as a detective with the Cornell campus police, Ellen Brewer had downgraded herself to patrolwoman in exchange for regular hours. She wanted to spend more time with her daughter, who'd been born at twenty-six weeks and had been allowed home only after four harrowing months in the hospital. Officer Brewer's daughter was now two years old, and regular hours meant the night shift from 11:00 p.m. to 7:00 a.m.

Campus police chose their own routes inside their assigned patrol zone. Typically, Officer Brewer turned left or continued straight after pulling out of the parking lot at Barton Hall, but on the night of June 17, 1998, she turned right toward Collegetown. She wanted to pick up a magazine and sunflower seeds for the night ahead, a decision that would haunt her for many months. She'd barely advanced a hundred yards along Campus Road when she noticed off to the left a tall, silhouetted figure moving slowly across the engineering quad.

The man appeared to be dressed all in black, incongruous for a campus in summer where students wore shorts, T-shirts, and sneak-ers. Officer Brewer felt a whisper of danger. She slowed her car, and the shrouded figure began loping toward her. He raised a hand and hailed her as if she were a taxi. As he drew closer, she thought he must be the victim of an assault, perhaps in need of medical assistance.

Suddenly, as if in a single stride, the tall, heavyset man was at her window. His florid face, shiny with sweat, was lowered close to hers. He was muttering distressed and incoherent things; his rusty beard and hair were wildly matted, and she thought again he'd been attacked or had perhaps fallen into the gorge. He seemed to be say-ing that he might have killed someone, his girlfriend or perhaps a windup doll. Officer Brewer radioed in the strange encounter, re-quested backup, and got out of her car.

Though she wasn't sure why, Ellen continued to feel the man might be injured as well as disoriented, that he was a victim who needed something from her. He was also in the middle of the roadway, and though there wasn't much traffic, she needed to get him over to the side. When she touched his shoulder, the man jumped back, his hand balled into a fist at the ready. Stepping back herself, she coaxed Mi-chael to the side of the road. The sense of danger mingled with the feeling that he was in distress, and she continued to wonder if he'd been assaulted. She stood with Michael as backup arrived.

The police station was all of a hundred yards away, and officers were already coming toward them, some on foot, others in cars. Patrolman Bobby Payne pulled up and suggested getting Michael into the back seat of his cruiser. Something told Ellen it would not be a good idea to fold this big man, who had just made a large fist, into a small car. She and Bobby escorted Michael to Barton Hall, the looming stone fortress that the campus police shared with the athletics department.

As he walked beside them, Michael continued muttering darkly. When Officer Payne asked him what was wrong, he told the patrol-man he might have killed his fiancée or a windup doll "because I thought she was going to have me sent away again." Where had that happened? Hastings-on-Hudson. Asked if he'd brought any luggage, Michael said he didn't want to talk about it, but he did explain how he came to be bleeding: "I used a knife and she moved her arm and the knife cut me in the hand."

Once they were in Barton Hall, Michael was installed in a small interview room that doubled as a processing room. The warm room had no windows or air-conditioning; there were metal file cabinets, a small table, and what the officers called a "bull ring"—a metal ring bolted to the wall, to which one end of a suspect's handcuffs could be attached if necessary. But Michael was still being treated as more of a mystery than a suspect.

Interviewed in quick succession by several officers, he continued to sound as much like a victim as a perpetrator. "I'm upset," he told Sergeant Richard Gourley when asked how he was. "I'm frightened." Sergeant Gourley offered him a drink. "Water, soda or something?"

"Something cool to drink would be nice," Michael said. He was given a Pepsi.

Michael didn't need much prodding, or any, to answer questions, but whenever he mentioned possibly harming his girlfriend, sometimes referred to as his fiancée, he added "or a windup doll." Even Hastings-on-Hudson had a fanciful sound, like Brigadoon, if only because it was 170 miles away.

Michael's outlandish statements mingled with mundane particulars, which made it even harder to gauge whether he was offering a confession or sharing a delusion. One exchange sounded like this:

Sgt. Gourley: Do you have a car up here?
Michael: No.
Sgt. Gourley: Anything I can do for you?
Michael: Well I know that, I know that I, I know that, I know that I, I know that I tried to kill Carrie or the windup toy that was Carrie 'cause and that she was trying to have me

locked up. (pause) I traveled a long way by car to Binghamton and then I got money at an ATM machine and then I
got a bus to Ithaca.

His semi-confession was oddly equivocal. He might have tried to
kill Carrie, but he didn't know if she was Carrie or a windup toy,
and he wasn't sure if he'd killed her or had only tried.

Everything had that indeterminate aspect. When Michael mentioned a lawyer, it sounded speculative, more like thinking aloud
than making a request. He was, in any event, easily diverted.

Sgt. Gourley: So you've been on the road a long time then, huh?
Michael Laudor: I don't know how long. (pause) I'd like to see.
    I think I need a lawyer.

Sgt. Gourley: Did you have supper?
Michael Laudor: I think I had a doughnut.

Sgt. Gourley: We have a candy machine. . . .
Michael Laudor: I don't want anything.

Asked if he'd ever been to campus before, Michael replied that
he was there in the summer of 1980. In fact, he'd been on his way
"to that house" to get the people there to help him contact the police
"because I knew I needed the police." When Officer Gourley asked
what house he meant, Michael told him, "Telluride."

Sgt. Gourley: You lived at Telluride when you were here in 1980?
Michael Laudor: Yeah, I think so in the summer.

Somehow that grand hub of intellectual achievement, the high
point of Michael's precocious adolescence, had become the place you
go when you need the police. The officers all knew what Telluride
House was, but who travels 170 miles to get the cops? It did not make

sense either as a lie or as the truth. Officer Gourley asked Michael if he'd made it to Telluride House, and Michael explained that he hadn't gotten that far because he saw the police car.

Strange as Michael's story sounded, there remained the blood on his clothing. When Sergeant Philip Mospan, the officer in charge that night, asked Michael if he was hurt, he received a simple no. In that case, "Where did the blood all over your person come from?" Michael told him it was Caroline's blood.

"Who is Caroline?" the sergeant asked.

"She's my girlfriend," Michael told him. "I hurt her. I think I killed her."

Was Michael sure about that?

He thought so, but asked, "Can we check on her?"

"Yes," Sergeant Mospan told him. "We would be glad to check on her well-being. What is her name and where is she?"

"Her name is Caroline Costello," Michael said, "and she lives at 19 Maple Avenue."

"Maple Avenue in Ithaca?"

"No," Michael said. "In Hastings-on-Hudson."

"That's pretty far away," Sergeant Mospan said. "Did this occur today?"

"Yeah, she was threatening to have me put away," Michael explained, "so I might have killed her or her windup doll, I'm not sure, can we check on her?"

His concern seemed urgent and genuine. So did his need to know, as if he were as surprised and perplexed as anyone. Michael had a dark foreboding about something he himself had done. He needed answers even if the investigation pointed to him. He needed the police to check on Carrie, and possibly on him too.

Michael knew something awful had happened that he hoped wasn't true. Perhaps an investigation would show that it hadn't happened after all, or if it had, that there would be time to do something about it. But Sergeant Mospan was asking how he'd gotten there so fast. Michael explained once more about driving Carrie's car to Binghamton, taking a bus to Cornell, spotting a police car, and running toward it.

A bus from Binghamton? asked the sergeant. Yes, Michael said, he paid $8.45 for the ticket.

Perhaps it was just to keep Michael talking, and to see what else he might disclose. It's also possible it was so unusual for someone to stab a person in Westchester, drive for three hours to a university, take an hour bus ride to another university, and there flag down a police car in order to report what he thought he might have done in the first location, that they were still seeking alternate possibilities, or looking for holes in the story.

Or maybe they just wanted to get the facts straight. Sergeant Mospan wanted to know when the events in Hastings had transpired. Michael said they'd happened that day. Did he remember what time? He did not. It was almost midnight, the sergeant said. Could Michael say if the events had transpired in the morning or after lunch?

"After lunch, I think," Michael told him. His agitation was mounting. "Can we check on her, I think, I don't know, she may be dead." Sergeant Mospan said they could do that. Did Michael know if Hastings had its own police department? If so, he'd call and ask them to check on Caroline. Michael said he thought they did.

"Wait here," Sergeant Mospan told him. "I'll call them and ask them to check on her. It's Caroline Costello at 19 Maple Ave?" Michael confirmed Carrie's name and address and thanked the sergeant, who went back to his desk to make his call.

Sergeant Mospan prefaced his request to the Hastings dispatcher by saying, "This may sound off the wall . . ." The dispatcher asked him to wait a moment, and then a detective came on the line. "Hold him!" the detective said. "He did just what he said he did." They had people on the scene, which was ghastly. The woman was dead, her head nearly severed. "Don't let him go!"

When Sergeant Mospan shared this information with Officer Brewer, she rose into the air and did what the sergeant later referred to as a 180 pirouette. It wasn't a joyful jump but a retroactive jolt of adrenaline. That she'd been so unguardedly proximate to a murderer—who, by the way, had been left sitting in the processing room—was a sobering reminder of "the fatal funnel" they warned you about in the police academy. The fatal funnel was the way they taught you how easy it was to go from a safe place to a place where you've lined yourself up for something bad to happen.

Officer Brewer had gotten out of her patrol car and stood with Michael by the side of the road without knowing who he was. She'd been drawn by compassion despite the whisper of warning she'd felt. Despite the incoherent but troubling talk of killing, even if it was only a windup doll, and his martial reaction to her touch. Once inside the fatal funnel, you could end up dead in a whole lot of different ways.

After the call to Hastings, Michael was formally arrested, read his Miranda rights, and handcuffed by his left wrist to the metal ring bolted to the wall about three feet off the ground. Officers from Hastings wouldn't retrieve him until morning, but now that they knew what they had, the Cornell PD began working the case from the Ithaca end.

Michael had exercised his right to an attorney, and asked for a phone call. Soon after a lawyer called the precinct to say that he was representing Michael and insisted on being present for any further questioning. Michael wasn't asked about killing Carrie, but there was information they needed from him that required no words. Blood also told a story, and Michael had flagged down a police car with hands that were literally stained red.

As it happened, Ellen Brewer, who'd spent time in the department's investigative unit, was the officer most qualified that night to serve as the evidence tech. She'd recently been certified as a crime scene technician. Michael was considered a crime scene in and of himself.

Despite her leap of retroactive fear, Officer Brewer had no trouble immersing herself in the slow, meticulous process of gathering and labeling evidence from the top of Michael's head to the bottom of his feet. It helped that she was being assisted by the largest officers on the force, and that Michael was attached to the wall.

Both for her safety, and because Michael needed to be undressed layer by layer, Ellen spent most of her time in the hallway, coming into the processing room mainly to direct the two big officers attending him. One was Bobby Payne, who'd helped her walk Michael up the hill and was nicknamed the Bull. The other, Dan Murphy, though not as big as the Bull, was a defensive tactics instructor. Assisting Ellen in the hall was Chuck Alridge, a young patrolman new to the force with a genial disposition and the build of a linebacker.

The painstaking work took hours. Each item of Michael's clothing had to be removed and examined. Hair had to be collected with tweezers; blood had to be swabbed. Anything with fluids had to go into a paper bag to prevent mildew. After each particle of possible evidence was bagged and tagged, it was conveyed by Alridge to a large room down the hall, where he arranged it all carefully on an open stretch of floor, like cards in a giant game of concentration. The assemblage grew steadily hour by hour until it covered a vast expanse.

Elsewhere, the circle of evidence was also widening. A murder did not need to be a mystery to require investigation. Luckily, Wednesday was a "fat shift," the one day of the week when every officer in the Cornell PD reported for duty. Nearly all of them spent the night working on Carrie's case.

The effort was coordinated by Sergeant Mospan, who was in charge of the shift that night. He stayed in constant contact with Hastings, which was in contact with Yonkers. He sent officers to find the Shortline bus that Michael had taken from Binghamton, which someone realized was spending the night in one of Cornell's perimeter lots waiting for its morning run. They found the driver, too, who remembered a bloody passenger with a wild look, changing seats.

As word of the case spread, Sergeant Mospan seemed to get a call every five minutes from local agents at the Bureau of Criminal Investigation—the plainclothes detective division of the state police—offering their services for what was promising to be a high-profile homicide. He sent the BCI agents to help the state troopers he'd contacted when he couldn't get through to the Binghamton city police. The troopers had found Carrie's black Honda in the lot Michael had described, with a big chef's knife inside, and towed it to a state facility to be processed for blood and hair.

A second knife was presumed missing but a great deal of progress had been made, considering it was the middle of the night. Everything had to be approved up the chain of command, logged, copied, coordinated, filed. A local judge had to be found to get an arraignment for the morning. All those rules and procedures that Michael's law school seminars had vaulted over to get to the interesting stuff needed to be followed with care, or a bureaucratic bungle could derail the case the DA was building before it even went to trial, and alter whatever defense Michael's attorneys decided to mount.

Every fifteen minutes, Sergeant Mospan walked down the long hall to see how the collection of evidence was progressing. He wanted to make sure that Michael was still cooperating and that Ellen, who had been working with the precision of a slow surgeon, was comfortable now that Michael was down to his last layer. His body was the final piece of evidence, and every cut and scratch on his skin had to be photographed. Some of his wounds were defensive, inflicted by Carrie as she fought back.

Michael's mood had ebbed and flowed in the course of the long night. In the early phase, he'd seemed agitated, overwhelmingly remorseful, and largely cooperative. He'd told Sergeant Mospan, who'd been a young officer at Cornell when Michael was at Telluride in 1980, how much he'd loved being there eighteen summers before. Telluride House was a place, Michael said, where he thought he could find some solitude and peace.

He'd seemed more lucid then, too, though always with that elsewhere quality that had intensified and mingled with darker moods as the night wore on. Initially, he'd refused to remove any clothing without a lawyer present. Gradually he'd settled into sullen compliance, eyes averted, silent and withdrawn.

At last, they were at the end. Having refused at the start to remove anything, Michael had ended by refusing to put anything on. They'd been offering him a Tyvek suit, one of those zip-up jumpsuits made of papery plastic that the CSIs wear, which was all they had to cover him. His clothing had all been peeled into evidence.

Michael was huddled in a chair in the corner of the small, hot room. He was completely naked, though half obscured by the metal file cabinets. Eyes averted, he was folded into himself, deeply withdrawn.

A naked man sitting in a chair in the corner, hunched toward the wall, hardly seemed a threat. They'd removed the handcuff that had shackled him to the bullring, but he still wouldn't dress or speak. He'd been told they were planning to move him to a more comfortable room. There was a small table in front of him, and he did not seem exposed when Officer Brewer came into the room, as she'd done from time to time in the course of the long night.

Later she would watch the video and see what she'd missed, the jaw clenching beneath the ruddy beard, the hands balling into fists. But that night, intent on her work and flanked by a protective detail of burly cops, she felt free to kneel with tweezers to extract a strand of Carrie's hair from a final item of uncataloged clothing. It wasn't until Michael sprang up without warning, a frightened, furious, naked man, that it dawned on her, too late, she was in the heart of the fatal funnel.

Though everything happened with extraordinary speed—his leap from the chair and simultaneous bending down, as if from a great height, to bring his enraged face inches from her own—there was also a feeling of suspended motion. She had plenty of time to burn a copy of his face, eyes narrowed with pitiless rage, into her brain while she thought, "He's going to hurt me. I don't know how but I know it's going to happen and I know it's going to be very bad."

Then Michael slammed his fist into her mouth and the world went dark.

When Ellen regained consciousness, her head was ringing with pain and she was lying in the hallway, where one of the officers had tossed her for her own protection. She was just outside the room where a great struggle was underway. She couldn't see, but she heard the sounds of the three big officers grappling with Michael. It did not sound like it was going well.

She'd crashed into a metal file cabinet before hitting the ground, and her face was wet with blood. Her jaw was dislocated and four front teeth had been flattened upward against the roof of her mouth. There was nothing she could do to help.

Touching the wall for guidance, she began to grope her way down the hall, dragging herself on all fours through darkness lit by inward flashes of crimson light, those mental sunspots that follow head trauma. Sergeant Mospan, who'd heard a scream and shouting, found Ellen crawling along the floor. He asked her if she thought she could make it on her own. Yes, she said, go help them.

Amazingly, they seemed to need it. Chuck, Bobby, and Dan were his biggest guys. Not only had they not managed to subdue Michael, he was flinging them with what seemed superhuman strength against the walls of the little room, made smaller and less safe by the file cabinets. One of the men went down.

Sergeant Mospan stood outside the door watching the framed scene of the grappling men. Michael was in the middle of the hot room, completely naked and too slippery with sweat and blood for the men to hold on to. Wild with adrenaline and psychotic rage, he was breaking through all three guys, even Bobby the Bull. Dan taught techniques for gaining physical control of people. None of that mattered.

Dan had pulled out his nightstick, one of the old "hickory sticks" in use before the collapsible kind. It was a formidable weapon in skilled hands. Sergeant Mospan watched in astonishment as Dan delivered a femoral blow, designed to cut the nerve and drop a man like a sack of oats, that produced no effect on Michael whatsoever.

If an impact weapon didn't work, the next level of force available was a firearm. Sergeant Mospan took a step back and put his hand on his holstered gun. Michael wasn't armed, but if they did not stop him, he was going to harm somebody. All this was happening in the blink of an eye.

The sergeant unclasped the leather strap on his sidearm, weighing whether or not to draw his gun. Dan Murphy had been thrown to the floor but still had his hickory stick in his hand. Lifting himself up on one knee, he delivered a second femoral blow with the force of desperation. The strike worked and Michael went down.

The men recuffed and shackled Michael. Eventually they got him into the Tyvek jumpsuit and zipped it up. Meanwhile an ambulance arrived and rushed Ellen Brewer to the ER. The station returned to a semblance of order. Sergeant Mospan reattached his holster strap, wondering if he had really been about to shoot a naked, unarmed man.

It had been less than two years since an Ithaca police officer had fatally shot a mentally ill woman who'd leapt out of the bathroom where she'd barricaded herself and stabbed the officer's partner in the neck with a steak knife, killing him. Ithaca was a small town where the police all knew each other and the stabbed investigator was the first member of the Ithaca police force ever killed in the line of duty. But it was the surviving officer, the one who'd shot the woman, who haunted them all.

Traumatized by his partner's death, and by the death of the woman he'd killed, accused of murder by mental health advocates, the tormented officer seemed a living emblem of a larger breach police were continually being sent to repair with tools unsuited to the job. This wasn't the first time the slain investigator had made a "check on the welfare of" visit to the woman who killed him. He'd no doubt assumed it would end like the others when he called through the locked door, "Mary, are you all right?" Though Mary was known for having cut open her own belly with a penknife to deliver her baby, a pattern of hospitalization and quick release must have made the situation feel manageably familiar.

They were all in the fatal funnel, and Sergeant Mospan was lucky to have escaped it as he had.

A dentist saved Ellen Brewer's four front teeth, but she missed four months of work, and it would take a lot longer for her to return to active duty. For months she was awakened by a recurring nightmare: Michael's enraged face inches from her own. It was only with the therapy that Sergeant Mospan encouraged her to pursue, at a time when it was still taboo on the force, that she began to reorganize her life and find a new calling inside the old one.

Officer Brewer would tell the story, and other lessons learned that night, in a training lecture she gave to officers around the country. Her lecture was about trauma, safety, the fatal funnel, the dangers of complacency, and the importance of mental health awareness for both police and the general public. She called her lecture "The Three Faces of Michael Laudor."

CHAPTER FORTY

CAIN AND ABEL

Westchester County District Attorney Jeanine
Pirro would not disclose a motive or say
whether Laudor's mental problems played a role.
"What you have here are two young, well-
educated people, and unfortunately one is
dead and the other is charged with second-
degree murder," Pirro said. "Not a happy ending."

—*New York Daily News*, "Lawyer Held in Knife Slay:
Suspect Fought Long Battle vs. Schizophrenia,"
June 19, 1998

On their way to Ithaca to retrieve Michael early Thursday morning, June 18, the Hastings detectives stopped in Binghamton
to arrange for the transport of Carrie's car back to Westchester.
The district attorney, Jeanine Pirro, was preparing to indict Michael on second-degree murder charges, which carried a sentence of
twenty-five years to life. "This is a particularly vicious crime," she told
a reporter, "and there don't appear to be any mitigating circumstances."

People from the DA's office spent the morning in Manhattan
interviewing Carrie's colleagues, who had initially been told not to
leave town, but Benno and some of the others used their influence
so everyone could be cleared in time for an afternoon flight to Chicago. The stunned and grieving tech team had been given the option

of staying home but decided, as Tom put it, that "Caroline would *not* have us stewing in our beer." It wasn't her way, and for her sake they would hold it together and get the job done.

Tom told the assistant district attorney interviewing him about Carrie and Michael, and the "family emergency" of the day before. The man was a young, sympathetic listener who seemed to understand the complexity of Michael's illness. The ADA only surprised Tom when he asked him if he'd known Carrie was pregnant, which he hadn't, and if she'd ever talked about a doll or teddy bear. Tom puzzled over the idea of a stuffed bear or some other soft, inanimate creature. Perhaps it was a code word for the baby, like "fuzzy bunny" or "our little teddy"? Nobody seemed to know.

Michael had barely spoken since his naked scrimmage with the campus police, though after he'd settled down and accepted a soda, they asked him why he'd punched the officer, and he explained that he'd wanted a lawyer. Since then, he'd been arraigned before a local judge in Ithaca, a securing order had been signed, and he'd been transferred to the Ithaca City Jail, where the Hastings officers went to claim him. When they told Michael who they were and why they'd come, he asked if they could take him back to Carrie.

In addition to some of the brass from the state police, who usually showed up hoping for face time on the local station, an unexpectedly large crowd of reporters and cameras had assembled outside the Ithaca jail. The story Carlo heard that morning, and quizzed his colleagues about in the Edison offices, was just the beginning of a growing media frenzy.

Even without Google, launched later that year, reporters had begun to learn that Michael's name was connected to Brad Pitt, Ron Howard, Yale Law School, and *The New York Times*.

Michael seemed entirely oblivious of his surroundings as the

Hastings officers escorted him to their unmarked car. Asked if he was comfortable, Michael said only, "I'm afraid." Asked if he was hungry or thirsty, Michael said no or mutely shook his head. The officers reminded him it was a long ride and suggested he take some food. "I don't deserve any," Michael told them.

The following day, the *New York Daily News* reported, "Authorities said he was nearly catatonic during the four-hour drive back to Westchester." The *Daily News* wasn't the only paper waiting for Michael's return that afternoon. The River Edge apartments and the nearby police station were swarming with television crews, photographers, and reporters for newspapers and wire services. Cameras shot B-roll of a gardener clipping the hedges outside the River Edge, while the building's manager likened Hastings-on-Hudson to Mayberry, the idyllic television town that made Ron Howard a child star.

Mingled with the horror of a murder in the little village was the dawning realization that a celebrity had been living in their midst. A delivery boy from Villaggio Sereno described the couple's taste in pizza, and told reporters, "When the guy answered he was kind of weird—he wasn't creepy, he seemed kind of innocent." The woman "was nice" and tipped him three dollars for a fourteen-dollar pie. The manager of Hastings Video said they were a quiet couple who "always seemed happy." She took her oath of customer privacy seriously, and refused to say what movies they'd rented.

It was late afternoon by the time Michael arrived. The photographs taken as he was helped out of the car and led to the police station would be in every major newspaper by morning. He was wearing a pale blue jumpsuit with the words Ithaca City Jail emblazoned on it, and what the newspapers called "green prison slippers." He was shackled. His cuffed wrists, attached to each other, were also tethered to a leather strap that wound around his waist. His left hand was bandaged.

His bearded face looked strangely bloated; his eyes smaller, unfocused, but fixed with fury on some invisible inward point. For many old friends and former classmates, that was the face that went with their discovery of what had happened. *The New York Times* ran the photograph with an article on the cover of the Metro section, in the same spot where "A Voyage to Bedlam and Part Way Back" had appeared two and a half years before.

The profile that had brought Michael so much seeming good fortune, and inspired so many people, had been subtitled "Yale Law Graduate, a Schizophrenic, Is Encumbered by an Invisible Wheelchair." The new article also emphasized the Ivy League aspect of his journey: "From Mental Illness to Yale to Murder Charge." In the place where they'd run the photograph of Michael leaning open collared against a pillar in the law school was a picture of Michael rising dazed and shackled out of the back of an unmarked police car.

A version of the photo was also on the cover of the *New York Post*, which devoted its entire front page to his capture. In the *Times* photo, Michael's body was partly obscured by the open door of the car he was being helped out of, as if something obscene were curtained off. The photo in the *Post* was taken at a later point in the perp walk, and Michael's body filled the frame. The zipper on his prison jumpsuit had worked its way open, exposing a wedge of hairy chest that pointed in a V toward an unexpected expanse of belly that seemed to mirror the bloated, bearded face. Michael wasn't wearing his glasses, but that couldn't account for the way his eyes, glassily focused on nothing, narrowed with suspicious intensity that made him seem both mad and menacing.

Above the photo was a massive one-word headline, printed in white on black "knockout type" to make it pop:

PSYCHO

The headline was even bigger than the bloodred screamer the *Post* had run for Son of Sam—**CAUGHT!**—in the summer of 1977

at the dawn of the Murdoch era. **PSYCHO** was so big that if someone had added an exclamation point, or increased the font size by a
single pica, it wouldn't have fit on the page.

To see Michael looking out from the far side of that black-and-
white tabloid window like the Son of Sam, or anyone else we were
never supposed to be, was shocking. The photo filled the left side of
the page; the right half announced, also in white-on-black type big
enough to be the headline on a normal front page:

Twisted genius

charged with

savage slaying

of pregnant fiancée

In the bottom right was a picture of Carrie smiling with the
hopeful innocence of a yearbook photo. It was one half of a snapshot
of Carrie and Michael that the *Times* had run whole on the inside
jump of its story. A footer running the length of the page flagged
coverage of Michael's ill-fated movie: "Universal Studio honchos on
hot seat page 32."

Like Michael himself, the movie had come to seem part of an
emblematic promise. It was only after the killing that I came to appreciate what Michael had meant to millions of people desperate for
recognition and representation, and what a personal devastation his
fall must have been for them. *Psychiatric Times* called its article about
Michael "From Poster Child to Wanted Poster." Michael was often
referred to as an ethics consultant for the New York State Psychiatric Institute, until a spokesperson from the institute told the Associated Press that Michael was just a volunteer who had never attended
a meeting.

The word "psycho" blotted out a world of goodwill, hope, and achievement. The National Alliance on Mental Illness had worked hard to get a *Psycho* doll taken off the shelves, and here was the *New York Post* putting Michael in its place.

"I heard about this first thing this morning, and I have to say I broke into tears," Laurie Flynn, the executive director of NAMI told *The Washington Post*, when asked to comment on the killing. The paper reported that Flynn's organization had been consulting for the movie about Michael's life, and that her own daughter considered him a hero:

> "He was a tremendous inspiration," she said of Laudor. "We are so grateful when we see these wonderful stories of people who succeed despite the difficulties of mental illness. It's inspiring to so many people like my daughter, people who need to be accepted and who need these role models."

Elyn Saks, now tenured at USC law school, had been thinking of writing a memoir about her own struggles with schizophrenia when she heard the news about Michael. "The heartbreaking story happening on the other side of the country only increased my ambivalence," she later wrote. In fact, it persuaded her to abandon her efforts. Eventually she would decide the opposite: that the tragic violence, and the sensational public reaction to it, were reasons to tell her story, lest Michael's tragedy appear to speak somehow for her and millions of others with schizophrenia.

At the time, Michael's story made her feel as if her own were impossible to tell. He, too, had made it through Yale Law School. Would her friends and colleagues identify her with him? "Maybe, once they knew the truth, they'd see me as too fragile or too scary to trust as a professional colleague or an intimate." In the book she eventually wrote, she recalled the fear she'd felt years before reading coverage of Michael's story: "Maybe they'd believe that a tragic, violent breakdown was inevitable."

When Elizabeth Ferber saw Michael on the cover of the *Post*, she got on a train with her young son and went to be with her mother, grieving in New Rochelle. Michael had lived in Dr. Ferber's big Victorian house, and sometimes when Jane got home late after working a full day at Creedmoor and seeing private patients at night, Michael would cook her dinner and sit with her while she ate. "I never liked to think," he'd told Elizabeth, "that she was sitting there alone, having dinner."

Elizabeth's mother no longer lived in the grand house by the water but on Crawford Circle, closer to Wykagyl. Michael had been a fixture in that house, too, a part of the family during all the years Elizabeth's father was gone. There was even a family notion that Michael bore a certain facial resemblance to her own husband, some buried Ashkenazi Jewish blood tie. But the expression on Michael's face she'd seen in the *Post* was so *not* Michael that he no longer seemed even to resemble himself.

Elizabeth had grown up hearing her mother talk about all the reasons people with serious mental illness were ignored: they don't contribute to society, they don't make money, they're difficult, they're disenfranchised—who's going to pay attention to them? Until something tragic happens; then it's a nightmare. This was the nightmare.

As Elizabeth's taxi pulled up to her mother's house, a reporter who had jumped out of a hastily parked car was calling out to her brother, who had come outside to meet her. "Are you Josh Ferber? Can I ask you some questions about Michael Laudor?"

The reporter had somehow gotten hold of Michael's address book and was contacting everyone in it.

"No," Josh told the man, and went inside.

Someone from *Time* magazine left a message for me at work—*I understand you were a friend of Michael Laudor*—that I decided to ignore. I got a call at home from someone at *The New York Times*. I told him I didn't want to talk on the record, that I didn't remember any stories about Michael, and that I didn't really have anything to say.

I told myself that silence was a gift I could give Michael, who had suffered from too many words already, trapped in stories he could never live up to, let alone tell. But I got off the phone feeling like Peter denying Jesus—*Sorry, never met the guy.* Of course, Jesus hadn't killed his pregnant girlfriend; on the other hand, he hadn't been my best friend in childhood.

The truth is I didn't know what to say or how I felt. Or rather, I was feeling too many things at the same time. When I'd first learned what had happened, I felt physically sick and flooded with a terrible sense of sadness. Overwhelmed by the tragedy of it, I was near tears all day. I paged Mychal at the hospital where she worked; she told me later she thought from the sound of my voice that my father had died.

I kept thinking that Michael himself had been murdered, and when I caught myself in the mistake, I felt confused and guilty. I wondered if killing someone was in itself a kind of death. But behind that speculation was the pregnant woman he had actually killed, strangely eclipsed by the horror her death aroused in me.

I was stunned to discover how swiftly the door of memory and identification swung open. The smell of the Laudor house, laundry detergent and burned American cheese, how it looked and felt, papers on the staircase, the Indian print, scattered books in all the wrong places. His warfare with his clever, shouting brothers; his booming take-no-prisoners father. The way he hugged his cat Dusty, with gentleness and a complete absence of irony. The time we rolled on the floor of his room laughing hysterically because we'd called our sixth-grade science paper "The Skin of Our Teeth: And Various Other Parts of the Body."

I'd been instantly thrown back into some primal version of myself bound up with Michael. I felt ashamed of my resentments, which had outlasted the onset of his illness, my jealousy that he'd sold his story to Hollywood and a fancy publisher while my own book was still unsold. And the wild disproportion of my enduring competitiveness, which was only brought home to me now.

I felt guilty for thinking, when I'd read the *Times* profile, "But you *can* be violent"—knowing he'd patrolled his house with a kitchen knife before getting treatment—but laughing with him when he told the story of the bigots who dared ask such stigmatizing questions so that I didn't feel vindicated so much as implicated now that my qualms had been grotesquely realized.

I felt guilty for being sane and healthy after all, and for wasting so much time imagining I wasn't. A high school friend I hadn't talked to in years, who also hadn't been able to sleep since hearing the news, called to talk about Michael. "It's terrible to say," he told me, "but I can't help thinking that the best thing he can do now is kill himself."

I wasn't going to say *that* to the *Times*. Or tell them that I dreamed I'd stabbed someone and was holding a bloody knife. Whether I was Michael or myself in the dream, and whom I'd killed, I didn't know. Only that I was both the watcher and the doer, and terrified. I felt I wasn't supposed to be there, like Cary Grant in *North by Northwest* when he puts his hand on the handle of a knife someone else plunged into the back of the man who has stumbled into his arms at the moment the photographer's flash explodes.

But Cary Grant was framed, and in my dream I'd really done it. I wasn't entirely sure *what* I had done, only that I was guilty and covered with blood. In fact, I was literally drowning in a pool of blood, possibly my own, but at the same time standing on dry ground.

When I woke it was as if some barrier had broken down and I could sense Michael's guilty terror, and see his mother in their house weeping. In that twilight mood it was impossible for me to think about anyone without becoming them for a moment, a frighteningly porous state I feared was a kind of madness in itself, until morning came and dispelled it.

It was my mother who told me that Carrie had been pregnant. I'd missed it in the day's reporting. When I got off the phone, I went into the bedroom, sat on the bed in the dark, and burst into tears. I couldn't remember the last time I'd cried, but there I was trying to have a child, praying desperately to become a father, and Michael had killed his own wife and child. Even if they weren't married and the baby wasn't born yet. To destroy your own family was awful beyond awful.

Mychal had been in the living room when I was on the phone getting the news from my mother. She came into the bedroom, sat beside me on the bed, and wept herself.

That night I dreamed my mother told me not to go home, but I went home anyway and found Michael waiting for me in front of my apartment. He was bloody and holding a knife, but instead of saying, "I killed my wife," he said, "I killed *your* wife." I knew he was lying because I'd talked to Mychal before leaving work, but how could I be certain he was lying when he was covered with blood?

I said, "Michael, you need help," and he said, "*You're* going to need help." I ran down the stairs and he ran after me; he'd always been faster than me, but he was heavy now and dazed. I ran to the Eighty-Second Street police station and yelled for help, and the cops came out and tackled Michael and cuffed him. In the dream, I was panicked to the point of tears and madness myself, paging Mychal over and over to make sure he hadn't killed her. Finally, she called and an officer handed me the phone, and it was her and she was okay.

I'd been lying in bed trying to write a letter to Ruth Laudor when I'd fallen asleep and had the dream. Later I wasn't sure if it was a dream or a waking fantasy, constructed in a kind of trance. It felt so much like it had really happened that I wondered if I was myself delusional. I considered myself a sane person by then, if prone to panic, though better in that department even after going off Prozac because we were trying to have a baby. Michael killing Carrie seeped in at the deepest and most disturbing level, an undertow pulling me backward.

What was the connection between the smart, gentle, bookish boy I had known and the man who had murdered his pregnant fiancée? And what was the connection between that man and me?

I had another dream. Two men were fighting, surrounded by a crowd of spectators. It was a very brutal fight; they were big men. One man struck a triumphant blow and turned to face the crowd with his arms outspread. The other man ran up behind him and drove a knife into his back. It was sickening to watch. He pulled out the knife and seemed to wipe the blood on his shirt, or the other man's shirt. This happened more than once. It was clear he was going to kill the other man. The strange thing is that the man who drove in the knife somehow *was* the big man who turned to face the crowd. There were two men but in a sense there was only one. And yet there was a feeling of murder.

I woke with a tremendous sense of danger, violence, and death. I felt disgusted with myself for being unaware of all the suffering in the world, and for not knowing how to deal with violence.

I also dreamed I was in prison. It was a very strict place. Michael was there, though I didn't see him. An overseer with glassy blurred eyes, like the single clouded eye of the checkout guy at our local supermarket, arrived when we were all in the mess hall. He was cracking his whip. He singled me out and took me to see the warden. She was an Indian woman playing with her children. She was actually very kind. I wanted to know when I'd be able to leave, but she couldn't tell me. Ask me next time, she said.

The feeling wasn't so different from what I'd felt ten years before, hearing about Michael's breakdown: that I was implicated, involved in Michael's nightmare. A destabilizing conviction that anything can happen, that life is fragile. But there was something more specific, deeply connected to me and to Michael, that made us secret sharers, though of what I couldn't quite say.

It was weird to feel, if only fleetingly, that a particle of Michael's madness had infected me in some sense, almost as if it needed a new host. Schizophrenia is not of course contagious. Neither is dementia, but I'd experienced the way my father left a fine powder of confusion on the faces of everyone close to him, like pollen. Michael's assault on Ellen Brewer had rewired her brain with a single punch, inducing PTSD, a mental illness, though a treatable one, which caused her to see his furious face on an endless nightmare loop. These ripples of spreading pain were not Michael's illness, but they were connected to it, like his friends' inability to reconcile the most extreme mani-festations of his illness with the person they knew and loved.

When Michael was psychotic, he thought his parents were im-posters and, later, fatally, that Carrie was a windup doll or robot. Now Michael's friends saw him as he'd seen Carrie. He had become unrecognizable to them. The *Daily News* quoted Randy Banner, who was a friend of both Michael and Carrie:

> "I look at his eyes, which I have many, many times, they are somebody else's eyes," said Randy Banner, a journalist who has known Laudor for 13 years.
> "If you can fathom that, they are somebody else's eyes. When he was well, he was the healthiest person you could ever want to know," Banner said. "But when he was ill, he was simply someone else."

When *People* magazine ran a photo of Michael being returned to Hastings in his Ithaca prison jumpsuit, Officer Ellen Brewer recognized the terrifying expression, clipped the picture out, and put it into her folder. Eventually she incorporated the image into her training presentation. It was the third of the three faces of Michael Laudor, the one she saw in her nightmares every night for three months.

Eddie Schecter told several of the papers, "The Michael Laudor I know is not the Michael Laudor who committed this murder."

I remembered visiting Michael at Columbia Presbyterian for the first time after he was committed, when he'd wanted to study the story of Cain and Abel. Why, Michael kept asking, was Cain's sacrifice rejected? And why does he kill Abel?

How odd that I should feel like Cain when he was the one who had killed somebody.

I remembered how Ruth Laudor used to ask me to call Michael whenever I ran into her, as if, after all those years, I was still his primary friend and wielded special influence. Childhood friendships last in the minds of parents, the way their own children remain in their minds even after they've become adults, and perhaps seem more real in that form than any other. It wasn't only dementia that prompted my father to say, when I spoke of Michael, "I keep thinking about that poor little boy sitting in his prison cell contemplating what he's done."

I had called Michael not so long before he killed Carrie. He was vague, equivocal, even as we picked a date to see each other that I suspected, perhaps hoped, would pass like the others. The date was still in my calendar. But it was clear that he was sinking, had in fact sunk. That was when he said, "I have to go. I'm having bad thoughts I need to not be having."

I knew something was wrong in a new and dreadful way, but I

buried that abject statement, and kept myself from considering its meaning. It came back to haunt me now. Years before, Michael had run away and left me to get pummeled. Now it was my turn. I was already running, and had, in fact, been running for a long time.

Michael was kept in the cell block on the ground floor of the Hastings police station. There were no cameras in the cells, and Lieutenant Vince Schiavone told the officer on duty to check on Michael every fifteen minutes. "I want you to know what he's doing," Vince said. "He's sitting on the bunk, he's laying down, he's sleeping, he's sitting on the toilet, I don't care what it is. *Note* it."

He'd learned enough from Ruth, and from decades as a cop, to know that Michael needed to be on suicide watch. Vince was informed at intervals that Michael continued to sit in frozen silence. When an officer offered him some cold water, Michael looked at him "like he was from outer space." The lieutenant figured Michael had surrendered himself to the fact that he'd done something horrible. Unless, and this, too, seemed possible, he didn't know what he'd done. He never asked about Carrie. Never asked about his mother. Never asked about anything. He just sat and waited and didn't say a word.

Meanwhile, reporters were everywhere. They filled the foyer of the police station, and one had tried to follow Vince home for dinner. *Daily News* reporters rang Ruth Laudor's doorbell, and when she "refused" to "discuss the killing," they reported on her refusal: "'This scrutiny is painful,' she said, peering through the door of her home." Michael's brother Danny was answering Ruth's phone: "The family will be making no statement whatsoever."

Television cameras set up on Mereland to film the outside of the house, which was henceforth "a Tudor-style home on a quiet tree-lined street." *Larry King Live* was preparing a full hour on the killing.

The house was also shown on the ten o'clock nightly news, which referred to Michael as "a self-admitted schizophrenic."

The segment featured a still photo of Michael from better days, morphing into a negative image of itself. *He had the world on a string; then, the string snapped.* Network news did something similar at eleven: *A genius; now, a killer.*

To get to the Hastings courtroom for his second arraignment of the day, Michael would have to pass along a hallway lined with journalists, and ascend a staircase crowded with photographers like roosting crows. Lieutenant Schiavone requested calm. "Folks, listen to me. We have to bring Mr. Laudor out, take him up to court. I would appreciate it if there was no *rush*. Don't stick any *cameras* in his *face*. Don't *ask* him anything. He's not communicating. I would like to do this. I can't have *chaos*."

Whether it was the force of Vince's words—a humane soul, Vince was also a large man with a gun—or whether there was something persuasive about Michael, and the aura of his illness, even the aggressive New York City press remained largely silent when he was brought out. The only sound was the locust whir of snapping shutters as the big, subdued prisoner, flanked by armed officers, shambled down the hall and slowly climbed the steps with chained ankles.

Michael was charged with second-degree murder. His lawyer did not enter a plea, but there would be later occasion to do that. There would be a grand jury hearing, and psychiatric evaluations, though Jeanine Pirro would tell Larry King that Michael's history of mental illness should not be a "get-out-of-jail-free card."

Because it was a homicide, no bail was set. But Michael's lawyer did ask the judge that Michael receive psychiatric care and medication. Now that he'd killed the person he loved most in the world, and would live forever on the far side of tragedy, it was no longer necessary to prove that he was an *imminent* danger to himself or others to get the care and medication he needed. The state, eager to have him fit to stand trial for murder, would provide him with both.

CHAPTER FORTY-ONE

THE ETERNAL OPTIMIST

About the victim, less was immediately known.

—*The Washington Post*, "Schizophrenic Lawyer's
Triumph Turns into Tragedy," June 19, 1998

As chief of the Sex Crimes and Elder Abuse Bureaus of the West-chester DA's office, ADA Barbara Egenhauser dealt with ter-rible things on a regular basis. This did not make them easier, but it made her the right person to escort Carrie's parents to the morgue to identify their daughter's body when the Costellos flew in from Bos-ton on Friday.

Vince Schiavone was assigned to go with her. The lieutenant would always remember the excursion as one of the worst things he'd ever had to do as a police officer.

He knew Barbara from past cases, and from the lectures she gave to the department about domestic violence and sex crimes. Vince ad-mired her combination of toughness and compassion and was glad the ADA was going with him.

Even in their afflicted state, William and Marilyn Costello seemed to Vince the kindest sort of people. He and Barbara stood with them outside the room where their daughter's body was being readied for identification. They would not have to enter the refrigerated room;

indeed, they weren't allowed in. There was a big curtained window in the wall that they would look through when the moment came.

The arrangement was like a cruelly inverted version of a hospital nursery, where parents gathered behind glass to spot their baby on the other side, wearing the tiny hat and wristband.

"Listen," Vince said softly, "we have to do this. I don't know what we're going to see when we open up that curtain, but we have to do it. If you can make the identify, and then we'll . . ."

There wasn't a single sentence that could meaningfully be finished. From that point on, everything ended in ellipses. Long afterward, Vince was still resorting to pantomime: "When they opened up that curtain and I saw that poor thing laying on that gurney I went like this. . . . The look on their faces . . . there is no way to describe, she just started, you could just, and I'm going like *this* cause I'm getting . . ."

Carrie's mother had immediately begun to sob. Her father turned and gave Vince a look that crumpled his soul. Vince counseled himself inwardly to be strong, to look the part and do his job. Barbara was saying something in a low voice, and then it was done.

They drove back to the Hastings parking lot near the police station in silence. There seemed to be no protocol for such a thing, though this nightmare happened to someone every day. "I'm so sorry," Vince said in parting.

He retreated to the station, where he sat in his office, thinking, "I should have been a fireman," which is what he always said when the dark side of policing reared its head. It was a macabre joke he shared with his wife, whose father had in fact been a Yonkers city fireman.

The ADA remained in the car with the grieving Costellos, who still had to meet with Jeanine Pirro, the district attorney in White Plains. Pirro would describe the meeting in her legal memoir, *To*

Punish and Protect: Against a System That Coddles Criminals, which devotes a chapter to the county's case against Michael. The chapter is called "The Laws of Madness."

The Costellos entered looking "shell-shocked, numb, their eyes distant and unfocused," the telltale marks of families who have lost "one of their own to sudden, violent murder." The DA ordered them sandwiches—"The last thing they wanted to do was eat, but I knew they would need their strength for the ordeal ahead"—and briefed them on the case, leaving out as many gory details as possible. Eventually, though, they would have to be prepared to look at gruesome crime scene photos as the case moved to trial.

"What hurt them the most," the DA wrote of the Costellos, "was the way Carrie disappeared in the frenzy of public discussion about her famous killer. Nobody was talking about Carrie's hopes and dreams and ambitions. It was all about Michael Laudor."

Pirro, who referred to Michael as "the most famous schizophrenic in America" and "the schizophrenic du jour," wrote that "while the media focused on Michael Laudor's regrettable lapse into madness, the woman who had been his greatest supporter barely earned a line or two in the news reports."

Pirro didn't see Michael as representative of schizophrenia, or of an individual's ability to triumph over the disease. She saw him as the embodiment of something that threatened the entire criminal justice system: "Before our eyes, in a perverse makeover, the murderer becomes the victim." The ultimate symbol of this tendency in the courts was the insanity defense, which the DA described as "one of the greatest travesties in this rush to forgive and excuse."

The psychiatric evaluations wouldn't begin until July, when Michael—who was refusing the medication his lawyer had requested for him—would explain his belief that medication was part of a conspiracy to poison him, much as the crisis intervention team his mother and Carrie had arranged had been planning to torture and kill him. But whatever the DA thought of the insanity defense—and she didn't believe in it—those who encountered Michael found it possible to imagine that he was not in fact in his right mind.

The Hastings officers who transported Michael from his arraignment to the Westchester County jail in Valhalla weren't allowed to question him, but if Michael offered unsolicited observations as he sat in their car, they could pass his unguarded utterances along to the DA.

"A lot of people tried to help me," Michael told the officers, "but I was trying to prove to my mother I wasn't gay." He added, "They have a tape of me killing Carrie. Either a tape of me killing Carrie or the fake Carrie." He then "talked about his E-ZPass."

Vince often recalled something he'd learned from Barbara Egenhauser about the way suffering expands outward from every crime, like the ripples created by a stone thrown into a lake. At the center was the victim herself, of course. But the "circle of victimization" grew in concentric rings to encompass an ever-widening world of people.

Carrie's parents were obviously inside that circle; so was the sister who had called Tom, and the sister who hadn't. So were their husbands, who would help carry the coffin at a funeral that couldn't take place until the autopsy was complete, and their children, who would grow up inside a calamity.

Ruth Laudor was in the circle, planning to go to the funeral of a woman she loved and considered part of her family, who'd been killed by her son. Michael's brothers were there, too; Danny was scribbling notes in the gallery during Michael's arraignment, the middle child managing the demands of a family crisis that neither life nor law school had prepared him for, to say nothing of the psychiatric dimensions wedded to the legal ones. They reached out for advice to Michael's stupefied law professors, who were themselves gathered up in their mortification.

As the rings of victimization expanded, they encompassed more and more people, all affected in real and lasting ways. There was Eddie Schecter, who would wonder for years if *The Lonely Man of Faith* was a mistake; perhaps if he'd given Michael a different book. . . . There were the officers Vince sent to the River Edge who'd been met with bloody horror, as well as the guys working the case, like Tommy O'Sullivan, a soulful former Marine who'd been a detective for only six months and was shaken to his core by Carrie's brutal killing.

There was Vince himself. And Barbara Egenhauser, who'd had to tell the Costellos their daughter was pregnant, doubling their already overflowing measure of pain and grief, *before* she'd had to take them to see Carrie's dead body. Barbara would have to retrace Michael's steps to build the DA's case, standing on the bridge where Michael stood, trying to put herself in his head as he turned his back on the ravine and suicide and headed toward Telluride House, only to run into Ellen Brewer's cruiser.

Officer Brewer was of course inside the circle of victimization, but so were the big officers who had fought with Michael, whose physical bruises would heal faster than their abiding sense that they'd failed to keep a vulnerable colleague safe. So was Sergeant Mospan, haunted by what would have followed if the nightstick blow had failed and he'd shot Michael, and perhaps killed him.

Michael, though he was the perpetrator, was clearly suffering from an illness that caused him anguish whether or not it proved exculpatory. Barbara's boss, Jeanine Pirro, didn't think psychiatrists should have a role in criminal proceedings, and hoped to put Michael away for as long as the law would allow, which was the rest of his life. But Michael, too, was half inside the circle.

Ellen Brewer, who was prepared to testify before the grand jury despite her immobilized jaw, replayed her violent encounter with Michael on a nightly loop, thinking a great deal about Carrie. Over time, she would come to think about Michael's trauma too; not only as part of her own therapy but as part of a desire to help others understand and avoid the fatal funnel.

You didn't need to see the ripples of victimization to sense their invisible progress as they traveled to Chicago with Carrie's colleagues on a 3:30 p.m. flight, once the DA's office cleared them. Her friend Barb wept the whole way, holding tight to Tom's arm.

Tom had called each member of the tech team into his office one at a time to tell them what had happened. Wave after wave of grief, tears, and raw emotion broke over him as the news swept into the corridors faster than he could share it. Barb had screamed when she heard that Carrie was dead.

Once they'd all decided to go to the Chicago conference, their grief had mingled with a kind of purposeful stress. Everyone was still hysterical, Tom thought, but it was a manageable hysteria. They were doing it for Carrie, and the schools and kids she cared about. Barb would have to make some of Carrie's presentations, but Carrie's computer was in Hastings, part of the crime scene, and nobody was going to bother the family for permission to claim it. She went into Carrie's office to gather up what materials she could.

Barb would never forget staring out Carrie's window at the world her friend would never see again. She thought, "We can't do this without her. God has put too much in front of us." But she found most of the printed material she needed among the chaotic stacks on Carrie's floor. And Carrie had of course backed up her work to the server. With Tom's help, Barb pulled it together.

Reporters had been calling for Tom nonstop since his arrival at the Chicago hotel. It was strange that this outsize journalistic inter-est had nothing to do with the magnitude of their loss, and that if Carrie had been killed by someone else, nobody would have called at all. Tom made an exception for *The New York Times*, but after that he told the front desk to disregard all calls for him. For the next six months, he didn't read a newspaper or listen to the radio.

That evening, while Michael was being arraigned in Hastings, Tom hosted a memorial service for Carrie in the Chicago hotel. He planned it with Barb, who found the perfect room to use as a chapel. It was a large room, all white, where the hotel collected the flowers it distributed to all the suites. Barb turned to the woman showing them around. "We just lost someone very dear to us," she said. "Could we have some white tablecloths and some of these flowers to make a semi-altar?"

They set up sixty or seventy chairs, lit candles, invited Carrie's closest friends and coworkers, people converging from around the country. Some were only just hearing the news. Others drifted in unsure what was happening, new teachers or technology instructors who had never met Carrie, or who had only spoken to her, but who quietly took seats. Candles flickered when people entered the room. To Barb it felt like Carrie was there with them.

They sat in silence for a good ten or fifteen minutes. Then Tom got up and spoke about Carrie. He talked about drawing strength from her, about her unexpected booming laugh, and how she was re-lentless, tireless in a happy, driven, purposeful way. They went around the room, and people shared their thoughts, grieved aloud, told favor-ite memories. Barb talked about driving with Carrie in a blizzard to visit a school outside Detroit, the street signs hidden, laughing and lost, but Carrie intrepid behind the wheel.

The next day, the *Times* gave its readers their first glimpse of Carrie as more than a corpse in the kitchen. The article described her as Michael's "37-year-old pregnant fiancée, Caroline Costello, a technology administrator at the Edison Project, the private firm that manages public schools," before saying where and in what condition she was found. It mentioned, too, that her parents had flown in to identify her body and speak with investigators.

Tom's voice was in the article, which described Carrie as "a wisp of a woman who typically worked 60 hours a week." Tom explained that she hadn't come in Wednesday, claiming "a personal emergency."

Most of the article was about Michael's struggle with his illness, and about his brilliance. "Mr. Laudor's successes in the face of his schizophrenia were so striking that he was the subject of an article in *The New York Times* in 1995," the *Times* reported, recapping highlights of the earlier story. But the article ended with a quote from Tom honoring Carrie:

> "She was a very 'up' person," Mr. Boudrot said. "I think it would take a person of that inner grain to look at a relationship that most people would say, 'Hey, this isn't for me,' and give it a fair shot. The eternal optimist. I think that's what most people would say about her."

CHAPTER FORTY-TWO

ENDINGS

"He had success, fame and fortune," says
Hastings police lieutenant Schiavone. "Now
the end of his story will have to be rewritten."

—*People*, "Into the Abyss,"
July 6, 1998

All that summer, as Michael was resisting medication in the West-chester County jail, doubting that Carrie was dead, and fighting his horrified awareness that he'd killed her, his story was abroad. It passed from hand to hand and newspaper to newspaper, given different meanings and applications at every turn. It ceased to be a single story, and it ceased to be his, though that change had taken place long before.

The *New York Post* had gotten hold of his proposal for *The Laws of Madness* and put Michael on the cover for the second time, three days after the first. They treated his book proposal, once the high-water mark of his prospects, as a sort of jailhouse confession: **MY DEMONS**.

This time, the photo on the front page was of the old Michael; he was wearing a winged-collar shirt with a black bow tie. It was his half of the divided picture of Michael and Carrie. His ironic eyebrows and trimmed Vandyke beard gave him a thoughtful, faintly Mephistophelian look. "I forgot he was so handsome," my mother said, but the caption read "Michael Laudor: The monkeys are eating my brain!"

The words that had won him a book contract and a movie deal were testifying against him now. Excerpts from the proposal, interspersed with summaries, ran inside across a two-page spread under the headline A HOTSHOT, HAUNTED AND "HUNTED." Vivid passages about the messages beamed into his head from television shows, informing Michael that the "medical unit" was going to start "removing limbs from me any minute, without anesthetic," no longer read like conquered delusions transmuted into compelling prose. Instead of showcasing the dangers he had passed, Michael's proposal, reframed and renamed, had become a window into the mind of a killer.

His illness itself became a blurred thing. "The goblins of schizophrenia invaded Michael Laudor's life without warning," the *Post* story began, echoing Michael's own pulp-fiction predilections. His illness was torn repeatedly from its medical context by overheated tabloid prose, but it had long been distorted by premodern ideas of demonic possession, postmodern ideas of social construction, Sigmund Freud's metaphors, Joseph Campbell's mythology, and Michel Foucault's obsessions with power and control.

Small wonder error and confusion seemed to be everywhere. There were literal errors, of course, of the sort newspapers inevitably made in the daily rush to print. A *Times* story, in which a friend recalled Carrie confiding her wish to have a baby with Michael, attributed mental illness to Chuck as well as Michael, forcing the paper to run a correction, while raising a question I'd never asked before.

> Because of an editing error, an article on Saturday about a fatal stabbing in Hastings-on-Hudson, N.Y., misstated the medical history of the father of the suspect, Michael B. Laudor. Mr. Laudor's father, Charles, did not have a history of mental illness; however, there was a history of mental illness among some members of Charles Laudor's family.

Perhaps the confusion about Chuck was the result of the newspaper's stylistic tendency to describe individuals as having "a history of schizophrenia," like a family, rather than simply having schizophrenia, as if baldly naming the illness were impolite. The disease waxed and waned but it didn't come and go, and couldn't skip a generation inside a solitary individual. What did it say about stigma if you had to denature something before you acknowledged it?

Two years before, the *Times* had referred to Michael as "a legal scholar with a history of schizophrenia" in an article headlined MEDICAL STUDENT FORCED INTO A HOSPITAL NETHERWORLD. The headline suggested a land of no return, and Michael had expressed outrage that a student who'd stopped taking medication for his bipolar disorder, and was alarming psychiatrists and fellow students with what they considered violent and threatening behavior, "lost five weeks of his life" to forced hospitalization. But who among Michael's friends would not have wished now that the same had happened to him, if those five weeks could have helped return him to the treatment he needed, saved Carrie's life, and prevented his own destruction?

In the bitter aftermath of Carrie's killing, it was harder to ignore the delicate evasions that ramified into policy, or the widespread pieties intended to spare the feelings of the desperately ill population that people were purporting to help while leaving their most basic needs unmet. A woman with schizophrenia wrote in the *Hartford Courant* about the "terrible irony" that Michael was "acceptable as a schizophrenia poster boy, but only so long as he wasn't noticeably schizophrenic!"

Michael's psychiatrist had decided to pursue a psychiatry residency in 1967 after reading Erving Goffman's *Asylums*, the 1961 landmark study that made "institutionalization" not merely a policy but a mental condition more damaging than whatever psychiatric illness might have sent someone to a mental hospital in the first place. Those illnesses had not much interested Goffman, a sociologist who only stopped putting quotation marks around the phrase "mental illness" after his wife's suicide some years later.

Some errors were harder to correct than others, running along tracks laid down long before by older stories, careless assumptions, or wishful interpretations. "It is so unfortunate that people only hear about schizophrenia in the context of violence," Dr. Jody Shachnow, the associate director of social work at the Westchester psychiatric hospital where Michael's original day hospital had been, told the *Times*. "These dramatic cases—Weston, Laudor, Ted Kaczynski or John Hinckley—are not the typical stories of schizophrenia. Mostly it is a story of quiet suffering."

But people hadn't learned about Michael because he was violent. His eloquence and quiet achievements, despite his schizophrenia, had made him a symbol of hope to thousands of people who had discovered him from a profile in that very newspaper, where he derided the association of violence with schizophrenia as "a common and painful stereotype."

Michael was certainly associated with violence now, and having claimed the mantle of role model, his rejection of medication, bloody crime, and terrifying appearance posed a special problem to those who had embraced him.

The head of one advocacy group chastised *The Washington Post* for suggesting the relevance of Michael's illness to the story of his arrest with its headline SCHIZOPHRENIC LAWYER'S TRIUMPH TURNS INTO TRAGEDY—though the article acknowledged that "it is not yet known what role, if any, Laudor's mental illness played." The same advocate had written to the *Times* after its profile of Michael three years before to "congratulate Mr. Laudor on his decision to go public with his struggles," and to praise the newspaper for demonstrating that "the majority can and do recover if given the same things everyone needs, such as social support and job opportunities."

Yale itself had helped elevate Michael to the eminence from which he fell. It was in the nature of the place to confer intellectual authority with its name alone. It served as perfect shorthand for the story of Michael's brilliance, and turned up in articles almost as often as schizophrenia.

"For more than a decade," one *Times* story began, "Michael B. Laudor had wrestled with the demons of schizophrenia, managing to eke out startling victories over the delusions and hallucinations, like a degree from Yale Law School and more than $2.1 million in book and movie contracts for his life story."

Were the extravagant measures of meritocratic success that Michael and I had always striven for really the markers of "victory" over a debilitating thought disorder, as if Yale and Hollywood certified mental health? Did they matter more than the extraordinary strength needed to take slow steps along an uncertain path, enduring treatments that were always trade-offs, never cures, which made the struggle all the more courageous because the journey never ended and the battle was never won?

Yale Law School, which loomed so large in all the stories, was something far more complicated than an emblem of academic triumph accessed with the aid of invisible ramps. It was the "day hospital" where Michael had found refuge, attended by humanistic professors who considered him brilliant, though incapable of functioning as a lawyer or law professor. Still, they felt him deserving of the place they'd created around him in the academic sun.

Bo Burt had been stunned when Bonnie called to tell him what had happened. Michael had seemed manic but good humored the last time Bo saw him, joking about casting and Danny DeVito. Then he'd withdrawn from the world to write his book, or so Bo told himself.

Bo had lost track of Michael, though he'd received Bonnie's Cassandra phone calls periodically. She let him know that the Network celebrated each new stimulus, whether book or movie deal, law school, or Michael's quest for an academic position, considering it all good. But it wasn't good. Michael wasn't bathing; he obviously wasn't taking his meds. He stank; his clothes were dirty; he was in big trouble.

But nobody, Bonnie included, had imagined what had actually happened. Even Carrie's parents, who the papers reported really did object to Michael as a prospective son-in-law on both religious and psychiatric grounds, assumed that while Michael might do harm to himself, he would never hurt Carrie. Bo had never allowed his mind to go to self-harm, or worse possibilities. He'd listened to Bonnie and hoped Michael was all right.

Ruth Laudor, with the pragmatic desperation of a grieving mother, called Bo after Michael killed Carrie. She called Owen Fiss too. She asked the professors if they would meet with her and Danny to review Michael's legal options. Someone chose a restaurant in Stamford, Connecticut, midway between New Haven and New Rochelle. Michael's mentors drove there together.

The professors left the abstractions of the classroom to discuss a defense strategy against four counts of second-degree murder. There were many meetings but no good options. Ruth was intent on saving her son from prison if nothing else. She was seconded by her second son, a comedian turned lawyer rising to a horrible occasion.

Bo's advice was that Michael should plead guilty. This was not done out of a desire to see Michael punished for a crime he didn't believe he'd knowingly committed, but because he thought Michael would serve less time if he was criminally convicted than if he was found not guilty by reason of insanity. He was familiar with lawsuits involving differential placement, and the data were clear; people who were diverted from the criminal justice system into civil commitment served many years longer.

And while second-degree murder carried a sentence of twenty-five years to life, if Michael pleaded guilty with extreme emotional disturbance—which wasn't the same as an insanity plea—the murder charge might be reduced to manslaughter, and his sentence might be reduced to fifteen or sixteen years, which was better than twenty-five to life. It was a risk, but one that seemed worth it to Bo.

Somehow the marriage of law and psychiatry engineered by experts decades ago had come to this. Bo Burt, a trustee of the Bazelon Center for Mental Health Law, agreed with Jeanine Pirro, whom he referred to as "that bastard district attorney," who also thought Michael ought to go to prison, though they had different reasons.

In the chapter devoted to Michael in *To Punish and Protect*, Pirro, referring to Michael as "evil," writes that "insanity should not be used as an excuse for getting away with murder." Bo, on the other hand, worried that if Michael were found insane, and committed to a psychiatric facility, he'd never get released.

Even if Michael wound up civilly committed, he would have to demonstrate to a psychiatric review board that he was no longer a danger to himself or others, and how, Bo asked, was he going to show that? Better to go to jail for a finite amount of time.

Ruth rejected this suggestion out of hand. For one thing, she thought prison would destroy Michael. For another, she took "not guilty by reason of insanity" to mean just that; you were not guilty. And if Michael wasn't guilty, then as soon as he started taking his medication again, and stopped being a danger to himself and others, they would let him go home.

Without medication, which he was still refusing, he was unstable and getting worse. His lawyer was already raising the possibility of transfer out of the mental health unit of the county jail to a forensic hospital where there would be better psychiatric supervision and a greater likelihood of compliance.

Michael punched a prison guard in the Westchester County jail and was arraigned at the end of July on two counts of assault. By then, two court-appointed psychiatrists had found him unfit to stand trial, though the DA was asking for a third evaluator of her choosing.

The stories about what was actually happening to Michael were always smaller and harder to find than the big opinion pieces or the grand summaries, like the article in *People* magazine that ran with color photos. The news stories about his court appearances suggested a grim decline.

"In court today," the *Time*s reported, "heavily bearded and manacled at the wrists, Mr. Laudor seemed disoriented, staring straight ahead with glazed, unresponsive eyes. He did not speak—Mr. Rubin entered a plea of not guilty on his behalf—and he did not appear to acknowledge one of his brothers, who sat near the front of the courtroom." The assault charges would add a year to his sentence if he was convicted of murder.

Paradoxically, it was because Michael seemed palpably insane that Bo thought he should plead guilty and go to prison. With Michael so floridly psychotic, Bo figured the prison would move him to a mental hospital anyway. He'd get the care of a psychiatric facility, and the benefit of a prison sentence, without having to persuade a commitment board when the time came for him to leave.

This hardly sounded like the best of both worlds to a distraught mother, or anyone else for that matter. And pleading guilty to murder was a high-risk decision. But whatever plea Michael entered, Bo knew he would be in for a long, long confinement.

Vince Schiavone continued to follow the case with proprietary interest. He kept a growing file of press clippings, including the article in *People*, which ended with a quote from him. "'He had success, fame and fortune,' says Hastings police lieutenant Schiavone. 'Now the end of his story will have to be rewritten.'"

He shared Ruth's concerns about Michael and prison. The lieutenant had encountered Michael on only one or two occasions, but his persuasive alien strangeness had made a deep impression. He'd also read about Michael's intellectual background. Vince had worked in a prison for three years where, as he put it, "their tolerance levels are not real good."

No doubt there were plenty of people with schizophrenia in the prison system, but Vince couldn't see Michael surviving in a place like Attica or Dannemora, let alone Sing Sing, where he could be sent for murder. Michael's mentors, who had not worked in a prison, came at the question from a different direction, though Joe Goldstein, who found the whole situation too horrific to think about, turned his back on the matter and Michael with it.

A month after Carrie's killing, another gruesome event eclipsed and extended Michael's story. A man named Russell Weston walked into the East Front entrance of the Capitol Building in Washington, DC, setting off the metal detector and shooting a Capitol Police officer in the back of the head with a .38-caliber revolver. He exchanged shots with another officer, wounding him and a tourist, then raced down a corridor and through a door that led to a suite of offices used by Majority Whip Tom DeLay and Representative Dennis Hastert. A plainclothes detective who was inside the suite had heard shots and told the staff to get under their desks just before Weston burst in and shot the detective in the chest.

It did not take long to discover that Weston suffered from paranoid schizophrenia, rejected diagnosis and treatment, and was severely delusional. He had stormed the Capitol to retrieve the Ruby Satellite stored in the Senate safe, which was the only way to avert the cannibal apocalypse and plague that were about to destroy the world. He was untroubled by the deaths of the officers he'd mistaken for cannibals and shot because, as he explained to psychiatrists, the Ruby Satellite had the power to restore the past, and so the men weren't really dead. It was just a matter of "washing time in reverse" to bring them back to life. It had all happened before. He himself had died many times.

Michael Laudor was immediately joined to Russell Weston as if he, too, had stormed the Capitol. They were paired despite radically different backgrounds; in some sense it was their differences that made the pairing irresistible. Without proper treatment, the illness they denied in different ways became a binding commonality.

The psychiatrist E. Fuller Torrey wrote about the two men for *The Wall Street Journal* in an article called "Why Deinstitutionalization Turned Deadly." It began with the "Yale Law School graduate," who allegedly killed his pregnant girlfriend, and "the drifter" from Montana who stormed the Capitol, allegedly killing two police officers. Their stories, the psychiatrist wrote, "are only the most publicized of an increasing number of violent acts by people with schizophrenia or manic-depressive illness who were not taking the medication they need to control their delusions and hallucinations."

Frank Rich, a columnist for *The New York Times*, wrote about Michael and the Capitol shooter in "This Way Lies Madness," which was read into the *Congressional Record* at the memorial service for the officers. Rich quoted Weston's anguished father, Russell Sr., about the impossibility of helping his son. "He was a grown man. We couldn't hold him down and force the pills into him."

Weston's father could do nothing, Rich wrote, because "a comprehensive system of mental-health services, including support for parents with sick adult children who refuse treatment, doesn't exist. If it had, the Westons might have had more success in rescuing their son—as might the equally loving family of Michael Laudor, the Yale Law School prodigy charged last month with murdering his fiancée."

There was something a little incongruous in President Clinton denouncing as "a moment of savagery at the front door of American civilization" the violence of an unmedicated psychotic man nobody felt authorized to treat. Diagnosed six years before, Weston had spent fifty-three days in a state hospital after threatening someone with a knife. Once he no longer seemed imminently dangerous, he was released with pills he didn't take because he did not consider himself ill. Instead, he'd traveled to CIA headquarters to report his conspiratorial fears to those best equipped to handle them.

For politicians, the outrage of *after* was different from the work of *before*. But as Torrey pointed out, after *was* before. "The total number of individuals with active symptoms of schizophrenia or manic-depressive illness is some 3.5 million," he wrote, adding that "the National Advisory Mental Health Council has estimated that 40% of them—roughly 1.4 million people—are not receiving any treatment in any given year. It is therefore not a question of whether someone will follow Michael Laudor and Russell Weston into the headlines. It is merely a question of when."

Unlike Bo, who came to speak of Michael's collapse as "a tragic inevitability," Torrey, author of *Surviving Schizophrenia*, did not see it that way. He did not believe that the one thousand deaths caused each year by people with unmedicated schizophrenia should indict the vast population of those suffering from the illness, but he did want to prevent those deaths, a greater number of suicides, a growing number of mentally ill homeless people, and a prison population swelled by people suffering from mental illness who received no care. His sister had schizophrenia and he did think there was a difference between being in your right mind and being out of it.

Every opinion piece seemed to outrage somebody. Michael was part of every argument on the subject, just as he had always been, except now they were all going on without him. I wasn't ready to think about Michael in relation to law or public policy, which I never thought much about anyway. But when Jeanine Pirro told a newspaper that "it would be an insult to every mentally ill person in this country to say that because someone is mentally ill that they are more prone to violence," I did not feel she was championing the rights of people with mental illness. When Torrey suggested that the disability checks Russell Weston received, once he'd been diagnosed, should have been tied to his receiving treatment, I thought he was.

What Laurie Flynn called "The Michael Laudor Tragedy" in a NAMI press release issued the day after the killing was a personal heartbreak for her and her daughter but did not shake the foundation of her work or her crusade against stigma. The problem wasn't acknowledging a potential for violence in those who were untreated, but a system that requires you "to go to court to get your loved one into treatment," Flynn told the *Times*. "Families feel enormously frustrated and quite helpless because they have to sit and watch someone they love deteriorate, and they are unable to get them help until they become dangerous."

Torrey had told *The Washington Post* the day after Michael killed Carrie, "There is no evidence that people on medication are more dangerous than the general population, but people off medication are more dangerous." The second half of the sentence, and the context that went with it, often fell out of the discussion.

In the weeks before Michael killed Carrie, newspapers had been filled with articles about the recently published MacArthur study on mental illness and violence, which ran under headlines like the AP's MENTALLY ILL NOT ESPECIALLY VIOLENT. In an opinion piece, Sally Satel, the psychiatrist Michael had criticized the year before, referred to Michael as only "the most spectacular recent case" to expose flaws in the study, which had focused on patients who received and responded to treatment quickly in acute care facilities, excluding anyone in a jail, forensic hospital, long-term care facility, or state hospital. The study, which eliminated anyone who was living on the streets, or who was unwilling or too incapacitated to participate, blurred the distinction between psychotic disorders and other types of mental illnesses; 40 percent of the study's participants suffered from depression, while the majority of those who opted out had schizophrenia.

Parents were in no hurry to see their suffering children further stigmatized, but like Satel's co-author, D. J. Jaffe—who helped care for a relative with schizophrenia—many had lost patience with destigmatizing campaigns divorced from efforts to provide quality psychiatric care to those least able to request it. Satel and Jaffe quoted Carla Jacobs, a NAMI board member from California who "became an activist for involuntary commitment after her mother-in-law was fatally stabbed and shot by a mentally ill relative."

"We used to think it was stigmatizing to acknowledge violence," Jacobs told them. "Now we recognize that violence by the minority tars the majority, and makes communities less likely to welcome the community-based housing that can facilitate treatment and reduce violence." Besides, she added, "too many of our relatives are hurting others, and winding up in jail. The first step to helping them is admitting there's a problem."

Michael's law school classmate James Forman Jr. read "From Mental Illness to Yale to Murder Charge" in the break room of the legal aid office in Washington, DC. Stunned by the tragedy, he could not help thinking about it in the context of the work he'd been doing for the past four years. James had recently represented a man who was accused of raping a child and who had seemed, when he first met him in his cell block, completely out of his mind. The man was sent to St. Elizabeths Hospital and forcibly medicated until he was considered fit to stand trial, which took a year. The transformation was remarkable; he appeared lucid at his trial, which was important because James wasn't arguing insanity but casting doubt on the prosecution's case.

James got his client acquitted. The man was free to go, and James accompanied him to St. Elizabeths to help him gather his belongings and try to enter him in some kind of outpatient treatment program. This wasn't simple even for a Yale-trained lawyer, but at last they found the right office and did the paperwork. The man was told to come back in three weeks, not for treatment, but for an intake interview. James tried to explain, without revealing too much, that the man had been taking medication that was helping him, and it was the kind where if you went off it you might not go back on. He needed an appointment for tomorrow or right now! But he did not get one.

He was no longer James's client, just someone James was trying to help. James tried calling him before his appointment but the man had moved on. The government had called the man a "monster" before he'd been sent for treatment, when James himself had considered him "raving." He *thought* his client was innocent, but you never could be sure. What would happen if the man returned to the state he had been in?

Like most of James's clients, the man was poor, Black, and without resources. The criminal justice system had been robustly interested in him after he'd been accused of a crime; the mental health system did not seem interested in him at all. Michael, he assumed, had access to a far more supportive community, but somehow, he, too, had been failed by the mental healthcare system.

Michael was found unfit to stand trial by summer's end, when the psychologist requested by the district attorney came to the same conclusion as the two court-appointed psychiatrists. The *Daily News* reported that Michael "can't believe he killed his fiancée," and quoted a "confidential report" by the psychologist explaining that "Mr. Laudor's fears of reliving the horror of what he has apparently done on the one hand, and his fear of being sent to prison on the other, are both sources of extreme fear and anxiety."

Michael would be sent to a forensic hospital, where it was easier to administer the medication that his lawyer had requested, which he was still refusing to take. He would be reevaluated after a year. Jeanine Pirro remained optimistic about a trial. "I accept the doctor's statements," she said, "but I also expect that he will be brought to the bar of justice."

Two weeks after Michael killed Carrie, Frank Rich had published an article called "Hollywood's Mental Block," urging Imagine to make "the Michael Laudor story" anyway.

Rich, who had been the *Times*'s theater critic before becoming a columnist, interviewed Chris Gerolmo, the director-screenwriter who was trying to keep the project alive but who also wondered, as Rich wrote, "if the mental-health community, which had looked at Mr. Laudor as a 'poster boy,' would welcome the idea of a revised, tragic version any more warmly than might bottom-line-driven Hollywood."

Rich was arguing that there needed to be more than horror movies on the one hand and saccharine falsifications on the other. He pointed to the movie *Shine*, "which blurs the nature and causes of mental illness while tacking on a simplistically triumphant denouement," though it had been a huge hit two years before, and a possible contributor to the excitement about *The Laws of Madness*. On the other side was *Psycho*, which, Rich ruefully noted, Imagine had just announced plans to remake. All the more reason for them to move forward with a complex, truthful portrait.

"In mass culture," he wrote, "where so many battles are fought for American public opinion, no one may fare worse than the mentally ill." A complex, honest story need not be a stigmatizing one.

Rich quoted Rona Purdy, another NAMI member, endorsing his call for "the Michael Laudor story" to still become a movie. "Ms. Purdy feels that people should 'see the horrible pain of Laudor's mother and fiancée as they tried to get him care in the last days' when he abandoned his medication and may have been forcefully resisting any kind of medical intervention. 'There's no such thing as a simple intervention,' she says. 'In the end, it's the moms that are left with these great big sick sons.'"

Rich had more than a passing interest in mental illness and the failures of the mental healthcare system; his mercurial stepfather, encourager of his theater dreams, had suffered from what was presumed to be bipolar disorder, and had driven his car at high speed into a wall, killing Rich's mother, who was a passenger.

Michael had gone from being an exemplar to a cautionary tale. He could not go back to being the first, but could he perhaps be both? Gerolmo was convinced that *The Laws of Madness* could remain true to Michael's story and still be a great movie. He wrote new endings that incorporated the killing, and tried out a coda that leapt forward in time, allowing the earlier triumph to stand but following it with an acknowledgment of Michael's tragic collapse at the end.

"We could do it like this," he explained to Grazer and Howard. "*It would be really good!*" The Imagine suits didn't necessarily disagree with that assessment, they just weren't going to make a movie that wasn't commercial.

Gerolmo understood this, but for a month or so refused to give up. He was determined to make Michael's story work, not only out of a genuine commitment to the material but because he was poised on the brink of a dream he'd spent his entire career working toward. Ron Howard had handed him the reins of a $50 million picture on an important subject with one of the world's most famous movie stars. If it fell apart, he knew he would never get back there again.

Unable to find an ending that would allow the story to remain an "uplifting affliction picture," Gerolmo devoted himself to cocaine, with pills to help him sleep, until that, too, came to an end when he found himself at three in the morning half sitting up in bed, like someone doing a stomach crunch, convinced he was getting smaller every time he exhaled. Frozen with horror, he realized he was going to simply disappear. Somehow, he lapsed back into sleep before breathing his last, and the night became a turning point that helped him pull back from the abyss. It also taught him a lesson about the awful psychic pain that went with believing in a horror even if it wasn't real.

In reality, *The Laws of Madness* had ended the day Michael killed Carrie. As it happened, the June issue of *Vanity Fair* contained an excerpt of a new book about a brilliant mathematician named John Nash. His career had been cut short by paranoid schizophrenia, but he'd won the Nobel Prize in Economic Sciences in 1994 for work he'd done decades earlier, before psychosis had overwhelmed him.

The biography, by *New York Times* reporter Sylvia Nasar, was called *A Beautiful Mind*. The excerpt, appearing between glossy covers the same month that Michael killed Carrie, had all the elements that had drawn the Imagine team to Michael's story. It took the summer for Imagine to negotiate a deal with Nasar for her book, and with Nash for his life rights. By then, Michael had been indicted by a grand jury on four counts of murder. By summer's end, *Variety* was reporting on Imagine's new project, which it summed up neatly in a single sentence: "A triumph over adversity story, 'Beautiful Mind' tells of a brilliant man with matinee-idol good looks who becomes mentally ill but overcomes his condition in time to receive a Nobel Prize."

The article mentioned that this was not the first time Grazer and Howard had been involved in a project about someone with schizophrenia. There was also *The Laws of Madness*, which told the true story of Michael Laudor, who "came down with schizophrenia"—it sounded like a bad case of the flu—but with the help of his father "overcame it to complete law school and become an attorney."

Though the reporter wrote that it was "unclear now whether the project will ever be filmed," it was clear that *The Laws of Madness* was a past-tense story: "That project was to have Chris Gerolmo directing Brad Pitt, but it took a tragic turn when Laudor relapsed and killed his girlfriend and their unborn child."

The fate of the movie was as obvious as the difference between the two stories. "Unlike Laudor's, Nash's story is an inspirational one, with a starring role likely to be a magnet for young leading men."

NO GOING BACK

Reality is the beginning not the end.

—WALLACE STEVENS,
"An Ordinary Evening in New Haven"

Unlike Russell Weston, whose lawyers succeeded in keeping him unmedicated for three years of solitary confinement and mental decompensation—after which he never did recover competency to stand trial—Michael's lawyers and family wanted him medicated. By the end of August 1999, following a year of treatment at Mid-Hudson Forensic Psychiatric Center, Michael had recovered sufficient sanity to be declared fit to proceed to trial by doctors working for the New York State Office of Mental Health.

Anticipating an insanity plea, DA Jeanine Pirro hired Park Dietz, a renowned forensic psychiatrist known to have a high threshold for insanity. He had found John Hinckley Jr. and the Unabomber legally sane, and testified as an expert witness that Jeffrey Dahmer was sane—and Dahmer had not only killed seventeen men and boys, and had sex with their corpses, but cut them up and eaten them. If Dr. Dietz thought the "Milwaukee Cannibal" was sane enough for prison, he would surely think Michael was too.

But Dr. Dietz stunned the district attorney's office in March 2000 by concluding that Michael had stabbed Carrie thinking she was "a nonperson, a robot or doll" who had been sent to torture and kill him. Like the forensic psychologist who had found Michael unfit for trial the year before, Dietz wound up agreeing with the defense.

By the time Dietz met him, Michael had been evaluated and reevaluated; he'd spoken to psychiatrists, psychologists, and lawyers, which meant, as Dietz put it, "what I'm interviewing is not the man who was arrested." The challenge was to capture Michael's state of mind at the time of the killing.

Dietz gave much greater weight to Michael's encounters with the Cornell campus police when he was still inside the fog of unfolding events not formalized by retelling. Michael had asked the police to check on Carrie even as he appeared to admit killing her. He'd fled Hastings fearing a murderous conspiracy, recoiling from real actions taken in response to imaginary dangers, and showing all the faces Ellen Brewer came to identify. Above all he showed confusion about "whether he had killed a person or a not-person" when he flagged down her police car, still wearing bloodstained clothes.

At the trial of Jeffrey Dahmer, Dietz had testified that the killer got drunk before murdering and eating his victims because he knew what he was doing was wrong, and planned to dissolve the evidence in acid for the same reason. Though a "sexual psychopath," he'd worn a condom before sex with his victims, casting doubt on the argument that he couldn't resist his impulses had he wished to. Michael thought his life was being threatened by a nonhuman agent of destruction, which put him in a different category.

The district attorney would have had no trouble proving that Michael killed Carrie. She had the car, the murder weapon, bloody clothes, his mother's call to the police. But she could hardly persuade a jury to disregard the findings of her own forensic expert. Though Pirro had been confident that Michael "would be brought to the bar of justice," in the end there would be no trial.

In reality, Michael was a minority of a minority; the insanity defense was used in less than 1 percent of all criminal trials, and succeeded in one quarter of those attempts. The real tragedy was that a finding of delusional thinking, which could exonerate Michael after the terrible fact, hadn't been sufficient to medicate him before it.

Even without a trial, Michael had to appear in court. The hearing was held on May 11, 2000, the day before his birthday. He was turning thirty-seven, the age Carrie had been when he killed her.

Lisa Foderaro, who covered the hearing for the *Times*, reported that "Mr. Laudor, who had successfully battled schizophrenia, had stopped responding to medication and had become severely delusional." In fact, Michael had stopped taking his medication. It had never wholly eliminated his symptoms, and produced side effects he hated, but the fact that he was competent to attend his hearing after months of mandatory treatment suggested a more complex relationship to its effectiveness.

The judge asked Michael a few questions, making sure he understood the nature of the proceedings, and accepted his plea of not responsible by reason of mental disease or defect. He ordered Michael evaluated once more to determine treatment, though Michael told the judge that he expected to be returned to Mid-Hudson. Was it possible that after two years it was where he wanted to be?

"Although his voice was breathy and strained," Foderaro reported, "his answers were lucid, and he seemed deeply distraught, his face red and contorted, as he listened to the angry and emotional statements read by Ms. Costello's mother and sister."

Ruth Laudor had gone to Carrie's funeral, but two years later the Costellos and the Laudors were no longer two families united by grief. Michael's lawyers tried to prevent the Costellos from making statements at the hearing, arguing that the law permitting victims or their families a chance to address the court before sentencing did not pertain because Michael wasn't receiving a sentence. Nevertheless, Carrie was still a victim, and the court allowed the Costellos to speak. In *The New York Times*, Lisa Foderaro offered a brief account:

"As parents, it is horrifying for us to accept that our daughter was murdered by someone she loved and trusted," said Marilyn Costello, whose husband, William, stood at her side. "It is horrifying for us to accept that our daughter died all alone, bleeding, terrified and in pain. This is a nightmare that haunts our waking as well as our sleeping hours."

The AP reporter, noting that "the victim's mother and sister railed against the idea that Laudor was not responsible for Costello's death," added a last line the *Times* left out: "Michael Laudor alone must bear the responsibility."

It has been twenty-five years since Michael killed Carrie. For most of that time he has lived at Mid-Hudson Forensic Psychiatric Center, a "secure psychiatric facility" fifty-five miles northwest of New York City. Mid-Hudson is in the picturesque Hudson Valley, not far from the foothills of the Shawangunk Mountains, surrounded by a sixteen-foot-high fence topped with razor wire. Michael lives there with 280 men and women sent there by court order, and twice that number of staff.

Mid-Hudson opened in 1973 after changes in the state criminal code transferred the care of unconvicted mentally ill prisoners from the Department of Corrections to the Office of Mental Health. It is a maximum-security psychiatric hospital for those not fit to stand trial, and an unofficial prison for the unconvicted found not guilty by reason of insanity. Many of its residents have done terrible things, for which they are legally blameless but still need a place to go. They are sent to Mid-Hudson as wards of the Office of Mental Health, which grants them a hearing every two years to evaluate their fitness for release.

It has been Michael's home longer than any other place he has lived. It is a hybrid institution born out of the paradoxes of deinstitutionalization. In its first year, the fence around the perimeter was eight feet high, and twenty-three of its involuntary inmates escaped. That soon changed.

Mid-Hudson was one of several institutions designed to replace the notorious Matteawan State Hospital for the Criminally Insane, which the Department of Corrections shut down for good in 1977. Many of its prisoners were sent to Mid-Hudson, which also took patients considered too dangerous to remain among the general population from state hospitals.

Inmates in state prisons who were too ill or violent to be released, but who could no longer be held legally once their sentences were up, were also sent to Mid-Hudson. Because it is operated by the Office of Mental Health, it isn't a prison. It is a "secure adult psychiatric center that provides a comprehensive program of evaluation, treatment, and rehabilitation for patients admitted by court order."

The New York Times was still referring to it as "a state psychiatric hospital for the dangerously criminally insane" when Michael was first sent there at the end of August 1998 to receive treatment, after being found unfit to stand trial. A few weeks before he arrived, a patient strangled his roommate to death using a pair of socks as a ligature, then ghoulishly broke each one of the dead man's fingers.

The strangler had been sent to a state prison and was serving fifteen years to life by the time Michael moved in. If you were found insane for killing someone on the outside, they sent you to Mid-Hudson; if you killed someone in Mid-Hudson, they sent you to prison.

The region is layered with the remains of older institutions that tell their own story. Mid-Hudson grew out of the ruins of a reformatory for delinquent boys known as "the Farm," which was opened by the City of New York in 1916. It was a place where tough kids from the Lower East Side, like the future middleweight boxing champion Rocky Graziano, were sent to learn discipline away from the malign influences of urban life. They farmed the famous black-dirt region, growing food for local penitentiaries, working in the reformatory's dairy, orchards, vegetable gardens, and vast root cellar that may yet lurk somewhere under Mid-Hudson's modern buildings. The reformatory was taken over by the state and swallowed up in its vast penitentiary system until the early 1970s.

Mid-Hudson opened as state hospitals were closing, beds for mental patients were vanishing, managed care was ignoring the need for long-term care, and the population of prisoners with mental illness was expanding. This was a nationwide trend that would soon make Los Angeles County's Twin Towers jail the largest mental health facility in the country. By 1998, more than 16 percent of the state prison population was considered mentally ill.

Putting the Office of Mental Health in charge was a way of acknowledging that state hospitals had not been replaced by community mental health centers but persisted in shadow form inside the prison system. Many people got care for psychiatric disorders only after they'd been arrested. The Network that had watched over Michael had been so determined to save him from the system that they'd hidden it away even from themselves, like the spinning wheel in "Sleeping Beauty." Michael had fallen into it after all.

I had a six-month-old daughter in the spring of 2000 when Michael was returned to Mid-Hudson Forensic Psychiatric Center. That was also the year I helped to settle my father into a nursing home after he'd been hospitalized for a medical crisis. Technically, he was going to the Jewish Home and Hospital for rehab, but the crisis had convinced my mother that she could no longer care for him at home, even with aides. It soon became clear that this was where he would remain until he died.

If he hadn't had dementia, I feel quite certain we would have brought him back to my parents' apartment, and not only because his articulate protestations would have broken our resolve as well as our hearts. The resolve wouldn't have been there in the first place.

Even before the episode that set my father's removal in motion, my parents' old friend, an esteemed psychiatrist, had told my mother, "Bob is a shell, you have to let go." It's possible he'd said this because my mother seemed to get angry at my father in inverse proportion to her acceptance of his Lewy body dementia. It took a long time to recognize that the man she loved, who had wooed her with poetry, had lost his mind. "I would rather have Zelda a sane mystic than a mad realist," F. Scott Fitzgerald told his wife's psychiatrist.

We did not say we were committing my father to an institution, but that is what we did. He received "custodial care," which made him sound like a piece of furniture to be dusted. The dread word "custodial" had been synonymous with the warehouse wards in state hospitals where neglected mental patients weren't treated, weren't a danger to themselves or others, and weren't released.

It was the old with unnamed dementias who had swelled the ranks of state mental hospitals in the first place, adding to the gloomy sense of mental illness as a one-way ticket to oblivion. An early name for schizophrenia was "dementia praecox," premature dementia, though that disease does not move inexorably toward decline. Nursing homes were better regulated by my father's time, though vigilance was necessary. Helpless populations are always vulnerable.

I had dodged the young man's bullet that had caught Michael, and moved beyond the fear that his fate would be my own, but seeing my father parked in the hall while Mr. Luther, the kind Indian-born nurse, pushed his medication cart down the aisle, forced me to recognize that I hadn't dodged the larger question of competence and compliance, or the need for asylum.

Pretending it is someone else's problem will only make the decisions harder for the people who will have to make them: my wife or children, or even, God forbid, the state. I am not Michael, but questions at the heart of his story are mine in ways that have only grown more immediate the farther away I move from that time.

Ruth Laudor came to shiva for my father, who died in 2003. By then I had two children and a new job. Ruth gave me her condolences and an old business card with her work info crossed out and the phone number of Mid-Hudson Forensic Psychiatric Center written on the back. Everyone had gotten married, she said, everyone had children, everyone had a job, except Michael. She spoke with bitter sorrow. His friends had all "moved on" with their lives. She begged me to call.

I put the card on my desk but I did not call Michael.

Some years after that I was in the lobby of a friend's building waiting for the elevator when the door slid open and there was Greg Morrison, beloved history teacher from long ago. Retired, bearded but not in protest, a pack of cigarettes in his breast pocket and a large book in his hand. He'd been playing bridge, which was an area of expertise. We caught up quickly in the lobby, and he asked if I had visited Michael.

I shook my head no. "You should," he said.

We had coffee not long after, and Greg suggested again that I visit Michael and offered to go with me. It turned out he had not been for a long time. It was hard.

I decided to call Michael, but didn't. My wife urged me. She trained hospital chaplains and believed in direct contact. I didn't need a plan or a reason. Childhood was itself a reason.

Our younger daughter was the age I had been when I moved to Mereland Road. She had a best friend, an intense attachment. Is that what we had been like? She seemed so small and so large at the same time.

I called Mid-Hudson and was connected to a social worker. He was a wry, chatty guy who seemed happy to be talking to an outsider. There was a sudden cry in the background and he said, "That's one of the nurses—you can imagine what the patients are like. . . ."

To arrange a visit, he told me, he just had to inform Michael I was coming and, if Michael didn't object, he would get me a "release" and put my name on a list. Would Michael remember me? I thought so but couldn't be sure.

The social worker called me back the next day. "Michael remembers you and would like to see you. He said you were the kid who was hit by a motorcycle. You flew through the air. Was that you?"

"Yes," I said. "That was me."

He gave me basic visiting advice. Go in the main entrance, leave your phone and wallet in the car, take your driver's license. There are lockers, but things disappear. Food gifts have to be x-rayed. No syringes, cash, dope, pornography, firearms, electronic devices. The list was long, amusing, tragic.

He warned me that Michael might not believe I was who I said I was, or might tell me there was human flesh in the food. Michael could also "be normal," he assured me. He was very fond of him—"You can't help but like the guy"—and had seen him "lose it" only once on the ward. Still, the "look in his face, you could see how he did what he did. . . ."

The metal fence around the perimeter topped with concertina wire seemed staggeringly high as I looked for the gate to get buzzed in. Remnants from the old penitentiary, redbrick buildings still used as dorms and offices, were visible through the steel slats of the high fence.

A lot of security measures had been added just a few years before Michael arrived, after two residents with prison records escaped. John Casablanca, described in the *Times* as "a former Mafia enforcer given to depression," had killed a bartender while on parole from a sixteen-year prison sentence, then killed a friend who criticized him for killing the bartender, before being sent to Mid-Hudson. There he met Herbert Arnold, who had served eight years in prison for murder before being sent to Mid-Hudson for raping a teenager while on parole and threatening to blow up a building. The men had gotten hold of a gun, which they held to the head of one of the Therapy Aides, who drove them to Brooklyn, where things went south as their medication wore off.

After a week, Casablanca gave himself up to two cops writing a ticket in East New York who described him afterward as "a little dirty and babbling." Arnold went peacefully the same day. Both men had been on the front page of the *Times* every day as dangerous, insane killers on the loose, though the director kept insisting, "This is not a correctional institution." For that reason, the new security was concentrated on the perimeter.

There was a security area with armed guards who buzzed you into an outer vestibule to look you over. The door behind you locked before the door in front of you opened, like an air lock. From there, you were buzzed in to a larger though still narrow area where uniformed officers with guns wanded and patted you, emptied your pockets, and sent you through a metal detector.

Even the pastrami sandwich I brought for Michael was examined by hand and x-rayed like a suitcase. Then I signed my name with a floppy pen, which looked like a novelty item but was designed to prevent stabbings. After that, a heavy door was unlocked from the other side, and I was admitted into the visiting area, where I signed my name again in a giant ledger using another ballpoint noodle and sat down to wait.

Residents weren't allowed to know you were coming in advance. Only after you'd arrived and cleared security was a call placed to an inner office, and a therapy aide dispatched to find Michael. If he felt like seeing a visitor, he'd be escorted by the TA to the meeting area. If he didn't, you'd drive home.

The visitor area of Mid-Hudson was a large, drab, fluorescent room that looked surprisingly like our junior high school lunchroom, with Formica-topped tables bolted to the floor and plastic chairs bolted to the table. There were vending machines along two walls and a television set positioned so that the guard behind the long bar-like desk could watch TV while keeping an eye on the visitors and residents.

There was a handwritten hymn taped to the visitors' bathroom. I was always surprised the makeshift poster was still there, taped to the door, even after months had passed. I'd assumed the first time I saw it that it had gone up that morning and would be down by the end of the day. I eventually memorized it while waiting for Michael.

> *May the Mind of Christ*
> *My Savior, live in me*
> *From day to day by his love*
> *Power be in all I do and say.*

At the bottom was the name of the woman who had copied it out in an array of colorful Magic Markers. At some point I found out she was a local woman who had stabbed her three-year-old daughter to death in 1998. She was pregnant at the time and had been sent to jail, where she stabbed herself in the belly but had survived and given birth. The baby had survived, too, and was taken away, while the mother was sent to Mid-Hudson.

The first time I visited, the wait was so long I was thinking of leaving, when I saw Michael on the far side of the glass door at the opposite end of the big room. That door, too, had to be unlocked before he could come in with his escort. He seemed enormous, bulky and bearded in a padded jacket as he stood looking around the almost empty room. He continued scanning even after I'd stood up to catch his eye.

Not knowing who had come to visit must have contributed to the confusion. He always looked around blinking like someone suddenly brought up into bright sunlight, when in fact he'd been outside crossing the grounds to get there.

He told me afterward he hadn't recognized me because my hair was so gray, though at the time it barely was. Still, if he pictured me as a twelve-year-old flying through the air, I could see why he was confused. When his gaze did settle on me, he broke into a smile of true recognition, or so I hoped.

He chose a table that allowed him to sit with his back to the wall.

"I like to see the whole room," he explained.

This could have been a manifestation of paranoia, but I'd been warned that bad things did sometimes happen before guards could step in. Michael's vigilance may only have been pragmatic. I liked to look around from time to time myself, though I never witnessed anything beyond a few placid patients eating McDonald's takeout with their visiting families, or playing an occasional game of cards.

It was hard to fathom the sorrows of families who were often the victims, visitors, mourners, and consolers at the same time. A staffer I got to know told me that the annual Family Sunday was epitomized for him by the woman with one eye visiting the son who had blinded her. He'd hit her in the face with a baseball bat after clubbing his little brother to death while he slept.

"Do you know why you're here?" the woman asked her son.

"I had a fight."

"I miss my younger son," the woman cried. "And my eye."

Often Michael and I were the only ones in the room.

That first visit we talked about the motorcycle and the schoolyard that he'd remembered me by, though Michael's memory was that I had refused to give ground. I told him I'd been paralyzed with fear, but Michael said, "You were braver than that." In fact, he was quite certain I had run at the guy in sheer defiance. This didn't seem like a point to argue over, especially because he clearly meant it as a compliment.

"I always liked to start a new school with an accident," I said. "Crutches for Albert Leonard, a face bandage for high school."

Michael laughed—he still had a sense of humor—but grew sober at the reference to my high school beating. He had a way, when distressed, of shaking his head from side to side quickly, like a pitcher shaking off a bad sign.

"I wasn't much good to you then," he said apologetically.

Strange that something that had so divided us made me feel closer to him now.

Michael was an extraordinary fusion of delusional paranoia and familiar personality. Talking about the groups he attended, he told me one was for relaxation.

"Yoga?" I asked.

"Some kind of diaphragmatic breathing," he said. "But it's hard to relax when someone's punching you in the nuts under the table over and over."

He was grateful for the deli I usually brought, and liked to quote a line from the movie *Diner*: "Are you using that pickle?"

I'd leave a few singles in my pocket to get us each a soda. He always read the ingredients. Studying the label of my pomegranate seltzer, Michael said, "It's good for you. It's got antioxidants."

"That's right," I agreed. "They trap free radicals—not that I know what those are."

To which Michael, after a pause, said, "I'm not that radical. And I haven't been free for a long time."

"I'm so sorry you've been sick," I told him.

"Thank you," he said. "I got tetanus, typhoid, TB, and several other diseases—they gave them to me. But a lot of them are gone now." He never did mention schizophrenia.

Michael told me he avoided the library because the only history of England he'd found devoted many pages to Gladstone and only a few to Disraeli, which he took as evidence of antisemitism. But he said he couldn't read anymore anyway.

However paranoid his thoughts may have been, he greeted everyone who passed with a friendly nod, including a guy with the bottoms of his pants rolled up who'd been shouting about the Sandy Hook shootings when I got there. He was a small, trim, energetic man with a beard but no mustache, like Thoreau or an Islamic scholar. He came over, put his hands on Michael's shoulders, and said approvingly, "You always salaam when I see you."

He asked Michael, "How are we going to get the Jews, the Muslims, and the Christians together?"

"Everyone in Jerusalem gets along," Michael said.

"That's right," the man responded. "You know how we can all get along? We can all get along because we all speak the same language: God."

"I thought the salt was arsenic," Michael told me once. "I thought pepper was the ashes of our people."

"What do you do with a thought like that?" I asked him.

"Suffer."

Sometimes there was no past tense. When I suggested his birthday was coming up, and asked if I had the date right, he looked around uneasily before telling me in a low voice that he didn't want to confirm it out loud. Someone might be listening who could "jump back in time and kill me in the cradle."

Did Michael believe, like Russell Weston with his Ruby Satellite, that time ran in both directions when he fled to Telluride House, or asked police to take him home to Carrie? For Park Dietz, it mattered more that Michael had fled "to escape persecutors whom he believed would torture him." In which case, he said, flight "stops being evidence of knowledge of wrongfulness and it becomes evidence that his delusion was pervasive."

Michael did not talk about the killing—at a recent hearing, he'd referred to Carrie as "living in France." Nevertheless, his words often felt like cloaked confessions, though perhaps this was a delusion of my own. Once, talking about the difficulty of writing, he quoted Faulkner's dictum, "You must kill all your darlings." It only meant edit your own words ruthlessly, but there was something in the way Michael said it that made me wonder. People at Mid-Hudson were housed by legal finding rather than illness. Michael shared a room with three other men who had also been found not responsible "by reason of mental disease or defect" in accordance with criminal procedure law 330.20. The dorm for 330.20s had a refurbished basement where, early in his time there, he'd played guitar with a young man who'd killed his girlfriend in a drug-induced psychosis. They both had copies of *Rise Up Singing* and taught each other songs. Michael taught him "Wildfire," popular when we went to camp, about a ghost woman on a phantom horse who's coming to carry the singer away. And "I Know You Rider," which the Grateful Dead made famous. "Gonna miss your baby, from rolling in your arms." Then Michael had gotten worse, his guitar disappeared, and the men drifted in different directions.

I didn't ask Michael about killing Carrie, or anything else I thought might cause him distress. But I mentioned her name the first time I visited, by way of vague acknowledgment. "I'm so sorry about what happened with Carrie," I said. To which he responded that it wouldn't have worked out anyway. He was Mossad, she was Opus Dei.

After that, we talked about our childhood, which seemed a neutral place he enjoyed remembering, and he remembered an extraordinary amount. The names of all four brothers who cut hair in George's Hair

Fort; the cost of a slice of pizza. But childhood gave way to other things.

When I asked him if he remembered reading *Lord of the Flies* in Miss Waldman's fifth-grade class, he responded, "And they wept for the loss of innocence." Then added in a sorrowful tone that it was the adults who were weeping. "I think they're British sailors," he said. "The adults come because there's been a death. That's why they wept."

Many of our exchanges were like that, as if we were actually talking about the thing we were avoiding. Once I told Michael that I'd watched *Shane* with my kids, and the western had so bored my younger daughter that she'd fallen asleep on top of me soon after the opening credits. Michael smiled but immediately said, "The book's better than the movie."

I remembered him carrying that little novel around, and asked why it was better. He spoke in the familiar explanatory style, slightly robotic, as if delivering a memorized speech, though when was the last time anyone had asked him about *Shane*? I'd been hoping to carry us back to the schoolyard.

"In the book," Michael said, "Shane is an ambiguous character. He wears a black hat, like the villain." He proceeded to recount the climactic scene at the end, after Shane puts on his hat and the old guns again, shoots all the bad guys, and starts riding away, when the boy runs after him, begging the gunslinger to come back. But Shane tells the boy, "There's no going back from a killing."

Was Michael telling me, in his encrypted way, that he knew he had killed Carrie and felt a terrible load of guilt? That there was no going back from a killing? Or did he identify with Shane and believe he had stood up to evil?

Either way there would be no going back. No matter how much we sat and talked about our childhood, we were still in the visitors' room of the Mid-Hudson Forensic Psychiatric Center. Once, when

I stood up at the end of my visit, Michael said, in a small voice, "I'd like to go home." Before I could stop myself, I asked him where home was. His face filled with panic and confusion, but only for a moment. He stood up slowly and shrugged the question away.

It was easiest when Mychal came with me, because our childhood memories could be told for her benefit. His only regret, he once told me when I was there alone, was that he did not know in advance when Mychal was coming so he could shower.

Once, Mychal asked Michael how we had spent most of our time together as kids.

"Talking," Michael said, without hesitation.

When it was time to go, he began putting on the bulky jacket he'd been wearing when he was escorted in and that he had removed at some point without my noticing. It was a plaid jacket lined with gray sweatshirt material.

"I like that jacket," I told him.

"This is Nino Scalia's hunting jacket."

"The Supreme Court justice?"

Michael nodded. He was putting on the jacket carefully, with dignified slowness.

"A friend got it for me," he said.

"Laudor, move over there!" the mild attendant suddenly barked when we were on the point of leaving. We'd said our goodbyes and Michael had drifted with us too close to the door. She was pointing to a spot on the floor several paces away.

Michael dutifully stepped back in his looming but somehow tip-toeing way, allowing the woman to unlock the door with a key attached to her belt. He was watching with a complicated expression as if already on the far side of the glass door he'd come through at the opposite end of the room.

It was often how I recalled him. The bulky hunting jacket over his own bulk, gray sweatpants and Velcro shoes below, rusty beard and thinning hair above. He wore the jacket on several more visits until it vanished one day, as many of his belongings and even his glasses seemed to do, as he explained with a resigned shrug. At one point, he mentioned that Guido was the friend who had delivered the jacket.

I was aware of being afraid of Michael even as I felt love for him. Hugging him goodbye was like putting my head in the mouth of an old and toothless lion, softened by age but still capable of crushing me. The awareness was very different from the nightmares of anticipation I'd had before my first visit. It was a little like the difference between an irrational fear of driving that keeps you off the road, and the feeling of relaxed vigilance once you are behind the wheel, even if you know that forty thousand people are killed by car accidents every year, and your children are in the back seat.

I sometimes found myself wondering if it was even remotely possible that the former dean of Yale Law School had given Michael the hunting jacket of a Supreme Court justice. It seemed unlikely, if only for reasons of judicial philosophy. But I reminded myself that Justice Scalia and Justice Ginsburg, both still alive at the time, were friends, and that stranger things had happened, though it turned out that Guido had not visited. None of his professors had.

Joe Goldstein died in 2000, before Michael's insanity plea had been accepted, so I cannot ask him certain questions that weigh on my mind. Before he died, he told Elyn Saks that he "faulted Michael for not killing himself after he killed his girlfriend." This was, as Saks put it tactfully, "nonunderstanding."

This is a personal story rooted in childhood, tangled in the history of the twentieth century, and told in the third decade of the twenty-first century by a writer past the midpoint of his life, looking back at a friendship that began when he was ten years old.

In some sense it is easier to remember 1973, the year I moved to New Rochelle, than 1998, the year Michael killed Carrie. That doesn't mean I remember more of that time, but my memories are tapered by experience and the narrow immediacy of childhood. I had one street, one school, one family, and one best friend. I had no job, no car, no smartphone, no wife or children, and no idea what the hell was going on in the world. The shadows of other worlds fell across me, some of them very dark, but it never occurred to me to try to understand them or translate them into words, which is probably why I remember them too.

For her quotation in the Newton North High School yearbook, Carrie chose a line from "The Love Song of J. Alfred Prufrock": "In a minute there is time for decisions and revisions which a minute will reverse." To the young and hopeful, even a fatalistic phrase like that can sound like a promise of infinite possibility. It did to me. At Telluride, we took the words directly preceding that line—"Do I dare disturb the universe?"—and modified them into an affirmative command for our T-shirt: "Disturb the universe!"

I always felt Michael had fled to his childhood when he took that Shortline bus to Ithaca, to a time when his brain was his friend and not his enemy. But according to Dr. Dietz, he was also afraid that Carrie was "a nonperson, a robot or doll" sent to torture and kill him. Michael was fleeing pain, not pursuing happiness. I could not help fitting him into a familiar frame, much as I tried not to.

Identification, I was beginning to learn, like empathy, can displace understanding and obligation as well as encourage it.

One surprise was discovering how many people lived next door to Michael, too, if not as literal neighbors then as metaphysical ones, bound by something beyond proximity.

Linus Yamane, who had reintroduced Michael and Carrie the summer he'd shared an apartment with Michael, and fretted about their going out, visited Michael in prison and then in Mid-Hudson. He knew Carrie would want him to go, and he went for her sake.

Jim McDermott, Michael's old roommate, had been overcome with guilt after Michael killed Carrie. I'd lost touch with Jim, and when I looked him up discovered to my sorrow that he had died of melanoma at the age forty-nine, on New Year's Day in 2013. I wrote his wife, Mary, who had been Jim's girlfriend in college, and we spoke on the phone. She had become a doctor; Jim wrote plays and made small independent movies. They had three children.

Mary remembered Michael bantering with Jim in their Silliman dorm, and at Naples Pizza, and she remembered the toast he gave at their wedding. It was one of the only things she remembered from the day, she told me, laughing because Michael had already been diagnosed with schizophrenia and still his words stood out. He told a parable about sticks that are stronger when they are bound together but easily broken when they're by themselves.

After Michael killed Carrie, Jim wouldn't come to the phone on the rare occasions Michael called, and didn't answer the letters Michael sometimes sent. Even in college Jim had a streak of moral severity under his easygoing exterior that I'd associated with his faith. In fact, he'd left the Catholic Church, shaken by the priest abuse scandals, a wrenching experience, Mary told me.

Leaving the church wasn't giving up on God, his brother Drew, a Yale computer science professor, explained. Jim had explored Greek Orthodoxy and other forms of Christianity, and joined Mary's Presbyterian church. His guilt about Carrie never left him, that strange feeling of unwitting complicity I knew as well.

All anyone ever did, Jim told Drew, was worry about Michael. Jim could not forgive himself for failing to worry about Carrie. Of course, Michael had deserved their compassion and concern, and all the late nights Jim spent listening to his laments. But what had their empathy and efforts at accommodation done? On his deathbed, Drew told me, Jim had wept for Carrie.

Marilyn Costello, Carrie's mother, wrote to tell me that the pain is too great to speak about. One of the Hastings detectives, Tommy O'Sullivan, couldn't talk about it either. "You say Michael Laudor," he told me, his voice filled with emotion—anger, I thought, smothered by sorrow—"and I think Caroline Costello." And Caroline isn't here to speak for herself.

I was stunned when I came upon Michael's name in the last chapter of *The Center Cannot Hold*, and realized that Elyn Saks had laid aside her memoir for years after she learned that Michael had killed Carrie, then decided she *had* to write it for the same reason. Fear of being eclipsed by Michael's experience, or judged by its dark light, gave way to a determination to interpose her own story between Michael's tragedy and the world.

I flew to Southern California to talk to Saks, who is on the faculty of the USC law school, where she goes to work even when the school is closed for vacation, as it was when I was there. The routine helps keep her organized, she told me in the empty law building, like the notes she scribbled on scraps of paper to help her remember what she wanted to say and stuffed into the deep square pockets of the jacket she wore like a lab coat. Saks remains one of the most impressive people I have ever met, combining fierce intelligence with a kind of innocent openness.

Practically the first thing she told me, once I was settled across from her, was that she'd spoken to her analyst that morning trying to understand why she had never done what Michael did. She's had "a lot of violent ideation, feelings and thoughts and fantasies" over the years, she said. Though she "never acted on them at all," she couldn't help wondering what had restrained her. "I mean, hell, I brought a kitchen knife and a box cutter in my purse to sessions in England."

She thought "partly it may just be demographic stuff"—she'd been "a late young adult woman from a middle-class family, so even in the face of threat, which I sometimes felt, my response wouldn't be to hurt them but to run away." I remembered the knife from her memoir, and the thoughts that went with it—"I must kill her, or threaten her, to stop her from doing evil things to me"—and had put the same question to a psychiatrist I interviewed that she'd put to her own: "Why hadn't Elyn acted like Michael?"

The psychiatrist told me that being a man was itself a risk factor for violence, which gave Elyn an advantage from the start. She didn't find the demographic explanation, or any other, wholly satisfying. "Partly I think it's just luck," Elyn said. "And I thank God that I never really acted on my thoughts and feelings."

I couldn't help thinking that her ability to wonder aloud about her illness with such intellectual honesty might in itself have been part of the reason for her success. She was like someone who has donated her body to science while still alive, turning to the outside world to learn about herself, including the paranoia that undermined her trust in the world she was turning to. She invited even a stranger to look on, though she was curious about me in return: "May I ask if you have a major mental illness?"

The Center Cannot Hold records the many times Elyn ditched her medication, always with disastrous results, until she finally accepted that she was really ill. She made her peace with medication only after her psychiatrist told her he couldn't treat her anymore if she didn't take it. It was a submission that put her more in charge of her life, which got so much better that she hasn't gone off medication since.

She has achieved everything Michael seemed destined for—a MacArthur "genius grant," a law professorship, a bestselling memoir bought by Hollywood, though if it is never made, it will not alter the balance of her life. She is married, employed, struggling but inspiringly open. Even after suffering a brain bleed, cancer, and schizophrenia, she quotes a neurologist friend who told her, "For an unlucky person, you're very lucky," laughing in amused agreement.

She was so open that I couldn't help asking if she was aware that in her magnificent TED talk, about the psychotic break she suffered at Yale Law School, she told the story of being body-slammed onto a gurney and clapped in restraints without mentioning the six-inch roofing nail gripped in her fist that she'd refused to relinquish just beforehand. It is a moment described with great power in her book, and she looked amazed when I informed her it was missing from the talk.

The nail wasn't eliminated by design, she told me. On the contrary. She hadn't realized it was gone. "Did I mention violence at all?" she asked.

Violence and mental illness have been legally entangled ever since dangerousness, rather than illness, became the necessary prerequisite for hospitalization. Because a hospital would only produce a bed, or mandate treatment, for someone actively threatening harm, you could hardly blame the general population for mixing up the very sick and the very violent, or mental hospitals and prisons. And you could hardly blame advocates for wanting to erase even the suggestion of violence as a precondition for eliminating stigma.

Michael had become famous for denying the stereotype, and infamous for conforming to it. Because he'd been my friend, and we'd grown up together, I could not shake the feeling of doubleness. When

I asked Elyn Saks if she felt that, too, given how she'd written about him, she told me, "Yeah, it's a—it's a really good question because part of me completely identifies and then part of me kind of repudiates parts of him that are not part of me, you know?"

I asked Guido Calabresi if he could hold Elyn Saks and Michael Laudor in his mind at the same time, as a sort of point and counterpoint. Guido was the author of *The Cost of Accidents*, which emphasized a shared distribution of responsibility and damages, and had taught a course called Tragic Choices, about legal and moral trade-offs. He'd also presided over Yale Law School, the training ground for law clerks, judges, presidents, and professors, before becoming a judge himself.

Guido paused to reflect, as if testing the proposition. *Was* it possible to acknowledge Elyn Saks's story and Michael Laudor's simultaneously?

"I don't know," he said.

For Laurie Flynn, the question wasn't an abstract one. She didn't know Michael's family personally, she told me, "but in a larger sense he was everybody's child. So many, many, many of the members of NAMI had that promising young child, that golden boy going off to Ivy League, that whole scenario suddenly implode."

What was remarkable about Flynn's words was that they could apply to Michael before and after he killed Carrie. Though not someone to break down on camera, it was almost impossible for her to speak when interviewed about Michael in the immediate aftermath of the killing. She kept getting calls from local leaders facing the same dilemma, as if they were all experiencing publicly the very private trauma that they'd created NAMI to help relieve.

The National Alliance on Mental Illness had been growing by leaps and bounds at the time, and Michael had seemed so emblematic of a new era, promising the rejection of shame and stigma,

that news of the killing sent the organization spinning. It "called
into question everything we had been saying and doing," Flynn
told me.

She described that message as "It's not true that they are dangerous and scary. Hardly any of them are ever violent, and yet it's always
blown up as a big deal, and that 'psycho killer' thing." All they asked
was that people "stop, listen, and learn about this, because you know
someone with this problem, or someone that you know has this in
their family or across the street."

I did know someone across the street, and he was Michael. All
the confusion, guilt, and uncertainty I'd viewed as personal and private turned out to be part of a larger conversation both practical and
philosophical. In some sense, Flynn told me, the internal debate at
NAMI has never stopped.

It wasn't that their message had been false, only that there were
parts of the story that weren't publicly addressed. Michael's killing
of Carrie became part of a complex reckoning that filled many in
NAMI with the understandable fear of stigma. Others trusted it
would be possible to explain how ordinary the lives of people with
severe mental illness could be, and that even those without treatment
were far more likely to take their own lives, or to become victims of
a crime than to commit one, while still making room for studies that
showed the extent to which devoted, desperate parents were often
afraid of the very children they were trying to help. Why should
parents have to hide their own scars in an effort to win better treatment for their children because society, in the name of honoring their
rights, had washed its hands of them?

Without a fuller understanding of the nature of serious mental
illness, how could people help those who suffered from it? Or appreciate the way prisons were replacing mental hospitals if they didn't
understand the elevated risk of violence among a portion of the pop-

ulation with serious mental illness who didn't take medication when they needed it, didn't know they needed it, or didn't respond to it if they did take it? Or understand that using recreational drugs, including marijuana, increased the odds of becoming psychotic for those already predisposed, and the chances of becoming violent for those already ill?

Officer Ellen Brewer, now Ellen O'Pray, talked to me in the processing room of the Ithaca campus police early in the morning, so she could tell her story "graphically," as she put it, without fear of traumatizing anyone passing through the office. I asked her if she had noticed that we were speaking on June 17, only to learn that for her it was an annual day of solemn reflection. She kept it even after all these years, when the premature baby whose birth had been the reason she'd taken the quiet night shift was in college.

Ellen's life had been transformed by that night, by the trauma she suffered and learned to address, and by a determination to care for frontline workers. It was because of that night, she told me, that after the planes flew into the World Trade Center, she'd gathered up wagonloads of apples from local orchards around Cornell and driven them to New York City to give out to workers sifting through the mass grave.

The interrogation room where we were sitting had been transformed because of Michael too. The file cabinets were gone, and they'd finally replaced the bullring with a metal bar that a prisoner can move along laterally with a handcuff. In her "Three Faces of Michael Laudor" lecture, Ellen stressed the importance of being aware of the needs of the person in custody, not simply Miranda rights, as she put it. Recognizing how people literally cornered might respond was part of her understanding that acknowledging potential violence, as she feels she had failed to do, was the best way to prevent it.

The law professors I was lucky enough to speak to overwhelmed me with their openness, and interest in reckoning with a reality that even today remains urgent and elusive.

"I have thought to myself from time to time," Tony Kronman, no longer dean, told me, "'Gee, if I hadn't been so busy being proud of what a great place the Yale Law School was to have admitted Michael Laudor, I might have paid closer attention to him, and had been more attentive to things that perhaps I would have seen. . . .'" But Michael had seemed so gratifyingly emblematic of what Yale valued most about itself that it was hard to see him any other way.

He seemed emblematic to a lot of people. To Cynthia Ozick, Michael was the culmination of my parents' search for the perfect street, where "the apotheosis of the Suitable Playmate" lived: "There's something almost mythical about two friends who together begin gloriously, until one ends in basest ignominy." Or as Hamilton Cain put it, quoting the movie *Capote* as commentary on my friendship with Michael, "I feel like we grew up in the same house, only he walked out the back door and I walked out the front." That was not how I thought about it, but Jacob and Esau, like F. Scott and Zelda Fitzgerald, or Cain and Abel, were always hovering.

Stories were like molecules in the house I grew up in, the building blocks of life. It's much harder, it turns out, to see things *not* as stories. The forensic psychiatrist Park Dietz had to unmake whatever stories he'd received about Michael in order to arrive at the assessment that he'd been driven by his delusions to kill Carrie and flee to Cornell.

When I interviewed Dr. Dietz, I asked him how he was able to do the work he does and keep himself from the darkness.

"Well, for one thing, I'm not as neurotic as you," he told me. "That helps."

Bo Burt understood immediately what a polarized charge there must have been between "two smart Jewish boys" growing up on the same street. He was retiring from the law school when I met him but still teaching a class on the book of Job with Jim Ponet, the Yale rabbi who performed my wedding, and who warned me, when I told him I was writing this book, not to go mad myself. Bo's engagement in this project, his willingness to wonder aloud about what he might have done wrong, made me feel this was his reckoning too. When Bo drowned swimming in his favorite lake two years after our conversations began, the loss was personal.

I told Owen Fiss that I thought Yale Law School was a great gift for Michael. If the university could not replace the old asylum for people as sick as Michael, it was nevertheless a place that for a time gave Michael what was once called moral care.

Fiss did not let himself off so easily.

"It was a *gift*," he said, catching my word. "But maybe it was a destructive gift. I think it's a gift I would probably give again, but there's something destructive about the gift."

And then, as we continued our conversation: "I wouldn't say it was a devil's gift, but there's a dark side to the gift that really emerged." The more he talked, the more the dark side widened, and what he wouldn't say it was began to sound like what, in fact, it might have become—though with the best of intentions.

Perhaps that is because some things aren't meant to be a gift, and when they are turned into gifts, other forces are unleashed in both the giver and the receiver. "Was the article a devil's gift?" he asked about the profile in the *Times*. "I mean, they're all sort of continuous, I think. One feeding on the other. Was his admission to the *Law Journal*? It doesn't just happen that one player in all this is the devil and everyone else . . ."

He wasn't questioning the worthiness of the accommodating impulse but wondering at the distinctions that were lost along the way, the questions unasked or elided. I'd talked about the incongruity I felt knowing Michael had armed himself with a knife against his imposter parents while reading the *Times* article where he explained the insult of being asked by prospective employers if paranoia had ever made him violent.

The problem of stigma wasn't only thinking that everyone with schizophrenia might end up like Michael, when only a very small percentage of people do. The problem was an environment that saw even an inquiry into the possibility of violence among the untreated as stigmatizing. If the key to reducing stigma is the normalization of mental illness as a disease and not a character flaw, then surely a discussion of symptoms, treatments, and interventions is part of the process. I told Fiss that I wished the *Times* had been able to raise the question in a way that would not have been seen as shaming.

"But why shouldn't the *Times* have asked that question?" Fiss asked me. "Why shouldn't Guido have asked that question? Why shouldn't *I* have asked that question? We should have all asked the question. We didn't. Carrie could have asked that question. She was getting engaged to him. I'm sure he threatened her for some significant period."

He had already warned me not to blame Hollywood, which after all was in the business of fudging facts and telling stories to make people feel good. Fiss went on connecting dots, noting that while the *Times* gave Hollywood its story, "the Yale Law School gave *The New York Times* the story that it gave to Hollywood. That's what I want to say. And maybe his friends before that . . ."

I know there is no going back to the time before Michael killed Carrie, any more than it is possible to go back to the vast hospitals that ceased to be worthy of the concept of asylum that created them in the first place. Just as there is no going back to the utopian visions of the people who destroyed them, whose faith in their own expertise, and dream of community care—without a practical plan for long-term hospital beds for those who need them, or follow-up care for people whose rejection of their illness is one of its symptoms—failed to fulfill their promises to the people whose desperate need had justified the demolition. I also know that there can be no going forward without a reckoning, however partial and imperfect, so that the reckoning will also no doubt require a reckoning of its own.

Owen Fiss's parting admonition—"If Hollywood is to blame, we all are"—was delivered like the lines at the end of *King Lear*, insisting that "the weight of these sad times we must obey, speak what we feel, not what we ought to say." It seemed like a good starting assumption.

One of my sister's college friends once asked my father—a challenge more than a question—if he believed in progress, to which my father replied, "Not if it ends at Auschwitz." I'd shared that story with Michael and it became a sort of running joke, as it was between my sister and me, in the darkest vein of Jewish humor. It worked for almost any occasion. "Going to the prom?" "Not if it ends at Auschwitz."

It wasn't of course funny in a normal way, or funny at all, if you thought about it. A public television series Michael and I had watched in the early 1970s, *The Ascent of Man*, had devastatingly ended one of its segments at Auschwitz. The program was hosted by a Polish British Jewish mathematician and literature scholar named Jacob Bronowski, who had a nearly round head, old-growth eyebrows, and round glinting glasses. Michael imitated his accent with the same voice he used for my father.

The program was a grimly celebratory history of scientific inquiry and the imagination by a humanist for whom the Western intellectual tradition was a flame in the darkness, nearly extinguished by its shadow side in a war that had killed fifty-five million people and left half of Europe in totalitarian winter. Bronowski's dark optimism and spirit of wonder about our common origins were also part of the world Michael and I grew up in. His humanism, rooted in the intrinsic worth of the individual, had an almost religious quality.

But after hours devoted to heroes of the Renaissance and the Enlightenment, cave paintings, steam engines, stars, and atoms, there was Bronowski at Auschwitz, squatting beside a pond into which he said the ashes of four million people had been flushed, including those belonging to many members of his family.

They were not killed by gas, he told us, they were killed "by arrogance." They were killed by people who believed they were gods, in possession of "absolute knowledge with no test in reality." There was only one way to counter this delusion, Bronowski said, his glasses flashing white: "We have to touch people." Then he thrust his bare hand into the pond and scooped up a handful of mud.

What made the moment so powerful was that it wasn't an argument; it was a plea for humility that took it for granted that we shared, as we did, his belief that denying the worth of the individual was an evil delusion. This was a paradox, because the only way to avert murderous arrogance was to acknowledge the possibility that we might be wrong: "Every judgment in science stands on the edge of error."

But even that essential scientific skepticism had to rest on a moral foundation that was also an aspect of the civilization he was defending. How could you safeguard the sanctity of the individual unless you believed there was right and wrong, and good and evil, or pursue science unless you believed truth could be tested, even if you couldn't know for sure that you had found it?

There are many kinds of delusions. Michael's were caused by severe mental illness. He had stopped taking the medication that might have helped him recognize his false beliefs for what they were instead of thinking his fiancée was an alien creature and killing her. Someone who accepted his delusion as an alternate perspective rather than a symptom of madness would betray both of Bronowski's precepts, scientific skepticism and the sanctity of life.

Bronowski spoke about the human mind's unique ability to imagine something that did not exist as a necessary tool for both the artist and the scientist. It was one of those singular traits that made us human and gave us a past and a future. That was one of the reasons it was so hard to come up with medications for schizophrenia, a researcher once told me: There are no true animal models for the disease. You can give a rat cancer but you can't give a rat a thought disorder.

Instead of a hoped-for solitary gene "causing" schizophrenia, hundreds of predisposing genes have been identified, interacting in complex and as-yet-unknown ways with environmental factors. The brain has billions of interconnected neurons. Schizophrenia doesn't attack a single region but affects networks connecting multiple parts of the brain, including those involved with our ability to imagine things that don't yet exist, along with our ability to believe in what we imagine. In that regard, it is the most human of disorders, a reminder of how remarkable our minds are. It's like the Tin Man realizing he has a heart because it's breaking.

Madelon Baranoski, a Yale forensic psychologist, told Michael's story at the Sandy Hook Advisory Commission, convened in the aftermath of the 2012 school shooting in Newtown, Connecticut, where Adam Lanza killed twenty children between the ages of six and seven, and six adults. Dr. Baranoski described Michael as "a well-meaning young man, very empathetic, very caring, took on advocacy, and very sick, and that's not picked up." It would be picked up "in clinical risk assessments," she said.

For Dr. Baranoski, Michael was an example of how "we get lulled by successful people" and fail to "appreciate how severe mental illness can be." That was why so many professionals "end up suiciding because we don't recognize the level of depression." To me she said, "We must learn from Michael Laudor!"

Eddie Schecter, the rabbi of Temple Beth Shalom in Hastings-on-Hudson, showed me the bronze plaque he'd put on the wall of the synagogue lobby in memory of Carrie. I caught myself looking for a second plaque until I remembered with a strange pang where he was and why.

Acknowledgments

The Best Minds took a long time to write and I have many people to thank. Some appear in A Note on the Sources as well, but cannot be thanked too much. I am grateful to my friend Stephen Dubner for his early encouragement and advice, and for introducing me to his agent extraordinaire, Suzanne Gluck at William Morris Endeavor, who understood what I was hoping to accomplish long before I'd done it. Suzanne found the perfect home for me at Penguin Press with Scott Moyers, a brilliant editor whose vision, patience, and generous enthusiasm made this book possible. Scott encouraged soaring without letting me fall into the sun. I am grateful to Helen Rouner, Scott's editorial assistant, for help with everything; Mia Council; Marlene Glazer, associate general counsel of Penguin Random House; and the designers and copyeditors who gave this book so much careful attention. I am grateful to Liz Calamari, Lauren Lauzon, and their colleagues in publicity and marketing for working so hard to usher this book into the world.

I have received an overwhelming amount of generosity and goodwill from people affected by the tragedy at the heart of this book who shared their memories, helped me reconstruct what happened, and trusted me to tell this story.

I never met Caroline Costello, but her childhood friends, classmates, and colleagues made me feel as if I had. Her coworkers at the Edison Project were generous not only with their time but their willingness to return to events steeped in pain and loss, even as they gave me a sense of Carrie's bright vitality and loving nature. I am so grateful to Tom

Boudrot and his husband David Elliott, Barbra Stoddard, Allison All-tucker, Nancy Hechinger, Carlo Schiattarella, and Patti Shane—who saved the binders Carrie filled with "perfect technical documents," mar-veling at the way "everything she touched had this clarity." Philip Averbuck—who first noticed Carrie at Newton North High School when he heard her read aloud in English class and thought "What a beautiful voice!"—told me that long after Carrie had been killed, he continued to recall her voice, with its mysterious quality of kindness. I can only hope some echo of what he heard found its way into this book. Carrie's friends Linus Yamane, Jacob Tanenbaum, and David Tanen-baum, who were also Michael's friends, inspired me with their human-ity and grace.

I am grateful to Nick and Amanda Wilcox, who welcomed me into their home and inspired me with their tireless advocacy of the Califor-nia treatment law named for their murdered daughter, Laura.

I learned a great deal from the psychiatrists who spoke to me, in-cluding Paul S. Appelbaum, C. Christian Beels, Robert Cancro, Park Dietz, Willard Gaylin, Sam Klagsbrun, E. Fuller Torrey, Howard Zonana, and David Taylor, who has also been a dear friend for forty years. Madelon Baranoski, professor of psychiatry at Yale School of Medicine, was inspiring even in a brief exchange. The Yale law profes-sors I interviewed were generous not only with their time but their willingness to think aloud about a tragedy that touched their lives too. I am especially grateful to Guido Calabresi, Owen Fiss, Tony Kronman, Stephen Wizner, Stephen Yandle, and Bo Burt, who is greatly missed.

Many of the people who helped me tell this story also carry it with them. I am deeply indebted to Rabbi Eddie Schechter, Lieutenant Vince Schiavone and his wife Ann, who contributed a great deal to our inter-view, and to Lieutenant Philip Mospan, Officer Ellen O'Pray, and other members of the Hastings and Cornell campus police departments who spoke to me about the events of June 17, 1998 and their aftermath. I am grateful to Laurie Flynn, who spoke as a parent as well as the executive director of NAMI as she recalled the trauma of those days. I am grateful to Ellen Baer who arranged my stay at Telluride House in Cornell.

This book has been a journey back as much as an act of remembering. Julie Cohen and Danny Goldman, beloved friends from New Rochelle, were there from the beginning. So was my sister Anna, to whom this book is dedicated. And how moving to spend time with grown-up versions of my childhood friends; I am grateful to Pat Rind, Jo-ann Sternberg, Andy Miller, David Kramer and Evan Ackiron, and my fifth-grade teacher, Miss Waldman, who turned into Marcia Gingold.

I don't know how many times you can say "this book wouldn't exist without" in one set of acknowledgments, but I wouldn't have gotten past the gate without Greg Morrison, a brilliant teacher and generous friend, who helped reconnect me to the past while reminding me to write out of the self I have become. The same is true for Elizabeth Ferber, who treated me like an old friend when I called her after reading her remarkable essay, "Because I Am Not My Father's Religion." Her generosity, humor, and devotion to truth, her deep concern for the care given and denied people with mental illness, and her openness in talking about her beloved mother, Jane Ferber, and the network that played such a large part in Michael's life, encouraged me to recognize the story I was telling as a public reckoning as well as a personal one. Elizabeth introduced me to members of her mother's remarkable circle of friends and colleagues. I am especially grateful to Bonnie Horen, Myrna Ruben, and Elin Weiss, who enriched this project immeasurably. Elizabeth also reconnected me to Dylan Schaffer, a deeply sensitive witness to Michael's world, and his own. Dylan led me to Josh Ferber, who shared memories of his parents, New Rochelle, Michael, and their struggles in the attic, with insight and openness. Josh led me to his father, Bodhicitta, back from his Indian wanderings, practicing psychiatry once more, and eager to reflect on his remarkable journey with warmth and candor.

I am grateful to Eric Rubin, another child of New Rochelle,

community psychiatry, and Yale, for his perspective on the past and his friendship in the present. The same goes for Michael Curtis, who entered into my journey with great generosity of spirit, as if it were an aspect of his own. I am grateful as well to Bianca Calabresi, Nina Calabresi, Mary McGrae McDermott, Drew McDermott, Mel Powell, Eric Halpern, Johanna Cohen, Scott McLemee, and James Forman Jr., whose brilliant book *Locking Up Our Own* was a model for how to investigate a story of moral, practical, and personal complexity.

I am grateful to Andrea Kocsis for allowing me to spend time at Futura House and for her lifelong devotion to improving the lives of people with severe mental illness. I am grateful to Maree J. Webster, executive director at Stanley Medical Research Institute, who showed me her brain lab and spoke to me about schizophrenia research. I am grateful to Elyn Saks, who also appears in my sources, and remains an awe-inspiring figure. I am grateful to Rabbi Jim Ponet for his cosmic perspective, and Rabbi Joanna Katz, who has devoted herself to the spiritual needs of people who are neglected, incarcerated, and mentally ill.

I am grateful to Hamilton Cain, Jane Rosenman, Chris Gerolmo, and Frank Rich, gifted editors and writers who grappled at close range with the tension between illness and narrative, and helped me understand it better. I am grateful for my exchanges with Debra Spark, whose powerful essay about Michael and Carrie appears in my sources.

Where would I be without the friendship and loving counsel of Cindy Spiegel, who turned up providentially in International House. Cindy, who read this book with extraordinary care, remains the best gift to come out of Berkeley, along with Saul Rosenberg and Josh Weiner, friends of a lifetime—much better than a PhD. I can't imagine this journey without them, or the friendship and bottomless hospitality of Julie Sandorf, Michael Weinberger and Sarah Weinberger. In addition to giving me encouragement, comfort cooking, a refuge from the city, and a job, Julie was the first to teach me about the crisis in care for mentally ill homeless people. She introduced me to the work of E. Fuller Torrey, who had inspired her to create the Corporation for Supportive Housing, and taught me about the heroism of Tony Hannigan and Ellen Baxter, who saw people drifting among the ruins of deinstitutionalization and managed, without fanfare or utopian fantasy, to create places where vulnerable people could live with dignity and support, a story that still needs to be told.

Daphne Merkin gave me generous suggestions and encouragement. Yossi Klein-Halevi gave me hope. Carolyn Hessel and the Sami Rohr Jewish Literary Institute gave me a community. Bari Weiss gave me courage and demonstrated that there is a world elsewhere. Many other friends accompanied me on this long journey in ways too numerous to list. I am very grateful to Sam Magavern, Blake Eskin, Nessa Rapoport, Tobi Kahn, Peggy Kuo, Jonathan Mahler, Jonathan Wilson, Esther Schor, Seth Lipsky, Amity Shlaes, Laurie Muchnick, Sarah Blake, Lizzie Leiman Kraiem, and Ruben Kraiem. Matthew and Miyoko Olszewski helped me keep my body and mind together.

My mother, Norma Rosen, talked to me a great deal about my childhood, Michael, writing, and the reckoning she understood my book represented, and though she did not live to see it finished, I am so grateful for the time we had before she died at the age of ninety-six. I am grateful to her dear friend Cynthia Ozick for being an electric presence in my childhood and a source of illumination in the murky present. I am blessed with loving siblings and siblings-in-law on all sides: Jonathan Springer; Tamar Springer, Steve Stancroff, and Ethan, Seth, and Noah Stancroff; Anna Rosen, Jon Rosen, and Isaac, Celia and Ella Rosen.

Finally, this book wouldn't exist without the love, wisdom, patience, and executive functioning of my wife, Mychal Springer, whose faith in the journey I was making, even when I was lost, made it possible. Our children, Ariella and Tali, grew up with this project and are a part of it. They hauled me out of rabbit holes when I fell in and threw me carrots when I couldn't get out. I am grateful to them, as always, just for being born. Also, Ariella made me spreadsheets to keep track of all my changes, and Tali took my author photo and even got me to smile.

A Note on the Sources

The Best Minds grew out of memory and experience, supplemented by hundreds of interviews, diary entries, letters, law journals, newspapers, court records, police records, television investigations, and books. The story I've told is personal, corroborated with oral and written sources; it is also a public history that extends beyond the boundary of individual memory, told against the backdrop of cultural and institutional changes that are themselves part of the story.

I've listed below only a small portion of the books I used in my research. They are the ones I found especially helpful, illuminating, or provocative. Some I returned to repeatedly, like Gerald Grob's sweeping history of America's treatment of people with mental illness, *The Mad Among Us*, and E. Fuller Torrey's more focused accounts of deinstitutionalization, beginning with *Nowhere to Go*. I also found Torrey's humane and informative *Surviving Schizophrenia*, now in its seventh edition, indispensable.

Michael E. Staub's *Madness Is Civilization* and Don Lattin's *The Harvard Psychedelic Club* were touchstone reminders of a cultural and intellectual mood, something hard to capture but part of the incubating air that hatched many of the changes reflected in my book. Psychiatry itself, torn between subjectivity and science, has been shaped by legal, cultural, and political upheavals as well as by advances in medicine, brain science, and genetics. Eric Kandel's *In Search of Memory* was a wonderful evocation of all that neuroscience can do; Sally Satel and Scott D. Lilienfeld's *Brainwashed* was a reminder of all it can't do—or rather, of how exaggerated or unsupported claims about neuroscience can misrepresent the mind as easily as psychoanalysis once did.

Thomas C. Leonard's *Illiberal Reformers: Race, Eugenics, and American Economics* was an essential book about the evils of scientific certitude—whether the science is biological or social—yoked to state authority and the sort of utopian idealism whose shadow, still sometimes mistaken for sunlight, hovers over the tragedy in my book. It was also a cautionary reminder of the danger of seeing single causes—whether bad genes or bad ideas—where complex interactions are much more likely. The antidote was Peter Kramer's argument for a psychiatry that can accommodate listening *and* neuroscience, and Andrew Solomon's generous study of family difference, both models of empathetic investigation with room for complexity and paradox.

To understand the tangled relationship of psychiatry and law, I often consulted Rael Jean Isaac and Virginia C. Armat's *Madness in the Streets: How Psychiatry and the Law Abandoned the Mentally Ill* and Paul Applebaum's *Almost a Revolution: Mental Health Law and the Limits of Change*, a book as valuable for its moral complexity as its history of psychiatry and law.

Laura Kalman's rich history of Yale Law School in the sixties, populated with figures still present in Michael's time, was enormously helpful. That book, along with Kalman's history of legal realism at Yale, and her biography of Abe Fortas, was part of my education in the paradoxes of postwar legal liberalism and its roots in the New Deal, when the country granted FDR what the *Times* called a "unanimous power of attorney."

There are many excellent memoirs by people living with schizophrenia; I've included only Elyn Saks' extraordinary *The Center Cannot Hold*, which discusses Michael, and Lori Schiller's *The Quiet Room*, a powerful, unsentimental book that takes place primarily at Futura House in White Plains, where Michael also lived, and gives family members and caregivers a voice.

The Halfway House: On the Road to Independence was published when

Michael was living at Futura House. Its coauthor, Andrea Kocsis, had become the director when I contacted her, and in addition to generously allowing me to spend time at a suburban group home she administers, and explaining how things had changed since Michael's time, she urged me to read *I am Not Sick, I Don't Need Help*, the first book on the list below, which focuses on persuasion rather than compulsion even as it acknowledges the imperative of helping people suffering from serious psychiatric disorders.

Books were often bound up with people who modified their meaning. Spending time at Futura House with residents fighting daily battles, saying their long goodbyes to former selves whose imprint was palpable in their present struggles, filled me with humbling realizations. "Recovery is every day" the social worker told me with that combination of unsentimental toughness and casual almost offhand godliness characteristic of people capable of giving real care to very sick people on a daily basis. She was a young Black woman with a bright smile and a Hebrew name whose mother had grown up in the New Rochelle projects and had sent her to a Jewish day camp every summer. Her mother turned out to be my year at New Rochelle High School, and though I didn't recognize her name, and the projects were beyond my ken in childhood, the encounter made me feel I had come full circle.

Some of the people I interviewed—like Vincent Schiavone, the Hastings police lieutenant who led the investigation into Carrie's killing, and Michael Shae, who was Michael's Telluride factotum before becoming an editor at *The New York Review of Books*—gave me clippings saved over the years about a tragedy that affected them too. Michael's Yale classmate, Debra Spark, wrote about Michael and Carrie in "The Dangerous Act of Writing," an essay published in *Agni* in April of 2015. Debra had known them both, and generously shared memories and research with me. So did Eric Halpern who, the year before, had published a recollection of Michael in *Ricochet* called "Insanity and Guilt" that argued for a bipartisan mental health bill then before congress.

Michael came to the world's attention when *The New York Times* ran a profile of him in 1995. After he killed Carrie in 1998, articles of a very different sort appeared; some quoted from his eighty-page book proposal. Several versions of his story were read into the congressional record. His lawyers' attempt to prevent Carrie's family from reading an impact statement became part of "Carrie's Law," a bill designed to protect a victim's right to make a statement in court even if the defendant has been found not guilty by reason of insanity. Michael appears in a TV documentary called *Shattered Mind*, in law and abnormal psychology textbooks, and in the transcripts of the Sandy Hook Advisory Commission convened by the governor of Connecticut in 2013.

E. Fuller Torrey turned out to have written articles about Michael. So did Sally Satel and D.J. Jaffe, whose *Insane Consequences* explains how $147 billion of federal mental health spending—for a single year!—bypasses the needs of the ten million Americans with the most serious psychiatric disorders. Jaffe, Torrey, and Satel all saw in Michael's story the familiar failure of a mental healthcare system they had been chronicling for years.

In her legal memoir, the former Westchester County district attorney Jeanine Pirro treats Michael's case, which never went to trial, as evidence of a failed criminal justice system, telling Michael's story from the perspective of Carrie and her parents in a chapter she called "The Laws of Madness," borrowing Michael's title for her own.

There were so many partial versions of Michael's story that fragmentation itself came to seem a feature of the tragedy I was trying to understand, suggesting something broken in the way we imagine and discuss mental illness. So too, perhaps, was my desire to make the kaleidoscopic pieces fit together. I tried to remain mindful of this, and to remember that behind these sources were people who were themselves contending with the written and remembered past, and trying to figure out its symbolic and actual meaning. And like the screenplay based on

Michael's life that Chris Gerolmo generously shared with me, many accounts were bound up with Michael's own telling and retelling of his struggle with schizophrenia, a process that began years before he killed Carrie.

I grew up surrounded by people who wrote things down, and wrote things down myself. My mother published an account of my getting hit by a motorcycle while playing touch football with Michael and other friends that may have formed our shared memory of that day as much as the experience itself. Cynthia Ozick sent me her written memories of my family's move to New Rochelle and my friendship with Michael. Dylan Schaffer, a year behind Michael and me in school, wrote a wonderful memoir that explored dark areas of his New Rochelle childhood that were helpful for this book. Linus Yamane shared a beautiful chapter about Michael and Carrie from an unpublished memoir. Elizabeth Ferber, whose family played such a large role in Michael's life, published an essay about her psychiatrist father's devotion to the Bhagwan Shree Rajneesh that moved me to get in touch with her, a transformative moment that in many ways made this book possible.

Elizabeth told me to read *God's Hotel*, a book about the role that time once played in mental healing—the very thing erased by modern life, managed care, and the restrictions placed on Medicaid reimbursements for people needing long term psychiatric hospitalization. She guided me through the world of community psychiatry that her revered mother, and the network of her mother's friends and colleagues, poured themselves into, and that loomed so consequentially in Michael's life. She gave me a copy of "the book of family therapy" that her father had edited with other prominent therapists, a time capsule all its own, including its lowercase title, with the name of Michael's psychiatrist mysteriously written inside.

I've left out many books, in some cases because the authors are mentioned in *The Best Minds* and are easy to find. They include Michel

Foucault, Thomas Szasz, John Paul Sartre, Franz Fanon, Erving Goffman, Betty Friedan, Sigmund Freud, Anna Freud, Aldous Huxley, Gregory Bateson, Ken Kesey, Joseph Campbell, and various Beat writers who weave in and out of my larger story and played an outsize role in the psychiatric, psychedelic, literary, and musical counterculture that had ceased being counter by the time Michael and I were growing up. Several of these writers are represented in a volume that I do include, devoted to the 1975 Schizo-Culture conference that brought artists, activists, and intellectuals foreign and domestic—including the as-yet untranslated authors of *Schizophrenia and Capitalism*—to Columbia University where, on a single panel, R. D. Laing and Michel Foucault discussed "Prisons and Asylums" with the founder of the Insane Patients' Collective and an aboveground member of the Weather Underground, still six years away from her participation in an armed robbery that ended in murder and a prison sentence of seventy-five years to life.

Other writers whose work is important to this book are represented only by epigraphs. In a couple of instances I've left off the source of a quotation, so as not to overwhelm a short phrase, but the context matters. The quotation from D. W. Winnicott about not being found, at the beginning of chapter three, comes from "Communicating and Not Communicating Leading to a Study of Certain Opposites" published in 1963. The quotation from James Baldwin about not being known, at the beginning of The House of Dreams—one of the four sections dividing this book—is taken from Baldwin's 1963 "Lecture to Teachers."

I've included only one book about Allen Ginsberg and the Beats, a memoir by the poet Bob Rosenthal that stands in for many others. I've also included a collection of letters exchanged by Allen Ginsberg and his father, the poet Louis Ginsberg, because father and son were haunted by Naomi Ginsberg's schizophrenia, lobotomy, and death in radically different ways, and the crack that ran through their arguments—about politics, poetry, mental illness, inspiration, freedom, and responsibility—ran through the world Michael and I grew up in, and still runs through contemporary culture unhealed.

I Am Not Sick, I Don't Need Help: How to Help Someone with Mental Illness Accept Treatment, Xavier Amador (Vida Press, 2000, 2020).

Almost a Revolution: Mental Health Law and the Limits of Change, Paul S. Appelbaum (New York: Oxford University Press, 1994).

Murder in the Model City: The Black Panthers, Yale, and the Redemption of a Killer, Paul Bass and Douglas W. Rae (New York: Basic Books, 2006).

The Shame of the States, Albert Deutsch (New York: Harcourt, Brace, 1948).

Pillars of Justice: Lawyers and the Liberal Tradition, Owen Fiss (Cambridge, MA: Harvard University Press, 2017).

Law and the Modern Mind, Jerome Frank, with an introduction by Brian H. Bix (New York: Routledge, 2017).

The Inheritance: How Three Families and America Moved from Roosevelt to Reagan and Beyond, Samuel G. Freedman (New York: Simon & Schuster 1996).

The Killing of Bonnie Garland: A Question of Justice (reissue), Willard Gaylin (New York: Penguin Books, 1995).

The Perversions of Autonomy: Coercion and Constraint in a Liberal Society (revised and expanded edition), Willard Gaylin, (Washington, DC: Georgetown University Press, 2003).

Family Business (selected letters between Allen and Louis Ginsberg), edited by Michael Schumacher, (New York: Bloomsbury, 2001).

The Halfway House: On the Road to Independence, Sylvia Golomb and Andrea Kocsis (New York: Brunner-Routlege, 1988).

The Mad Among Us: A History of the Care of America's Mentally Ill, Gerald Grob, (New York: Free Press, 1994).

Madness in the Streets: How Psychiatry and the Law Abandoned the Mentally Ill, Rael Jean Isaac and Virginia C. Armat (New York: Free Press, 1990).

Insane Consequences: How the Mental Health Industry Fails the Mentally Ill, DJ Jaffe, foreword by E. Fuller Torrey (Amherst, NY: Prometheus Books, 2017).

The Fall of the House of Roosevelt: Brokers of Ideas and Power from FDR to LBJ, Michael Janeway (New York: Columbia University Press, 2004).

Out of Bedlam: The Truth about Deinstitutionalization, Ann Braden Johnson, (New York: Basic Books, 1990).

The Guardians: Kingman Brewster, His Circle, and the Rise of the Liberal Establishment, Geoffrey Kabaservice (New York: Henry Holt, 2004).

Legal Realism at Yale, 1927–1960, Laura Kalman (Chapel Hill: The University of North Carolina Press in association with the American Society for Legal History, 1986).

Yale Law School and the Sixties: Revolt and Reverberation, Laura Kalman (Chapel Hill: The University of North Carolina Press, 2005).

In Search of Memory: The Emergence of a New Science of Mind, Eric R. Kandel (New York: W. W. Norton & Company, 2006).

Simple Justice: The History of Brown v. Board of Education *and Black America's Struggle for Equality*, Richard Kluger (New York: Vintage, 2004).

Listening to Prozac: A Psychiatrist Explores Antidepressant Drugs and the Remaking of the Self, Peter D. Kramer (New York: Viking, 1993).

Ordinarily Well: The Case for Antidepressants, Peter D. Kramer (New York: Farrar, Strauss & Giroux, 2016).

Schizo-Culture (2-volume set): *The Event, The Book*, edited by Sylvère Lotringer (New York: Semiotext(e) Journal, 2014).

Pathologist of the Mind: Adolf Meyer and the Origins of American Psychiatry, S. D. Lamb Baltimore, MD: Johns Hopkins University Press, 2014).

The Harvard Psychedelic Club: How Timothy Leary, Ram Dass, Huston Smith, and Andrew Weil Killed the Fifties and Ushered in a New Age for America, Don Lattin (New York: HarperOne, 2010).

Illiberal Reformers: Race, Eugenics, and American Economics, Thomas C. Leonard (Princeton, NJ: Princeton University Press, 2017).

Shrinks: The Untold Story of Psychiatry, Jeffrey A. Lieberman, MD, with Ogi Ogas (New York: Little Brown and Company, 2015).

The Unraveling of America: A History of Liberalism in the 1960s, Allen J. Matusow (Athens: University of Georgia Press, 2009).

What Is Mental Illness?, Richard J. McNally (Cambridge, MA: The Belknap Press of Harvard University Press, 2011).

Joining the Club: A History of Jews and Yale Dan A. Oren (New Haven, CT: Yale University Press, 1986).

To Punish and Protect: Against a System that Coddles Criminals, Jeanine Pirro, with Catherine Whitney (New York: Simon & Schuster, 2003).

Straight Around Allen: On the Business of Being Allen Ginsberg, Bob Rosenthal (Beatdom Books, 2019).

The Center Cannot Hold: My Journey Through Madness, Elyn R. Saks (New York: Hyperion ebook, 2007).

Refusing Care: Forced Treatment and the Rights of the Mentally Ill, Elyn R. Saks (Chicago: University of Chicago Press, 2002).

The Trouble with Testosterone and Other Essays on the Biology of the Human Predicament, Robert M. Sapolsky (New York: Scribner, 1997). (I often revisited Sapolsky's superb lectures on schizophrenia and depression, part of a series of twenty-five lectures delivered at Stanford in 2010–201, https://www.youtube.com/playlist?list=PL150326949691B199)

Brainwashed: The Seductive Appeal of Mindless Neuroscience, Sally Satel and Scott D. Lilienfeld (New York: Basic Books, 2013).

Life, Death & Bialys: A Father/Son Baking Story, Dylan Schaffer (New York: Bloomsbury, 2006).

The Quiet Room: A Journey Out of the Torment of Madness, Lori Schiller and Amanda Bennett (New York: Warner Books, 1991).

Madhouse: A Tragic Tale of Megalomania and Modern Medicine, Andrew Scull (New Haven, CT: Yale University Press, 2007).

Is There No Place on Earth for Me? (Second edition), Susan Sheehan (New York: Vintage, 2014).

Far From the Tree: Parents, Children, and the Search for Identity (reprint edition), Andrew Solomon (New York: Scribner, 2013).

Madness Is Civilization: When the Diagnosis was Social, 1948–1980, Michael E. Staub (Chicago: University of Chicago Press, 2011).

God's Hotel: A Doctor, a Hospital, and a Pilgrimage to the Heart of Medicine, Victoria Sweet (New York: Riverhead Books, 2012).

Hippocrates Cried: The Decline of American Psychiatry, Michael Allen Taylor, MD (New York: Oxford University Press, 2013).

American Psychosis: How the Federal Government Destroyed the Mental Illness Treatment System, E. Fuller Torrey, MD (New York: Oxford University Press, 2014).

The Invisible Plague: The Rise of Mental Illness from 1750 to the Present, E. Fullerr Torrey, MD, and Judy Miller (New Brunswick, NJ: Rutgers University Press, 2001).

Nowhere to Go: The Tragic Odyssey of the Homeless Mentally Ill, E. Fuller Torrey, MD (Perennial Library, 1989).

Surviving Schizophrenia, 6th Edition: A Family Manual, E. Fuller Torrey (New York: HarperCollins e-book, 2013).

9 Highland Road: Sane Living for the Mentally Ill, Michael Winerip (New York: Pantheon Books, 1994).

Index